ARCHITECTURE IN THE SOUTH PACIFIC

THE OCEAN OF ISLANDS

To all people of the South Pacific

First published by
Editions Didier Millet Pte Ltd
121 Telok Ayer Street, #03-01
Singapore 068590
www.edmbooks.com

Published in North America by
University of Hawai'i Press
2840 Kolowalu Street
Honolulu, Hawai'i 96822 USA
www.uhpress.hawaii.edu

Library of Congress Cataloging-in-Publication Data

Taylor, Jennifer, 1935– author.
Architecture in the South Pacific, the ocean of islands / Jennifer Taylor and James Conner.
pages cm
Includes bibliographical references and index.
ISBN 978-0-8248-4672-5 (cloth : alk. paper) 1. Architecture—Oceania. I. Conner, James, author. II. Title.
NA1610.T39 2014
720.995—dc23
2014008082

Designed by Nelani Jinadasa
Printed by Tien Wah Press Pte Ltd, Singapore

Printed in Singapore

19 18 17 16 15 14 6 5 4 3 2 1

ARCHITECTURE IN THE SOUTH PACIFIC

THE OCEAN OF ISLANDS

'No part of the world exerts the same attractive power upon the visitor, and the task before me is to communicate to fireside travellers some sense of its seduction...'

Robert Louis Stevenson
In the South Seas

JENNIFER TAYLOR   JAMES CONNER

HAWAI'I

University of Hawai'i Press
Honolulu

‘Oceania is vast, Oceania is expanding, Oceania is hospitable and generous, Oceania is humanity rising from the depths of brine and regions of fire deeper still, Oceania is us.’
Epeli Hau‘ofa

THE OCEAN OF ISLANDS

'The Pacific is inconstant and uncertain like the soul of man.'
William Somerset Maugham

The ocean is large and seemingly almost empty, stretching endlessly. Its very spirit lies in extremes – the miniscule floating in the huge – the small far-flung islands within the vastest body of water on earth. This is its primary quality. In partnership with this emptiness is its instability, its volatile force that regularly changes the static into the dynamic, with devastating winds and heaving ocean floor. With this unpredictable nature, longevity and permanence appear to have little meaning.

Comparatively few descendants of those who first came and of those from other times and places live on the remote fragments of land scattered through these subequatorial waters. These are tropical places in the sun – places of vibrant colour and full of life. Geographical factors shaped the lightweight, loosely assembled construction of the traditional shelters that leave few marks on the land. It is an architecture of acceptance – not of resistance. In essence, this is a world virtually the antithesis of the increasingly urbanized worlds beyond the seas, from whence the new settlers came and continue to come. The juxtaposition and interweaving of the legacies of contrasting worlds are fashioning the contemporary South Pacific – the new Oceania.

'A JOURNEY OF A THOUSAND MILES ...

We ascribe names to regions to enable us, with ease, to make generalizations about the collective ensemble. A common perception of the South Pacific fails to appreciate the layers of diversity that characterize the islands and the people of the islands. The South Pacific is a complex region with a unique population structure of different racial groups. While there are shared characteristics among the indigenous people and basically similar geographic conditions throughout the region, inherent differences, settlement patterns, cultural developments and the circumstances of colonial and post-colonial experiences have engendered dissimilar political and economic conditions that find expression in the still-young emerging architecture of the South Pacific of today. Yet common to all remains the South Pacific setting and all that that means, and the persistence of a shared awareness and continuing consciousness of the early cultures of the islands that have been and continue to exist at the core of the life of the towns and settlements. Examples of traditional buildings of note, both historical and contemporary, carry forward lessons demonstrating the direct logic of concept and the arresting imagery of the simple geometry of form in the vernacular. Regional types persist, such as the ever-adaptable fale, which continues to appear throughout much of the Pacific, accommodating the present in contemporary variations of its many guises. Given the remote location, the splendid matchless setting and the distinctive ethnic mix, the potential is there for a unique and appropriate contemporary architecture with an Oceanic identity to evolve.

... BEGINS WITH A SINGLE STEP' Laozi in the *Tao Te Ching*

This book tells one part of the saga related to the making of the new South Pacific. The genesis of the work lies in an invitation received in 1986 to write a chapter on Oceania for Banister Fletcher's *History of Architecture*.[1] It soon became evident that while there was well-documented information on Australia and New Zealand and a substantial amount on Papua New Guinea, the small island lands produced virtually a blank slate, with the exception of some studies on the vernacular buildings.[2]
Needing telling was the overlooked story of the buildings and towns of the South Pacific's smaller islands engendered by the European presence. While this became the primary focus of the study, traditional Pacific buildings, practices and expressions take their place as a part of the new architectural mosaic. In 1998, research for the 'Oceania' section of the book *World Architecture 1900–2000: A Critical Mosaic*[3] revealed that little further information on the architecture of the smaller island countries was available and gave a reminder of the still-awaiting task. There are many opinions as to what constitutes Oceania with the definition mainly adopted here being 'the coral atolls and volcanic islands of the South Pacific'.[4] While there are buildings of note from the nineteenth century, the principal building programmes of the settlers commenced in the twentieth century, with the majority of development on the islands occurring after 1980. Hence, the study began to be defined in terms of structure, subject, scope and time. It was not until 2003 when Jim Conner joined the team that the opportunity to undertake such an extensive project presented itself and the travelling commenced.

Given the unchartered field of the architecture of Oceania, the approach has been, by necessity, an empirical one and the research required one, and often more, extended visits to each of the island countries. With virtually no texts and few records on architecture, information came 'from the grass roots', and the storehouse of material and opinions on which the book is based was built up, almost exclusively, by visiting, looking, photographing sites, and by searching museums, libraries and the limited archives for any possible record of, or oblique reference to, building. Much was learnt from listening, primarily to architects, planners and engineers, but also to conservationists, residents, churchmen, curators and politicians.[5] In Oceania architects are few in number, but for the generous assistance of the few we are very much appreciative. *Varangue*, the annual magazine of the Order of Architects of New Caledonia, published since 1990, was a most welcome light within a dark sea of absence. Archival material is rare, and documents and drawings commonly have not been retained or have disintegrated in the adverse climatic conditions. Further, as there is limited publication of work, architects could provide little documentation or illustrative material of publication quality. The fragile existence of many buildings in the South Pacific was a further major problem, especially as records are rarely kept.

Architecture in the South Pacific does not have aspirations to be a fully documented history. Rather, the material is presented as a collection of themed essays – a structure that lends itself to the disparate stories of the region. Our 'history' does not follow a linear sequence, and the chapters are but loosely ordered with regard to developments through time. The essays are intended to serve as starting points for further research. We have attempted to present as informed a recording as possible, but given the exploratory nature of the study, it is to be expected that the text will have shortcomings, and we hope future scholars will remedy deficiencies. We wish them as rewarding an experience as we have been privileged to enjoy with the people of the Southern Seas.

During our seven years in the South Pacific there were many hundreds who, in one way or another, contributed to the making of this book, and to whom we wish to express our sincere gratitude – to you all, thank you.

But even with those exceptional Pacific-wide contributions, this book would not exist in its present form without the guidance of friend and scholar Made Wijaya and the advice of Professor Xian Ruan and Professor Ron Knapp, who introduced us to EDM, and there is no way in which we can adequately thank Didier Millet and the press for accepting the project. It has been a great pleasure working with them all from the very first day when we visited the office in Singapore and met the general manager, Charles Orwin, whose support has been ever present throughout the process to the realization of the publication. The whole team has been outstanding, but we would like to especially tell of the charm and meticulous attention of our editor Rachael Morris, the talent and detailed care of our designer Nelani Jinadasa, and the guidance and coordination of our editorial directors, Douglas Amrine and Martin Cross. Thank you, thank you – we will miss you.

CONTENTS

Part I

THE WORLD OF OCEANIA

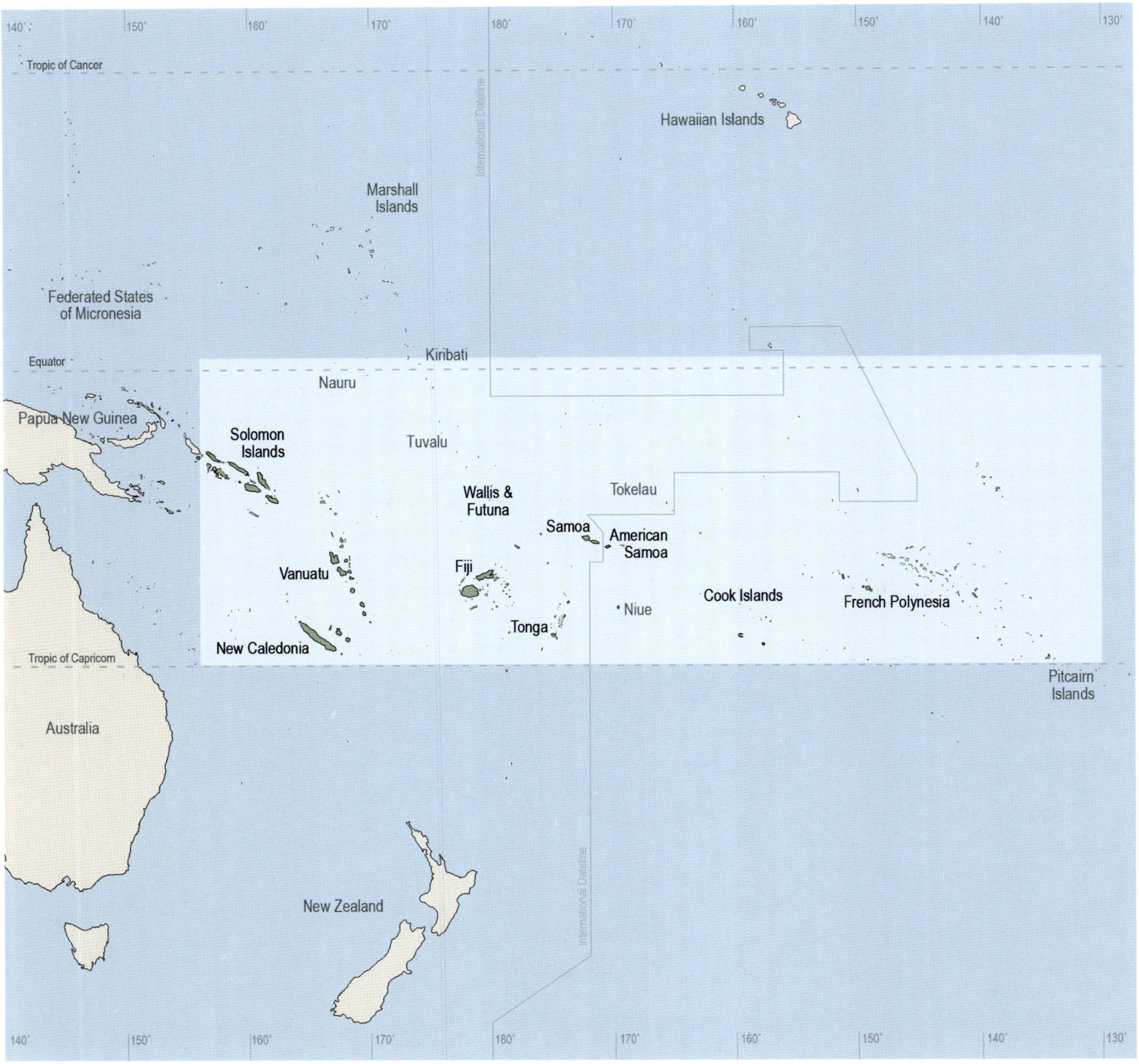

Map of the Study Area within the Pacific Ocean

MAR DEL SUR
THE SOUTHERN SEA

'For all those who venture within this, the world's largest ocean, and who have made it their home the ocean influences every aspect of life. It has done so for millennia.'
Epeli Ha'uofa

The Pacific Ocean, at 165.25 million square kilometres, covers one third of the earth's surface. The International Date Line divides the Pacific east and west, and the equator subdivides it into the North Pacific Ocean and South Pacific Ocean. The subequatorial Pacific is the subject of this study. The Pacific Ocean was named Mar del Sur ('South Sea') by the Spanish explorer Vasco Núñez de Balboa, who crossed the Isthmus of Panama in 1513. The later name, 'Pacific', was given in 1521 by the Portuguese explorer Ferdinand Magellan, and while it is derived from the Latin *Mare Pacificum*, meaning 'Peaceful Sea', it is anything but peaceful in geological terms.[1]

The South Pacific is a dynamic region formed and programmed in landform and climate, and thus culture, by the movement of the tectonic plates at the ocean's floor – notably the Pacific plate and the Indo-Australian plate. Approximately 85 per cent of the world's annual release of seismic energy occurs within the Ring of Fire (the circum-Pacific belt). Located around the edge of the Pacific plate, it produces 80 per cent of the world's largest earthquakes. Where the western edge of the Pacific plate meets the Indo-Australian plate the movement and collisions of crustal plates create an earthquake belt that runs north-east from

New Zealand, up the east coast of Tonga to Samoa, and continues up the south-west side of Vanuatu and the Solomon Islands to New Britain.[2] Dispersed throughout the waters of the South Pacific are numerous islands that are generally grouped in archipelagos. The islands are formed by geographical upheaval or volcanic activity that leaves peaks in various stages of formation. Over time, volcanoes disintegrate and sink back into the sea. The volcanic lava core becomes the central island, and flat coral reefs develop about the sunken rim of the crater, commonly enclosing lagoons. Islets, or motus, appear on these coral reefs. Where there are no promontories other than reefs and islets (i.e., the central core has sunk under the sea), the reef is described as an atoll. Natural disasters are frequent in the region in the form of cyclones or hurricanes,[3] earthquakes and tsunamis, and the tolerances available for the preservation of a harmonious ecological balance are fine. Due to these destructive forces, buildings of the South Pacific are constantly threatened and commonly destroyed.

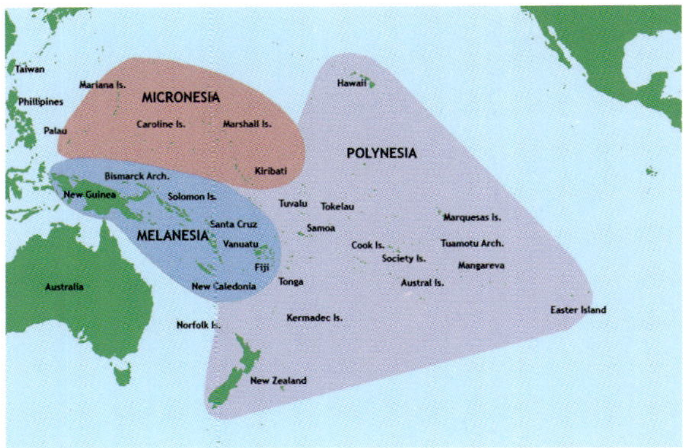

Ethnocultural areas of the Pacific Ocean. *Courtesy of Wikipedia* (Map information based on K R Howe, *Vaka Moana: Voyages of the Ancestors: The Discovery and Settlement of the Pacific*, 2008).

Oceania

The Pacific contains approximately 20 000 islands, the majority of which are found south of the equator.[4] The islands are remote and isolated, with Tahiti over 6000 kilometres from Sydney and over 6000 kilometres from Los Angeles. Early aviation pioneers, such as Charles Kingsford Smith, proved that flights across the Pacific were possible, and after World War II the islands, which had previously been dependent upon the shipping lines, developed aviation links with the outside world. The countries of the South Pacific vary in size from Papua New Guinea down to Tuvalu, which at twenty-six square kilometres is the fourth smallest country in the world.[5] Only a small percentage of the South Pacific islands are occupied, and Pitcairn Island, with only forty-eight inhabitants, is the least populous and most remote jurisdiction in the world.[6]

The islands of the South Pacific form part of various territories or nations, and are mostly in a post-colonial stage of development. Due to previous settlement and governance by foreign powers, English and French are widely spoken in addition to the 450 Oceanic languages of the indigenous peoples.[7]

People of Oceania

Passage out of Asia

Ethnographically, Oceania is a large cultural area including the subregions of Melanesia, Polynesia and Micronesia. Melanesia is in the subequatorial zone in the west, and Polynesia is dispersed through the eastern Pacific with New Zealand in the south-west and Hawaii to the north. As the islands of Micronesia lie to the east of the Philippines and primarily north of the equator, the ethnographic subregion generally is not considered to be in the subequatorial zone. Hence, the study concentrated on the Melanesian and Polynesian island states, covering the Solomon Islands, Vanuatu, New Caledonia, Wallis and Futuna, Fiji, Tonga, Samoa, American Samoa, the Cook Islands and French Polynesia. The small states of Niue, Tokelau, Tuvalu, Pitcairn and Easter Islands are not included due to the absence of work seen to be relevant to the study, nor are the small western islands along the coasts of Australia and Papua New Guinea that are rightly more associated with those countries.

The history of the region is one of migrations. It is thought that as long as 60 000 years ago Archaic Papuans (Australoids) migrated southwards from Asia and occupied parts of the Solomon Islands; these were the first islanders of the Pacific. Approximately 4500 years ago a wave of Austronesian-speaking settlers arrived from Southeast Asia. The Lapita culture (1600–500 BC) represents the first substantial Austronesian colonization in the Pacific. These were seafaring people, and their progress across the Pacific can be traced by the remains of their distinctive pottery. They first moved down through the Bismarck Archipelago and the Solomon Islands in Near Oceania and then spread to the islands of Vanuatu and New Caledonia in Remote Oceania some 3300 years ago, reaching Fiji 100 years later.[8] Beyond were the great seas across which these remarkable mariners migrated in their double-hulled sailing canoes, to populate the islands of the central Pacific Ocean. They arrived in Samoa around 1200 BC, where, in western Polynesia, there developed a specific Polynesian culture. Recent scholarship[9] suggests that they colonized the Society Islands around 1025–1120 AD and settled in the remaining eastern, northern and southern Pacific islands (including Hawaii and New Zealand) around 1190–1290 AD, establishing the 'Polynesian Triangle' in 'the greatest maritime expansion known in history'.[10]

Passage out of Europe

The Western trespass over three centuries took many forms and changed much of the South Pacific, but 'that transformation was co-directed by the same Islanders who were the product of tens of thousands of years of continuous Pacific history'[11] and which, in turn, expanded the horizons of Europe. However, due to the dispersion of the islands over a large area, certain Pacific Islanders were among the last people on earth to have contact with Europeans – some as recent as only fifty years ago.[12]

Exploration and Colonization

After the initial explorers charted and opened up the Pacific to European contact in the sixteenth, seventeenth and eighteenth centuries, the activity of traders, who took natural products such as whale oil, bêche-de-mer and sandalwood, followed.[13] Alongside the traders came those who were dedicated to conversion of the people to the Christian faith. So these waves of migrations in the South Pacific arose from both religious zeal and the spread of capitalism in Europe, which demanded sources of materials for exploitation. Thus, in the nineteenth century European settlers and missionaries established themselves on the islands, and their migrations led to the colonization of most of the inhabited islands of the South Pacific, primarily by France, Britain and Germany, and subsequently the conversion of the people to Christianity. The twentieth century brought a fresh generation of interest and some small-scale occupation by America and New Zealand. There was little colonization following World War II, with American interests primarily concentrated on the islands of the North Pacific.

Reconstruction of Lapita Pot with Faces. *Courtesy of Christophe Sand* (Christophe Sand, *Lapita: The Pottery Collection from the Site at Foué, New Caledonia, Vol 7, Les Cahiers de l'archéologie en Nouvelle-Calédonie*, Département Archéologie, Service territorial des musées et du patrimoine, 1999).

Global Paths

The Second World War

Of all the recent outside incursions, World War II had the most far-reaching and transformative impact on the South Pacific Islands. While combat in the region was limited (with the exception of the Solomon Islands), the presence of US army military bases nevertheless had a marked influence across the Pacific. US forces employed local labour and paid high wages, creating an economic boom. They produced a wealth of equipment never before seen in the islands, and basic infrastructure such as roads, electricity, water supply, drainage, sewage, aerodromes, wharfs and hospitals quickly appeared to support the fighting forces. This effort and investment to sustain the US war machine changed the islanders' perceptions of what was possible within a Western society and, among other factors, indirectly led to later independence movements designed to end colonial rule.[14]

Tourism

Tourism is a substantial factor in most island economies, although this varies considerably from country to country. In 2010 the small South Pacific nations had an estimated population of 2.5 million people, and between them they attract 1.5 million visitors a year. The tourist impact on the Pacific Islands is both positive and negative. Major benefits derived from tourism are employment, and foreign exchange and investment – as long as returns remain in the local economy. The negative physical impact of tourism, however, is extreme in terms of the generation of environmental negatives, such as traffic, which is a major pollutant. Many islands have limited sources of potable water and generally are dependent upon the importation of increasingly expensive diesel fuel for electricity generation, but alternative sources of energy are being sought. Eliminating or recycling waste products is also a major problem for small island states. Without the proper infrastructure, contamination of the environment is inevitable.

Being in the New Pacific

After World War II various colonies sought self-rule, and independence was granted to Western Samoa in 1962, the Cook Islands in 1965, Fiji in 1970, the Solomon Islands in 1978 and Vanuatu in 1980. American Samoa is an unincorporated territory of the United States but gained limited self-governance under a constitution that became effective in 1967. The islands under French control have overseas territory status and remain linked to France's administrative systems, although some steps towards increasing self-government are in train in New Caledonia. Politically significant was the 1947 decision to form an intergovernmental organization, the South Pacific Commission (SPC), to enhance relationships between countries in the South Pacific. Renamed the Secretariat of the Pacific Community in 1997, it now acts across the Pacific to heighten cooperation between the member countries and to represent their interests.[15] The headquarters are located in Noumea, New Caledonia, and the commission has been headed at the political level since 2000 by the Pacific Islands Forum Secretariat (PIFS), Suva, Fiji, which was founded in 1971 as the South Pacific Bureau for Economic Co-operation (SPEC). In 2008 the secretariat of the recently recognized Melanesian Spearhead Group (MSG) was formally established in Port Vila. The MSG is a regional organization of five members that share similar cultural heritage and ties and are in agreement to work together for the common interests and solidarity of the people in Melanesia.[16]

The most urbanized country in the South Pacific is New Caledonia, where more than half the population lives in the capital of Noumea. New Caledonia has had active immigration programmes and is the only country that, like Australia, had an early convict base to its population. The highest annual population growth rate in the region is in the Solomon Islands (2.7 per cent) and the lowest is in the Cook Islands, Samoa and Tonga (0.3 per cent).[17]

There is a wide spectrum of economic performance across the South Pacific with the per capita income of New Caledonia forty times that of the Solomon Islands.[18] Setting aside the two French overseas territories of New Caledonia and French Polynesia, the remaining South Pacific nations have been performing relatively poorly economically.[19] In many countries there is evident high unemployment, and social and political instability, as well as substantial health and environmental problems. This disparity in economic growth and well-being has led to an increase in emigration, with the more mobile people moving to places offering both education and enhanced employment opportunities. Substantial island populations have now relocated to countries around the Pacific – up to 210 000 in New Zealand, 150 000 in America and 65 000 in Australia. Some countries, such as the Cook Islands, have more of their populations living abroad than at home.[20] This outward migration remains the pattern, as does the sending home of money to support extended families, which accounts for as much as 39 per cent of the gross domestic product in Tonga.[21] Urbanization, however, is expanding in most countries as the rural-to-urban drift continues. The provision of adequate services and infrastructure in these urban centres is an ongoing problem.

Today, it is Asia – notably China – and to a lesser extent Europe, America and Australia, permeating the region and providing the needy Pacific countries with extensive financial assistance. This provided largess commonly is gifted buildings, direct investment in projects such as resorts, or as funds to open up investment potential for the development of regional industries, including tourism. In return, political support may be sought and rights for the extraction of resources including fish and forestry supplies that the South Pacific states can provide.[22]

The Making of Architecture

Traditional Making

While there are distinct regional practices in design and construction of the vernacular throughout the South Pacific, common is the tradition of minimalist, even temporary, building construction comprised primarily of vegetative materials. This is in response to availability, the benign climate and the unpredictability of the moods of the Pacific. Building types mostly are limited to the dwelling and various ceremonial buildings, and the functional and symbolic importance accorded the roof is widespread. Given that the roof is the principal element of South Pacific building, it becomes a powerful representative form in architecture.[23]

Regional materials and tried ways and means of planning and spatial enclosure make for a kinship between individual buildings in the village, with building skills, functional use and importance giving rise to differing expressions. Structures of social and religious hierarchies determine locations for special-use buildings. In remote areas across the Pacific, a rich, diverse range of specific answers to the dictates of place and custom, within a family of shared materials and forms and planning traditions, still can be found. As modern materials and technology are overlaid, traditional building skills are being lost.

Technological Making

As architects are not in the South Pacific in large numbers, architects from outside the region design many significant works – but this is changing. There are no universities that offer degrees in architecture in the small South Pacific countries. Those speaking English attend universities mostly in Australia, New Zealand and Papua New Guinea, and sometimes England, while those speaking French almost exclusively have received their degrees in France. There are some Melanesian and Polynesian architects primarily educated in Papua New Guinea and occasionally Australia or New Zealand, and these also are increasing in number. While building regulations do not exist across all islands, insurance companies pressure designers to meet building code standards from nearby developed countries such as Australia or New Zealand. There can be difficulties associated with building in the South Pacific, many of which stem from geological instability and the variable weather conditions. Further, in much of the region there is a low level of technology available plus a shortage of skilled workers, tradespeople and construction materials. Yet, these conditions have not precluded the construction of buildings of distinction.

The Oceanic Identity

As was the situation in other colonial countries, Europeans in the South Pacific seem to have found little precedence in vernacular structures for the building types they required. Throughout the short history of European settlement, the acceptance and application of architectural solutions existing elsewhere – notably Europe – has been normal practice, with the modification of these forms, as demanded by Pacific conditions. Recognition of the appropriateness of some vernacular building types for new uses appeared towards the end of the nineteenth century, as with the churches of Tonga, which adapted the fale to accommodate the Christian ritual. In the mid-twentieth century, vernacular forms and details were appropriated by the tourist industry. Although most investors and architects remain of expatriate origin, recent decades have seen an increasing appreciation of the applicability of certain qualities of the buildings and arts of the indigenous people of Oceania, and sensitivity is emerging that blends the universal and the local.

Part II

IN TRANSITION

SETTLEMENTS IN THE SOUTH PACIFIC

1

TWO TOWNS

Port de France: Noumea

Unlike most of the islands of the South Pacific, New Caledonia was not formed by recent volcanic uplift; rather, it is very old, being a breakaway fragment of the Gondwana supercontinent.[1] It shares, however, the cyclonic weather patterns found across most of the South Pacific region. New Caledonia consists of the large island of Grande Terre, the Loyalty Islands of Ouvéa, Lifou, Tiga and Mare to the north-east with the coral atolls of the Île des Pins to the south. The country is situated approximately 2000 kilometres north-east of Sydney. The location of New Caledonia is of strategic importance in the western Pacific, and the country became a major US base during World War II. New Caledonia, a special territorial collectivity (*sui generis collectivity*), is of particular value to France due to its location and its rich supplies of nickel.[2] Following the export of nickel, tourism is the primary source of income, with visitors numbering approximately 150 000 per year, of which one third are accounted for by cruise ships, coming primarily from Australia.[3]

Excavated pottery dating back more than 2500 years evidences the early settlement of the islands of the New Caledonia archipelago by the Lapita people.[4] European contact occurred in the eighteenth century, with the landing of James Cook in 1774 and the naming of the archipelago as New Caledonia. Traders followed in the early nineteenth century, with the London Missionary Society arriving in approximately 1840, and the Catholic Marist priests in 1846. In 1853 France annexed the country to protect the floundering Catholic missions, and from 1863 it served as a penal colony.[5] At the time of the 1996 census, 44 per cent of the total population of New Caledonia were indigenous Melanesian, 34 per cent were European and the remaining 22 per cent were made up of those from the nearby islands of Wallis and

Futuna, as well as from Indonesia, Vietnam, Vanuatu and elsewhere.[6] The first uprising over the French occupation of Melanesian land occurred in 1878–79.[7] Further unrest has continued, and the Matignon Accords and the Accords of Noumea, of 1988, sought to redress these issues, but the country remains divided by pro-France and independent sentiments.

Port de France

Noumea occupies a splendid site on one of the largest harbours in the world and spreads for fifteen kilometres along a hilly and deeply indented peninsula in the south-west of the island of Grande Terre. A considerable part of central Noumea is built on reclaimed land and thirty-nine kilometres of its coastline have been artificially formed. While some reclamation took place for the building of the port in the nineteenth century, most has occurred since the economic growth at the end of the 1960s.[8] Unlike most South Pacific countries, due to nickel mining, New Caledonia is financially solvent. The early name for Noumea of 'Port de France' still rings true today (although in 1866 it was changed to avoid postal confusion with Fort de France in Martinique), as Noumea is primarily European in character, with buildings and settings quite akin to those of the Mediterranean.[9] It is a dichotomous city for, while central Noumea still operates as a political, business and transportation hub, it has shown little development as a residential or tourist centre. Few apartments or hotels of status were built in central Noumea after the Hôtel de la Gare of 1905, and the original city became overshadowed in the second half of the century by extensive growth along the peninsula to the south.

The Town

The sleepy colonial town of Port de France grew along Baie de la Moselle. The plan of central Noumea, which runs inland from the bay, was originally laid out in 1855 by the chief of the battalion, Paul Coffyn, with an approximate north-south grid of streets placed irrespective of landform.[10] Coffyn's plan centres on the square of Place des Cocotiers[11] with rue de la République to the north, flanking the extensive grounds of the high commission of the Republic, and defined to the south by the major twin streets of Avenue Henry Lafleur and Avenue de la Victoire, forming an axial mall that leads to La Caserne, the extensive stone army barracks of 1869.[12] While there was a considerable number of buildings occupied by the penal establishment, major civic buildings were few in number.[13] Apart from the barracks, Noumea boasted the Bank of New Caledonia on the Place des Cocotiers that was designed by Henri Marchand and built in 1875. In 1882 it became the Noumea Town Hall.[14] The Catholic Cathedral of St Joseph, 1888,

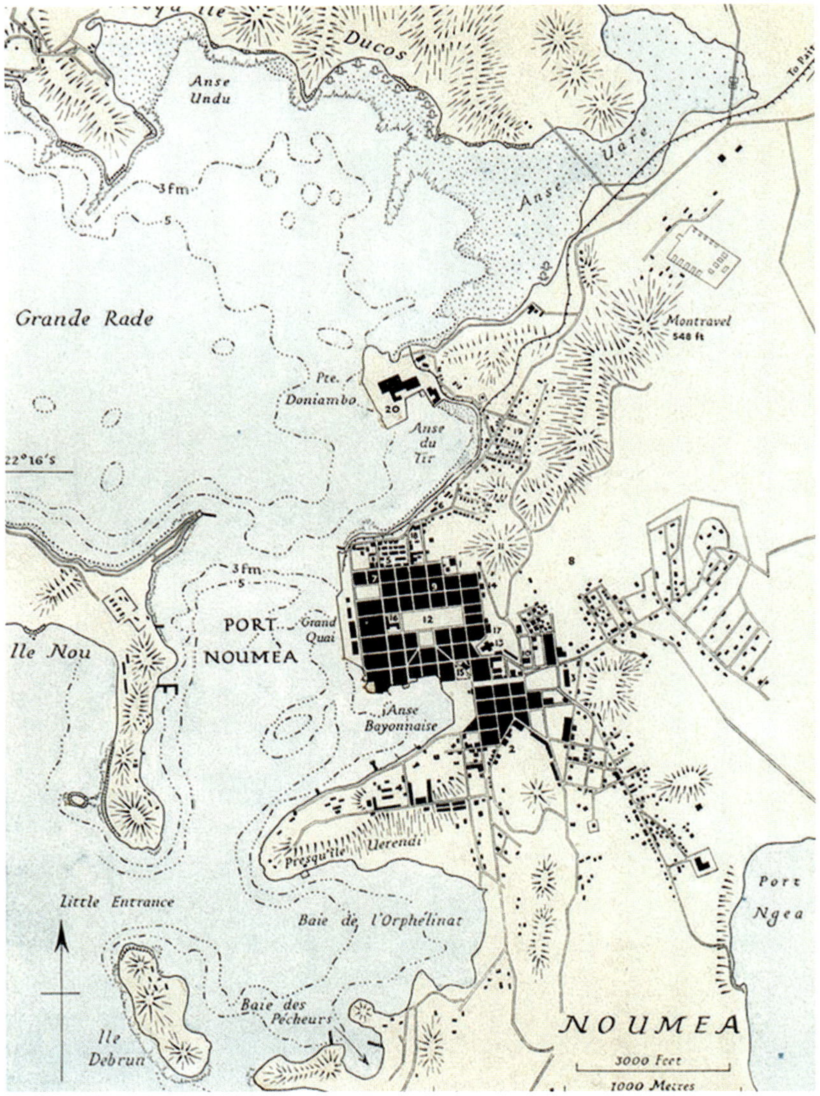

splendidly located on a hill overlooking the town and Baie de la Moselle, still dominates the town, while the restrained Temple of the Reformed Church, 1893, was built on lower ground in central Noumea. The latter two, among others, were constructed using convict labour. From central Noumea the long island of Nouville (connected to the mainland by a causeway in 1972) runs off to the west, forming to the north the protected cargo ship harbour, the Grande Rade. Nouville has

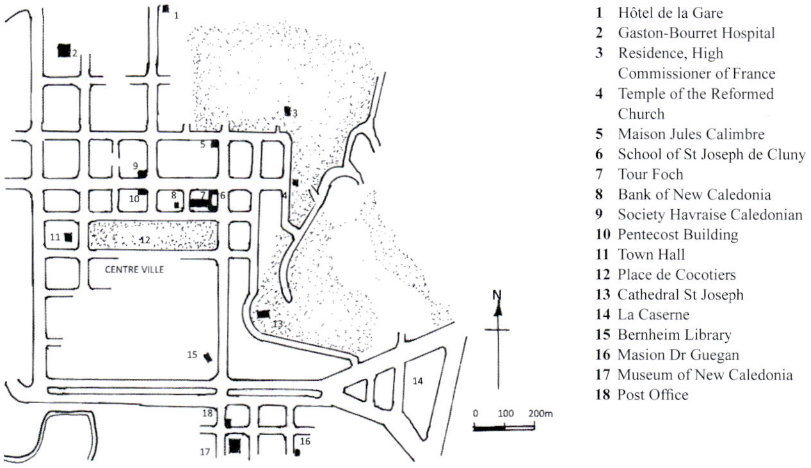

OPPOSITE: Noumea Port Plan, c. 1920, showing the Coffyn Plan for Central Noumea (1855). *Courtesy of University of Texas Libraries, the University of Texas at Austin.*

PREVIOUS PAGE: La Caserne.

ABOVE LEFT: Cathedral of St Joseph, Noumea, 1888.

TOP RIGHT: Plan of central Noumea showing early buildings.

ABOVE RIGHT: Temple of the Reformed Church, Noumea, 1893.

Bank of New Caledonia, Noumea, 1875. Henri Marchand. *Courtesy of Archives New Caledonia: 1 Num 4-05.*

been occupied since the nineteenth century for military use, with the first convict prison and associated structures in the country.[15] The residential areas of Vallée des Colons grew to the east, and Vallée du Tir and Ducos to the north. There was little expansion to the south, but this was to change dramatically after World War II.

The selection of Noumea as the US military headquarters for the Pacific operations was to have an instant and lasting effect on its development and on the facilities of the town and its surroundings. While the headquarters of General Patch, the commander of the US forces in New Caledonia, were established in central Noumea, the camps, general service and amenities buildings were located to the south along the beautiful bays of Baie des Citrons and Anse Vata at the end of the peninsula, opening up new areas for future growth. The construction of Magenta Airport on Baie de Magenta encouraged development to the east.

Nickel and the New Prosperity

Between the end of the war and the nickel boom of 1968–72, when world nickel prices soared by 50 per cent, Noumea developed slowly, with the major economic stimulus for the city coming from the sporting facilities built for the Pacific Games of 1966. The discovery of nickel in 1863 had a great impact on the city, not only because of the prosperity that it brought, but also because of the large numbers of people who flocked to New Caledonia due to the increase of the nickel exports in the late 1960s, with most settling in Noumea.[16] The industrial zone expanded to the north, and the building of the Société Le Nickel (SLN) smelter, Doniambo, attracted Melanesian workers from outside the town, many of whom moved into the nearby crowded Vallée du Tir. This pattern continued and between 1969 and 1978, 50 000 people entered the country. Of those, 6000 stayed.[17] Many large multi-storeyed housing estates were built by the government to help accommodate the mass migration of workers from Europe, Asia and Polynesia, as well as from nearby countries and from within New Caledonia itself, to work in the nickel mines and processing plants. In all, 2250 minimal units, in towers similar to those of the European housing estates of the time, were constructed in Magenta and in several centres to the north.[18] Of note among these was the 1974 Magenta Housing Complex designed by Louis de Hoym de Marien from Paris in association with Miloç Hristic, as architect in charge in Paris. Local Noumea architects André Maikovsky and his then partner Yves Cormier were responsible for the supervision of construction.[19] The estate consists of 844 units incorporated within twelve tower blocks ranging in height from three to fourteen floors. The complex represented state-of-the-art European planning of the 1960s, with a staggered arrangement of the multi-storeyed residential blocks arranged around a shared central green area and serviced by an external ring road. The Magenta Housing Complex was the subject of a revitalization study by Maikovsky in December 2006.[20]

One further result of the upswing in nickel production was the upgrading of transportation services, with extensions to the ports and a new airport capable of receiving jumbo jets, being constructed north of Noumea at Tontouta. The first terminal, designed in France, was completed in 1971.[21] It is a competent if conservative modern building of concrete columns and slab construction with a double-height departure lounge enclosed by a glass façade facing the parking and arrival points. La Tontouta International Airport made a considerable contribution towards the future growth of Noumea. To the east of the city, the 1995 Jean-Marie Tjibaou Cultural Centre also brought further life and activity to that region.

It was, however, along Baie de l'Orphelinat, immediately to the south of central Noumea, and Port Plaisance, further down the south-west coast, that have witnessed the remarkable changes that occurred after 1990. Following the withdrawal of the US troops, the region retained its political importance, with Anse Vata chosen as the location for headquarters of the 1995 South Pacific Commission, the most important regional organization in the South Pacific. But primarily this southern part of Noumea is the home of tourists and those comfortably off, with hotels, expensive

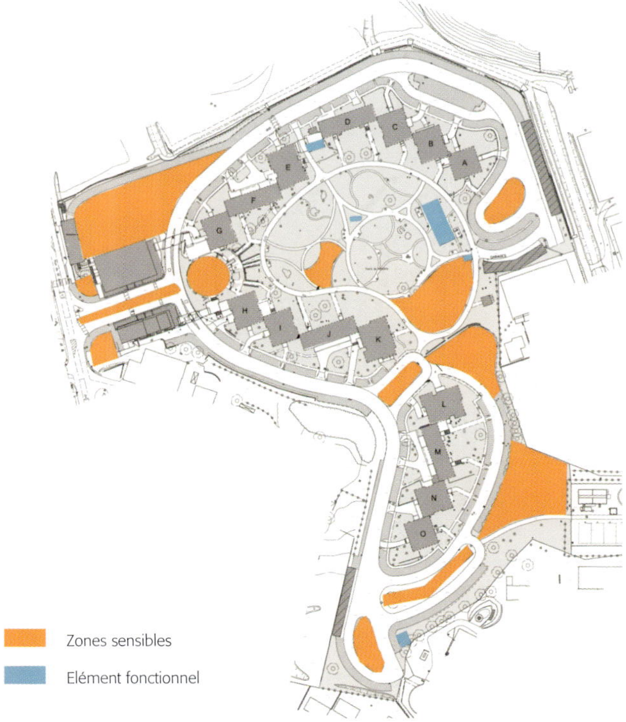

LEFT: La Tontouta International Airport, Grande Terre, New Caledonia, 1971.

ABOVE: Magenta Housing Complex, Noumea, 1974. Louis de Hoym de Marien and Miloç Hristic. Site plan: André Maikovsky, 2006.

apartments, shopping centres and restaurants. The central city was promised fresh life in 2010 when Noumea authorities held an international competition for a new master plan for the Noumea waterfront. The scheme was to include accommodation, a conference centre, museums, and a marina and market to serve as a gateway to the city. Seventeen entries were received and seven firms were selected to enter stage two of the competition.[22] In 2011 the project was awarded to the Australian firm of Woods Bagot. As at 2013 the waterfront master plan was moving to a new phase of consolidation, with the ambition to start construction in 2014.[23]

The twentieth century saw the development of Noumea from a small French colonial and convict outpost into the most cosmopolitan town of the South Pacific, due primarily to the dominant French presence. It grew as a dispersion of small communities of diverse nature and economic status around the central hub of the old town. Significant for the nature of the urban structure was the distribution of the prosperous section of the population along the spine of the peninsula to the south, branching from the rest of the town and virtually creating two Noumeas. Today, urban growth is occurring to the city's north.

'Water from a Basket': Papeete 1950–70

French Polynesia consists of thirty-five islands and eighty-three atolls in five archipelagos: the Society, Austral, Tuamotu, Gambier and Marquesas. These small islands, scattered to the east of the Cook Islands, are distributed across the sea from south-east to north-west, and in aerial terms cover approximately the same area as the continent of Europe. There is substantial variation between the island groups, with some being volcanic and others of coral formation. The Society Islands, consisting of the Windward Islands of Tahiti and Moorea and the Leeward Islands including Huahine and Bora Bora, are of recent volcanic origin, and the steep mountainous terrain restricts the habitable land to the ocean fringe. The Tahiti group consists of two joined islands, Tahiti Iti and the larger Tahiti Nui, with the capital of French Polynesia, Papeete, located on its north coast. Cyclones are rare in East Polynesia, but Papeete did suffer considerable devastation from the cyclone of 1906.

Papeete in Transition

Modern Papeete is the outcome of a rapid and profound transition that occurred over a very short period in the 1960s, when its links to the rest of the world expanded extensively, and it was forced into prominence following the establishment of France's nuclear Centre d'Expérimentation du Pacifique (CEP) base in 1963, with the atolls of Moruroa and Fangataufa serving as nuclear testing sites between 1966 and 1996.[1] Papeete was in a wretched state in the 1950s, and the demands caused by the drastic changes over the next decade were disruptive to the town and increased the social deprivation and poverty in the urban environment. Primarily due to the remarkable efforts of Jean Charles Sicurani, the governor of the territory of French Polynesia from 1965 to 1969, many of the difficulties were overcome and through judicious controls, incentives, and extensive planning and building programmes the town became better prepared to handle its new status and functions. Today, Papeete ('Water from a Basket') is the most bustling and dynamic town in the South Pacific, yet there is something still of the early settlement about it, and its streets, as in the past, seem to wander at will.[2] The town wraps around the busy working harbour, with ships, sheds and bristling cranes a part of the everyday scene. It is an active place with 105 000 people, that is, 51 per cent of the population of French Polynesia, living in the urban zone of its communes.[3] Due to the topography of Tahiti, Papeete is spread out thinly around the waterfront and includes the communes of Faa'a, Papeete, Puna'auia, Pirae and Arue.

Pre-war Papeete consisted primarily of three sections: first, the colonial military and administrative centre and the royal palace and governor's palace around Avenue Bruat, centring on the historic Broche district to the west; second, the waterfront, with important buildings including the leading hotel, Hotel Stuart, the post office and the US Embassy, and third, to the east, the commercial centre containing the cathedral, the Bank of Indochina and the markets, with the town hall and convent further beyond.[4] In the 1940s many of the fine old nineteenth-century houses and colonial buildings were still standing, but most of the more recent additions had been hastily built and were of poor quality and infested with termites. The Chinese community, primarily traders descended from workers who had arrived between 1872 and 1911, had established itself in the region near the markets, and the expansion of Papeete in the post-war years occurred principally in this eastern section of the town.[5]

Papeete entered the second half of the twentieth century as a still-small trading port with a population of 28 000, over 80 per cent of whom were Polynesian and

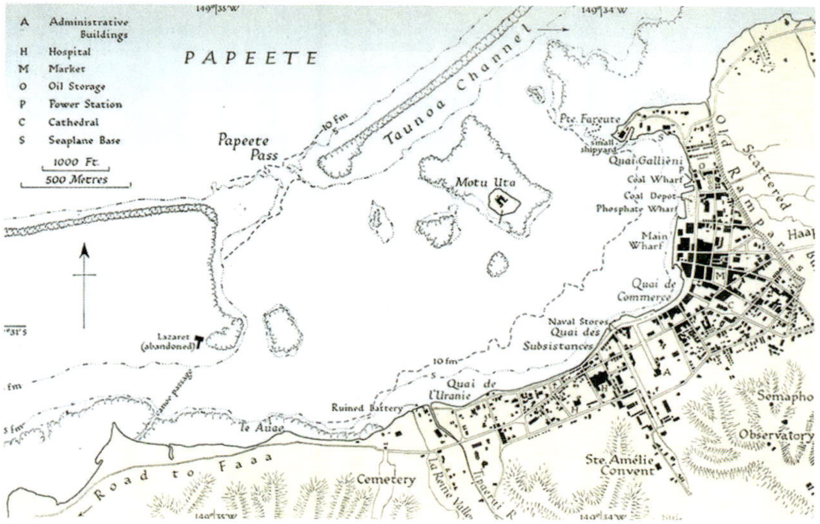

Papeete Town Plan, Tahiti, French Polynesia, 1931. *Courtesy of University of Texas Libraries, The University of Texas at Austin.*

Mid-century Papeete port facilities. *Courtesy of the French Polynesia Archives.*

5 per cent Chinese.[6] The Chinese minority were important to the commercial life of the town, and the first major Chinese stores were opened in the 1950s. The town was isolated from most of the world due to primitive communication systems and, apart from the Bora Bora airstrip, it had limited transportation connections.[7]

Unlike World War I, in which, during 1914, German warships attacked Papeete, World War II had little physical impact on the town, as the French naval hydroplane base at Fare Ute closed in 1941 and most of the American activity was confined to the island of Bora Bora.[8] The population of Papeete was greatly increasing, with a doubling of the number of inhabitants between 1921 and 1951, but there were inadequate services including communication, power, and water and sanitary drainage. There were no daily newspapers, little broadcasting and limited electricity.[9] A small number of streets were paved, but most were chaotic dusty tracks on which a few cars joined the carts and pedestrians.[10] There were no planning proposals or controls, and lots were subdivided in random fashion – not in accordance with the street layout. 'The commune created in 1890 never had the money (or the will?) to carry out the necessary public works and infrastructure and successive administrations never really faced the major problem of the town's burgeoning population growth.'[11] To add to the depressing situation, dancing had been stamped out by evangelism!

The Young Planners

In 1950 Robert Auzelle, Professor of Theory at the Beaux Arts and the Institute of Urbanism in Paris, went to Tahiti to undertake an urban study of Papeete.[12] When, at thirty-seven years of age, Auzelle arrived he was 'little prepared for the disgraceful sight and the misery that the town presented; he went inside the courtyards of Chinese houses in the centre of town and in the sordid narrow streets of certain peripheral quarters. White ants were eating many of the houses and there were terrible pools of stagnant and polluted water and sewerage material was draining straight into the lagoon.'[13] He immediately applied himself to the town's problems, proposing slum clearance and new housing programmes.[14] He commissioned the photographer Adolphe Sylvain to make a photographic study of the town as a record of its condition, and with Sylvain, Auzelle undertook an aerial photographic survey of possible sites for the proposed new airport.[15] After five months of work Auzelle submitted his report, Plan for the Management of the Agglomeration of Papeete, which was accompanied by justification and annexed documents indicating how the plan was to be realized, 'but the politicians did not have the courage, heart or political will to adopt the plan,' so it was set aside.[16] Auzelle published the work in *La Vie Urbaine*, No. 60, April 1951, providing 'a lucid examination of the situation in 1950 and the first modern urban study done concerning Papeete'.[17]

Auzelle's work paved the way for the appointment in 1952 of Michel Prévot, who was twenty-seven years old when he came from France with a contract with the government for a post as architect and urbanist.[18] Prévot had studied at the Institute of Urbanism, Paris, and graduated with a diploma from the School of Special Architectural Studies.[19] Despite the plan set forth by Auzelle, the situation in Papeete remained unchanged as 'they had no planning and the money was very scarce'.[20] Prévot's proposals for Papeete followed closely on those of Auzelle, and he extended this work to projects for the outer islands. Prévot established his own practice in 1955 and was to design the major public, political and cultural buildings of Papeete in the 1960s and 1970s.

In 1959 Claude Bach,[21] a thirty-year-old architect from France who had won the Prix de Rome in 1958, arrived in Tahiti on contract to SETIL[22] to do a further urban plan for Papeete, of which 59 per cent was still of wood construction at the time. Auzelle's plan of nine years before had never been implemented, and the town was much as it had been when he left office. Bach further expanded it into a new proposal that he submitted in 1960 but, as with Auzelle's plan, Bach's plan was not officially adopted.[23] Bach did, however, complete several architectural projects for CEP, including offices and housing for the commune, the plan for Faa'a airport, and his later submissions, such as his proposals for the second plan for Papeete, the seafront of Papeete and the town of Pirae, contributed to their urban improvements.

In addition, Bach was architect for the important Gauguin Museum, built in 1964, which provided the first cultural exposition offering insights into Tahitian life. In this, Bach was assisted by a young German architect, Rodolphe Weinmann, aged twenty-seven, who had studied at Strasbourg and graduated in 1959. He arrived in Tahiti in 1963 and worked for SETIL and in association with Bach on the museum. His new bride, Claude Boyon, an interior designer, accompanied him.[24] While with SETIL, Weinmann was involved in construction and planning. During the period 1964–65 he presented plans for Pirae, Faa'a, Taravao and Papeete, and in 1966–67 undertook building projects such as the school at Blue Lagoon, housing and the markets at Pirae. Weinmann established his own office in 1970, and his projects included many commercial structures for the Chinese community and several notable buildings including the Papeete Post Office, 1980, and Town Hall, 1990.[25] He returned to France in 2004.

The early 1960s witnessed a major turning point for Papeete. While the first air route between Paris and Papeete had commenced in 1950, prior to 1961 all entry by aircraft to French Polynesia was via the airstrip built by the Americans on Bora Bora in 1942. From there passengers travelled by seaplane to Papeete. In 1961 Tahiti's airport at Faa'a went into operation, permitting direct international access to Papeete. Due to the mountainous terrain of the island, the airport was constructed mainly on reclaimed shelves of coral reef off the north coast of Tahiti Nui. In the same year Pan Am, UTA and TEAL inaugurated jet air travel to Tahiti, and in 1964 the terminal was completed. The building of the airport at Faa'a made possible the next momentous change to come to Papeete, as it became feasible for General de Gaulle to transfer to the Pacific his nuclear testing programme from Algeria. The phosphate mining reserves, which had provided a considerable percentage of French Polynesia's income since 1911, were exhausted in 1966, and the territory was facing an economic recession. To remedy the financial situation the assembly agreed to the establishment of the CEP. This resulted in the introduction of vast infrastructure and construction projects on Moruroa and Fangataufa and on the advanced CEP bases at Hao and Tahiti. Critical to the running of CEP was the construction of new port facilities for the handling of materials and personnel related to the nuclear sites. The port project commenced in the early 1960s, and amenities and services were considerably improved with the reclamation of the reef and the building of Port Autonome during 1964–66.[26] In 1966 France's spending in Tahiti at the height of the construction boom was 76 per cent of Gross National Product.[27] 'The massive, and continually increasing injection of public funds (civilian and military) secured for the territory resources unparalleled in preceding cycles and caused significant disturbance.'[28]

Jean Charles Sicurani

When Jean Charles Sicurani took up the post of governor in 1965, Tahiti 'had the appearance of a crumbling society', and Papeete was in a chaotic state.[29] Sicurani was a highly capable leader, and for the next five years he steered the country through a turbulent period of change.[30] Early in his administration Sicurani collaborated with the Council of the Governor and the elected territorial assembly and gained support and consent for his many programmes. The arrival of thousands of French to work on the CEP nuclear station had resulted in a major disruption to the island community. This was compounded by the migration of workers and their families from the outer islands to Tahiti, mostly to Papeete, to work on the building of the new airport, to profit from the thousands of new CEP jobs or to work for high wages as helpers or as extras for MGM during the 1961–62 filming of the second version of *Mutiny on the Bounty*.[31]

There was inadequate infrastructure, housing or facilities for the increasing numbers, and further slum communities soon formed again. The agglomeration of Papeete spread around the newly extended port facilities to Pirae and Faa'a. The city was congested and in a deplorable condition, with crowding and consequent social tension. Fortunately, the endowments from France to the territorial assembly, and income from the American film industry and the CEP nuclear station, by way of both wages and expenditure in the town, provided funds to help the city adapt to its new role. To help cope with the exploding urban growth and protect the environment, Sicurani established the Urban Planning and Housing Office, which significantly raised the amenity and the quality of life in the city through many notable landscape projects, such as the realization of the Boulevard de Mer and the reservation of Park Bougainville. In addition, he renovated the commercial centre and introduced a large construction programme across many building types, including government and cultural buildings, a television station, housing, schools, port offices, hospitals and airport landing strips on the outer islands. Among the many other projects he initiated were the Olympic Pool, the Olympic Stadium at Pirae,[32] the hospital at Mamao and the renovation of the cathedral.[33] Sicurani encouraged proposals that were Polynesian in spirit, including government buildings such as the Territorial Assembly, the Tourist Bureau and the Cultural Centre.

Notwithstanding the negative world attitudes that prevailed with the establishment of CEP, tourism was still considered to be a potential source for investment in French Polynesia. In order to support incentives, Sicurani had a tourist bureau built on the waterfront in central Papeete, and encouraged and regulated tourist growth, including the introduction of tax concessions for tourist facilities. In 1966 he adopted two important measures: first, he created the Office of Development and Tourism (ODT), and second, he introduced an investment code for developers. For his building programme Sicurani had the professional advice of Bach who, after the rejection of his 1960 plan for Papeete, had turned his attention to tourist facilities. Bach's reports and proposals, plus Sicurani's initiatives, led to the completion of a number of major projects, including two international hotels, each of 200 rooms: the Tahara'a, funded by American investors, including Pan Am Airways, and the Maeva Beach Hotel, with finance from UTA, the Caisse des Dépôts and the Bank of Indochina.[34] Numerous other major projects to boost tourism were undertaken including an international standard golf course at Mataiea,[35] the Museum of Discovery at Port Venus, the restoration of the tomb of Pomare and a number of communal/sacred gathering places – the 'marae'.[36]

While the growth in tourist numbers followed the introduction of convenient and frequent air travel with the completion of Faa'a International Airport, Sicurani's role in improving conditions in French Polynesia was critical. The impact of the airport on the town was dramatic – not only were there many tourists passing through town and spending US dollars, but the introduction of mass tourism also meant more jobs. Therefore, migration to Papeete continued, placing further stress on the urban fabric. By 1971 the population had increased to 64 451, and with the prosperity of the next decade it continued to grow.[37] The affluence of the 1970s was evidenced by the opening of the central major shopping complex of Viama Centre. Sicurani was far-sighted enough during his tenure to establish a working group to explore development options after CEP was disbanded.[38] Before his departure Sicurani started two further important projects, 'which would never have been realized without him': the establishment of the Centre of Polynesian Culture and Science at Puna'auia, which had scientific, cultural and tourist programmes, and the establishment of a new centre at Vairao for the exploration of marine resources.[39] The land for the cultural centre was purchased in 1966 but the complex, later named the Museum of Tahiti and Its Islands was not built until 1977.

Despite the local commune leaders' lack of interest in, let alone commitment to, the infrastructure and physical fabric of Papeete, four young, newly graduated designers and a dedicated governor took up the challenge of injecting some order and amenity into the chaos of Papeete in the 1950s and 1960s. They worked hard to find solutions to a number of problems – both material and human – to enable Papeete to adapt to its new conditions and status, and to embellish the town and enrich the lives of its inhabitants. When Sicurani left Tahiti for France in 1969, the ramshackle town of Papeete had grown into a busy, but still congested, city, though one with an emerging structure, greatly improved facilities and services and, importantly, some sense of identity.

BUILDERS AND BUILDINGS 2

Early 'Architects' of New Caledonia 1900–1980

The date of arrival as well as the amount and geographic spread of European architecture varied considerably throughout the South Pacific. In the early decades of the twentieth century, buildings of the church and those of the colonial administration, mostly designed in Europe, continued to dominate the landscape of the towns. In New Caledonia little development occurred outside Noumea until towards the end of the twentieth century. In Noumea, however, some accomplished buildings, builder-designed, prefabricated, or based on French pattern books, were constructed early in the century. There were no trained architects, but there were a handful of builders who introduced innovative ideas and new materials from overseas. Some military personnel in Noumea were called architects, but it appears they were primarily engineers. The term *architecte-voyer* was loosely used, as in *architecte-voyer de la ville*, a title given to those in charge of construction in the municipality. The role existed up until 1957, but the appointees were administrators and sometimes engineers rather than architects.[1] The first accredited architects arrived in the post-war years.

New Buildings for the New Century

For the most part, the twentieth-century architecture of Noumea was primarily of European derivation. Some regional input, by way of ideas and materials, came from Australia, as the countries are close and the climate of New Caledonia is similar to that of Queensland. Further, access to Noumea from the rest of the world historically was through Sydney.[2] The London Missionary Society had not been as successful in New Caledonia as it had in most parts of the Pacific. The French missionaries also struggled, but with French settlement and annexation, Catholicism became the dominant religion, and

LEFT: Church of St John the Baptist, Vallée des Colons, Noumea, Grande Terre, New Caledonia, 1923. Father Gaudet.

PREVIOUS PAGE: Museum of New Caledonia.

with the exception of the Temple of the Reformed Church, Protestant churches tended not to be of particular architectural significance. The first major building for the Catholic Church in the new century was the Church of St John the Baptist in the Vallée des Colons district of Noumea, consecrated in 1903 but not completed until the steeple was erected in 1923. The cathedral in Noumea could not house the congregation, and the Church of St John the Baptist was built to help with the overflow. The Reverend Father Gaudet, a Marist missionary, was appointed to this task.[3] Throughout the Pacific it was normally the local priest who was entrusted with the erection of churches. In this instance, however, it would seem likely that the design, or at least the instruction, came from Paris. The traditional and academic brick architecture of St John the Baptist is uncommon for early Catholic churches, which, usually being designed locally and by fresh untrained eyes, tend to be simple and inventive. Typical are the 1913 Thio Mission Church and the 1934 brick Church of the Sacred Heart at Bourail, which replaced a wooden church first built in 1878.[4] The Bourail church has an appealing basic form like a child's drawing and contrasts with the dynamic verticality of the Thio church.

In 1902 the prefabricated steel structure of what is now the Bernheim Library was erected in Noumea. The building was designed in France by the Parisian architect M Bley and installed at the 1900 Paris Exposition as New Caledonia's Pavilion Colonial de l'Exposition Universelle. It is claimed that the exposed, lightly framed steel roof trusses were designed by the French engineer Gustave Eiffel.[5] It later was demounted and shipped to Noumea and remounted on the present site.[6] Hence, the building was transported from Paris to constitute the environment it was originally intended to represent. The building served different functions before

ABOVE: Church of the Thio Mission, Thio, Grande Terre, 1913.

RIGHT: Church of the Sacred Heart, Bourail, Grande Terre, 1934.

LEFT: Bernheim Library, Noumea, 1902. M Bley.
ABOVE: Construction. *Courtesy of Bibliothéque Bernheim.*

becoming the library that it now is. The shipping of prefabricated buildings to the South Pacific continues, mostly from Australia and New Zealand, with some from America. The beginning of the century also saw the construction of the railway from Noumea to Bourail and, with that, the building in 1905 by entrepreneur Paul Mosnier of a hotel at the Noumea terminus, the Hôtel de la Gare.[7] The original hotel had only six rooms, but new wings were added up until 1926. In 1940, after the railway failed, it was renamed Grand Hôtel du Pacifique. It was famed throughout the Pacific and is claimed to have been of today's five-star standard.[8] During World War II it was used as the headquarters for General Patch of the US forces. While given over to various mixed uses and in poor condition, it survived as an evocative, primarily timber building with some masonry walls, wooden shutters, timber fretwork around windows and eaves, and cast iron balustrades. The design for the ornamental work probably would have been from a French pattern book or have been imported from France.

Towards the end of the nineteenth century several fine examples of New Caledonian houses were constructed. Outstanding examples include the 1892 Château Hagen, with a dominant central tower, that was designed by Jean Taragnat, a young Marist brother and professional mason who had come to New Caledonia as a missionary,[9] and Maison Célières, 1898, built by M. Géroso, which is a

FAR LEFT: Prefabricated Cottage, rue de Soissons, Vallée des Colons, Noumea, c.1905–06. Porch detail.

LEFT: Hôtel de la Gare, Noumea.

BELOW: Hôtel de la Gare, 1905. *Courtesy of Archives New Caledonia: 1 NUM 4-08.*

LEFT: Maison, 8 rue Paul Deligny, Noumea, c.1939. M Ritter.

BELOW LEFT: Maison, 16 rue Paul Deligny, Noumea, 1939. M Ritter.

BELOW: Maison Gaudriault, Noumea, c.1939. Georges Derquennes.

one-storey building with a central square plan dominated by four corner pavilions.[10] Finance for these investments was often gained from the nickel mines, as was the case with Maison Higginson, which was built for a wealthy industrialist, one of the founders of the Nickel Society of 1880.[11] Maison Higginson, 1901, a fine two-storeyed house of a more progressive design, has an asymmetrical plan with a gabled wing set forward towards the street. It is a well-proportioned building with handsome French windows, balconies and shutters on both levels.[12]

Early in the century a major hardware and materials importing firm, Ballande Barrau, established a permanent branch office in Sydney – thus an important connection with the Australian building trade was established.[13] In 1905–06, on rue de Soissons in Noumea's Vallée des Colons, M. Ballande erected three typical prefabricated cottages, imported from Australia for himself and the management of the nickel mines. The house at 13 rue Pasteur, Vallée du Tir, with four corner pyramid roofs, similar to Maison Célières, is typical of the builder houses of the prosperous class of the early twentieth century. It has an agreeable plan with verandas linking

13 rue Pasteur, Vallée du Tir, Noumea, 1933.

the corner pavilions and a central corridor with rooms on each side opening to the verandas. Records show that the land changed hands in 1917–18, so the house was probably built just after that time. It was rebuilt in 1933 in the aftermath of a cyclone and extensively renovated in 1994.[14] Around 1939 on rue Paul Deligny three mansions showing influence of the Art Nouveau style were built by an Italian builder, M Ritter, to similar plans but with different façades.[15] They are mature buildings with well-proportioned forms and spacious rooms of quality design and construction. The generous use of large windows is certainly uncommon for the time. Their style and evident classical spirit derives from their Italian builder, who left Noumea for California following World War II.[16] Also of interest is the work of a further builder, Jules Mary, who constructed some large and distinctive houses in Noumea in the 1930s and 1940s, including two adjoining houses, known as Maison Mary, between 1930 and 1934, in what is described as both 'northern Flemish' and 'neo-Basque' style.[17] It appears that another builder, Georges Derquennes, was involved with the drafting of houses for Mary, until draftsman Gilbert Allègre from Marseilles, who had married Mary's daughter, came to New Caledonia and displaced him.[18] Derquennes also built several houses to his own designs, including Maison Gaudriault, 1939.[19]

Reinforced concrete had been introduced early in the century and became a common building material in the 1930s and 1940s. Of interest is the use of concrete in the buildings of a Czechoslovakian builder, Martin Bottcher, who established his business in 1935 and built several houses between then and 1949.[20] Bottcher's idiosyncratic designs and concrete details impart a distinctive character to some of the older parts of Noumea. His houses have little to do with the climate or space of New Caledonia, nevertheless, this is innovative and competent work and must have been quite startling to New Caledonians at the time of construction. Maison Jules Calimbre is generally credited as the first architect-designed house in New Caledonia. Calimbre bought the plans from an architect in Paris, and the house was erected in central Noumea in 1938.[21] It is an uncommon dwelling, inspired by the Art Deco of France but with considerable originality evident in the strong geometric modelling of the form, the precast ornamental concrete

2 rue Bichat, Noumea, 1948. Martin Bottcher.

balustrades, the strange parapet to the roof and the handsome pair of coloured-glass entry doors. The generous spaces of the interiors are characterized by fine timber cabinetwork of doors and mouldings. The sheltered veranda zone is broad and accommodating. The house was burnt down in 1985 during a period of civil unrest and rebuilt to the original form and detail in 1992.

The American Arrival

The importance of Noumea during the war was primarily as a forward US army base in the South Pacific, and this period marks a further turning point in the history of the country. War-time Noumea was described as 'a pretty dreary place with service men by the thousands thronging the streets, standing around with nothing to do, and no place to go.'[22] With the American presence, the population of Noumea doubled, and new tent towns, such as Camp Barnes at Anse Vata and the camp at Baie des Citrons, emerged seemingly overnight. The first landing saw 30 000 troops come ashore and over one million passed through Noumea between 1942 and 1945. The naval base was established on Nouville, and five airstrips were built on Grande Terre as well as one on the Île des Pins.[23] Up to 125 ships crowded the harbour, with hundreds of planes on the ground at the airport. The Pentagon, a structure of considerable dimensions, was built in 1944 on the waterfront as a part of Camp Barnes and was overlooked by the American Chapel located on the hillside behind.[24]

Some prefabricated huts built for the military hospital remained in use for the Anse Vata Clinic as late as 2005 and were among the few buildings that still evidenced the American settlement. However, its presence lives on in the names of some of Noumea's suburbs, such as Receiving and Motor Pool.[25] The post-war salvaging of war materials was common and can be seen in the reuse of discarded corrugated steel for various structures, the occupation of Quonset huts ('*demi-lunars*') primarily as houses and in the recycling of left-behind steel sand tracks as fencing. The Americans found Noumea a small tranquil backwater and left it with a new set of values, a raised economy and a major network of infrastructure, including Magenta Aerodrome, which helped link the country into the global transportation systems.

Maison Jules Calimbre, Noumea, 1938
(rebuilt 1992).

LEFT: The Pentagon Building and American Chapel, Anse Vata, Noumea, 1944. *Courtesy of Archives New Caledonia: 1 NUM 9-13.*

BELOW: Camp Barnes, Anse Vata, Noumea, *Courtesy of Archives New Caledonia: 1 NUM 12-11.*

The Post-War Era and the First Architects

Following the war, New Caledonia settled down to a life of increased affluence. Builders continued to introduce new ideas, materials and technologies. Significant among these builders was Alexander Jamieson from Newcastle, New South Wales. Jamieson furthered Australian influence in Noumea, with many houses based on typical Australian designs, such as the 1949–50 house in the Anse Vata region, which at one stage was Jamieson's own dwelling.[26] In 1948 he also constructed the Pentecost Building on rue de l'Alma in the city – the first building in the country with a lift.[27] This is an accomplished streamlined corner building of four storeys with a curving façade of banded white concrete spandrels alternating with continuous strip windows, while the upper floor is set back with an open arcade of horizontal concrete sun screens forming a pergola.

New Caledonia was fortunate in that the first permanent practising architect, Pierre Raighasse, was an architect of considerable aptitude. He was also a talented painter.[28] Raighasse graduated in France and came to New Caledonia in 1946. He was responsible for several schools, and individual and multiple housing, in both a crisp modernist style and in a richly sculptural mode that was part Art Deco and part Art Nouveau.[29] Raighasse's most imposing house was built in 1956 for Dr Guegan. The design is somewhat idiosyncratic in that it presents a cantilevered curving bay window protruding from the street façade yet resembles Frank Lloyd Wright's Unity Temple on the side. Also among his early buildings was the Society Havraise Caledonian building erected in 1951 on a corner site facing the Pentecost Building on rue de l'Alma. Raighasse's building is less resolved than Jamieson's and consists of two long office wings

ABOVE LEFT: Résidence Dr Guegan, Noumea, 1956. Pierre Raighasse.

ABOVE RIGHT: Maison Jamieson, Anse Vata, Noumea, 1949-50. Alexander Jamieson.

LEFT: Pentecost Building, Noumea, 1948. Alexander Jamieson.

BELOW: Society Havraise Caledonian Building, Noumea, 1951. Pierre Raighasse.

OPPOSITE: Church of the Vow, Noumea, 1953. Pierre Raighasse.

with strip windows facing each street. The horizontal banding of the windows is interrupted at the corner by a curved wall with a heavy cornice, which serves as an advertising surface.

Raighasse bequeathed to Noumea one of its finest edifices, the Church of the Vow, built on the crest of a hill overlooking Anse Vata. During the conflict, the Monsignor vowed that if the Virgin Mary would save New Caledonia from the imminent invasion by the Japanese, the congregation would build her a new church. After the war, funds were raised and the church was completed in 1953.[30] The building has a restraint and elegance reminiscent of the finest war memorials. Its flowing lines seem to rise effortlessly from the hill on which it stands. The simplicity of the soaring space of the interior, lit by floods of clear light, echoes that of the exterior. Raighasse's most notable civic building, the Museum of New Caledonia, 1962–67, is one of the few of the period to respond creatively to the climate of New Caledonia. It is a white rendered brick building built around a large courtyard through which air constantly passes by way of the decorative open steel grills fabricated to Raighasse's design. The building also has high ceilings and makes use of Noumea's clear light and sun by presenting planar white walls that both reflect the heat and invite the patterns of the graceful movements of palm tree shadows.[31] Raighasse's last building was the Indoor Sports Hall, Magenta, built for the Second Pacific Games of 1966. Raighasse was a gifted architect and was unfortunately lost to New Caledonia when he committed suicide in 1966.[32]

After the war professional assistance had been needed, primarily for the planning of Noumea, and such persons were brought from France to work for the government. Among these was the architect Paul Pascalon, who arrived in 1949 to study the city's planning. At the time, the state of the town was chaotic with very few controls

and a poor infrastructure. He imposed planning regulations and in 1952 submitted an urban planning scheme to the general council. Most of his recommendations were passed, thus setting a framework for development in Noumea.[33] While he was engaged principally as a planner, Pascalon also designed some institutional buildings, including the School of St Joseph de Cluny, rue de Sébastopol, built between 1951 and 1954.[34] The school is an extensive complex arranged around a large rectangular courtyard in differing styles and at various stages. He later became disillusioned with practice in Noumea and returned to France.

Similarly, in 1959 Jacques Rampal, a New Caledonian by birth, returned to Noumea to take up the post of Chief of Urbanism but later opened his own practice. He had trained in France as an architect and planner and had worked with Le Corbusier. This influence is evident in buildings such as the Residence of the High Commissioner of France, a crisp white planar building in the International

ABOVE: School of St Joseph de Cluny, Noumea, 1951–54. Paul Pascalon.

OPPOSITE: Museum of New Caledonia, Noumea, 1962–67. Pierre Raighasse.

MUSEE

Style dramatized by the strong projecting cantilevered roof over the entry, and the Fédération des Œuvres Laïques, built in 1975 on a hill on the site of the old Masonic temple, which was destroyed in 1963.[35] This is a white geometric building in concrete with a pierced concrete block façade on the projecting upper floor.[36] His major architectural works were the Magenta Sports Stadium, partially covered by a cantilevered roof,[37] which was built for the Pacific Games of 1966, and 650 units of multi-storeyed housing for the nickel workers in Rivière Salée, built in the 1970s.[38] He also supervised the construction of the new airport at Tontouta that was designed by a former professor of his in Paris.[39]

The Australian input continued through to the 1970s. Douglas Snelling, an architect practising in Sydney, was engaged in the late 1960s by two local businessmen to design two houses: one at Mount Mou for Jean Nawa, 1968, and one in Noumea for Louis Nawa, 1969. Snelling, having spent time in the islands, was known in Noumea.[40] The large houses are well planned with clearly resolved relationships between indoor and outdoor rooms and the clever use of different levels. The inner-city Noumea house creatively responds to its raised corner site and the built-up nature of its surroundings with a large inner paved courtyard and other terraces and walled gardens. The work demonstrates a high level of construction and the crafting of details, notably in the interior, which is richly finished with panelling and doors of kohu wood. Snelling followed these with the 1970 house at Erakor Lagoon, Port Vila, for the entrepreneur and developer Pierre Bourgeois, who played a highly significant role in the development of Vanuatu in the 1950s and 1960s.[41]

The years of Raighasse, Pascalon, Rampal and Snelling in Noumea overlapped the early period of the long and significant career of Gabriel Cayrol.[42] Cayrol, who

OPPOSITE, LEFT: Magenta Sports Stadium, Noumea, 1966. Jacques Rampal.

OPPOSITE, RIGHT: Indoor Sports Hall, Magenta, 1966. Pierre Raighasse.

ABOVE: Rivière Salée Multi-Unit Housing Estate, Noumea, 1970s. Jacques Rampal. Wall Mural.

RIGHT: Residence, High Commissioner of France, Noumea. Jacques Rampal.

OPPOSITE: Résidence Nawa, Noumea, 1969. Douglas Snelling.

LEFT: Nickel Society House, Baie des Citrons, Noumea, 1957. Gabriel Cayrol. *Courtesy of the architect.*

BELOW: Swimming Pool, Ouen Toro, Noumea, 1965. Gabriel Cayrol. *Courtesy of the architect.*

opened his practice in 1955, was the country's first New Caledonian architect (fourth generation). He had worked with Raighasse before leaving New Caledonia to study architecture in France. After graduation from l'Ecole Spéciale d'Architecture, Paris, in 1955, he decided to return to New Caledonia.[43] Cayrol's familiarity with the architecture of the modern movement is evident in four early houses, built at Baie des Citrons between 1957 and 1974 for managers of the Nickel Society. These are modern white buildings with flat roofs and are designed to allow for free air circulation through vertical louvers and the easy use of outside spaces. Cayrol had been interested in the work of Richard Neutra, and the influence of this is clear in these houses. Stylistically related are the War Veterans Home, 1961, and the house of M. Claude Lafleur, 1963. Both were clear-cut white buildings with an emphasis on the horizontal plane. Two major projects followed: the Swimming Pool at Ouen Toro, built for the 1966 South Pacific Games, was a revolutionary modern building for Noumea – an elegant white lightweight structure in two parts, bridged by an open raised walkway.[44] For a site adjacent to the pool, Cayrol designed Noumea's first notable hotel since Hôtel de la Gare, Hôtel Château Royal, 1964.[45] Both pool and hotel were set in creative tropical gardens, an uncommon consideration at the time.

Perhaps Cayrol's finest building of this early period was his own residence and office combined with apartments below, which was completed in 1972. This white modern building, framed by tall swaying palms is set on the very top of a high peak above Baie de l'Orphelinat overlooking the harbour and is itself a landmark for Noumea. The house combines interior spaces and open terraces and pool with extensive orchid gardens. While in Paris, Cayrol also took a course at the l'Ecole Nationale d'Horticulture of Versailles on tropical gardens. He was an authority of international reputation on orchids, and his splendid collection enhances the rooms and terraces, greatly contributing to the enjoyment of the house.[46] The building has a sense of openness, providing a celebration of the extensive views. It is a mature and resolved work of modern architecture and a high point for Noumea architecture of the 1970s.

The early designers of New Caledonia were varied in their backgrounds and training. Designs and buildings imported from overseas took their place amid the work of talented churchmen and builders, as well as the sheds and depressing buildings of the economically deprived. The builder-designers, such as Bottcher, Mary, Ritter and Jamieson, introduced a spectrum of influences from many parts of the world. Further influence came from the war, and the impact of the American presence was more marked in New Caledonia than anywhere else in the South Pacific. The first works by qualified architects practising in New Caledonia did not appear until the second half of the century. Raighasse, whose career unfortunately was cut short, and Cayrol gave New Caledonia high quality buildings of modern architecture. The early 1970s saw a marked change in the profession with several talented architects from France opening practices in Noumea.

OPPOSITE AND RIGHT: Résidence Cayrol, Baie des Pêcheurs, Noumea, 1972. Gabriel Cayrol.

Part III

PLACES OF THE SOUTH PACIFIC

DOWN THE CORAL SEA TO FIJI

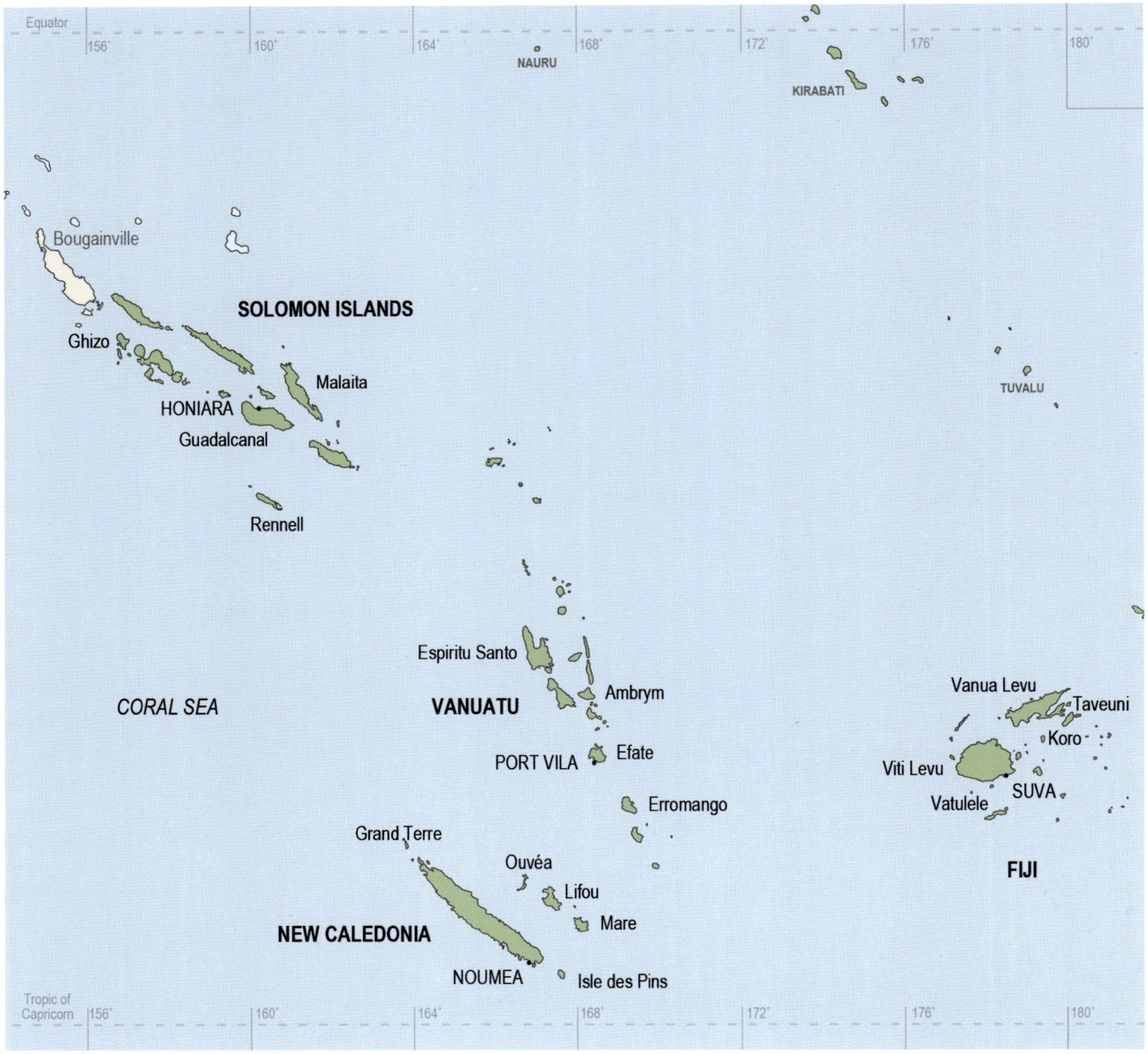
Equator
156°
160°
164°
168°
172°
176°
180°
NAURU
KIRABATI
Bougainville
SOLOMON ISLANDS
Ghizo
Malaita
HONIARA
Guadalcanal
Rennell
TUVALU
Espiritu Santo
Ambrym
VANUATU
CORAL SEA
PORT VILA
Efate
Erromango
Vanua Levu
Taveuni
Koro
Viti Levu
SUVA
Vatulele
FIJI
Grand Terre
Ouvéa
Lifou
Mare
NEW CALEDONIA
NOUMEA
Isle des Pins
Tropic of Capricorn

ISLAND LANDS OF WESTERN WATERS

Melanesia is a subregion of the Pacific embracing a chain of islands located south of the equator and to the north and north-east of Australia, and stretching from Papua New Guinea to Fiji. The islands of the Solomon Islands, Vanuatu and New Caledonia follow the Australian coast, bounding the Coral Sea to the west, with Fiji bordering the mid-Pacific to the east. Melanesia was settled by the Lapita people approximately 3500 years ago. Unlike the Polynesians the Melanesians are not sailors, and they tend to remain in isolated groups across the wide scattering of islands, hence the diversity of social and cultural values and languages – in contrast to the homogenous society of the Polynesians, which shares one root language.[1] The small island countries of Melanesia have come under different historical influences and patterns of colonization, with French being spoken in New Caledonia, English in the Solomon Islands and Fiji, and in Vanuatu Bislama and English, and also French.[2] Today, an intergovernmental organization called the Melanesian Spearhead Group, led by Fiji and Papua New Guinea, provides a forum for shared concerns and interests of the Melanesian people, for the benefit of all.

These countries are markedly different in terms of stage of development and level of Westernization. New Caledonia, with the urbane city of Noumea, exhibits a distinctive European ambience, while the Solomon Islands is one of the least developed of the larger countries of the South Pacific, with much of its population living on the wide scattering of small islands. They vary in population size – Fiji, 847 000; Solomon Islands, 549 000; Vanuatu, 245 000; and 254 000 in New Caledonia.[3] The major cities are located on the coast, with Suva on the south-east of Viti Levu; Honiara, the Solomon Islands, on Guadalcanal; Port Vila, Vanuatu, on Efate, while in New Caledonia, Noumea is sited on the south-west of Grande Terre.

DIVERSE IDENTITIES 3

Building the New Noumea

The architectural history of Noumea in the second half of the twentieth century was determined primarily by the nickel boom of 1969–72 and the violence of the uprising of *les Événements*, 1984, which cut short the building developments of the 1980s. The peace that ensued after the signing of the Accords in 1988 made the country once again attractive to both residents and tourists and consequently gave a boost to construction.[1] Thus, the architecture of Noumea in the late twentieth century was primarily produced in two phases: the buildings before 1984 and those after 1988.

Architects of Noumea

Before the 1970s many of the architects engaged for major works in Noumea had been based in France, but this changed with the prosperity resulting from the rise in nickel prices and financial advantages derived from the atomic-testing programme in French Polynesia. The resulting demand for architects led to an increase in the number of local professionals. Among these was Roland Osmont, who was born in Tahiti and, after completing his studies in Nice, moved in Noumea in 1969. He worked with Gabriel Cayrol before opening his own office in 1971. Further architects included François Raulet, also educated in France, who established his practice in New Caledonia in 1971. Richard Audoly, a 1971 graduate of the School of Architecture at Marseille, arrived shortly thereafter and initially worked on a number of projects with François Raulet and Pierre Lacombe, who had studied at the Paris School of the Beaux Arts and commenced practice in Noumea in 1972. These were followed by the young New Caledonian architects Daniel Leroux and Willy Porcheron. Leroux, a fourth-generation New Caledonian returned to Noumea in 1978 after receiving his diploma in architecture in Paris and, after two years as an architect during military service, joined Lacombe's firm. At the time of the civil unrest there was little work in Noumea, and Lacombe moved to Tahiti to open a branch office. In 1985 Leroux and Lacombe separated, with Lacombe continuing to practise in Tahiti. Subsequently, Leroux formed a partnership with Philippe Trouillat under the name of atelier 13.[2] Porcheron comes from a long-established family in Noumea.[3] He was accredited by the government after having trained with local architects for several years. He worked for Lacombe in Tahiti and returned to Noumea in 1988 to set up his own practice.[4] The first Melanesian architect was the urban designer Macate Wénéhoua, who, on his return from training in France, worked with Raulet between 1987 and 1989. Later he became involved in local politics, became mayor of the island of Lifou between 1992 and 1995, and subsequently returned to practise in Noumea.[5]

Architecture for Noumea

Apart from resorts, little architecture of note was built outside Noumea before 1970, and in the city there had been few additions in the central zone since the Pentecost Building of 1948 and the 1951 building for the Society Havraise Caledonian.[6] Between 1970 and the uprising of the 1980s, however, some buildings of significance were built in the inner city. Two buildings were erected on sites facing Place des Cocotiers: the office building Tour Foch on the long northern side of the square and the new Town Hall of Noumea, which occupies the entire block adjoining the square to the west. Tour Foch, 1970, the first tall building in the region, was designed by Cayrol for the Société Générale. Previously, in 1963, Cayrol had designed the Government Office Building on rue Paul Doumer – a modern six-storeyed slab office building with a glass and vitreous enamel façade.[7] Tour Foch, a landmark building for Noumea, follows Skidmore, Owings & Merrill's Lever Building model with a well-proportioned curtain-walled office tower of eleven storeys, built using lift slab construction techniques. The tower stands on a substantial podium that defines the corner of Avenue du Maréchal Foch and rue Jean Jaurès, edging the square. Considerably later, in 1999, the seven-storeyed Anthony Saru Building in Honiara joined Tour Foch as one of the only two office towers in the western Pacific.[8] A competition for the new Town Hall of Noumea, held in 1974, was won by the French architect G R Buzzi, who later collaborated with Jacques Rampal for design development and construction.[9] The large complex, completed in 1979, is an unassertive composition in both off-form concrete and pre-cast concrete elements, with a low

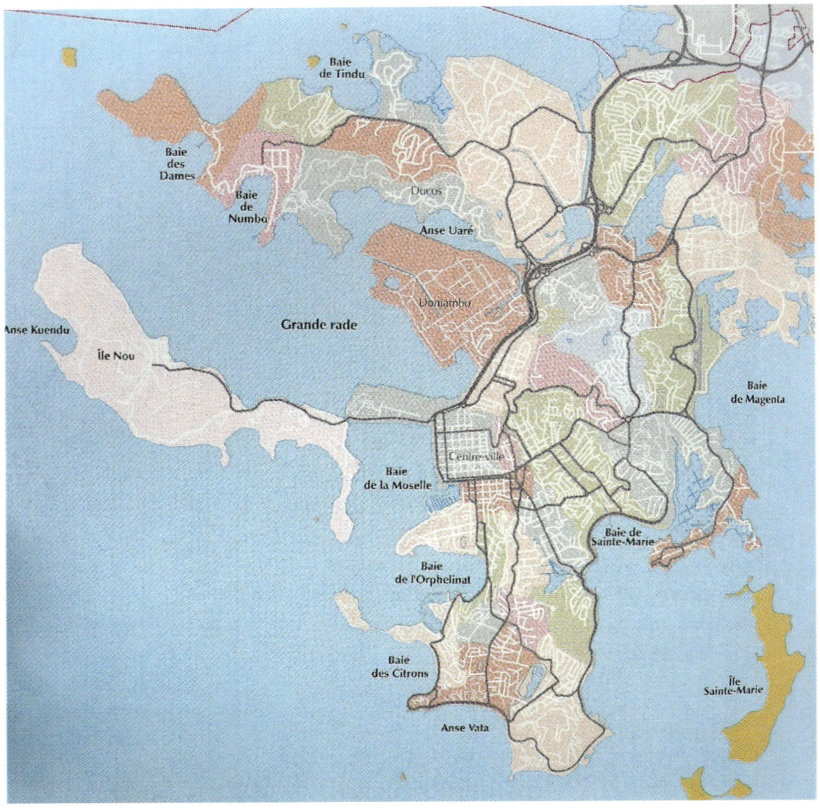

ABOVE: Plan of Noumea, 1999. *Courtesy of Editions Grain de sable.*

PREVIOUS PAGE: Tour Foch.

central reception block flanked by banks of offices with articulated vertical circulation towers.

Further expansion in central Noumea occurred on reclaimed land around an inlet of Baie de la Moselle north of avenue de la Victoire. In 1970 the area adjacent to Port Moselle boasted only one major modern civic building, Raighasse's 1967 Museum of New Caledonia located near the Latin Quarter, yet it became a major site for the expansion of Noumea into the 1990s. One of the earliest buildings was the distinctive Post Office, 1971, by René Lecourt from Rouen, with the New Caledonian architect Gilbert Allègre. The post office, a geometric concrete building enlivened by an expressive external structural frame with divided columns and

LEFT: Tour Foch, Noumea, 1970. Gabriel Cayrol.

ABOVE: Government Office Building, Noumea, 1963. Gabriel Cayrol. *Courtesy of the architect.*

a perforated hollow-block screen wrapped around the main postal hall, makes a distinctive statement in the architecture of Noumea. Closer to the city centre, a major addition to the Bernheim Library by Leroux was completed in 1981.[10] The new library block stands free of the old building and faces it across a shared circulation court. The two-storeyed building is in a neo-Colonial style, with a low-pitched roof and a wide veranda with a traditional cross-patterned balustrade. The library contains a generous internal space with a mezzanine level reached by a formal central stair.

After *les Événements*

The turmoil of *les Événements* prevented further building in this urban precinct for many years. In 1985 a competition was held that called for a pleasure port for 500 boats, the municipal market and a large commercial area with offices and accommodation, planned as a continuation of the expansion of the port on reclaimed land stretching along the waterfront. The commission was awarded to

Post Office, Noumea, 1971. René Lecourt and Gilbert Allegre.

OPPOSITE: Baie de la Moselle and markets seen from over the cathedral towers, Noumea.

Town Hall, Noumea, 1979. G R Buzzi and Jacques Rampal.

François Raulet and atelier 13. Leroux and Trouillat undertook the design of the market and Raulet the rest of the scheme, of which only the port offices were completed.[11] The municipal markets, one of the busiest places in Noumea, is easily reached from the central city and the areas to the south. It is an interesting complex of six small pavilions, on land and over water, with gleaming blue tiles cladding the low-pitched hexagonal roofs. The group of open-sided spaces are appropriate to the climate and the activities of the market and have a village scale, rarely encountered in Noumea.

In 1990 the striking raked form of the Southern Province Government Offices appeared on the southern end of Port Moselle. This important government building was the result of a competition won by the architect Pascal Picou in association with Jean Pierre Huvon and Willy Porcheron.[12] It is one of the most arresting buildings in the city, with a pyramidal form with sloping walls of metal bris-soleil. The staggered floors are defined by balconies with parapets clad with glazed blue tiles that continue the imagery of the roofs of the market buildings. More reserved is the nearby Annex to the Southern Province Government Offices, 2001, the result of a competition awarded to Gabriel Cayrol, atelier 13 and Willy Porcheron.[13] This is a refined, well-proportioned building of five storeys that successfully counterbalances the exuberance of the earlier structure. Strips of rectangular aluminium tubing screen the glass wall of the façade. The strong horizontality is relieved by the main entry, which is articulated by both the overlay of a broad vertical band of tinted glass and the bold cantilevered entrance canopy, supported on two round concrete columns.[14] Porcheron's previous Atelcom Building, built in 1996 on the outskirts of Noumea for France Cable and Radio is a small but interesting office building that introduced innovative ideas to practice in Noumea. Its exploratory nature is manifest in many aspects of the building, including a transparent roof over the central circulation zone and the horizontal sunscreens that are suspended by steel wires attached to round concrete columns standing proud of the walls. The solidity of the exterior belies the lightweight openness of the interior.

Prior to the Port Moselle project, Raulet had designed several notable buildings such as the Noumea Beach Hotel, 1981, and Bourail College, 1986–89, and in the 1990s many of the civic buildings for New Caledonia including the Archives of New Caledonia at Nouville, 1992.[15] His 1992 American Memorial built to

Southern Province Government Offices, Noumea, 1990. Pascal Picou, Jean Pierre Huvon and Willy Porcheron.

Annex, Southern Province Government Offices, Noumea, 2001. Gabriel Cayrol, atelier 13 and Willy Porcheron.

commemorate the fiftieth anniversary of the landing of US troops in Noumea, was installed in a park near the Latin Quarter. The simple arrangement of the memorial consists of a central mound representing the Pacific zone of the earth's sphere inscribed with the points of engagement of the US soldiers during World War II and surrounded by pillars painted in the patterns of the American flag. Raulet's atypical monumental extension to the Gaston-Bourret Hospital, designed in 1991 with Richard Audoly, is located in the north of the city. The principal block of the building is faced with honeycomb sun screening, and cantilevers dramatically from its sloping site, introducing a bold scale that is in contrast to the fine texture of the earlier buildings of Noumea. Audoly had previously designed the University of New Caledonia on the outskirts of the city. The university, completed in 1994, consists of a series of walk-up blocks arranged about a central walkway. The original additional protective covering of the roofs of white polymer sheeting over steel frames blew off in Cyclone Beti in 1996, but the fabric has since been replaced.[16]

Raulet's Noumea Overseas Passenger Terminal stands on the principal quay for docking the cruise ships, which make up a significant component of New Caledonia's tourist industry. The building was first erected in 1992 with a large umbrella roof of 1600 square metres covered with a skin of white polymer that had been designed by a Brisbane engineer and produced in collaboration with a local and a Brisbane-based firm.[17] The roof was destroyed by Cyclone Beti, and in 2001 a gently curving steel roof, structurally suspended from a tall central steel lattice mast, was erected. The building, which serves as an orientation space and a tourist market place, is appropriately festive in mood with a high, centralized space surrounded by mezzanine levels on all sides. An inverted pyramidal polycarbonate skylight allows natural light into the interior. Using different structural means but demonstrating

RIGHT, ABOVE: Atelcom Building, Noumea, 1996. Willy Porcheron.

RIGHT, CENTRE: Market Pavilion, Noumea, 1987. atelier 13.

RIGHT, BELOW: Little Sisters of the Poor Home for the Aged, Noumea, 2002. atelier 13.

a similar spirit is Raulet's Henry Millard Racecourse Grandstand, 2000 that was designed in conjunction with the engineer Christian de Lagarde of the French firm of France Galop.[18] The project was won in a competition in 1990 but took ten years to complete. The contrast between the disciplined muscular concrete structure and the elegant but dramatic cantilevered roof of the stand makes for an arresting composition. The structural members all but disappear when viewed from the racetrack, and the roof appears to float without support. The architecture of the grandstand demonstrates a complementary partnership between architecture and engineering, and provides one of the most accomplished examples of large-scale building in the South Pacific. Among Raulet's buildings at that time were the Vanuatu Cultural Centre, 1995, the French University, Port Vila, 1998, the airport terminals for Pekoa-Santo, Vanuatu, completed in 2000, and the new domestic terminal for Noumea at Magenta, 2003. In 2001, Raulet won the international competition for Bauerfield International Airport, Port Vila.[19]

The turn of the century saw the continuing growth of Noumea. The request of the Little Sisters of the Poor to replace the inadequate 1902 building they occupied as a home for the aged was initially rejected on the grounds of its historic value. The decision was rapidly reversed when the sisters responded by saying they would leave Noumea for elsewhere in the Pacific unless the project was approved.[20] The 2002 design by Leroux sympathetically acknowledges the previous building by incorporating some elements of its construction and by generally following its planning and character. The original wall and stair were retained and the convict-carved woodwork of the sacristy, the iron balustrades and posts, and the roof tiles were reused. While Noumea had seen the addition of many new important civic and educational buildings, office buildings had not been well represented. Leroux's Carcopino Office Building, 2000, which stands on a high site to the south of the city, is a simple rectangular glazed slab block enriched by the abstract geometric pattern of the concrete spandrel beams, which are set forward to act as sun screens. His uncommon 2001 Canal +,a mixed-use building with retail offices and parking levels, with a strongly modelled concrete frame, added a further landmark – this time on the low land of the central city.

Uncommon for the South Pacific, Noumea is home to women architects. In 2011 of the seventy members of the Order of Architects, ten were women. Among these is Agnès Gabet-Jézéquel, who was born and educated in Paris and came to Noumea in 1986. Before opening her own practice in 1990, Gabet-Jézéquel worked for Alain-Jean Formis for one year and Raulet for three before joining Alain Garcia.[21] The Territorial Music School, 1992, first brought Gabet-Jézéquel to the attention of the profession. The building took its starting point from the existing building on the site, the 1877 British Consulate, which had been used as a music school since 1950.[22] Gabet-Jézéquel extended the old building to the rear with a reinterpretation of its style in a contemporary design of brick construction, demolished interior walls and inserted an auditorium into its central space. The formal one-storeyed symmetrical building is faced with an enclosed veranda serving as a reception area and gives access to the performance hall, the library and various administration offices. In 1997 Gabet-Jézéquel completed two further projects in Noumea: the Aged Persons' Home at Magenta and the Rivière Salée Ecumenical Church. The home accommodates eighty units in a group of three-storeyed blocks arranged around a large informal garden, making for a pleasant non-institutional setting. The Ecumenical Church is an interesting building, perhaps indebted in part to Spanish Mission churches. The existing hall and the new church on a higher level are faced and united by a continuous pale-pink sculptural wall and a handsome set of integrated external stairs. The church on the upper level takes priority over the lower hall and its status is proclaimed by a rising of the façade over the entry to form a spire. This is enriched by a delicately painted religious figure around whom the various peoples of the world are assembled, symbolizing the ecumenical nature of the church. The portal provides a transitional space into a light-filled interior. Overhead, cranked beams rise steeply along the axis to the altar and change to

ABOVE AND RIGHT: Henry Millard Racecourse Grandstand, Noumea, 2000. François Raulet.

OPPOSITE, BELOW RIGHT: American Memorial, Noumea, 1992. François Raulet.

OPPOSITE, TOP RIGHT: Gaston-Bourret Hospital, Noumea, 1991. François Raulet and Richard Audoly.

OPPOSITE, LEFT: Overseas Passenger Terminal, Noumea, 1992. François Raulet.

a gentle low pitch as they spread out over the seating in the nave. This is an accomplished building in which the sculptural richness of the exterior is carried through into the spatial richness of the interior. Gabet-Jézéquel's ability to work with sculptural form, evident in the ecumenical church, is further demonstrated in the striking curved end façades of the 2004 Magenta Gymnasium. She extended her interest in gymnasium projects with a large indoor sporting complex that seats 3000 for the Pacific Games held in Noumea in 2011.[23]

A later noteworthy building for New Caledonia was the new Noumea Lagoon Aquarium, Anse Vata. A competition determined the outcome, with the selection of the proposal by Chambre and Vibert from France in association with Formis as the local architect. The aquarium was originally scheduled for completion in 2004, but the opening was postponed several times due to technical and logistical problems. It opened in 2008, with costs that had escalated from the original US$ 10 million mark to US$ 17 million.[24] The 3000-square-metre project received US$ 6.2 million in aid from the European Development Fund. The central premise of the design is that it is an aquarium, not a building containing an aquarium, so it is constructed as a concrete 'tank' and is mostly buried within a small hill.[25] The roof of the building – which does not have glassed openings so as to allow

OPPOSITE: Ecumenical Church, Rivière Salée, Noumea, 1997. Agnès Gabet-Jézéquel.

ABOVE LEFT: Gymnasium, Magenta, Noumea, 2004. Agnès Gabet-Jézéquel.

ABOVE RIGHT: Noumea Lagoon Aquarium, Anse Vata, Noumea, 2008. Chambre and Vibert Architects. *Courtesy of Chambre and Vibert.*

BELOW: Territorial Music School, Noumea, 1992. Agnès Gabet-Jézéquel. Section.

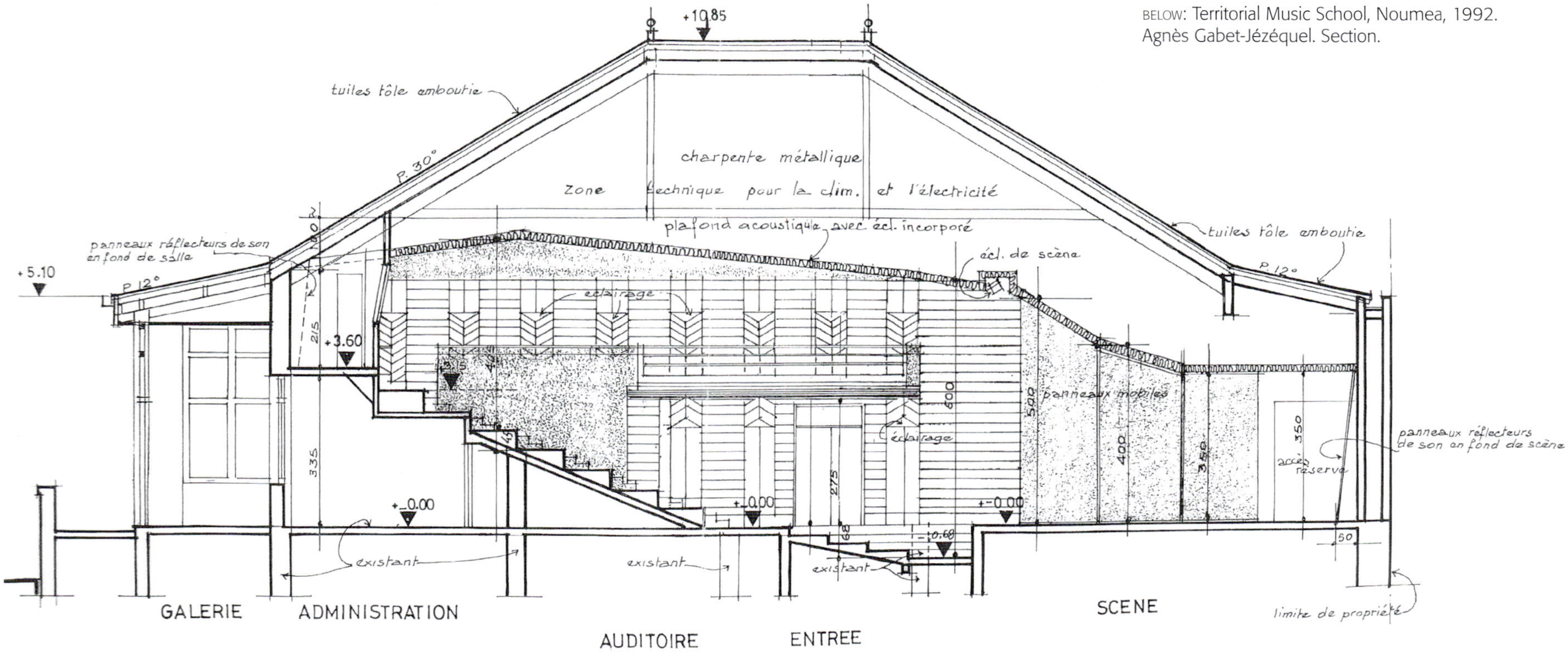

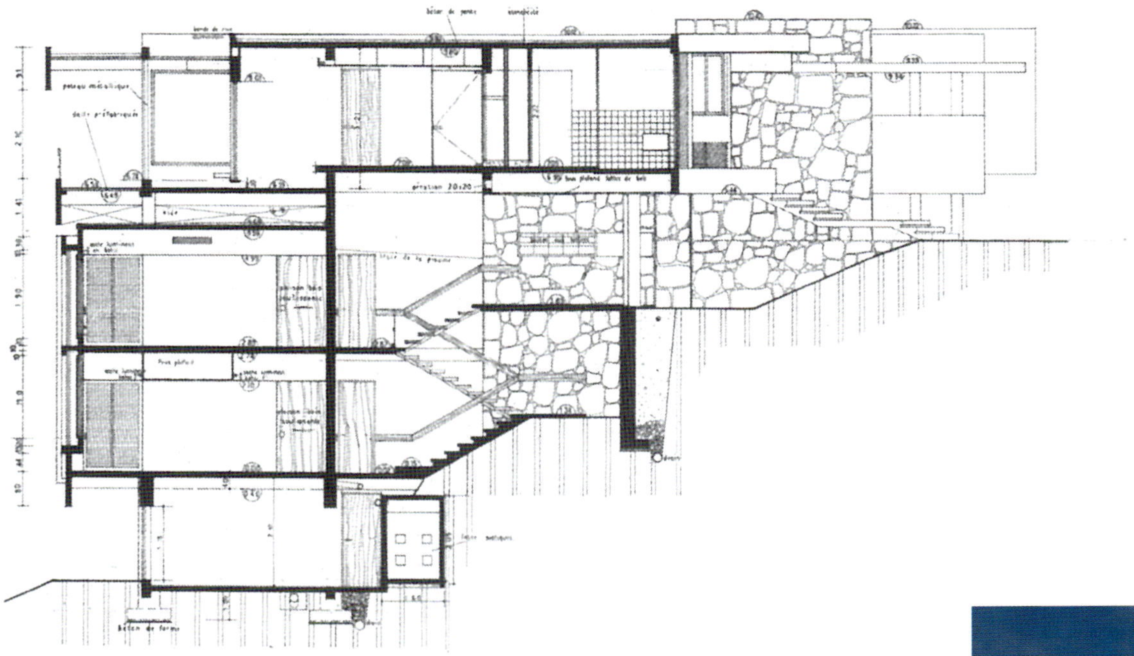

LEFT: Résidence Cayrol, Baie des Pêcheurs, Noumea, 1972. Gabriel Cayrol. Section.

BELOW: Jacaranda Apartments, Noumea, 1980. Gabriel Cayrol.

OPPOSITE: Building Morault, Anse Vata, Noumea, 1983. François Raulet.

the precise regulation of light inside the interior – is grassed, both for insulation and visual reasons.[26] The dramatic entrance is along a timber walkway that leads towards a doorway in the middle of the waterfall that cascades down along the full front wall, giving the sense of passing through to underwater. The seawater is pumped in from Baie des Citrons and out into the bay at Anse Vata. The aquarium is among the most modern in the world with specific control of such factors as the temperature of the water, its oxygenation and the use of ultraviolet radiation.[27]

Living at Cannes – Noumea

In the decades since the nickel boom Noumea has continued to grow and mature into a city of some sophistication. By 1996 it was accommodating over 60 per cent of the total population of the country. Over 80 per cent of the European population resided in Noumea, as did 90 per cent of those coming from other countries. Only 29 per cent of the Melanesian population lived in the capital city.[28] The city continues to grow, and in 2009 the population reached 163 723 inhabitants, or about 67 per cent of the total New Caledonia population.[29]

LEFT: Résidence le Catalan, Noumea, 1996. François Raulet.

OPPOSITE, TOP LEFT: Île de Lumière, Noumea, 1989. François Raulet with Andre Diaz and Miguel Harbulet.

OPPOSITE, TOP RIGHT: Résidence de la Plage, Anse Vata, Noumea, 2000. Roland Osmont.

OPPOSITE, BOTTOM LEFT: Commercial and Residential Development, Baie de l'Orphelinat, Noumea, 1990s. Roland Osmont.

OPPOSITE, BOTTOM RIGHT: Casa del Sole, Baie des Citrons, Noumea, 2002. Gabriel and Jean-Gabriel Cayrol, atelier 13 and Willy Porcheron.

The presence of numerous apartment buildings gives Noumea a unique ambience among the cities of the South Pacific. While the escalation in the construction of apartments did not occur until the end of the twentieth century, modern apartments, such as Raighasse's four-level apartments in rue de Sébastopol, 1950, had been built much earlier in central Noumea. It was, however, Cayrol who first explored the opportunities of a sloping site in 1972 with his own house and apartments. The two levels of apartments are stacked into the steep hillside, providing a platform for the residence at street level. The project exploits the terrain for the fine views of Baie de l'Orphelinat and demonstrates the potential of a steep building site. Cayrol followed this in 1980 with the Jacaranda Apartments, a refined, well-proportioned apartment block with split levels given strong horizontal emphasis from white bands of the balconies of the façade.

The first residential tower in Noumea was Raulet's 1983 Building Morault, Anse Vata, facing along the beach from the eastern end. It contains eighteen units, a private pool on the first floor and a tennis court on the roof of the car park. It is an unusual building, with two precast panels with turned-out ends edging the balcony floor slabs on each level. The juxtaposition of the inside curved ends of the beams creates a central spine with branching ribs so that the façade resembles a very powerful skeleton but is also suggestive of certain Pacific motifs. The same detail occurs at the top of the building over the service shafts, forming a well-structured transition to the sky. His next apartments, built in collaboration with Andre Diaz and Miguel Harbulot, the Île de France at Anse Vata and the Île de Lumière, both of 1989, are equally landmark buildings. The Île de France is conspicuous with its circular tower, and the two

30 202

LEFT AND OPPOSITE: Résidence Porcheron, Baie des Citrons, Noumea, 1993. Willy Porcheron.

dramatic up-curving roofs of the Île de Lumière create a tent-like form that adds a festive note to the slopes overlooking Noumea's markets. The blue sails of the roof extended the colour of the markets and the Hôtel de Provence Sud, adding to the band of blue around the bay.[30]

As with Baie de la Moselle, the foreshores of Baie de l'Orphelinat underwent extensive levelling and reclamation of land in the 1990s. This was later developed with a commercial centre by Osmont and multiple residential towers adjoining a large yacht harbour. Adjacent to this complex is Raulet's apartment complex of Résidence le Catalan that was completed in 1996. The centre section of this elegant low-rise building curves sensuously, softening the long form. The horizontality of the building is emphasized by the banding of the white floor slabs, blue balustrades and the patterns of the blue-and-white striped awnings. Osmont's Résidence de la Plage, Anse Vata, 2000, is typical of the new generation of apartments. The apartments form a long six-storey building, enlivened and given a residential scale through the articulation of the mass into sections of slightly different design and orientation. Completed in the same year was Résidence Monnin, Osmont's extensive apartment project, which is highly visible in the city due to its size, its location on a hilltop overlooking Baie de l'Orphelinat, and its large eye-catching green tiled roof. These were succeeded by his twin linked circular towers of eighteen storeys, housing 164 apartments and operating as the Ramada Plaza Hotel, 2001, near the Île de France at Anse Vata.[31]

In the new century, significant residential blocks continued to be built in the Anse Vata and Baie des Citrons area, including the Casa del Sole at Baie des Citrons, 2002, by Gabriel and Jean-Gabriel Cayrol, atelier 13 and Willy Porcheron, that introduced a different concept for apartment building on the peninsula.[32] The

OPPOSITE: Résidence Royal Vernier, Noumea, 2002. Willy Porcheron.

RIGHT: Résidence Copernic, Noumea, 2000. Willy Porcheron.

freestanding oval tower of seventeen floors, located on a level site at the eastern end of the beach, rises high above its surroundings, providing expansive views over Anse Vata to the east and Baie des Citrons to the west. The tower is accompanied by a low spreading commercial complex of two buildings with numerous first-class restaurants – primarily al fresco establishments under awnings – all contributing to make this one of the most chic settings in Noumea. Building continued on the ridge overlooking Baie des Citrons, including the extensive La Ballah residential scheme, covering a site 140 metres long. The La Ballah proposal contained housing, a future hotel site and two large retail centres linked by an esplanade.[33] By 2010 it had been partly constructed, with a southern section by Gabriel and Jean-Gabriel Cayrol, atelier 13 and Willy Porcheron, and a northern section by Australian architect Gerard Thomas. By 2012 these projects had been joined by the Mirage Plaza, by Lacombe's practice, Tropical Architecture, a complex of sixty-four apartments and twenty shops on the lower level of the slope facing the bay.

Several earlier residential buildings, including Porcheron's 1993 three-storeyed apartment block on rue Catalan are found in this area.[34] The western façade is clad with louvered shutters of pencil cedar that form horizontal bands of a warm and richly textured pattern across its width. The shutters allow for the adjustable control of sunlight and air movement, and create an unusual quality of space and light in the interior that is enhanced by the placement of the windows. Particularly innovative is the solution for the west wall where a continuous sheet of glass is installed below the principal shuttered windows, ensuring daylight to the interior and a view of the water of Baie des Citrons. Rich timbers – mainly kauri and kohu – and creative detailing contribute to the quality and interest of this assured design. Résidence Copernic, 2000, and Résidence Royal Vernier, 2002, are representative of Porcheron's later residential buildings, which are distinctive in Noumea's urban fabric. Copernic stands on a hillside looking north over central Noumea and is articulated into three attached blocks with a façade invigorated by the curved weaving levels of the white balconies and cornice. Résidence Royal Vernier, also on an elevated slope, overlooks the ocean at Val Plaisance on the east side of the southern peninsula. It is a large residence broken up in its mass and enlivened by a changing pattern of deep rose, beige and white walls. The complex consists of several articulated vertical units surrounding a central landscaped court containing an open stair that gives access to walkways on each level. It is an uncommon building characterized by the diverse components of the differing parts. The spacious balconies, the strongly defined floor slabs and the flying skillion roofs make for a vigorous complex, presenting constantly changing readings from differing perspectives.

The strong French connection, the concentration of the French population in Noumea and the prosperity of New Caledonia (when compared to the most of the rest of the South Pacific) have given rise to a particular social situation and hence pattern of living that is exceptional. The apartments of Noumea, built in response to the social and physical structures of Noumea, provide accomplished examples of New Caledonian architecture.

The city of Noumea's indented coastline, hilly terrain and continental European flavour make it markedly different to any other town in the South Pacific. Even its sister city, Papeete in French Polynesia, presents a distinct contrast with its port town atmosphere and more casual lifestyle. Despite the upheaval of the 1980s, the architects of Noumea have consistently produced a high standard of design and construction reflective of their education in the architecture schools of France.

The Solomon Islands: Guadalcanal and After

The Solomon Islands archipelago is made up of almost 1000 (widely scattered, mountainous, sometimes active volcanic) islands, enclosing numerous lagoons. Extending eastwards for 1667 kilometres from Bougainville Island in Papua New Guinea, the archipelago makes up a land mass bigger than that of Fiji. The highest of the mountains is 2447-metre-high Mt Makarakomburu on the large island of Guadalcanal. As with the other islands in this northern region, the Solomon Islands experienced the arrival of the Papuan-speaking settlers and later the Lapita people who both settled and moved through on their epic journey across the Pacific.

The archipelago was named the Solomon Islands (*Islas Salomón*) in 1568 by the Spaniard Álvaro de Mendaña de Neira, who, over the succeeding centuries, was followed by Dutch and French explorers. From the early 1800s Solomon Islanders increasingly came into contact with whalers, labour recruiters, traders and missionaries, and the first settlers arrived from Germany and England in the mid-nineteenth century. Subsequent to the Anglo-German Treaty of 1886, Germany established a protectorate over the northern Solomon Islands. In 1893 Great Britain declared the islands the British Solomon Islands Protectorate, although it was not until 1900 that Germany ceded the northern islands in return for Britain's promise not to prevent the German annexation of Samoa.[1] The protectorate was renamed the Solomon Islands in 1973. Today, the Solomon Islands archipelago consists of two states: the sovereign state of the Solomon Islands and the largest island of Bougainville to the north, which became an autonomous province of Papua New Guinea in 1975.

The Solomon Islands presents virtually the antithesis of New Caledonia in terms of ethnic balance, westernization, recent history, wealth and, consequently, architecture. Melanesians make up 93 per cent of the population, with about 75 per cent living in small villages engaged in farming and fishing.[2] Of the remaining population, 4 per cent are Polynesians and Micronesians. There are a few Chinese and Europeans. Given this ethnic distribution and life pattern, it is not surprising that there is little urban development. Further, around 88 per cent of all Solomon Islands land is held in customary tenure that neither the government nor expatriates can own. The other 12 per cent is known as registered land, half of which the government owns. Foreigners may hold leases of land only for a maximum of seventy-five years – the average life of a coconut tree.[3]

With the majority of the population living in rural villages, local building practices are very much alive. Bundles of woven and lashed sago palm leaves are the most frequently used materials for cladding walls and roofs, and internal spaces often are ventilated by panels hinged at the top and held open with a timber prop. Buildings are almost exclusively rectangular in plan. Being nearer to the equator than most other South Pacific islands, humidity and rainfall are high. Consequently, the sago palm roofs are steeply pitched, and buildings are frequently raised on stilts – both on land and over the shallow waters of the lagoons – to provide ventilation and to protect the timber structures from termites and flooding. Ceremonial buildings are often open with carved posts, and as is common in the South Pacific, the roofs of low structures commonly sweep to the ground for cyclone protection.

The War and After

Modest, appropriate vernacular buildings continue to be built throughout the islands, and there is little evidence of any significant European architecture dated before the 1960s. While there were the towns of Tulagi and Visale at Cape Esperence (north-west of Honiara) and isolated missions from the mid-nineteenth century, earthquakes, occasional cyclones and the devastation of war and civil strife have destroyed what little was there. In the years following World War II hotels and boarding houses, along with a few small cottages, could be found.[4] Among these were the fledgling hotels of the Mendana and the Hibiscus, which

Ceremonial Building, Honiara.

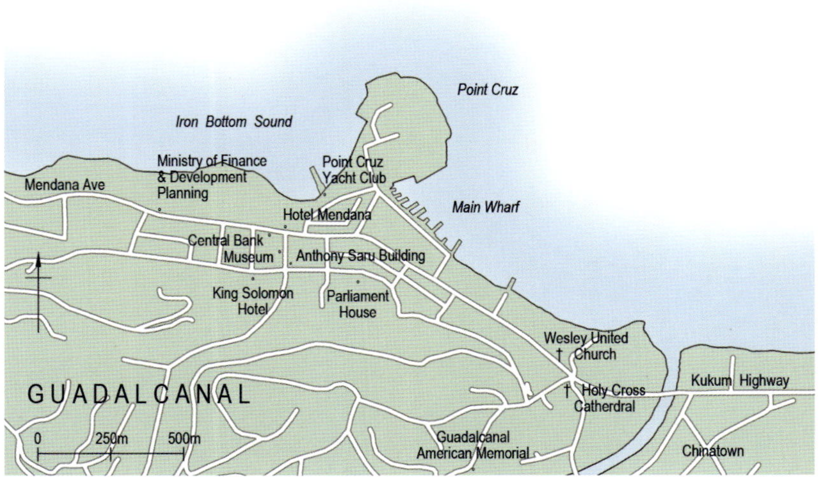

Plan of Honiara.

Guadalcanal American Memorial, Honiara, 1992.
Charles C Stevenson. *Courtesy of US Consular Agent, Solomon Islands.*

later were extended, but in general the Solomon Islands remained much as it had been.

Unlike New Caledonia and Vanuatu, which operated as US army bases during the battle of the Pacific, the Solomon Islands archipelago was invaded by the Japanese, who took the British capital of Tulagi, on Tulaghi Island, in April 1942. In August 1942 the Allied Forces' Operation Watchtower was launched, and the Battle of Guadalcanal became an important campaign whereby the Japanese were prevented from extending their airbase. This was a decisive factor in stopping their expansion in the South Pacific.[5] After the war, the destruction of Tulagi was so extensive that a new capital had to be found. At Honiara the US troops had built wharfs, accommodation and storage depots, and had upgraded the existing Japanese airstrip into Henderson Airport, the country's only runway capable of landing all but the larger jet aircraft (the present unremarkable terminal building was funded and built by the Japanese Government in 1996).[6] When the Americans withdrew, this ready-made Quonset hut town became the new capital. So, Honiara was born of the war. Quonset huts are still in use in the towns of the Solomon Islands, such as those on Mendana Avenue, Honiara, and on Middenway Road, the main street of Gizo in the Western Province.

The British returned after the war, and in 1975 the first governing council was elected. In 1976 the islands became self-governing and in 1978 were granted independence.[7] The Asian economic crisis of 1997, followed by racial disturbances within the Solomon Islands, greatly affected the export trade, resulting in the closing down of major industries.[8] Ethnic violence – known as 'the tension' – between various groups, such as the aggressive Malaita Eagle Force, broke out in 2000, further setting back the economy. In 2002 there was more unrest. The country was bankrupt and the capital in chaos. The government asked for overseas assistance to stabilize the situation, leading to the 2003 intervention by the RAMSI task force, an international contingent with the goal of helping to lay the foundations for long-term stability. RAMSI is led by Australia and New Zealand but includes members from thirteen other Pacific countries.[9] RAMSI's assistance has had a major effect on the use and upgrading of housing and other building stock. Among the aid gestures, architects were sent to help with projects, such as the reconditioning and extension of the hospitals. Further uprisings occurred in 2006, resulting in looting and burning of various part of the city including Chinatown and the Pacific Casino Hotel.[10] Of the few significant buildings that have been built, most were financed by donations from outside countries. These included the Nambanaen hospital, funded by the Taiwan Government, and the markets, funded by the Japanese Government.[11]

Designers in the Solomon Islands

Architectural commissions in the Solomon Islands are few and far between. For the most part, architecture in Honiara has been in the hands of draftsmen working in the Ministry of Works Infrastructure and Development and representatives of

Port Cruz Yacht Club, Honiara, 1980.
Charles C Stevenson.

overseas firms. The National Building Code was never gazetted, so there was no building height limit and virtually no monitored regulations regarding building design, except wind and seismic control based on Australian and New Zealand codes.[12] The New Zealand firm of Fletcher Construction has been engaged in design as well as building works since 1979.[13] The presence of engineering firms has not been consistent, and often the only engineering expertise on the islands resides within the Ministry of Works Infrastructure and Development.[14] Sporadic engineering services have been provided by the Australian Kramer Engineering Group, also practising under the name of Kinhill Kramer, and after 1998 as the Kramer Group. The New Zealand engineering firm of Murray-North was also engaged in the Solomon Islands in the 1990s, but there was insufficient work and it ceased practice.[15]

Among the early architects in the Solomon Islands was the Murray Cockburn Partnership from New Zealand and Fiji, which had opened an office in the Solomon Islands in 1981 and practised there intermittently for the next ten years. Its commissions included the Solomon Islands Technical College Assembly Hall, 1984, the Australian Chancery, 1989, with Fletcher Construction, and approximately 200 residences in the Naha Valley.[16] Representative of the small aid buildings gifted to the Solomon Islands is the Honiara Radio Station, 1981, by the Australian firm of Ancher Mortlock Woolley, which positively responds to the tropical conditions by placing the heavy sound-sensitive parts of the building along one side of a courtyard and protecting the remainder with hinged lattice shutters of local hardwood, which stand at different angles according to aspect and can be bolted so that they serve as storm shutters.[17] Also notable among the overseas architects in the 1980s was the Brisbane firm of Cameron McNamara, which designed the Central Bank of the Solomon Islands, 1985, in partnership with Kramer Engineering Group, and the National Provident Fund Plaza in 1986.[18] The Sydney firm of Gazzard Sheldon and Rosenberg was responsible for several

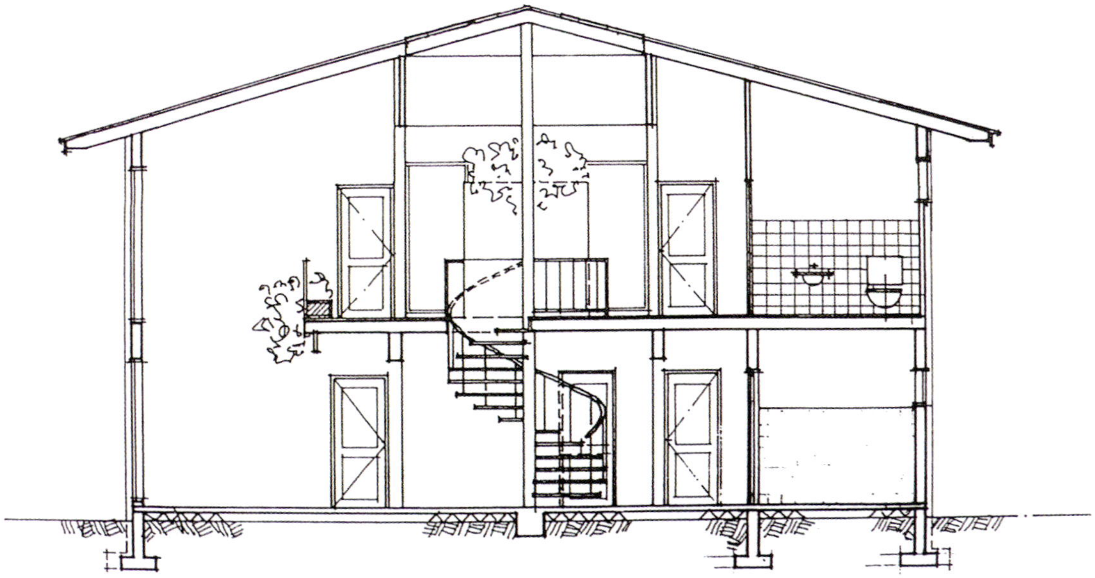

ABOVE: Chancery of Roman Catholic Church, Auki, 2002. Pacific Architects. Section.

TOP RIGHT: Ministry of Finance and Development Planning, Honiara, 2002. Islands Architecture with Murray-North.

RIGHT: Anthony Saru Building, Honiara, 1990. Fletcher Kwaimani Construction.

OPPOSITE: Parliament House, Honiara, 1993. Construction Battalion of the US Navy in association with the engineering firm of Martin and Chuck.

education buildings and the 1987 housing project for the Solomon Islands College of Higher Education, which was built from pre-cut, pre-nailed and pre-framed components manufactured in a specially set-up workshop.[19]

The last expatriate Chief Architect of the Public Works Department was John Coombes from England who, with the Melanesian Senior Architect, Osborne Van Gana, prepared the original designs for the proposed new Parliament House and State House during 1989–90, but the projects did not proceed.[20] Currently there are several Melanesian architects (primarily educated at the Papua New Guinea University of Technology, outside Lae) working in the Ministry of Infrastructure and Development. Aubrey Zeke, the first Melanesian architect in private practice, commenced his architectural education in Papua New Guinea in 1988 and after graduation spent some years working in Wellington, New Zealand, before returning to the Solomon Islands in 1997.[21] Zeke founded his firm, Wantok, in 2000.

The first private architect based permanently in the Solomon Islands was Charles C (Jock) Stevenson.[22] He was the only private architect practising in the country between 1968 and 1979. Stevenson had arrived in Honiara in 1963 to take up the appointment of Senior Architect at the Public Works Department. Among his projects of this time were the Honiara National Referral Hospital, Stage 1, and the Point Cruz Yacht Club, 1964. In 1968 Stevenson left the government and travelled to England. He returned later that year and set up in private practice. His commissions included Stage 2 of the Point Cruz Yacht Club, 1980,

consisting of two new buildings with a linked timber A-frame construction and fanciful flying thatched roofs; the Guadalcanal American Memorial, Skyline Ridge, 1992; various buildings for the industrial area of Kukum and a plan for the redevelopment of an education precinct for the island of Kiribati. Of particular note is the memorial, built to celebrate the fiftieth anniversary of the American landing in the Solomon Islands. It is a commanding composition of sculptural pieces, including a 7.2-metre-high federal memorial pillar and five other lower memorial walls all encased in South Australian red granite and standing on a black exposed aggregate concourse surrounded by a white painted concrete block wall. In 1994 Stevenson retired to New Zealand after thirty-one years in the Solomon Islands.[23]

In 1992 Islands Architecture, the New Zealand firm of Kayhan Khadem, won the competition for the proposed new State House and established an office in Honiara. Ken Grossmith from New Zealand was appointed as project director and took up the position in 1993, and Don Boykin, an American who had arrived from Los Angeles in 1993, also joined the practice.[24]

However, a change of government occurred, and while initial site works had commenced on the proposed new State House, the project was disbanded. Khadem returned to New Zealand in 1995, and Grossmith continued with the practice.[25] Grossmith carried out a number of notable commissions including the National Bank of the Solomon Islands, Ranadi, 1995, the residence of the archbishop of the Church of Melanesia, 2000.

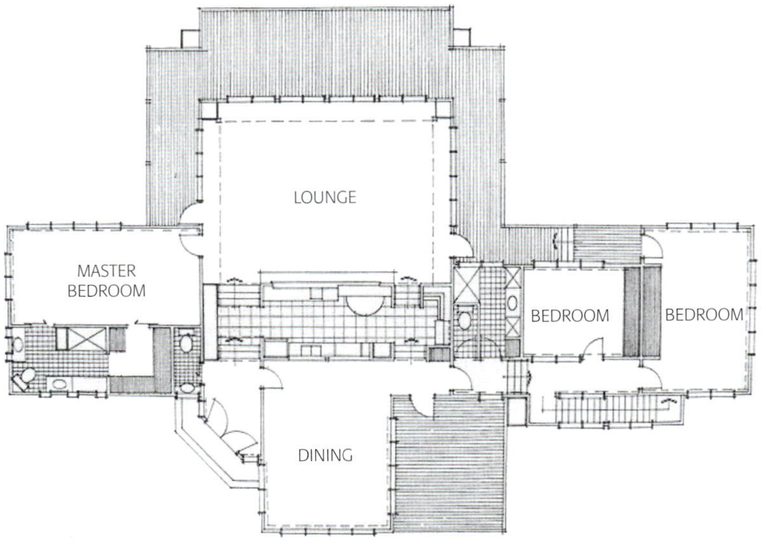

Grossmith later became the manager of the Solomon Islands buildings division for Telecom, and in 2009 he founded the private consulting practice of Nambawan Architects.[26]

Boykin has practised as Pacific Architects since 1995, and the firm remains the only current long-standing architectural practice in Honiara, with many quality houses and wide-ranging projects to its credit.[27] In Honiara, Boykin designed the additions to the National Referral Hospital, 1997, and a complex for the Pacific Casino Hotel, 1997, that included the freestanding waterfront buildings of the Fortune Restaurant and Supreme Casino, and the Patrick Leong Honiara Recreational Park with health spa and squash and tennis courts. Of particular note in Boykin's oeuvre is the Chancery of the Roman Catholic Church, Auki, Auki Island, Central Province. The simple chancery, built for the bishop of Auki, 2002, is a small two-storeyed concrete block building, entered on both levels and linked by a spiral stair encircling a large timber central pole. For such a simple building – essentially a twelve-metre cube – it is spatially expansive with a two-storey ground-floor foyer and three-metre-high windows with louvers and insect screening extending the sense of space and providing generous ventilation throughout. In 2008 the firm was commissioned to design the major project of the Parliamentary Office Building.

Honiara

Honiara, with a population of 68 000, is an uneventful small town with poorly maintained roads and inadequate services. Mendana Avenue runs along the waterfront for one kilometre, with cultural, office, banking and government buildings, hotels, the markets and the few shops to each side along its length. On the hills behind are residential areas. Where there once were squatter towns, the slopes, which afford excellent views, now contain the houses of professionals, government figures and administrators. Among the more substantial buildings lining Mendana Avenue are the Central Bank, the Ministry of Finance and Development Planning, the Mendana Hotel and the Pacific Casino Hotel. The Central Bank, 1985, was the first major institution in Honiara. The bank, while only of three levels, has a dominating presence in the town, due to its white classical form and the large scale of the building elements. Internally it has high quality finishes and is uncommon in that it contains locally crafted furniture and fittings, and Solomon Islands artwork displayed in permanent settings. Since then only two major office

OPPOSITE, LEFT: Butterfly House, Tasahe Ridge, Honiara, 1996. Pacific Architects. Plan.
OPPOSITE, RIGHT: Interior.

RIGHT: Nautilus House, Tasahe Ridge, Honiara, 1999. Pacific Architects. Plan.
BELOW: Interior.

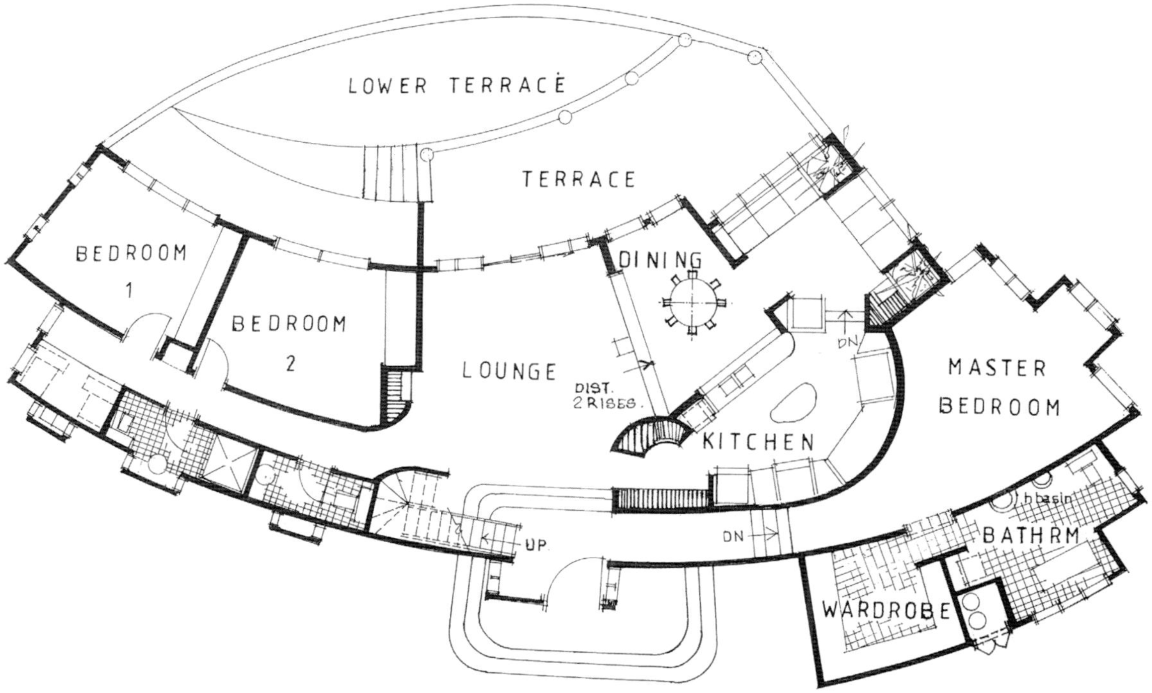

buildings have been built: the commercial 1990 Anthony Saru Building, set back from Mendana Avenue, and the Ministry of Finance and Development Planning, completed 2002. The Anthony Saru Building, which was sponsored by the European Development Fund, was a design-build project by Fletcher Kwaimani Joint Venture. The seven-storeyed office block consists of a two-level podium, with shops and conference and social amenities, and an exposed-concrete framed tower with setbacks and balconies. The building is crowned with a battened pitched roof over the service plant. The Ministry of Finance and Development Planning was designed by Islands Architecture in association with Murray-North, who jointly won it on a competitive bid. The previous ministry had been destroyed by arson, and the requirement for the new building was that it stand on the same long narrow footprint and reuse the remaining three-level stair and service units that survived the fire.[28] It is a low-maintenance building with bold blue external columns and a pre-coated aluminium panel cladding. The ministry was erected in a very short time, with most of the building elements coming prefabricated from Fiji.[29] The large concrete building of the Parliament House, 1993, is situated on a small hill adjacent to the central intersection of the town, and further to the east is the Holy Cross Cathedral, 1978, that provides a welcome landmark on the edge of the town.[30]

LEFT: Holy Cross Cathedral, Honiara, 1978. Noel McKernan.

ABOVE: Wesley Uniting Church, Honiara, 1989.

ABOVE RIGHT: St Barnabas Provincial Cathedral of the Church of Melanesia, Honiara, 1975.

Tasahe Ridge

Among the houses on the slopes above Honiara in the Tasahe Ridge area is a group of houses by Boykin, planned with thoughtful consideration for the site and humid climatic conditions. The 1996 Butterfly House, originally built by the architect for his own use, is a large dwelling partially elevated off the ground and built on a raised site with sea views. Setting the house apart from most of the domestic architecture of the area is the extensive provision of outside space with wide verandas encircling the principal living space and an extensive terrace off the dining room. The wish to provide views of the sea from all bedrooms and living spaces resulted in a multi-level plan stepping down from the rear of the building, with the dining room, kitchen and the living area arranged on tiered floors leading towards the open upper deck. Views to the sea from the dining room are maintained by a three-metre-wide opening linking the space through the kitchen to the living room below and beyond to the seascape. From the entrance, the living space is strongly directional towards the view and light coming through a tall band of glazed doors opening on to the north-facing deck at the far end of the room. Overhead the pitched roof is open, with a raised translucent ridge-cap admitting light and ventilating the space. The house has a generous sense of space and louvers, mesh screens, overhangs and pergolas keep it shaded and well ventilated. The composition of the natural timbers with the varied geometries of the grids, screens and louvers create intricate patterns on the exterior walls. The louvers are even more striking from within with the light forming ever-moving silhouettes along their blades. The later Nautilus House, 1999, inspired by the nautilus shell, expands and spirals up through multi-level overlapping mezzanine floors forming a central atrium. The atrium, containing the entrance and principal living area, is defined by intersecting angled wall planes. The partially enclosed upper levels are laid out as trays supported at different heights on the internal open timber frame, allowing for free air movement throughout the space of the house. The revealed timber construction, painted white, creates an intricate linear configuration on walls and ceiling, which is further elaborated by the upper windows, louvers and mesh screens that capture the light and ventilate the building, setting up a regular and controllable airflow. Boykin followed these two projects with many more designs for well-considered houses for the region.

The Church

Approximately 96 per cent of the Solomon Islands people are Christians, and as is usual throughout the South Pacific, the first major buildings to be constructed in the towns were those of the Church.[31] While important churches provide symbolic landmarks and places for major gatherings, in rural areas the essence of religion is celebrated in modest shelters built by villagers using local materials.

St Barnabas Provincial Cathedral of the Church of Melanesia, one of the earliest buildings of significance erected after the war, was built on the outskirts of Honiara, dedicated in 1968 and inaugurated in 1975. As was customary with important structures, the cathedral probably was planned and built by workers brought in by the Church. A sheltering, long simple tent-shaped building, it clearly relates to the vernacular meeting houses of the Solomon Islands. The flanking sides, under deep overhangs, are left open affording breeze and shade into the generous space under the roof. At the apse end the partially enclosed slatted-timber screening and the rich ochre-and-black patterns of wall panels throw into relief the simple white marble of the dais and altar.

The Holy Cross Catholic Cathedral, built in 1978 to a design by the New Zealand architect Noel McKernan, replaced the former Catholic cathedral at Visale, which was destroyed by bombing during World War II.[32] The church has a commanding presence imparted by its location on an elevated site and its wide, spreading A-frame profile, clearly defined by a deep-white fascia and the raised, steeply pitched ridge cap. Its imagery is further marked by the large white cross that stands in relief against the screen of multi-coloured glass panels of the west wall. The contrasting octagonal structure of the 1989 Wesley Uniting Church, built nearby in Honiara, is a wide spreading building, freely ventilated by many glazed doors on all sides.[33] The extensive metal roof, supported by large beams and radiating timber trusses, is edged with a wide upturned fascia, and resolved at the peak with an octagonal conical rooflight criss-crossed by the radiating ribs of the roof structure.

Outside Honiara

Apart from the vernacular villages, the only buildings outside Honiara are the locally designed resorts on various islands and the service buildings and shops of small townships, such as Gizo, on Ghizo Island, the provincial capital of the Western Province. This remote part of the Solomon Islands still retains an early South Seas character, with the small sleepy port of Gizo surrounded by villages. The waterfront market and the everyday buildings of the town give the place an active but informal character.[34] The small tourist industry targets a market segment at which it can excel, that is, diving – principally around numerous crashed planes and the wrecks of the thirty-seven Japanese and US warships that were sunk in the waters of the Solomon Islands during World War II.[35] Diving is serviced by specialized resorts, such as Sanbis in the Western Province. The protective political policy, however, plus instability, security issues, and limited infrastructure and transportation, hamper the growth of tourism. The cruise ships that take many tourists to the islands of the South Pacific rarely visit the Solomon Islands. With these limitations there is little incentive to build.

Gizo Airport Terminal, Western Province, Solomon Islands.

Due to the remote location, the dispersion of the people throughout the archipelago, the invasion in the Pacific War and its unsettled internal history over the past sixty years, the Solomon Islands is the least developed of the larger island states of the South Pacific. Because of this, the Solomon Islands largely presents as an archipelago where the western influence has penetrated to a minimal degree. There is therefore a lack of pretension and an elemental simplicity to the built environment, which has, in large part, been lost in much of the Pacific.

Vanuatu: The Amiable Isles

The islands of Vanuatu lie between New Caledonia and the Solomon Islands and represent a midway point between the two – not only by location but also in terms of politics, history, culture and architecture. It is a widely dispersed country consisting of eighty-two islands. The 2007 Happy Planet Index of the New Economics Foundation (NEF), which reports on human well-being and environmental impact, pronounced Vanuatu first out of 178 countries, using the indicators of life satisfaction, life expectancy and the ecological footprint for the country.[1] Today, Vanuatu is a moderate country with a 'low population and large land area, 2500 kilometres of coastline, a life expectancy of sixty-nine, a very rich and available land resource for growing crops, unique rainforests, little logging, an excellent democratic record, and next to no carbon emissions'.[2] It is, however, one of the most cyclone-prone countries of the South Pacific, suffering an average of eight cyclones per year. The winds can be of such severe force that roofs sometimes, by necessity, are held down by external rafters or tied down with cables.

The Austronesian-speaking people spread south from the Solomon Islands into Vanuatu and were followed by successive waves of migrants, and today there persists a diversity across the islands, with the people speaking over 100 different languages. The first European contact with Vanuatu was by the Portuguese explorer Pedro Fernandez de Quiros in 1606. This visit was followed by the explorations of Louis-Antoine de Bougainville in 1768 and James Cook in 1774, who named the islands the New Hebrides. In the early nineteenth century sandalwood traders came to the South Seas, and shortly thereafter the raids by colonial labour trade recruiters (blackbirders) commenced.[3] Members of the London Missionary Society arrived in 1839, with settlers following in 1865. Port Vila, on the south-west coast of the island of Efate, became the major settlement and port of the country.

The New Hebrides has a unique colonial history, having been governed up to 1980 by two colonial powers, Britain and France, concurrently, as both British and French colonists had settled in the islands. The 1904 Entente Cordiale brought an end to Anglo-French colonial rivalry, and in 1906 agreement was reached to establish a joint condominium to run the country.[4] 'This meant two languages, two police forces, two courts systems.'[5] At independence in 1980 the name of the country was changed from the New Hebrides to Vanuatu. The people of Vanuatu assumed the name of ni-Vanuatu, embracing both the ethnicities originating in Vanuatu and the nationals and citizens of Vanuatu – whatever their ethnicity.

Buildings of the Condominium

Given the history of cyclones in the New Hebrides, it is not surprising that very little remains of the buildings of the years of the Condominium. Because of the shared governance by Britain and France, there needed to be not only two systems of government but also, with the exception of the Joint Court, two of each official building. Consequently, there were two resident commissioner residencies, residencies for the French and British judges and a further residency for the president of the Joint Court, two hospitals and even two jails. The buildings were primarily timber structures prefabricated in Australia. Less significant colonial houses also were often shipped prefabricated but were sometimes built of bamboo, as with the local building practice.[6]

The British Residency was built in 1903–04 on high ground on land leased from the Presbyterian Church on Iririki Island, a short distance across the bay from the township of Port Vila. The original building was built from a set of specifications prepared by Alexander Dean and Son, an Australian building firm.[7] Iririki Island was also the former home of the Paton Memorial Hospital complex, built in 1911. The hospital was relocated to Port Vila in 1976.[8] The early British Residency was built with a prominent central core of concrete walls to withstand cyclones.[9] Presumably to reduce costs, the builder was instructed to omit many

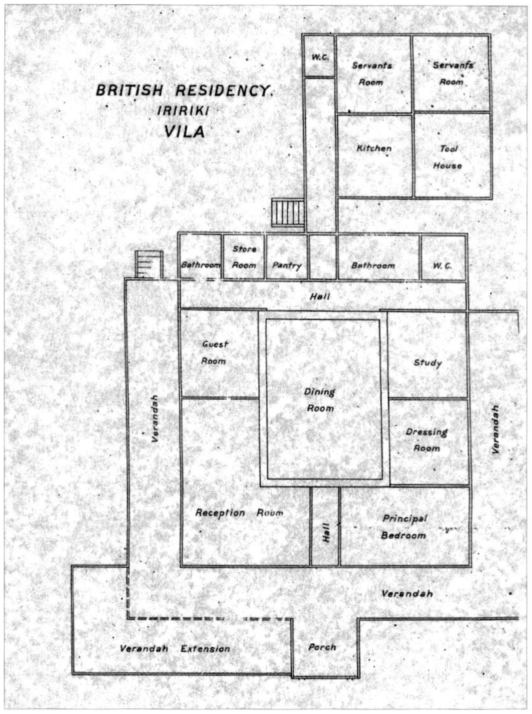

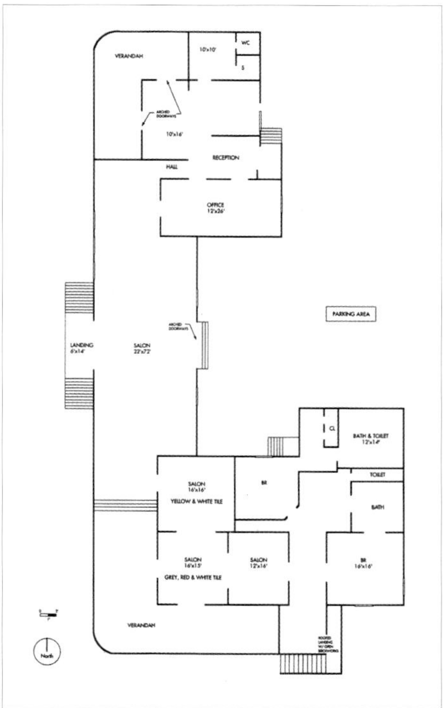

FAR LEFT: British Residency, Iririki Island, Port Vila, Vanuatu, 1907–08. Joseland and Vernon. Plan. *Courtesy of Margaret Critchlow Rodman.*

LEFT: French Residency, Port Vila, 1910. Joseph-Mare Coursin. Plan. *Courtesy of Margaret Critchlow Rodman.*

of the specification requirements, and consequently, the strength of the building was significantly reduced.[10] It was never judged to be satisfactory by its residents, and ongoing alterations were made and extensions were added. In 1907–08 the Australian architectural firm of Joseland and Vernon designed a major extension to the first residency, which consisted of a lightweight timber structure of rooms and verandas that encompassed the original inner concrete building.[11] By 1955 the building was in a poor state of repair, and the decision was made to build a new one on a site nearby. Plans by Australian architect Maxwell Hoskings were rejected, and Geoffrey Atkinson from the UK Colonial Office prepared new drawings for a very simple but functional bungalow, which was completed in 1957.[12] The residency was abandoned at Independence in 1980 and in 1987 lost its roof during the devastating Cyclone Uma.

The French Residency was erected in Port Vila in 1910 on land at a similar height as the British Residency, and the buildings faced each other across the bay.[13] It was a long, single-storey white building with a corrugated-steel roof raised off the ground on piers and entered by a centrally placed set of stairs. A continuous band of sliding louvers along the front veranda provided generous ventilation to the inside rooms. In 1980, at the end of the Condominium, it became the State House, the residency of the first President of Vanuatu. It, too, was seriously damaged by Cyclone Uma and was abandoned and left as a ruin.[14] It appears likely that it was designed by the French architect Joseph-Mare Coursin, who came to Port Vila from New Caledonia, where, for a short period, he had been instrumental in the planning of the town of Noumea. On arrival in the New Hebrides he worked for the Condominium and practised in Port Vila for fifteen years before returning to Noumea.[15] In 1910 Joseland and Vernon designed the post office, treasury and several houses in Port Vila including those for the president of the Joint Court, the British judge and the public prosecutor.[16] These buildings, notably those for the Joint Court and the houses of the judges, were impressive buildings. They clearly stated the presence and permanency of the Condominium, and the supremacy of the law.

The 1912 Courthouse of the Joint Court stood on a commanding site overlooking the bay.[17] It was a large two-storeyed building with prominent central bays with the entry portico reached by a grand double stair and long wings to

TOP: Original Joint Court, Port Vila, 1912. *Courtesy of Margaret Critchlow Rodman.*

ABOVE: Residence of the President of the Joint Court, Port Vila, 1910. Joseland and Vernon.

each side. It ceased to be used as the courthouse after World War II, and the Joint Court took up residence in the building formerly occupied by the president of the Joint Court.[18] The official residence of the president of the Joint Court was a fine timber colonial house of two storeys with wide verandas on each level.[19] A set of stone stairs, framed by tall trees, led up to a small covered porch opening into the projecting central bay. The house had an unpretentious but refined character, and its location on the slopes above the town gave it an imposing air. During the war it was occupied by the Americans, and after the military left it was taken over by the Joint Court. When the New Hebrides gained its independence, it became the Supreme Court of Vanuatu.[20]

The various British offices were built in a precinct called the Paddock that now contains several buildings of the government, including the Department of Home Affairs, the Department of Foreign Affairs and External Trade, and the offices of the prime minister. The Department of Home Affairs was previously the British Resident Secretariat of the Condominium, which was built in 1910 on land leased from the Presbyterian Church, and is the only important building of the Condominium remaining. It is a handsome timber building composed of two large bungalows to each side of the lower central section defining the entry. The bungalows have half gable roofs decorated with timber carvings. The wide verandas had fine horizontal timber louvers below the handrails, while above there were timber shutters that either folded or were removable.[21] A small adjacent annex was constructed in the 1920s for the resident commissioner's office.[22]

During the War

In 1938 the population of Port Vila was 1200. While the New Hebrides was a forward base for the US forces based in New Caledonia, the impact on the country was considerably less than on New Caledonia and the Solomon Islands. The principal bases were to the north on the island of Espiritu Santo.[23] There was, however, a sizeable camp centrally located in Port Vila, with the former official residency of the president of the Joint Court serving as the headquarters for General Rose, the US army commander. As in many countries of the Pacific, the American occupation changed the course of the country's development. Santo-Pekoa and Bauerfield airfields were built, and an infrastructure of roads, bridges, water supplies, drainage systems and telecommunication networks was put in place. Little physical evidence remains of the buildings of the Americans except for minor structures, such as some huts that have survived in Espiritu Santo.

After the war, Port Vila remained a quiet town lying along the Lini Highway that follows the shoreline of Vila Bay. 'It was still a small community and everyone

British Resident Secretariat of the Condominium, Port Vila, 1910.

spoke French.'[24] The cathedral, a converted Quonset hut, and the buildings for the Condominium were above or behind the township and apart from the markets there were no buildings of note along the waterfront.

In 1950 a remarkable entrepreneur, Pierre Bourgeois, came to the New Hebrides from France, changing the face of the tourist industry and, with it, that of the country.[25] As well as projects for hotels, Bourgeois built shops, the 1957 deep-water wharf, roads – including one linking the wharf to the town – and in 1960 he was instrumental in introducing the British-owned New Hebrides Airlines, which provided a scheduled and charter air service throughout the islands.[26] In 1962 Bourgeois was joined by Joe Mulders from Belgium, who actively promoted tourism in the New Hebrides.[27] Bourgeois' further contributions to the welfare of the country include the establishment of the first broadcasting station in 1967 and the first chamber of commerce and industry in 1982.[28]

In the 1960s the New Hebrides experienced a minor boom due to the opening of the manganese mines at Forari on the east coast of Efate. Forari became a centre of activity and, with a population of 2000, was the second largest town in the country, but mining was restricted and short lived due to disagreements over land titles and unclear government legislation regarding ownership of the subsurface. The mine closed in 1978, and it quickly became a ruin overgrown by jungle. During the short-lived prosperity, changes included the replacement in 1960 of the Centrepoint 'Old Shops' of 1920 with a new shopping complex, the Centrepoint 'New Shops'. The new dock and roads provided better connections to the town and the Port Vila Harbour deep-water wharf and the 1964 reconstruction of the US airstrip, Bauerfield, which had been allowed to degenerate into a state of disrepair, improved overseas communications. Among the early international arrivals was General Charles de Gaulle, who visited Port Vila in 1966.[29] In the early 1970s the US airstrip at Espiritu Santo was repaired and put into operation, and Bauerfield was strengthened to take jet aircraft in 1972. With these initiatives, the introduction of the international airline Air Vanuatu and the opening of small-scale resorts, built primarily on the island of Efate, Vanuatu increased its attraction as a tourist destination.[30]

The Church in Vanuatu

As with most of the Pacific countries, missionaries introduced various forms of Christianity to Vanuatu, but churches primarily are simple structures and do not assume a dominant role in the towns and villages. The majority outside the larger towns are straightforward open-sided structures erected by the local people. Even in Port Vila there are few conspicuous churches. The only large church is the Holy Cross Cathedral, 1977, by Renaud d'Hauteserre, which replaced the Quonset hut there previously. The cathedral is a prominent building with a long low portico leading to a large internal space defined by the high prow-like roof of steel and laminated timber construction.[31]

Of note is the 1964 Presbyterian Paton Memorial Church, a small elemental building that gains its landmark status from its arresting architectural qualities, the eye-catching blue-and-cream geometric patterns of its façade and its location in Independence Park.[32] It was designed in Australia by an architect member of the church, John Paul, and erected in 1964 to replace the 1907 church that was blown down in the cyclone of 1959.[33] Following vernacular precedence, it is a basic A-frame building with a steep roof to readily shed the torrential rains. The building is enclosed by an inexpensive panel system that can be totally closed or partially or totally opened through hinged panel doors across the façade and along the sidewalls, which also house an upper tier of pivoted panel fanlights. The flyaway roofs down each side, which provide sun and rain protection for the walls below, enliven the basic form of the building. The church is particularly appropriate to the climate as it is readily adjustable to the environmental conditions of the islands.

TOP: Holy Cross Cathedral, Port Vila, 1977. Renaud d'Hauteserre.

ABOVE: Wayside Church, Efate Island.

ABOVE: Presbyterian Paton Memorial Church, Port Vila, 1964. John Paul. Interior.
RIGHT: Exterior.

The blue of the exterior trim is matched in the interior, and by night the open church glows like a blue lantern. This church offers many lessons for building in the islands. It has an inexpensive, easily erected structure and cladding, with an A-frame form sympathetic to the place and familiar to the people of the islands. This is given a further artistic expression both by the colour and openings, which delineate the order of the wall system, and by the uncommon drama of the flyaway roofs, which are integral to the functional requirements and spatial logic of the architecture.

Architects of Port Vila

The context for building in present-day Vanuatu remains open. There are no building height controls, and there are few regulations for construction or fire safety, despite the location of the islands in an earthquake and cyclone belt.[34] It is necessary, however, to apply for permission to build under a draft code that has never been ratified, but compliance with its cyclone code is required for insurance.[35] With limited professional support, the architects tend to do their own engineering and the engineers their own architecture.[36]

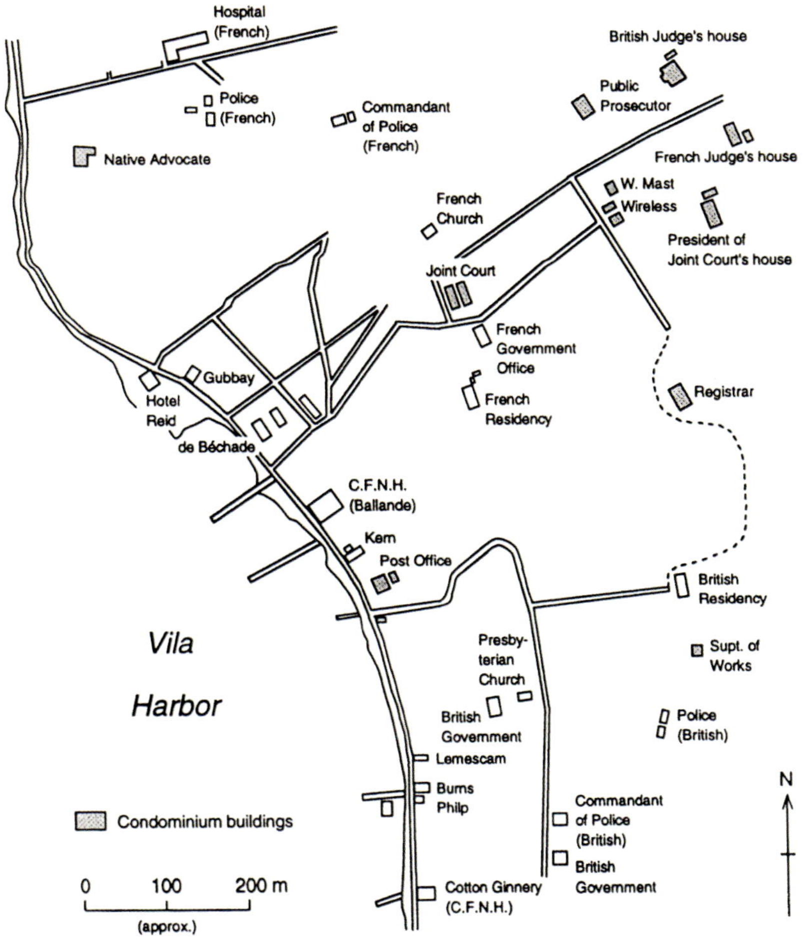

LEFT: Condominium Buildings, Port Vila. Plan. *Courtesy of Margaret Critchlow Rodman.*

ABOVE: Aerial view of Port Vila. *Photograph by Phillip Capper.*

By 1967 the population of the New Hebrides had reached 78 000, and that of Port Vila was 5200 – hardly large enough to support more than limited architectural and engineering services.[37] However, the improved communications, and the establishment of the New Hebrides as a tax-free haven in 1970–73 led to a small boom in the succeeding years.[38] The potential for development attracted construction firms, engineers and architects from abroad, as well as bankers, lawyers and accountants. Fletcher Construction began building in the early 1970s, the engineering firm of the Kramer Engineering Group was established in 1984–85 and the Australian architectural firm of Peddle Thorp and de Preu opened an office.[39] Other Australian architects undertook various individual commissions, such as Ancher, Mortlock, Murray and Woolley, architects for the Port Vila Radio Station, 1980, a precursor to their Honiara Radio Station in 1981. The practice of Peddle Thorp and de Preu was taken over by Renaud d'Hauteserre, a young French architect who had been serving in New Caledonia on National Service.[40] In addition to the cathedral, d'Hauteserre designed several of Vanuatu's most significant buildings of the 1970s, including a part of the Georges Pompidou Hospital, the French Embassy, police headquarters, and the new town hall at Luganville.[41] In 1976, the Singaporean firm of James Ferrie and Partners, represented by Geoffrey Feast, bought d'Hauteserre's practice and was soon busy with schools, houses, resorts and buildings for the Church. Feast was educated in New Zealand at the University of Auckland, and after graduation he worked in England. His travels took him to Singapore where he joined James Ferrie and Partners. His most prominent work in Vanuatu has been in the field of resorts, including the Iririki Island Resort, across the bay and visible from Port Vila. Feast has continued to practise in Port Vila, being the only architect of long-standing in the history of the country.[42]

Port Vila Development

Despite the fact there was no town plan, the development of Port Vila during the 1990s followed the urban form established under the Condominium, with a low-

LEFT: Parliament House, Port Vila, 1993. Chinese Government.

BELOW LEFT: Nasituan Building, Headquarters of the Works Department, Port Vila, 1991. Alexander and Lloyd Group.

BELOW RIGHT: Department of Foreign Affairs and External Trade, Port Vila, 2003. Eric Bourdet with European Union.

LEFT: Reef House, Port Vila, 2009. Peter Stutchbury. Entry Walkway. *Photograph by Michael Nicholson.*
OPPOSITE, ABOVE: Plan. OPPOSITE, BELOW: Diagrammatic Sketch. Roof Structure.

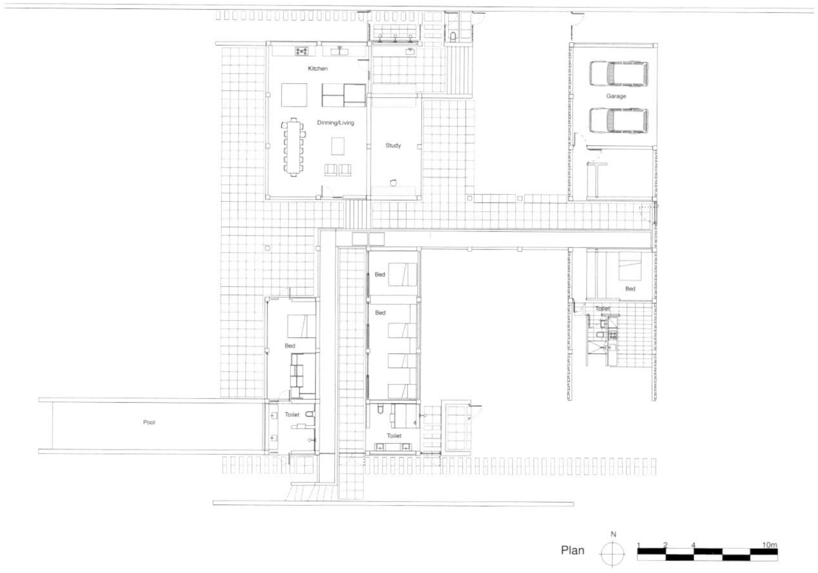

key commercial zone on the water, a loose scattering of houses and significant buildings on sites above and behind, and beyond those, the villages with their churches and kava huts. Villagers, utilizing any materials that come to hand, casually built the unpretentious kava huts, which are evident in all villages and towns. By the late 1980s multi-storeyed buildings housing financial institutions began to appear on the slopes behind the town, including the three-storeyed concrete building of the 1990 Reserve Bank of Vanuatu, by Colin Minton, who arrived in Port Vila after the 1987 cyclone.[43] A further major public building, the Nasituan Building[44] (the headquarters of the Public Works Department), was opened in 1991. The headquarters, by the Alexander and Lloyd Group, was a gift from AusAID to replace the previous building destroyed by Cyclone Uma.[45] While not as prominent in the landscape as the Reserve Bank, the Public Works Building is a large commanding two-storeyed building with a symmetrical composition dramatized by a central high vaulted space enclosed by walls of striking bright-blue louvers.

The Parliament House, 1993, designed in China, and the Vanuatu Cultural Centre, 1996, by the New Caledonian architect François Raulet, were constructed on adjacent elevated sites to the east of the town centre. While not visible from the commercial area, the large, dominant form of the Parliament House and its striking red roofs make a major visual impact on Vila Bay and the general ambience of the Port Vila locality. In contrast, the Vanuatu Cultural Centre is part of an unassuming complex of significant buildings celebrating Melanesian traditional culture. Following the culture centre, Raulet was commissioned to prepare a site plan and drawings for a regional institution building for the Agence Universitaire de la Francophonie (AUF), 1998, the first building of the small campus programme. The simple rectangular two-storeyed building is dramatized by the sweeping, over-sailing blue metal roof, which places it in the mainstream of Raulet's oeuvre. The government continued to be the major client for architecture in Port Vila and the town slowly grew with the addition of buildings such as the new police headquarters by Feast, 1998, and a market building by the Public Works Department at the turn of the century. In 2003 the new Department of Foreign Affairs was opened in the Paddock. The two-storeyed building, with a dominant central arch and a vivid-blue roof, was designed by architect Eric Bourdet in conjunction with the European Union design team, which was also responsible for a large number of schools in Vanuatu.

In 2002 Bourdet designed Chantilly's on the Bay, the first apartment-hotel of note on Port Vila's waterfront. Located on the fringe of Port Vila to the north, Chantilly's on the Bay is an accomplished three-storeyed, well-sited building with a curved façade that satisfactorily relates the building to its bayside setting. The sweeping lines of the façade of Chantilly's are activated by patterns of light and shade from the broken forms of the balconies and the syncopated rhythm of multiple protrusions of sun-screening panels. The building takes advantage of its waterfront location for cooling, but also by association, notably in the engaging relationship established between the cantilevered deck of the restaurant and the water below.

Further appropriate design for living in Port Vila can be seen in the Reef House, 2009, by Peter Stutchbury Architecture, Sydney. The house is fashioned around the geographic conditions of the tropical climate and the location of Port Vila in a cyclone belt. The rooms of the house are arranged as separate open pavilions around courtyards and are related to the central spine of the entry promenade.

This walkway, edged by a water channel, leads through the house and on to the open terrace and pool. The cooling features of water, breeze and gardens bring the landscape deep into and through the house. The exteriors of the pavilions are edged with tall folding louvered shutters, allowing them to be fully open or with partial or total enclosure. In response to the cyclonic conditions, the house is designed as two entities: the frame tied down to the ground by holding-down bolts to concrete frames, and the 'flying' roof, ventilated to allow the free passage of wind to pass underneath without obstruction. In this, the house uses concepts borrowed from local typologies but translates them into a language for contemporary construction.[46]

Speculative Developers

While land ownership is vested exclusively in customary owners, investment in leasehold property continues to rise in Vanuatu.[47] The early purchasers were primarily Japanese, but by the turn of the twenty-first century the market widened. Much of the land exploitation was directed at short-term profits, with projects aimed at quick sales and quick returns.[48] Too often, ruthless buyers exploited the customary landowners, and legislation was introduced that requires that each time a property is sold by a developer a certain percentage goes back to the original owner.[49] This legislation has helped to quell the rampant speculation.

Port Vila entered into a new phase of growth. Speculative housing sites, often with outstanding views, were developed on the hills behind the town. While most projects have been aimed at quick sales, there were schemes of quality, such as those by Feast and Bourdet. In 2007 Bourdet completed Amalfi Court, one of the more impressive apartment complexes above Port Vila. Amalfi Court contains eight strata title units and is on three levels with the upper level containing penthouses, served by the first residential lift in Vanuatu. The complex, set high on the ridge with sweeping views to the sea on the east, is situated in park-like grounds containing a tennis court, gymnasium and swimming pool.

While most of the rampant speculation has occurred outside downtown Port Vila, the scale and texture of the town was disrupted by the construction of the seventy-room De Port Palms Casino and Hotel, 2002.[50] Built on the waterfront next to the market in the centre of the town, the prominent curved form of the six-storeyed hotel, makes a visible intrusion in the townscape as seen from the bay, the commercial centre, and the slopes behind. The concept drawings for the De Port Palms Hotel, a speculative project by the French company Brunet Enterprise Genéralé, were prepared by the Brisbane architect Hubert van Hoof, but the building was engineered by the Kramer Group and the proposal developed without an architect.[51]

Similar to most of the larger towns of the Pacific Islands, Port Vila owes its location and urban structure to its role as a port. Throughout the twentieth century the number of buildings on the gentle slope of the hill rising behind the town slowly increased, yet with little disturbance to the early morphology. The Lini Highway in Port Vila remains much as it was in the 1970s. With the construction of the De Port Palms Hotel, the long-established growth pattern of Port Vila was interrupted.

But the amiable isles of Vanuatu remain amiable isles, and Port Vila retains its relaxed ambience and is one of the least changed towns of the South Pacific. It was not until the growth of tourism of the 1970s, made possible by the airlines and heralded by the resorts of Bourgeois, that the first resident architectural practices were established. The profession remains small – major projects are commissioned to overseas firms, while architects practising locally, with the exceptions of Feast and Bourdet, have worked in the country for temporary periods of varying length.

ABOVE: Chantilly's on the Bay, Port Vila, 2002. Eric Bourdet. Sun Screens.

OPPOSITE: De Port Palms Casino and Hotel, Port Vila, 2002. Hubert van Hoof.

PLAYING ALONG THE CORAL SEA

4

The Tourist: Beginnings 1970–90

'Perhaps the lure of Bali Hai is that it can be any island you want.' James A Michener

Until the 1970s the islands of the New Hebrides, the Solomon Islands and New Caledonia were outside the mainstream of tourist development, and they remained on the fringe until the 1990s. Earlier in the century these islands were not part of the major shipping routes that ran through the region and the later air routes crossing the Pacific, and so they were less visited and, consequently, less well known than those of the central Pacific. They were not entirely unknown, however, for as early as 1884 Burns Philp, an Australian shipping company, regularly sent ships to Papua New Guinea and the New Hebrides.[1] 'The company was selling holiday packages to the leisure classes of Australia and New Zealand, and from the 1910s Burns Philp cruise ships plied the islands'[2]

While the first flight from Paris to Noumea took place in 1932 and Air France flew the first commercial flight in 1949, these were seen as special destination routes and were not a part of the regular public transport flight paths of the Pacific.[3] After the Hôtel de la Gare, Noumea, 1905, and before 1970, the only hotels of note in the region were the Hôtel Château Royal in New Caledonia and the Mendana Hotel in the Solomon Islands. Modest boarding houses or private homes provided the principal accommodation. There were also some local hotels and small resorts, with New Caledonia boasting the Nouvata, Lantana, and Noumea hotels as well as the Relais de Kanumera and Relais de Koulnoué.[4] In the period 1970 to 1990 Vanuatu was the centre of tourist activity, but after 1990, while hotels and resorts were built in all three countries, it was New Caledonia that became the most sought-after destination for tourists.

In contrast, Fiji had a large tourist industry, and French Polynesia also became a major tourist centre due, to a certain degree, to its relative proximity to America. While, from the first visits of the early explorers, Polynesia was feted as a paradise of exotic scenery and sensuous women, this was not the case with the islands along the Coral Sea. Hence, they never attained the magical allure of French Polynesia and did not attract the painters and writers and film crews that helped to spread the word and enhance the image of Tahiti. An exception was American writer James A Michener, who wrote *Tales of the South Pacific* while stationed on Espiritu Santo in the New Hebrides during the war and based his fabled island of Bali Hai on the islands of Ambrym, Vanuatu, and Mono in the Solomon Islands.[5] While the Americans had bases throughout the Pacific, the Coral Sea was the location for the major battles of the war. On the other hand, French Polynesia was not a forward base and the servicemen stationed there are reputed to have led a somewhat idyllic existence, so it is not surprising that they carried the most colourful South Pacific stories back home.

The First Hotels Post-War

New Hebrides

Port Vila's most famous early hotel, the Rossi (originally a printery), stood on the waterfront in the centre of the town and from the 1930s was run by the Reid family under the name of Reid's Hotel.[6] The original small one-storey timber structure went through many alterations. When the hotel was taken over by Antoine Rossi in 1951, it had sixteen rooms and was extended in 1970 by a new block of twenty-four rooms.[7] The noted entrepreneur Pierre Bourgeois became involved in building later additions and in the running of the hotel.[8] As Port Vila's oldest hotel, it became an institution and with several further changes in planning, it continued in use as a restaurant and bar until its demolition in 2007.[9] Bourgeois followed his involvement at the Rossi by building the Hotel Vate in 1965, which was the second concrete building in the New Hebrides.[10] The Hotel Vate, well located on an important intersection, had twenty-four rooms on two floors separated from the commercial floor at street level by a cantilevered awning. The hotel was built by 124 Vietnamese workers with very few islanders involved.[11] The equivalent hotel in Noumea was the La Pérouse, a white modern building of five floors that was the tallest building in town when it was built in the late 1960s. Bourgeois' next investment was the 1966 Tanna Hotel, consisting of a group of bungalows on Tanna Island.[12]

LEFT: Tassiriki Estate, Port Vila, 1973. Subdivision Plan.

PREVIOUS PAGE: Le Méridien Île des Pins.

New Caledonia

The early hotels of the New Hebrides and Solomon Islands were of local design and lacked the distinction of Noumea's Grand Hôtel du Pacifique or the first professionally designed hotel, the Hôtel Château Royal, Noumea, 1964, by Cayrol. The original Hôtel Château Royal plan had two long bedroom blocks and a restaurant-casino with bedrooms on the upper floor, staggered back along the beachfront to provide a defined and protected outdoor space along the water. These units, of concrete block construction, had blue tiled roofs and open verandas with slender steel-pipe column supports overlooking the ocean. Cayrol travelled to Hawaii to study air conditioning for this building, which had the first water-chilled air conditioning in New Caledonia and probably in the region.

The Solomon Islands

In 1948 the nine-room Woodford Hotel was opened in some officers' facilities left from the war on an oceanfront site on the outskirts of Honiara. There was also a small lodging that later became the Honiara Hotel.[13] The Mendana Hotel replaced the Woodford Hotel in 1958, and in 1967–68 it was extended, to become the first hotel of note in the Solomon Islands.[14] The Fiji architects and engineers, Derrick Dignan & Associates designed the new Mendana as a simple, modern white building of two levels with rooms with balconies facing the sea.[15] The Mendana remained the only hotel until 1966 when Arthur Blum built a home-stay of fourteen rooms, Blum's Hometel, later known as the Hibiscus Hotel. In the succeeding years other hotels, such as the Honiara, were built or extended, and by 1974 the Solomon Islands had 151 tourist beds.[16]

TOP LEFT: Le Lagon Country Club, Port Vila, Vanuatu, 1969 (redesigned by Media Five, 1987).

BOTTOM LEFT: Hôtel Château Royal, Noumea, New Caledonia, 1964. Gabriel Cayrol. *Courtesy of the architect.*

TOP RIGHT: Hotel Vate, Port Vila, 1965. Pierre Bourgeois.

BOTTOM RIGHT: Rossi Hotel, Port Vila, 1930s.

FAR LEFT: InterContinental Island Inn, Port Vila, 1995. Architects Pacific. Reception. *Courtesy of Holiday Inn Vanuatu.*

LEFT: White Sands Country Club and Golf Course, White Sands, Efate, 1987. Michael Heffernan. Roof Construction. *Courtesy of the architect.*

OPPOSITE: Iririki Island Resort, Iririki Island, Port Vila, 1986. James Ferrie and Partners.

The Airlines

The New Hebrides/Vanuatu

The New Hebrides continued as the leading tourist destination of the region despite the international airport being located in Noumea. Overseas tourists normally flew in on airlines such as UTA to New Caledonia and from there were transferred to Port Vila.[17] Bourgeois, however, had seen that the future of tourism would depend on ready access by air and so played a role in founding Hebridair in 1964.[18] This opened the door to development and made feasible Bourgeois' large undertakings of Port Vila's next two hotels, Le Lagon Country Club, 1969, and the InterContinental Island Inn, 1975, both on Erakor Lagoon, which defines the western edge of the Port Vila peninsula.[19] Later in 1981, Vanuatu's government-owned flag carrier, Air Vanuatu, was established.

Le Lagon Country Club was built on 30.5 hectares of land that had once been a French plantation. The original 1968 buildings of Le Lagon, funded largely with French money,[20] are reported by Bourgeois to have been designed by a New Caledonian architect.[21] The twenty-five air-conditioned bungalows were arranged on the site in relation to a twelve-hole golf course and a striking group of central buildings, all with traditional roof forms with shingle cladding.[22] In 1973, in order to raise funds for his next project, Bourgeois sold Le Lagon to a Japanese company and UTH (the hotel arm of the airline company UTA) took over the management, adding it to their other Pacific hotels. Geoffrey Feast extended the hotel in 1980–81. Very few of the early buildings remain due to the destruction wrought by Cyclone Uma in 1987, and several later stages of intensive rebuilding. Following Uma, Le Lagon was redesigned by the Hawaiian firm Media Five with similar planning of freestanding bungalows and the addition of two-storeyed units related to the golf course.[23]

Bourgeois' next proposal was for the Tassiriki Estate, which consisted of sites for two large hotels and a housing estate at the northern end of Erakor Lagoon. To raise funds and interest, Bourgeois flew to America and formed an association with the developer Trammell Crow, who signed an agreement with Pan Am to build hotels for them in the Pacific, among these the Tassiriki project.[24] The InterContinental Island Inn, the only hotel of the scheme to be built, was designed by Bourgeois in collaboration with an architect from Dallas with Bourgeois flying to Dallas on several occasions to work with the architect, who did not visit Vanuatu.[25] While widespread destruction caused by the cyclone occurred throughout the Vanuatu resorts in 1987, the InterContinental did not suffer to the extent of others and remained virtually intact as an imposing hotel of 166 rooms, standing on a rise overlooking the lagoon. Islands of reclaimed land (maintained by Bourgeois as being the first of their kind in the resorts of the Pacific) were constructed, with beaches and accommodation units reached by bridges. The addition of an impressive reception area consisting of a high-roofed traditional thatched hall, by Architects Pacific, Fiji, was completed in 1995.

Two further exclusive resorts were built in Vanuatu in the 1980s: the Iririki Island Resort, 1986, and the White Sands Country Club and Golf Course, 1987. Iririki Island (the site of the earlier British high commissioner's residence) was chosen as the location for a resort, which was designed by Feast for the slope of the island and faces Port Vila across the lagoon, with bungalows arranged along paths at different levels, stepping to the pool terraces and open-sided reception building. The original

seventy units of prefabricated timber components from Australia were built in stages, with the first stage and the reception building completed in 1985. Following Cyclone Uma, when approximately two-thirds of the resort was swept way, it was rebuilt with pitched-roof cabins of timber stud construction standing on raised platforms.[26] The lower level cabins provide modest examples of the 'overwater' concept, however they are entered directly from the beach, rather than being placed out from the shore and approached along walkways as in Polynesia.

White Sands Country Club and Golf Course, originally a Japanese investment, was an environmentally sensitive resort located at White Sands Beach on the south coast of Efate Island.[27] The resort was alone in the region in demonstrating the aesthetic, construction and climatic possibilities inherent in the use of local materials and ways of building. It was designed by Michael Heffernan of Australia, primarily as a golf resort, with the cabins sited in a splendid palm grove. The buildings, constructed out of local material, coral stone and bush timbers, and built using local labour, survived Cyclone Uma.[28] Heffernan was a pioneer in terms of sustainability and respecting regional building practices, and White Sands was laid out along environmentally sound principles regarding climate control, passive solar heating, water conservation and waste treatment. Also significant was the emphasis placed on training indigenous

labour and the use of local skills. In 2010 a further group of investors introduced a new golf course subdivision at White Sands with houses by the Australian architect Bruce Henderson.[29]

Heffernan's next project was an unbuilt scheme for the proposed Eruiti Resort and was conceived as a complete zero-emission resort utilizing solar energy and a recycling waste treatment plant. In 1982 Heffernan had worked on the master plan for the low-scale natural resort, which was to be sited on 6.5 hectares on the island of Erakor in Erakor Lagoon across from Le Lagon. Here, he continued his exploratory projects for comfortable, low-energy living with cabins of various configurations. He undertook later projects for the island, including two interesting cabins in 1991, designed in collaboration with the Erakor elder, Alec Sualo, a local builder. The cabins were built with a three-dimensional development of a 'chieftain's truss' with forty-five-degree window openings that were able to catch trade winds and accelerate their velocity.[30]

Although Vanuatu continued to be the favoured destination in the region, the 1980s were generally not the best years for tourism in Vanuatu. The market image suffered from the devastation of Cyclone Uma and because overseas tourists incorrectly associated Vanuatu with the uprisings in New Caledonia. Tourism figures did not fully recover until the mid-1990s.[31]

New Caledonia

While some tourists came by flying boat from Sydney and some by sea (such as when the liner *France* called at Noumea in 1972) the destiny of the South Pacific islands as tourist destinations primarily lay in the hands of the leading airlines and, more recently, the regular visits of cruise ship companies. As with the majority of the hotels of the post-war years, Cayrol's Hôtel Château Royal was linked to an international airline, UTA.[32] A group of Americans who had been in Noumea during the war had returned to the islands and promoted the venture, which was later financially backed by the airline.[33]

By the mid-1960s the local regional airline Air Calédonie was starting to fly its own fleet of aircraft operating from Magenta Airport, Noumea (although the new terminal there was not completed until 1975).[34] Noumea's international terminal building was opened at La Tontouta International Airport in 1971, and AirCalin, the international arm of Air Calédonie, started operating in 1983. The recently completed runway was capable of taking a Boeing 747, which had come into operation, thus opening up the region for large-scale tourism.[35] While economic growth slowed with the fall of nickel prices in 1972, there was some response in Noumea to the potential increase in the tourist market, for example, the 1973 ten-storeyed extension to Hôtel Château Royal. Also built facing the sea in the area of Anse Vata were the Île de France, 1973, the Park Royal Hotel, 1977, and the Novotel Le Surf Hotel, 1981.[36] The Hôtel Château Royal closed in 1978 but reopened in 1979 as the Club Mediterranean after being renovated by Raulet with interior designer Gérard Colson. It was refurbished by Raulet again in 1988 but closed once more in 2001 when the lease terminated.[37] Raulet, with Colson, also designed the 100-bed Club Med Hienghène in the Northern Province, 1992, on the site of the old Relais de Koulnoué. At Hienghène, multi-coloured abstract patterns add a contemporary note to the Melanesian 'village' theme, with thatched cottages built to resemble the vernacular.

The Park Royal Hotel went through various phases: the first stage being the early Nouvata Hotel by Raighasse, built in the early 1950s.[38] The subsequent addition of 1977 is a visually strong, pink building of three floors with a regular rhythm in the façade established by columnar pilasters between the units and the columns defining the central bay.[39] Further focus is given to the entrance by the imposing projecting porte-cochère and the curtain wall of the stair lobby above, which also successfully breaks up the horizontal lines of the balconies. Leroux's Novotel Le Surf Hotel, built in stages between 1981 and 1999 (first stage with Lacombe), stands on the Anse Vata side of a dramatic headland

OPPOSITE: White Sands Country Club and Golf Course, White Sands, Efate, 1987. Michael Heffernan. *Courtesy of the architect.*

LEFT: Park Royal Hotel, Anse Vata, Noumea, 1977.

separating Anse Vata from Baie des Citrons. The accommodation is conventional, with wings of straightforward white rectangular blocks arranged in a lineal composition and with open balconies looking out over the water. These were the last of the major hotels in New Caledonia before the uprisings of *les Événements* of 1984 virtually put a stop to tourism and the building of New Caledonian resorts for a decade.

The Solomon Islands

Air Pacific had been operating varying services from Nadi to the Solomon Islands since 1960, and in 1962 Laurie Crowley started Megapode Airlines with charter flights from Papua New Guinea. Megapode Airlines was the initial genesis of Solomon Islands Airways (SOLAIR), which began flying internationally in 1981.[40] Despite these endeavours, the country had been little affected by the increase in air travel, and tourist development in the 1970s and 1980s remained minimal.[41]

Tourist activity in the islands bounding the Coral Sea commenced on a small scale, principally in Vanuatu and primarily through the perception and entrepreneurial interests of private enterprise, including the introduction of Air Vanuatu. Increased air access further directed the islands' tourism in the following decades, notably through the building of La Tontouta International Airport, but primarily due to the internal turmoil the major effect of this was not felt in New Caledonia until later.

The Tourist: Since 1990

'The Coral Sea is the marine equivalent of the Serengeti.' Hugh Possingham

While La Tontouta International Airport had set the scene for increased tourism there was little further hotel investment along the Coral Sea until the 1990s – in part due to local problems and in part to the world oil crisis. Towards the end of the century there was growth in tourism across the South Pacific, including the islands along the Coral Sea, which became sought-after holiday destinations. Of particular significance was the rising 'bubble' economy of Japan, resulting in Japanese property investments, notably in resorts in the western Pacific, including Australia and New Zealand. With increasing wealth, travel became more popular and affordable for the Japanese. In addition, with greater economic activity along the Pacific edge, overseas travel by Australians and New Zealanders also increased. No longer was location a problem for the islands, rather, with the upswing in the tourist market the islands of New Caledonia, Vanuatu and the Solomon Islands were highly convenient and readily accessible from the introduced air routes, and Vanuatu and New Caledonia became regular ports of call for cruise ships visiting the waters to the east and north of Australia.

Vanuatu

In the 1990s Vanuatu remained a popular tourist location. The central Windsor International Hotel, Nambatu, Port Vila, was built on the site of the earlier Solaise Hotel, which had been destroyed by Cyclone Uma. After Uma, it passed into Japanese ownership and was renamed the Windsor International, and subsequently it became the Melanesian. The 1993 wings of the new hotel, by Warren and Mahoney of New Zealand, designed in affiliation with Fletcher Construction, are agreeable simple versions of the white three-storeyed blocks of rooms with balconies that were commonly found across the South Pacific at the time.[1] The accommodation wings are arranged alongside a new central building with a rectangular administration floor on ground level and an upper circular floor containing a multifunction complex that overlooks the tropical planting of the setting around the central swimming pool.

Unique in the context of Vanuatu's hotels are Feast's villas of 1999, designed for the pleasant small resort of Tamanu on the Beach on the southern tip of Efate. Unlike other tourist resorts on the island, these distinctively different villas are characterized by their blend of the innocent with the exotic. The child-like elevations of the 'French Colonial-style' cottages with their front verandas belie the open spaciousness of the interiors, with airy bedrooms and, to the rear, Bali-style

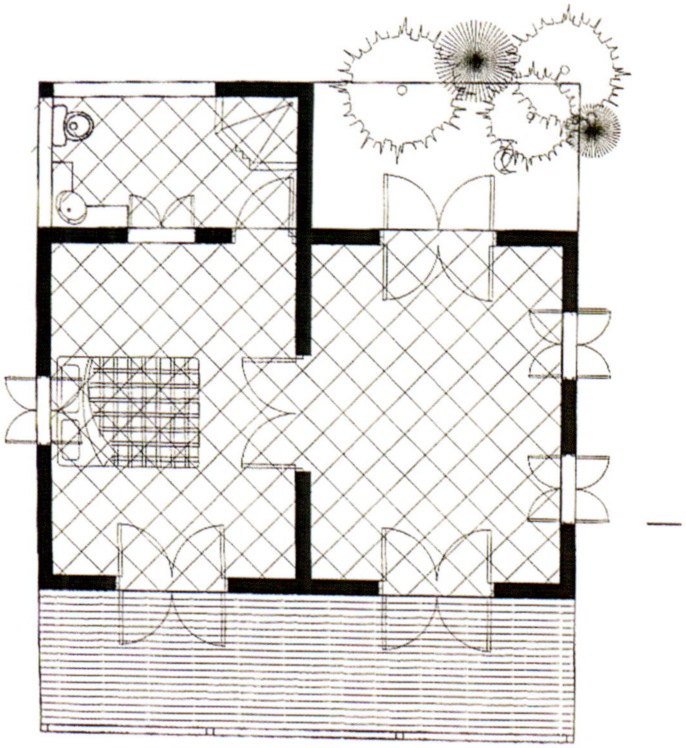

OPPOSITE: Melanesian Hotel, Port Vila, Efate Island, Vanuatu, 1993. Warren and Mahoney.

ABOVE: Tamanu on the Beach Resort, Efate Island, 1999. James Ferrie and Partners.
ABOVE RIGHT: Plan. RIGHT: Bali-style Bathroom.

open bathrooms built with coral stone from the beach. Further, for some of the villas Feast also selected coral stones for the principal walls, successfully mediating between the local context and the colonial image.

Other small private resorts appeared on Efate's coast, mostly within easy reach of Port Vila. Typical is the Paradise Cove Resort, 2000, with imaginative buildings that display the skills of the island craftsmen. The resort has a relaxed ambience with a spreading open restaurant, the Nakamal, and ten villas of differing designs set in luxurious gardens. The roof of the Nakamal is an intricate construction of thin poles and Natangora roofing with sago palm thatching from Epi.

LEFT: Paradise Cove Resort, Efate Island, 2000.
ABOVE: Restaurant Roof Structure.

New Caledonia

After the disruption to the country in 1984, tourism made a slow recovery with most of the subsequent projects being for hotels on the smaller islands. Noteworthy hotels of the 1990s on the main island, Grande Terre, were the Park Royal Nouvata Wing and Le Méridien Noumea. The curved façade of the 1998 Nouvata Wing, by atelier 13, faces the earlier Park Royal Hotel across an impressive large swimming pool of 3000 square metres, interspersed by islands of tropical planting.[2] The new section is complementary to the original hotel in its colour, massing and general proportions, but while the first building is a regular symmetrical design, the new section is dynamic. The façade's crisp lines, with a strong pattern of solid and void horizontal banding, are interrupted by the concave central bay that forms the high space of the generous glazed lobby. This is a confident building showing the maturity of New Caledonian architecture in achieving an appropriate regional expression without resorting to imitations of the vernacular. Le Méridien, which opened in 1995 on Pointe Mangin, is a large hotel of 256 rooms. It was designed by the French firm Arte Charpentier, with Raulet as resident site architect.[3] The hotel consists of a series of separate medium-rise blocks arranged in relationship to a large pool set in lavish tropical gardens. In 1998 Arte Charpentier, with the French urbanist and landscape designer Philippe Thébaud of TUP Paysagiste, also won a major competition for a significant complex at the old Pentagon building site, La Promenade Hotel, with parkland, tourist and commercial facilities and 164 self-contained units in three nine-storeyed buildings.[4] In 2001 the next major project, the twin eighteen-storeyed towers of the Ramada Plaza Hotel by Osmont, was added to the Anse Vata skyline.

La Tontouta International Airport received a major expansion in 2011 (with a new terminal designed by Jacques Rougerie) to accommodate the Airbus A380. The interior of the old terminal building was demolished, and the space incorporated with a new wing of the same size built parallel to it with gardens in between and linked by a rounded hall at the northern end.[5] This gave a stimulus for further facilities to house the expanding tourist numbers. Among these

ABOVE: Park Royal Nouvata Wing, Anse Vata, Noumea, New Caledonia, 1998. atelier 13. Site Plan.
RIGHT: Exterior.

was Tropical Architecture's Sheraton Hotel, located at Bourail on the west coast of Grande Terre, 165 kilometres north-west of Noumea. The hotel, which is due for completion by 2014, contains the usual central core facilities with accommodation being distributed around the site in sixty individual units, each carefully located near an iconic tall tree. The units are elevated on 'stilts' and capped with tall conical roofs that take something from the traditional Kanak 'case', while other conventional suites are located in two-storeyed wings.[6]

The Solomon Islands

In Honiara the Hibiscus Hotel of 1966 was renovated as the King Solomon Hotel and was later extended up a steep hillside to either side of a central funicular that serves bedrooms housed in separate wings on several levels. In 1995 Boykin designed the major addition of a reception and dining area, and worked with local tradesmen in the construction of two large canopy roofs. These are expressive vaulted structures consisting of fine Vasa wood frames bound in the traditional

LEFT: Le Méridien Noumea, Pointe Mangin, Noumea, 1995. Arte Charpentier and François Raulet. *Courtesy of Le Méridien Noumea.*

BELOW LEFT: Le Méridien Île des Pins, New Caledonia, 1998. atelier 13. Pool.
BELOW RIGHT: Restaurant. OPPOSITE: Beach Villa.

manner and roofed with sago palm thatching. These roofs were among the first structures in the Solomon Islands to adapt traditional building techniques to contemporary use.[7] Later hotels included Boykin's Pacific Casino Hotel, 2003, on the central waterfront of the town, and the 2008 Heritage Park Hotel, by the Bartlett Group, Brisbane, built on the site of the old Governor's Lodge. There was, however, no substantial increase in tourist facilities in the Solomon Islands until the construction of small, ecologically responsive resorts primarily built on the small islands after the turn of the twenty-first century.

Resorts of the Outer Islands

One of the striking changes to resort proposals in the 1990s came with the further opening up of the outer islands of the countries of the South Pacific. This was predominantly due to the expansion of the local airline companies such as Air Calédonie, Solomon Islands Airways, Air Fiji and Air Tahiti. This was accompanied by the building of new airport terminals such as the terminal by atelier 13 for the Île des Pins, 2002.

In the western Pacific, it was New Caledonia that exploited the possibilities that the new airlines offered, and it quickly replaced Vanuatu as the leading tourist centre in the region. Two informal resorts by Daniel Leroux for atelier 13 were built in the Loyalty Islands to the north of Grande Terre – Nengone Village Hotel, Cengeite, on the island of Mare, 1994, and the Drehu Village Hotel, We, on the island of Lifou, 1996. Both are based on the 'village' pattern with single-storeyed reception and restaurant pavilions and nearby villas with covered terraces, all linked by paths or boardwalks. In both resorts Leroux used timber construction, and the colours, textures and scale of the units relate well to their beachside settings. Leroux's resorts ushered in a new direction in tourist accommodation along the Coral Sea, leading to resorts that began to resemble

TOP: Hotel Paradis d'Ouvéa, New Caledonia, 2000. Isotope and François Raulet. Main Entrance.
ABOVE: Villa Interior (Yohji Yamamoto).

OPPOSITE, LEFT: Ouré Hotel, Île des Pins, 2002. Agnès Gabet-Jézéquel.

OPPOSITE, RIGHT: Kuendu Beach Resort, Noumea, 1995. Jean-François Beltrano. Overwater Bungalows (Resort, 1979. Henri Morini).

the style and sophistication of those of Fiji and French Polynesia, but on a considerably smaller scale.

In Leroux's Le Méridien Île des Pins on Baie d'Oro, 1998, the model of his Loyalty Islands resorts is carried into a more prestigious and larger project of thirty-nine units.[8] Le Méridien Île des Pins is situated on a picturesque spit of land, edged by the lagoon on one side and a small river on the other. The planning makes full use of the site by locating the central facilities near the lagoon, with most of the accommodation in villas and walk-up units on the other side of the spit. The shed forms of brown timbers and the carved friezes of the main buildings hint of local tradition. The villas, of dark wooden siding contrasting with white panelling, open with sliding walls to the generous verandas and landscape. These restrained buildings are well sited along the banks of the stream and on the white sands at the mouth of the river (see p. 98). The contrasting dark brown and white of the walls and the minimal, flexible nature of their interiors are akin to traditional Japanese compositions. The principal buildings of the resort open onto the lushly planted pool terrace with a fine composition of land and water elements that visually extend the gardens out over the lagoon.[9] The scale and distribution of the separate parts of the complex together with the selection of forms and materials complement the characteristics of the site. Akin to Le Méridien Île des Pins is Gabet-Jézéquel's Hotel Ouré, 2002, also on the Île des Pins. The reserved creativity of Gabet-Jézéquel's architecture, seen in the ecumenical church, is again evident here. At the Hotel Ouré twenty-five timber bungalows are located in a palm plantation on the edge of the beautiful Kanumera Bay. The main lodge, a long, open building under a dark low-pitched roof, is well sited, overlooking the quietly restrained garden terrace and pool and through the palms to the bay beyond.[10] Similar planning principles determined the site plan of Hotel Paradis d'Ouvéa, 2000, built along a wide sandy beach on the northern very small island of d'Ouvéa in the Loyalty Islands Group. The resort was a Japanese investment, designed by the Japanese firm Isotope in collaboration with local architect Raulet. The developers established a successful relationship with the island people who had an investment interest in the resort. Further, while many building products were imported from Japan such as the screens and steel pan-shaped roof tiles, the construction was primarily by builders of d'Ouvéa. The main reception hall is a large high-lit space approached through an impressive, ceremonial portal. The hall is scaled down towards the ocean side with a gentle connection from the dining room on a lower level and on to the beach. The cottages are simple but elegant, providing visual connections with the beach from the internal spaces. The interiors by the Japanese designer Yohji Yamamoto are minimal,

restrained and muted. Paradis d'Ouvéa offers a refreshing difference in the architecture of the South Pacific.

The 'Pacific' Experience

Following the building of the Hotel Bora Bora in French Polynesia in 1961, local vernacular precedent was drawn upon to impart a 'Pacific' ambience in tourist facilities across much of the South Pacific, but before the twenty-first century, this had rarely been the case in the islands of the Coral Sea. In 1995 Jean-François Beltrano added six overwater thatched bungalows, built in the Polynesian manner with access by raised timber walkways, to the 1979 Kuendu Beach Resort outside Noumea.[11] This would appear to be the first example of this type of Polynesian accommodation in this part of the Pacific. The next faux-'Pacific' resort, the Coral Palms Island Resort, 2004, was built on Îlot Maître, five kilometres off the coast from Anse Vata.[12] The resort is a sophisticated complex of sixty-nine units with land-based villas by Leroux and overwater bungalows by Porcheron. The resort has a dramatic approach down a long pier on axis to the central complex with its terrace, pool, restaurant and other public facilities. Having worked in Tahiti for several years, Porcheron is knowledgeable of the overwater villas there and his design for Îlot Maître is of the same spirit as the French Polynesian resorts, offering an elite interpretation of the vernacular with the precision of its details and the use of synthetic materials, including plastic thatch imported from South Africa.[13]

Coral Palms Island Resort, Noumea, 2004.
atelier 13 and Willy Porcheron.

Feast's Breakas Beach Resort, Vanuatu, 2003, offers a 'vernacular' ambience and is a remarkable contrast to his 'colonial' Tamanu on the Beach of 1999. Breakas was opened as an intimate resort, initially of ten villas, located on a wide sandy swimming beach on the tip of a peninsula to the south of Port Vila. The starting point for the resort was an existing long shed building that was upgraded and re-roofed in thatch, to serve as the main entry and restaurant. Feast's composition, formed by the addition of an outdoor restaurant along the face of the shed, a seating terrace around a large pool of diving training depth, a sunken bar and a pool café, successfully defines a central place focused on the beach and ocean. The new buildings of 2003 are of traditional construction and the resort exhibits fine examples of regional craft skills, notably the Natangora sago palm thatching.

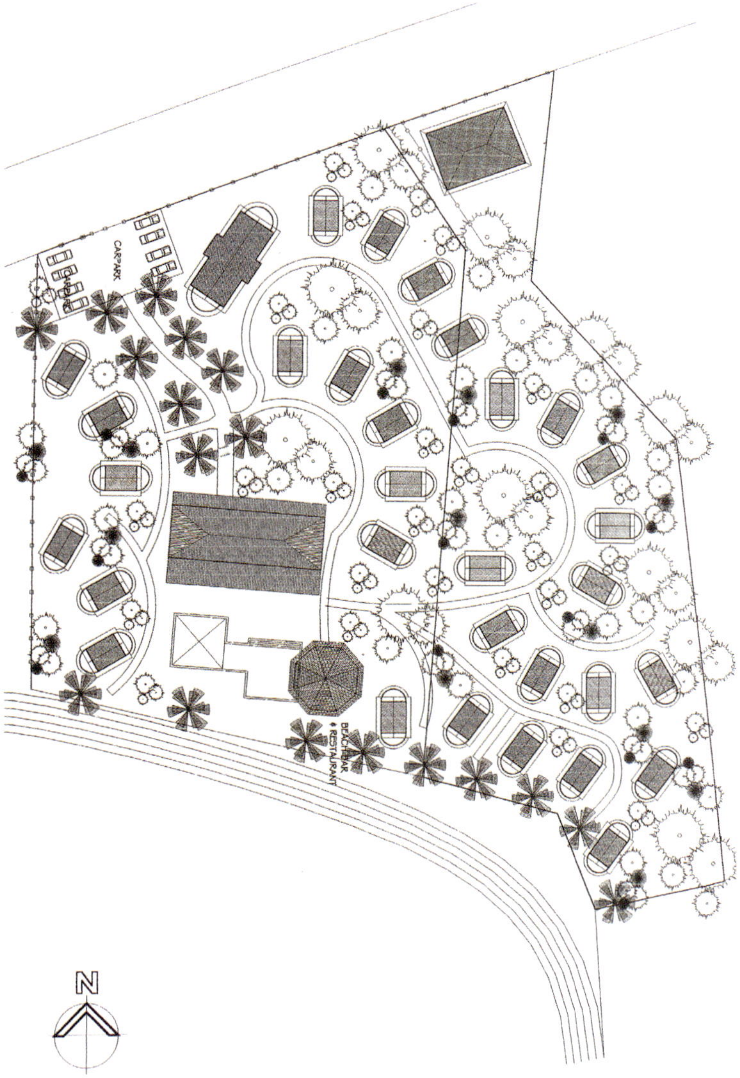

LEFT: Breakas Beach Resort, Port Vila. James Ferrie and Partners. Site plan.
ABOVE: Beach Villas, 2003.

Later Subdivisions

While the emphasis from the late 1990s remained on boutique resorts with perhaps ten to twenty units, there was also a tendency towards more complex and comprehensive settings, and some established operating resorts were intensely redeveloped. The land was further subdivided, and places that started out as small resorts with a low-key ambience were turned into high-density sites. The Iririki Island Resort subdivided much of the remainder of the island and sold it for individual home sites. Erakor Island was extended through the addition of new bungalows. This pattern of additions can also be seen in the later phase of Breakas Beach Resort, which was enlarged from ten to sixty-three units.

With a Difference: The Solomon Islands

The antithesis to most of the South Pacific is found in the Solomon Islands, where tourism is minimal and there are no large international resorts. Rather, outside Honiara the Solomon Islands generally offer low-key, often remote, establishments that are owner-built and operated. Some areas are without postal and telephone contact, and there can be few modern technological services. As there are sometimes no roads, access can be unreliable and can involve travel in open motor canoes in unpredictable conditions. The Solomon Islands Government tourist policy, which was passed in the late 1980s, encompasses guiding principles that insist on all tourist facilities being in accord with and respectful of traditional values and customs.[14] Overseas aid is available to help families to open simple, very low

OPPOSITE: Breakas Beach Resort, Port Vila, 2003. James Ferrie and Partners.

FAR LEFT: Fatboys, Gizo, Western Province, Solomon Islands, 2004. Andrew Duncan.

LEFT CENTRE: Sanbis, Gizo, Western Province, 2005. Hans Mergozzi. Roof Detail.
LEFT: Gilbertese Craftsman weaving Ridge Capping. BELOW: Entrance Pier.

technology resorts. Organizations such as UNESCO's World Heritage Committee and The World Wide Fund for Nature are working with the local people to protect the environment from exploitation and to establish eco-tourist lodges. Particularly noteworthy for such interventions is the beautiful Marovo Lagoon on the eastern seaboard of New Georgia Island. Marovo, with a length of over 100 kilometres, is the world's largest island-enclosed lagoon.[15] But concern for the preservation of eco-systems also characterizes many of the less basic resorts, such the early Tavanipupu Resort, Marau Sound, on the remote south end of Guadalcanal Island, and Vulelua Island Resort, off the coast near Honiara.[16]

The unspoilt region of the Western Province has attracted environmentally developments including resorts, restaurants and houses. Travelling across the water from the town of Gizo, the 2004 restaurant of Fatboys appears. Grant Griffiths from Australia, now a naturalized Solomon Islander, built Fatboys on the eastern tip of Mbabanga in 2004 to a design by Andrew Duncan, chief engineer with the Western Provincial Government of the Solomon Islands. The restaurant is a large open pavilion raised on timber pylons and sheltered by a spreading thatched roof. Due to the shallow waters in this area, Fatboys is built out over the lagoon far from the shore and is mostly approached by boat, but has access to the land along a jetty leading to a small cluster of beach bungalows.[17] On the western tip of Mbabanga Island, four kilometres south-east of Gizo, is a small resort that provides an example of ecological development practices in the islands. This exclusive resort, which was planned for ten guests only, is primarily targeted at divers and big-game fishing adventurers. Sanbis Resort is owned and built by a Swiss, Hans Mergozzi who, following many years in Australia, sailed to the Solomon Islands in 2002

OPPOSITE: Naru Island, Gizo, Western Province, 2006. *Courtesy of Shane and Sue Kennedy.*

FAR LEFT: Kennedy House, Naru Island, 2006. Andrew Duncan. *Courtesy of Shane and Sue Kennedy.*

LEFT: Gizo Hotel, Gizo, Carved Figurative Post at Entrance.

in his yacht. Mergozzi also owned Solomon Watersport and Solomon Connect, which provided transport throughout the Western Province.[18] Mergozzi used local materials and primarily island labour, including Gilbertese craftsmen, and personally oversaw the building of this delightful eco-friendly complex.[19] Sanbis Resort, which displays, notably in the roofing, fine examples of regional craftsmanship, was also planned to utilize sustainable resources and renewable energy. The buildings are carefully sited to conserve the existing vegetation, with the residential units placed along the sandy beach. The reception, dining and service areas are also located on the waterfront and linked to the landing stage by a long axial pier. In addition, 4000 plants were added to the island's native vegetation.

Beyond Sanbis, on the private island of Naru and sharing in the same spirit, is the Kennedy House, designed by Duncan. Shane and Sue Kennedy, also from Australia, bought both the King Solomon Hotel and the Gizo Hotel, 2002, and have used the hotels as vehicles for furthering local traditional building techniques and art. Notable in their projects has been the introduction of major pieces of woodcarving to the entrances and public spaces, principally posts carved by craftsmen of the nearby islands. In 2006 they bought the island of Naru and built the Kennedy house – an ideal environment to be in to further their interests in local art and culture – on an expansive sandy beach with views towards the north-west. The basic timber dwelling opens on to a wide veranda and a forecourt protected by a high pitched woven sago palm roof with leaves from the local island of Renonga. The roof is supported by impressive figurative posts from the islands of Rennell and Bellona. As with Sanbis, it was built using the structural traditions of the region, and local labour and materials were utilized, including Vasa wood, Rosewood and Coconut wood sourced from the nearby island of Vella Lavella. The Kennedy House is an idealized retreat that represents the acme of the traveller's search for the lost paradise of the South Pacific.[20]

As with the dominance of the architecture of the Modern Movement that threatened to cast the buildings of different climates and cultures into one mould, the popularity of the 'Polynesia' style is resulting in a certain sameness about the resorts of Oceania. Vanuatu, New Caledonia and the Solomon Islands were late in developing a tourist industry, and they were also late in taking up the Polynesian theme. Consequently, the resorts of the Coral Sea have retained a certain regional distinction.

THE SPECIAL CASE OF FIJI

5

Two Colonial Capitals

While French Polynesia lies at the centre of the waters of the South Pacific Ocean, Fiji lies at the centre of the islands. Fiji's position has been crucial to its development, as it is well placed to act as a focal point for activities in the region and to serve as a hub for transportation and commercial exchange in the South Pacific. Fiji is also directly linked to Australia and America, and further on to Europe, as it provides a convenient stopping point on the important Pacific sea and air routes. Having been a British colony English is spoken there, and this also has proved advantageous on Pacific crossings. In recent years its accessibility to Asia has become an important factor in attracting tourists from that region.

Fiji is the most easterly of the Melanesian islands, and its location has resulted in a pervasive influence from Polynesia, predominantly from Tonga, evident in such fundamental matters as the adoption of the strict chiefdom structure of the Polynesian countries. The name 'Fiji', though given to the islands by the Europeans, is of Tongan derivation. The relatively large population and the high proportion of Indians makes Fiji singular in the Pacific.[1] The Indians, now almost entirely Fijian-born, for the most part are the descendants of the 60 000 Indians who arrived between 1879 and 1920 to serve five-year terms on the sugar plantations, of whom over two-thirds remained. The Chinese also came as workers and were first officially recorded in 1911.[2] By the 1940s the Indians had outnumbered the Melanesians and this population shift contributed to the tension that led to the political coups between 1987 and 2006, when Melanesians sought to retain control of the country.[3] Many Indians left Fiji after the coups, and by 2007 the population distribution had changed to 57 per cent indigenous Fijians, predominantly Melanesian, 37 per cent Indo-Fijians, and others 6 per cent.[4]

LEFT: Levuka, Ovalau Island, Fiji.

TOP: Royal Hotel, Levuka, 1860s. *Courtesy of Gould Genealogy.*

ABOVE: Morris, Hedstrom, Ltd., Levuka Main Street, 1900.

PREVIOUS PAGE: Bank of New South Wales.

The Fiji islands cover a land area of some 18 376 square kilometres and form one of the largest archipelagos of the South Pacific. The land was created primarily through volcanic activity, with some island groups formed from coral outcrops. As is the case in most of the islands throughout the South Pacific, the Fijian islands are subject to earthquakes and hurricanes. Viti Levu (Great Fiji) is the largest of the 330-odd islands, 100 of which are inhabited. Viti Levu and the northern islands of Vanua Levu (Great Land) and Taveuni are ringed by small fringes of islands and beyond are the outer islands.[5] European explorers, including Abel Tasman, James Cook and William Bligh, sailed in Fijian waters in the seventeenth and eighteenth centuries without making landings because of dangerous coral reefs. The first contact Fijians had with Europeans was with traders seeking the sandalwood that was discovered at Bua Bay, Vanua Levu, in 1801.[6]

By the 1820s European colonists had established small towns, with the main centre being at Levuka on the island of Ovalau. It was not long before those spreading the word of the Bible turned their focus to Fiji, and as early as 1830 three converted Tahitian missionaries, sent by the ubiquitous London Missionary Society missionary John Williams, landed at Lakeba in the Southern Lau Group. Five years later British missionaries from Tonga arrived.[7] The first Catholic Marist missionaries settled in 1844 at Lakeba and were followed in 1851 by three brothers, led by Bishop Bataillon who moved to Levuka and established a mission.[8] The first Anglican minister, William Floyd, arrived in Levuka in 1870.[9] In 1871 King Cakobau, a Christian convert, was crowned at Levuka, and a modern nation-state was established with an elected government. Due to warring among tribes this had to be disbanded, and in 1874 Cakobau requested cessation to Great Britain. Fiji was granted independence as a dominion in 1970 after ninety-six years of colonial administration. As a sequel to the 1987 coups led by Lieutenant Colonel Sitiveni Rabuka, the 1970 constitution was invalidated, and Fiji was declared a republic.

The British Colony

Levuka

Levuka is a picturesque town on a narrow strip of level ground between the lush high mountain range and the sea, and as the major centre for Fiji in the nineteenth century, the principal buildings of the colony were built there. By 1870 Levuka, with a population of approximately 3000 Europeans, had acquired a reputation as a lawless port for sailors and whalers, and as a centre of traders, including those blackbirding for workers from the New Hebrides and the Solomon Islands. They were catered for by more than fifty-two bars and saloons in the town and three large hotels: the Royal, the Levuka and the Criterion.[10] The buildings of Levuka included the original store of Morris, Hedstrom, Ltd. (established 1898), a company which was to dominate the retail trade of the central Pacific,[11] the 1879 two-storeyed Levuka Public School – a notable building with an unconventional high central entry tower and wide open verandas on both levels[12] – the pseudo-Tuscan masonry Masonic Lodge of 1875, which was the first in the South Pacific, and the 1898 Queen Victoria Memorial Hall (later the Levuka Town Hall), an uncommon masonry building suggestive of the Spanish Mission style.[13] In 1904 the Ovalau Club, the first private club in Fiji, was established in an existing house of timber and corrugated-steel construction.[14]

Among the early buildings for the Anglican Church was the Church of the Holy Redeemer, the original timber buildings of which were destroyed by hurricanes on two occasions, before the church was rebuilt in concrete in 1904.[15] This fine church

TOP: Levuka Public School, Levuka, 1879.

ABOVE: Church of the Holy Redeemer, Levuka, 1904.

TOP: St John's Church and College, Cawaci, 1893–1900.

ABOVE LEFT: Church of the Sacred Heart, Levuka, 1891.

ABOVE RIGHT: Bishop's Tomb, Ovalau Island, 1922.

OPPOSITE: Marist Convent School, Levuka, 1893.

boasts high quality stained-glass windows from France depicting early settlers of Levuka.[16] As the seat of the Vicar Apostolic of Fiji, Levuka held a special place of prominence for the Catholic religion, and several large schools and churches were constructed. The original Catholic church was blown away in 1886 and was replaced by the Church of the Sacred Heart in 1889.[17] An imposing concrete clock tower was added later, dwarfing the low basilican form of the timber body of the church. The important Marist Convent complex, constructed in 1891 and extended in 1900, is the oldest Catholic mission school in Fiji, serving as the motherhouse for all others. This is a large symmetrical stone and concrete building with a central gabled porch and two gabled side porches, linked by a wide veranda providing circulation colonnades on the lower level.[18] In 1893 the Catholic mission bought land at Cawaci, to the north of Levuka, principally to build St John's Church and College to cater for the growing number of those seeking education. The mission is one of several built under the direction of Bishop Vidal, the first Catholic Bishop of Fiji. The impressive white complex, consisting of the chapel, the rectory, dormitories and classrooms, and two tall round towers, is one of the largest and finest missions in the South Pacific.[19] On a picturesque promontory nearby is the coral stone Bishop's Tomb, erected in 1922 in memory of Bishop Vidal. This is a formal commemorative building with a centralized plan and caped by a cupola. Over the few short years of its position as the capital of the colony Levuka was a microcosm of a British colonial town with all the 'essential' buildings of colonization, to present a replica of 'home' and to reassure and impress with all the trappings of 'civilization' in an alien outpost.

Subsequent to the annexation of Fiji, the British Government sought another capital as Levuka was proving unsuitable due to inadequate port facilities, the limitations on town growth due to its constrained site, and difficulties with 'the restriction on alienation of Fijian customary land'.[20] Despite this, Levuka remained a busy port until 1900 but the loss of status, the destructive hurricanes of 1886, 1907 and 1912, and the closure of German businesses during World War I meant a decline in its fortunes.[21]

Early Suva

Lautoka on the north-west coast and Suva on the south-east coast of Viti Levu were considered to be potential capitals. With the large-scale cultivation of sugar in the 1880s, many favoured Lautoka as the emerging centre of the industry, but Suva, which had been a failure in terms of sugar production, had the better port. In 1877 Suva was named capital, and in 1882 the government was officially relocated there.[22] Given the concentration of activity in Levuka in the nineteenth century, the

town of Suva had remained a small rural community with a few European settlers. The town consisted of the Fijian village of Suva[23] and 'three or four houses, a small disused church, a large disused sugar mill and this disused and deserted hotel'.[24] In 1882 there was, however, a population influx, and the small buildings and limited services of the town soon proved inadequate to serve the community.

Suva followed the usual pattern of urban growth in the South Pacific, with the first major buildings being those of the churches. The early churches included the Anglican Pro-Cathedral of the Holy Trinity, designed in timber by George Moore and consecrated in 1886. Despite severe hurricanes it survived and continued to be used as a parish church until 1952. In 1940 the foundation stone was laid for a new cathedral to replace this building on land vacated by the old government offices, but due to the intervention of World War II, building did not commence until 1948.[25] Stage 1 by the Government Architect C H Nettleton was completed in 1952 and Stage 2 by Derrick Dignan & Associates in 1974. St Andrew's Presbyterian Church, also of timber, was opened in 1883 but suffered major damage in the hurricane of 1895. The church was rebuilt in the same year, again in timber, under the direction of Reverend William Gardner from Melbourne, and despite damage from further hurricanes it has survived in virtually its original form.[26] The major Catholic edifice, Sacred Heart Cathedral, was built for Bishop Vidal under the supervision of Father Pierre Boudier to replace the small wooden chapel of St Paul of 1885. The foundation stone was blessed in 1894, and despite the demanding task of importing all the sandstone and construction materials from Sydney and the timber flooring from Quebec, the cathedral was opened in 1902.[27]

Victoria Parade

The Royal Engineers laid out Central Suva. In 1875 Colonel F E Pratt was appointed as Surveyor-General and Director of Works and given responsibility for the new town. While his proposed plan was quite accomplished, in reality, it was not fully implemented, and Suva grew in a rather disorderly fashion. Roads and services were in a poor state, and they were not much better in the new century.[28] Civic and trading buildings appeared in the small framework of streets that were laid out as the town. Suva grew out from the pivotal point of 'the Triangle', located at the four-way intersection of Victoria Parade, Renwick Road and Thompson and Central streets. Victoria Parade, the principal avenue of the plan, originally was a short one-sided street fronting the harbour, but despite its unsatisfactory condition, by the end of the century it boasted fine hotels such as the Melbourne Hotel, 1881, the imposing Club Hotel, 1883, and McDonald's Hotel, 1885.[29] In 1914 Victoria Parade was extended to serve the new Grand Pacific Hotel and to link with Thurston Park (now the Suva Botanical Gardens), which was opened in 1913. A bandstand and clock tower were added to the gardens in 1918.[30] With the reclamation of the foreshore for building sites, Victoria Parade developed into a major avenue with many of Suva's most prestigious buildings, such as the Queen Victoria Memorial Hall, the Carnegie Library, the Pacific Cable Board Building and the Suva Boys' Grammar School.

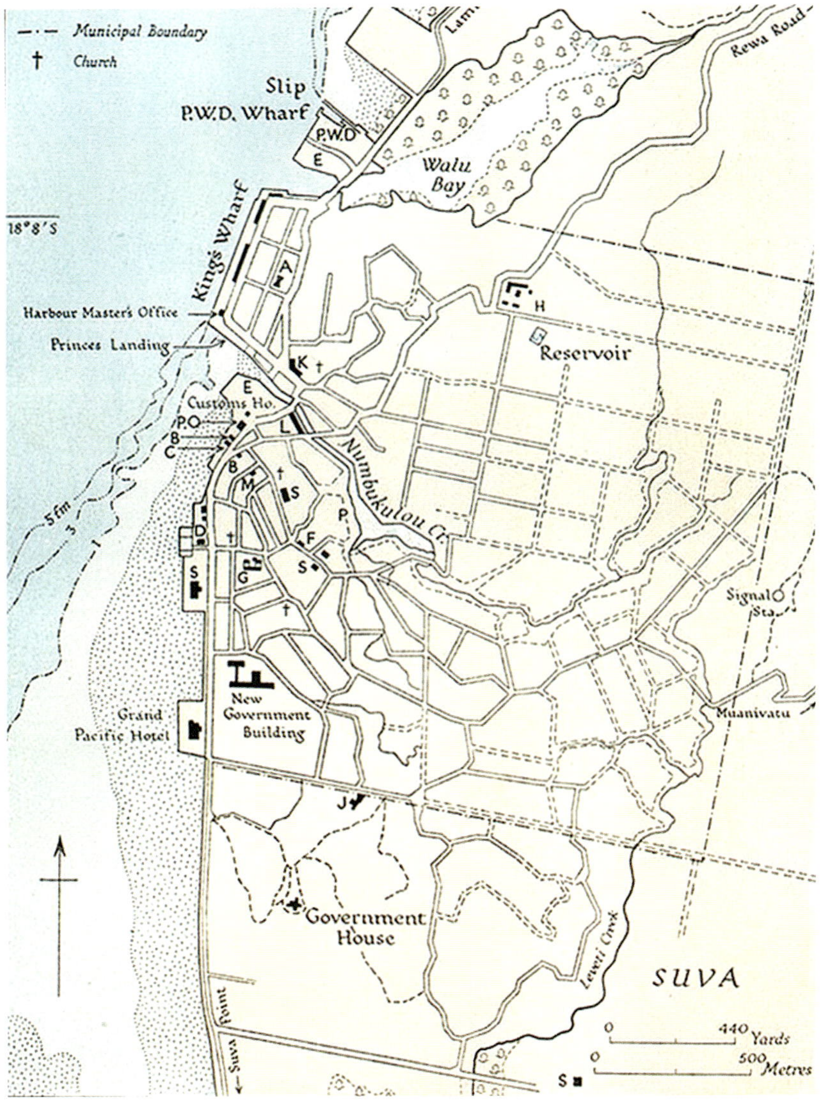

Plan of Central Suva.

OPPOSITE: Plan of Suva, c. 1930. *Courtesy of University of Texas Libraries, The University of Texas at Austin.*

Queen Victoria Memorial Hall, Suva, 1904. R Anrep. *Courtesy of the National Archives of Fiji.*

St Andrews Presbyterian Church, Suva, 1895.

One of the principal buildings of the colonial government was the 1904 Queen Victoria Memorial Hall, by the local architect R Anrep, which, as at Levuka, was later to become the Suva Town Hall.[31] The building consists of two sections: a two-storeyed block facing Victoria Parade with wide verandas with iron lace-work and a high and long auditorium built as a wing on the seaward side.[32] It was both the administrative and social centre for the town because in addition to serving in its role as the town hall with offices of government on the ground level, it was the venue for concerts and dances and had facilities for a museum on the upper level. It operated as the town hall until 1966 when the Suva Civic Centre, by Larsen Holtom Maybin, was opened nearby on reclaimed land.[33] Contributing to Suva's emerging civic presence was the 1909 Carnegie Library, built on a free site next to the town hall with a donation from American benefactor Andrew Carnegie. The building had to be re-roofed after its roof blew off six months after opening. In contrast to the Queen Victoria Memorial Hall, the Carnegie Library, also designed by Anrep, is a concrete building with a heavy 'temple' façade of four piers supporting an entablature and an uncommon pediment with ten columns. The library occupied the ground floor, and reading rooms were on the second level. Wings were added to the central block in 1929–30, doubling the floor space.[34]

Victoria Parade was given further definition by the construction of the fine Pacific Cable Board Building (Fintel Building), designed by A H Martin of Suva in 1926.[35] The building replaced the 1902 timber Cable Board Building that had been built on a site next to that of the future Council Complex. The early building was moved to another location, and the site was enlarged by reclamation to allow for much larger premises. The new concrete building is typical of colonial architecture, being of two storeys with wide verandas, but it shows an uncommon level of accomplishment in its proportions and the quality of the decorative timber verandas, with a suggestion of the influence of Art Nouveau in the design of the pierced timbers of the balustrades. The building also introduced new technologies, being roofed with special steel from England and 'concrete sheeting' that was used to roof the verandas.[36]

FAR LEFT: Pacific Cable Board Building, Suva, 1926. A H Martin.

LEFT: Carnegie Library, Suva, 1909. R Anrep.

BELOW: Grand Pacific Hotel, Suva, 1914. Salmond and Vane Architects. Elevation. *Courtesy of Architects Pacific.*

OPPOSITE: Henry Marks Store (later Morris, Hedstrom, Ltd, Nabukalou Creek, Suva, 1893–1912. *Courtesy of the National Archives of Fiji.*

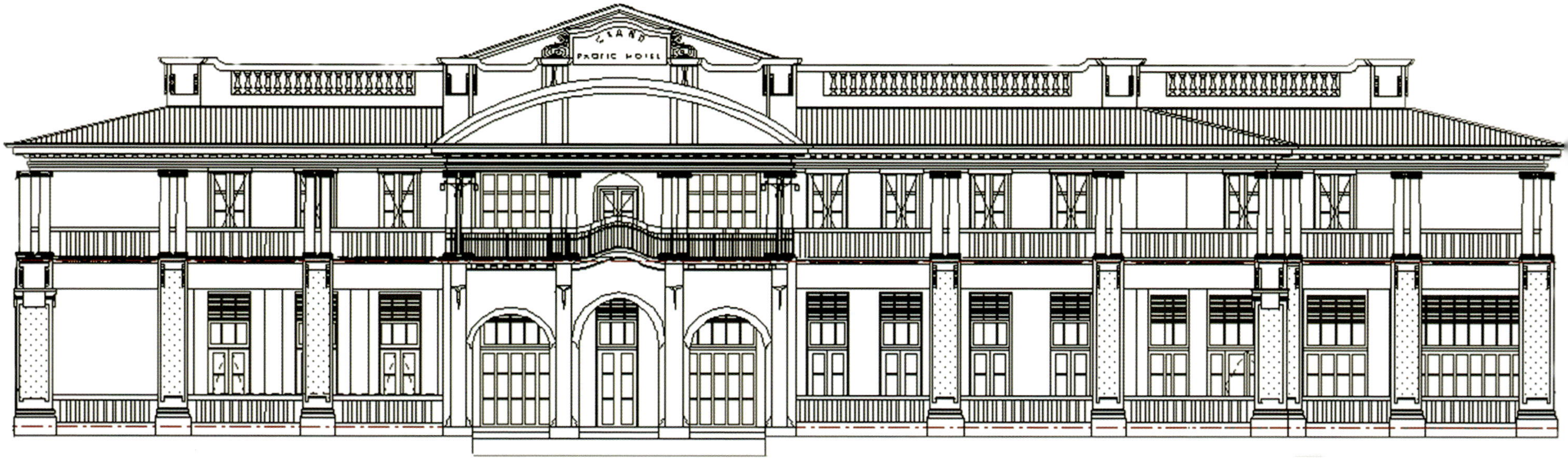

ESTABLISHED 1881
IMPORTERS
GENERAL MERCHANTS
MORRIS HEDSTROM

LEFT: Hedstrom House, Suva, 1907 (renovated as the Australian High Commissioner Residence, 1991. Adrian Sofield).

OPPOSITE, LEFT: Suva Boys' Grammar School, Suva, 1918. Owen Cross Ludolph.

OPPOSITE, RIGHT: Suva Girls' Grammar School (previously the Suva Boys' Grammar School and before that the Suva Public School), Suva. *Courtesy of the National Archives of Fiji.*

The Grand Pacific Hotel, 1914, became the social and business centre of Suva and a landmark building in terms of its physical presence. More significant were the first-class facilities it offered to guests, with the resulting prestige it brought internationally to the country. The Grand Pacific became known as one of the great hotels of the world, vying with such famed destinations as Raffles Hotel (1887) in Singapore and the Peninsula Hotel (1928) in Hong Kong.[37]

The Triangle

Suva's central area around the Triangle also was growing, and in 1912 Morris, Hedstrom, Ltd. moved its headquarters there.[38] In 1920 the company occupied a prominent building built in 1893 by the major trading firm of Henry Marks.[39] Their 'largest retail store of the western Pacific' originally was of single-storeyed timber-framed construction and stretched along the bank of Nabukalou Creek from Thompson Street to Renwick Road. In 1912 Henry Marks extended the building in height and width by erecting a concrete structure on reclaimed land on the creek bank and over sunken concrete piles in the water. The new upper-floor balcony, eighty-four metres long and three metres wide, overhung the public right-of-way along the creek, and access was provided by way of the colonnaded arcade, which made a substantial contribution to the urban definition of central Suva.[40] In 1907 the Hedstrom family built a timber colonial house in Tamavua, Suva, that was damaged by cyclone in the 1950s. The house was restored in 1991 by Adrian Sofield as the Australian High Commissioner Residence, which, with a new chancery and staff residences, makes up the Australian Government Embassy complex. More commercial buildings were built in the centre of the town, such as the 1930 building in Marks Road for the shipping company Burns Philp, which was the first building in Fiji to have a lift.[41] The imposing façade and central tower of their Suva office established the hallmark design of their buildings throughout the Pacific.

Between the Wars

In the decades after World War I several imposing buildings were added to Suva's streets, many of which were designed by Owen Cross Ludolph, the newly appointed Government Architect. Ludolph was born in 1883 to German parents living in South Africa.[42] He completed his architectural studies in England and sailed to Melbourne to take up employment there.[43] At the outbreak of World War I he moved to Fiji to fill the position of Government Architect, and during his term he gave Suva some of its most distinguished buildings.[44] His first major building was the Suva Boys' Grammar School of 1918 that, together with the Girls' Grammar School, provided schooling for European children. In 1917 the government resumed the site next to the Carnegie Library for the school and later reclaimed additional land for a sports field on the seaward side. Work was completed in 1923. The

Girls' Grammar School was moved into the building the Boys' Grammar School had vacated, originally built for Suva Public School.[45] It is a fine two-storeyed concrete building with a façade that has a central pediment and wide balconies. The Boys' Grammar School is of a balanced classical composition, similar to other major buildings throughout the empire, with a commanding façade characterized by a projecting central portico, square corner towers and generous open verandas on both levels.[46] Ludolph's concrete Colonial War Memorial Hospital of 1923–24 replaced the run-down nineteenth-century timber buildings of the old Colonial Hospital.[47] With its open verandas and lower arcaded colonnades, it is related to the Boys' Grammar School.

The first Government House, 1882, was of timber construction and was laid out as a related group of buildings of similar character to other civic buildings in Suva, such as the Suva Post Office and Customs House. These had steeply pitched gable roofs and were surrounded by verandas under single pitched coverings. Government House was burnt down after having been struck by lightning in 1921, and a new Government House was commissioned, which was completed in 1928 to a design by Ludolph.[48] While of a lighter composition than his previous Suva buildings, Government House is an imposing building in the pseudo-Renaissance style favoured by Ludolph, with round arched windows and deep arcades on two levels to each side of a protruding portico. The building consists of three interconnected two-storeyed pavilions facing the sea with an entrance portico on the south. Wide colonnaded verandas on all sides protect the main rooms of the house.[49] The governors of Fiji were also high commissioners to the former British Western Pacific Territories, and the grand size and character of the building reflects the importance of Suva as the core of British administration in the region.[50]

A further mansion, Borron House, which stands on a fourteen-hectare site at Samabula, high above Suva, was built in 1927 to a design by Australian engineer Ronald Albert Derrick for a Scottish plantation owner, James M Borron. The two-storeyed house has four bedrooms, beautiful Yaka archways and staircases, Vesi floors and portraits, paintings and furnishings that provide historical documentation of a long family history extending through generations in Scotland and Fiji.[51] Taken over by the US armed forces during World War II, Borron House was used as a guest residence and many history-making figures stayed there.[52] After 1980 the Fiji Government used the property as a VIP guest house, as requested in the 1977 bequest of the house and gardens to the National Trust.[53]

The last of the major structures of the first half of the century was the imposing Government Offices of 1939. Ludolph was unsuccessful in the competition of 1928,[54] which was won by W F Hedges, an architect and structural engineer from England, who had designed civic buildings in Asia, including the 1928 Telecom Museum, Kuala Lumpur.[55] This large office complex in grey stone occupies a key

ABOVE: Government House, Suva, 1928. Owen Cross Ludolph.
LEFT: Living Room. *Courtesy of the National Archives of Fiji.*

OPPOSITE, LEFT: Government Offices, Suva, 1939. W F Hedges.

OPPOSITE, RIGHT: Borron House, Suva, 1927. R A Derrick.

site in central Suva, facing out over the grass of Albert Park, which has served as a place for sport and general recreation for the people since Suva's early days.[56] The site originally was an old creek and swamp, and the building is set on piles. The offices have frontages of 163 metres to Albert Park and 90 metres to Victoria Parade, with the focus of the composition provided by the 35-metre-high clock tower.[57] Uncommonly, the building has ornamentation of Indian derivation in the entry portico and along the façade. The building exhibits some concern for tropical design, in being a long narrow building on the east-west axis with verandas to the north and open to prevailing winds.[58] Parliament met here until 1987, and the building later housed the Fiji High Court, the Prime Minister's Office and government members' offices.

The transitional building into the modern city was the 1940 Art Deco Bank of New South Wales,[59] designed by the Sydney architects Louis S Robertson and Son, that was built in a nodal location on the corner of Central and Thompson streets.[60] The building, ornamented by cast decorative infill panels typically found in other buildings of the bank in Australia, introduced a new note to the architecture of the Triangle (see p. 120). Development of the town, however, was slow, and it was not until much later in the century that the diversified practices of Larsen Holtom Maybin, Murray Cockburn Partnership, Lee Associates/Jaimi Associates and Architects Pacific made their contributions to Suva's skyline.

The Fiji islands have a history of two colonial capitals and consequently two groups of civic and religious buildings, each representative of the conditions in the colonial Pacific of its time. Due to the late date of the founding of Suva, the use of masonry construction and the quality of the early architects, much of the architecture built between Suva's establishment as the capital in 1882 and the mid-twentieth century has survived and still determines the character of much of central Suva. These buildings, together with those of nineteenth-century Levuka, provide the most complete collection of colonial buildings in the South Pacific.

Shaping Suva

Being on the fringe of the Pacific Theatre during World War II, Fiji was one of the least affected countries, yet, like the other nations of the South Pacific, its development slowed and recovery was not easy as it moved into a new era following the conflict. Fiji did not house large numbers of Allied troops, but it was in a key defensive location, and New Zealand forces were active, working on the airstrip at Nadi and, together with Fijian troops, manning the large gun emplacements on the coast of Viti Levu. Fiji's commitment of troops to the Allied forces was significant, with more than 6500 serving by the mid-1940s.[1] The contact this brought with ways and places beyond the islands changed perceptions and expectations.

The growth of Suva and its transformation from a colonial town into a modern city was a part of the overall growth of the country after the opening of the Nadi International Airport to jet aircraft in 1958. By 1960 the airport was servicing three international flights each way every day.[2] With an upgraded airport and flight connections, Fiji was well placed to host the first Pacific Games in 1963, but these early Games did not have a major impact on the development of Suva.[3] Yet, despite the international airport being at Nadi, Suva was fully established as the hub of the country by the 1970s. It had the major port and was the centre of government, industry, education and commerce. The selection of Suva again as the venue for the Pacific Games, this time in 1979, was a key event in the second half of the century that helped place Fiji on the international map. The minister appointed the firm of Larsen Holtom Maybin to design the two principal games buildings: the National Gymnasium and the National Stadium Grandstand (the second with design architect Murray Cockburn). The construction of the next major sports venue was not until the Suva Pacific Games of 2003, with the large 3300-seat blue-roofed Indoor Sports Arena, which was a gift from the Chinese Government.[4] Further contributing to the growth of Suva was the opening in 1980 of the University of the South Pacific (USP) (Laucala Campus), and this made Suva not just the educational centre for Fiji but also an important focus of education for the English-speaking regions of the South Pacific. The university is located on the site of the old flying boat base, built during the war and given to Fiji by the New Zealand Government.[5] Most of Suva's architects subsequently were represented with buildings on this large campus.

Fiji Development Bank, Suva, 1968. Larsen Holtom Maybin.

Indoor Sports Arena, Suva, 2003. Chinese Government.

Suva Civic Centre Complex, Suva, 1965–1969. Larsen Holtom Maybin.

Suva and its Architects

By the mid-1990s Suva, with a population of 167 975, had begun to resemble the city of today.[6] Its physical profile changed, but the general structure of the early plan served as the core for the horizontal expansion of the town. For the most part, the buildings of contemporary Suva were by local architectural firms – a notable exception being the bold 1970 concrete YWCA Building on Suva's waterfront, by the Australian firm of Daryl Jackson Evan Walker Architects. Architects of European descent dominate the profession, but those with Asian backgrounds, such as Ben Lee, Ron Seeto, Jitendra Narsey, Vijay Sharma and Jaimi Samarawera, are well represented. The first Melanesian architect was Udit Narayan, who trained in Auckland and practised in the late 1950s.[7] Prominent among current Melanesian architects is Filipe Tauva of Vitia Architects, designers of Fiji's Parliament House.

While Fiji's architects received their formal architectural training abroad (and still do), positive initiatives were introduced locally early in the century. The first classes in building construction were taught by R A Derrick, an engineer who had been sent from Australia by the Methodist Mission to establish a building construction class at Davuilevu on the banks of the Rewa River.[8] He was later placed in charge of technical education in Fiji. Derrick was a scholar of note and wrote several books and papers including *A History of Fiji*, 1946.[9] The first training school, named the Derrick Technical College (the precursor to the Fiji Institute of Technology), was designed by Gordon Larsen of Larsen Holtom Maybin (LHM). By the 1960s it offered a two-year full-time course in drafting run by correspondence from London.[10] The Professional Practice in Architecture course was introduced in 1981, and the Design Course in Architecture in 1982.[11] R. A Derrick and family made notable contributions to architecture in the South Pacific. His son, Brian Frazer Derrick was educated in Suva and at Melbourne University where he graduated in civil engineering in 1952, and in 1953 he started work at the Suva City Council as assistant city engineer.[12] In 1954 he commenced practice as a consulting engineer, and in 1959 he formed the firm of Derrick and Derrick with his older brother Alwyn, an architect. Alwyn resigned from the partnership in 1966 and subsequently, Derrick established the firm of Derrick, Dignan & Associates.[13] In 1967 Brian Derrick founded and became managing director of Naviti Investments Corporation, which was involved in hotel and resort projects throughout the South Pacific.[14]

Tony Sansom, who arrived in Fiji from Australia in 1974, also was a contributing figure in the development of the architecture of Fiji and played an important role in architectural education, both formally and informally. Sansom was born

in Zimbabwe and grew up in Tanzania and retained a major interest in tropical architecture and climate control. According to Sansom, 'I arrived in 1974 in Fiji and have been preaching about tropical architecture ever since.'[15] After completing an Architecture Association diploma, London, he enrolled in a Graduate Diploma in Tropical Architecture. On arrival in Fiji he gained three years experience in the Public Works Department and was associated with the Fiji Institute of Technology as a lecturer. After spending 1978–86 in private practice with Architects Pacific, Sansom rejoined Public Works to both practise and teach. A few months before the first coup in May 1987 he was appointed Government Architect.[16]

Larsen Holtom Maybin was the earliest of the major private firms to practise in Suva. It has played an important role in Fijian architecture for, in addition to a large portfolio of the practice's own notably commercial work, it has been the principal firm working with overseas practices on many of Fiji's noteworthy projects. These include the Fiji Regent Hotel, Denarau, 1975, with Black, Pagliuso, Kikuchi and O'Dowd of Honolulu, and the 2006 Suva Foreshore Redevelopment International Competition in association with Place Design Group of Brisbane. Gordon Larsen, 'a gospel churchman', arrived in Suva from Scandinavia in 1953 and established the firm of Gordon J Larsen & Associates.[17] In 1964 he was joined by Frank Holtom, an architect from Perth who had experience in the Papua New Guinea Ministry of Works, and the Irish engineer Patrick Maybin, and together they formed the firm of Larsen Holtom Maybin (LHM).[18] The three original partners are no longer with the firm, which continues to practise in Fiji under the directorship of Jitendra Narsey.[19] The initial Suva buildings by LHM include the City Council Complex of the Suva Civic Centre, with the administrative offices of 1965–66 and the subsequent auditorium of 1969, and some of the earliest multi-level buildings in central Suva. Among these were the robust Fiji Development Bank of six storeys, completed in the late 1960s, the ten-storeyed Courtesy Inn, 1976,[20] and the eight-storeyed Vanua House office and shopping complex, early 1980s. In these buildings LHM adopted a responsible position towards climatic control to reduce the demand on air-conditioning, but it was not until 1996 with the ten-storeyed Fiji National Provident Fund Place that they attained an expressive solution, with a skeletal frame held free of the building supporting multiple-layered horizontal sun hoods. In Lautoka, LHM, with project architect Paul Durrant from Auckland, completed the authoritative Supreme Court Building in 1975.[21] The court has an uncommon structure and expression for Fiji in being protected by a full-height colonnade of deep, generous concrete arches resembling those of an aqueduct.

OPPOSITE, LEFT: National Stadium and Grandstand, Suva, 1978. Larsen Holtom Maybin. Project architect: Murray Cockburn.

OPPOSITE, TOP RIGHT: Courtesy Inn, Suva, 1976. Larsen Holtom Maybin (refurbished 2002 by Shama Architects).

OPPOSITE, BELOW RIGHT: Supreme Court Building, Lautoka, 1975. Larsen Holtom Maybin. Project architect: Paul Durrant.

RIGHT: Fiji National Provident Fund Place, Suva, 1996. Larsen Holtom Maybin.

Murray Cockburn was among the earliest architects to establish a practice in the small islands of the South Pacific. He graduated from the School of Architecture at the University of Auckland in 1963 and in 1965 opened offices in Oamaru and Queenstown, New Zealand. He commenced practising architecture in Suva in 1971 as Architects Engineers Partnership and in 1973 founded the firm of Murray Cockburn Partnership, which has successfully worked in both New Zealand and Fiji and in other countries around the western Pacific, notably the Solomon Islands. Cockburn has contributed to the shaping of Suva in all three major arenas: the Pacific Games, Laucala Campus and the inner city. The Grandstand of the National Stadium, 1978, is a confident work with a simple but structurally expressive stand supporting the clearly articulated, oversailing cantilevered roof that follows the curve of the running track. Similar clarity is seen in the 1977 Student Union Building that is strategically located in the centre of the university campus. The union consists of three circular joined buildings, each lit from above through central roof cones. The inward-focused spaces of the units consist of the large common room, centred on a sunken conversation pit, a quiet reading room and a cafeteria encircled by a wide, surrounding veranda defined in the perimeter by the tapered blade piers. The union is built with concrete block walls, plastered and painted white, and an exposed-timber roof structure. The order of the geometry of the building is complemented by the lush plantings of its setting. Cockburn's inner-city buildings of the 1980s include the Kukurua Building, which offered a viable fresh model for living in Suva. The building, which combines offices and apartments over six floors, is expressive of its differing uses with the residential levels enlivened with balconies and plantings.

Lee Associates, and the subsequent practice of Jaimi Associates, was among the most successful architectural firms in the central South Pacific, with branches

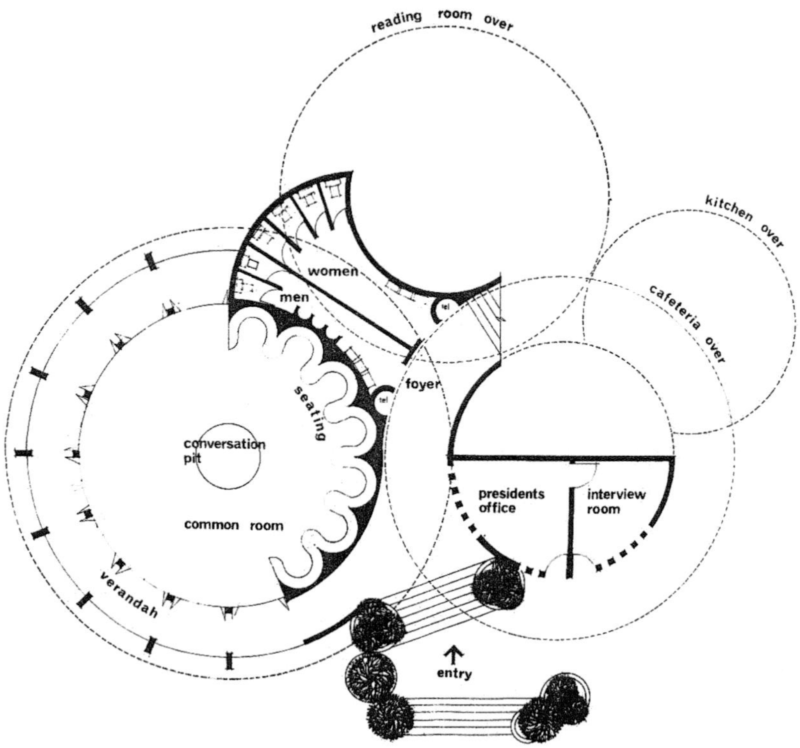

in Fiji and other countries of the region, notably Tonga. The firm is noted for its architecture for the Catholic Church, for meeting houses for the Great Chiefs of Fiji, and various USP campus buildings throughout the Pacific, including those of the Cook Islands and Tonga. Jaimi Samarawera from Sri Lanka worked for three years with the Murray Cockburn Partnership before joining the firm of John Rounds, Lee and Partners, and when Rounds retired in 1982, Lee and Jaimi founded the firm of Lee Associates. Lee left in 1989 and in 1990 the practice was re-established as Jaimi Associates.[22]

In 1982 Jaimi, for Lee Associates, won an important commission with the competition for the St Peter Chanel Chapel for the Pacific Regional Seminary. This centralized concept became the model for Jaimi's future churches. The building's regular form was generated by the octagon plan, the geometry of the roof construction with radiating trusses spreading from one major internal decorated post to columns on the periphery, and the high peaked conical rooflight that introduces natural light to the centre of the interior. A surrounding colonnade allows for the opening of the glass walls of the chapel, to admit the free movement of breezes though the building. A related configuration determined the dramatic space of Our Lady of Assumption, Lomary, 1992. The interior of the Lomary church, including the ceiling beams, focuses on the inverted apse, defined by two sculptural curving walls strikingly lit from the rooflight above and flanked by the ceiling-high glass walls with stained-glass panels. This basic form also generated Jaimi Associates' Roman Catholic Cathedral of St Joseph, 1994, Avarua, Cook Islands. The firm also designed the new apse for the Sacred Heart Cathedral, Suva, 1993. Typical of their buildings for the USP is the 1984 Industrial Arts Complex (later the Technology Building), in that it is a low-scale cluster of buildings arranged in relation to an open court.

The Ro Lalabalavu House, 1998, in central Suva was designed by Jaimi Associates in consultation with Sansom. This is an accomplished building, which was specifically planned for low-energy climatic comfort of the internal working environment. It is a long thin building on a narrow site located between Victoria Parade and the harbour on an east-west axis with the principal façade facing the favourable orientation to the north. While the building is air-conditioned, the solution aims to minimize the dependency on mechanical systems, and additional climatic protection of the building is achieved by the modulation of the façades, light louver screening and the astute use of planting. Jaimi Associates also won the limited competition for the Lautoka Magistrates' Courts, which were completed in 1997. The courts are in discrete sections, linked around courtyards. This is a regular modernist building enlivened in the central block by the modelling of the façade. As is commonly found in the work of this firm, the building was conditioned by considerations of low maintenance materials, environmental comfort and energy efficiency.

Architects Pacific is a prominent practice with commissions for China, Australia and New Zealand, as well as from other countries of the Pacific.[23] The firm's architecture is strongly conditioned by environmental concerns and the search for an appropriate contemporary architecture in a transitional tropical society. Architects Pacific was founded as Architects Pacific Design Partnership by Stuart Huggett and his architect wife, Gilly, in Suva in 1971.[24] The work ranges across a wide spectrum from individual houses to major resorts to new town developments, as well as urban redevelopment proposals including the Savusavu Foreshore Development Plan, 2003. Architects Pacific's main office in Suva is located in Huggett's house, and is structured around a close personal working relationship between staff members. Huggett's firm has also been important as a training school, acting as a mentor for many architects newly-arrived in Fiji, who work there for several years and are exposed to his ideas regarding a suitable architecture for the Pacific.

OPPOSITE: Student Union Building, University of the South Pacific, Suva, 1977. Murray Cockburn Partnership. Plan.

LEFT: Our Lady of Assumption Church, Lomary, Viti Levu, 1992. Jaimi and Associates.

ABOVE: Chapel of St Peter Chanel, Suva, 1982. Lee and Associates.

LEFT: Reserve Bank of Fiji, Suva, 1985. Architects Pacific.

TOP: Ro Lalabalavu House, Suva, 1998. Jaimi and Associates.

ABOVE: Administrative Centre, University of the South Pacific, Laucala Campus, Suva, 1980. Architects Pacific.

OPPOSITE: Suva Foreshore Redevelopment Concept. Place Design Group in association with Larsen Holtom Maybin. *Courtesy of Place Design Group.*

Stuart Huggett left Fiji for New Zealand after the 2006 coup, but Architects Pacific continues to practise in Fiji.[25]

Huggett, who came from Bath, England, completed his architectural education at the Roger Williams University School of Architecture, Art and Historic Preservation at Bristol, graduating in 1965. As a student he travelled to India, Iran and Ethiopia on various study tours run by the university. On graduation he undertook further travel in northern Nigeria and worked in London for Sir Basil Spence in 1967 and 1968. Stuart and Gilly Huggett then decided to migrate to Australia and on visiting Suva on the way they chose to stay. Huggett worked from 1968 to 1971 as a project architect at the USP and was engaged on the transformation of the NZRAF Flying Boat Base into the Laucala Campus for the university. In 1972 he travelled extensively in Europe, India and Africa and once back in Fiji worked with Walter Collins of Belt Collins on preparing the first Fijian tourist master plan.[26] He was also assisted in his early practice by Peter Wimberly of Wimberly, Whisenand, Allison, Tong and Goo, who invited him to work on extensions to the Fijian Hotel, 1975, and the Mocambo Hotel, 1976.

While buildings of Architects Pacific are found throughout Fiji, few have been constructed in central Suva, with the notable exceptions of the Reserve Bank of Fiji, 1985, which is a dominant form in the city, and the Fiji Womens' Crisis Centre of 2006. The Reserve Bank, with fourteen floors, is the firm's only tall building and is atypical of their general portfolio. The concrete framed tower satisfactorily addresses the street, as it rises from a low stepped base and is enlivened with a two-level entry portico and extensively planted cantilevered terraces. Architects Pacific's buildings are well represented on the Laucala Campus. The USP School of Social and Economic Development, 1979, and USP Administrative Centre, 1980, are Brutalist buildings of poured concrete evidencing Huggett's training in England in the 1960s. The Administration Centre consists of two levels with wide circulation balconies edged by the luxurious growth of the sculptured planter boxes. The irregular bent plan consists of four segments that define an informal open forecourt. The later university projects such as the Lecture and Library Complex, 1997, show an increasing concern to encourage natural ventilation, even in extensive buildings that house large numbers, as in the lecture theatres consisting of three interlinked units where the simple step of planning with generous spacing of the seating has improved air circulation and increased coolness.

While Suva's most important growth period occurred in the 1980s, the town continued to expand steadily and uneventfully in the decades that followed. The most consequential urban design change in the period was the opening in 2000 of Suva Central, a shopping-business centre by Ignite of New Zealand. This complex provided a focal point for the town that previously had been rather loosely ordered in relation to the Triangle. While there was little architectural development in central Suva early in the new century, three political complexes of consequence for Fiji's future were built in Suva's suburbs: the Ryoichi Jinnai Conference Centre, Muanikau, by Architects Pacific; the Parliament House of Fiji, Nasese, Suva, by Vitia Architects; and the Great Council of Chiefs' Meeting House, Draiba, by Jaimi Associates. In addition, in the new century Suva's future was the subject of planning initiatives. Foremost among these were the winning submission for the Suva Foreshore Redevelopment International Competition and the 2006 Foreshore Reclamation Master Plan, by Place Design Group in association with LHM.

IN SEARCH OF SHANGRI-LA 6

Escaping to Fiji

'Fiji: You can't get any further away before you start coming back.' The Truman Show

Today Fiji is a major world playground. While initially visited primarily by travellers passing through on the South Pacific sea route, the country now also enjoys visitors from Asia. Tourism has long been a major component of Fiji's income, and in 2010 it made up about 18 per cent of the gross domestic product.[1] Following independence in 1970 the Fiji Government lost no time in exploring means to encourage investment in property, to insure that the country's biggest and most important industry was sustained. While speculators offered all manner of inducements for the Fijians to sell their land – particularly to the tourist industry – the nineteenth-century colonial administration had the foresight of investing native title and its administration in the Native Lands Trust Board. While there is a certain amount of freehold land and some native title can be leased on certain terms, the ownership of native title was deemed to be non-negotiable.[2]

The Ocean Liner Era

As a major stopover port on the Pacific route and the administrative centre of the British Empire in the South Pacific, there was a need for a large number of hotels for drinking, socializing and to provide accommodation for the numerous travellers that called in at its ports – notably Levuka and Suva. While offering differing levels of comfort and amenity, the hotels were similar: usually two-storeyed timber construction with bars and other public spaces on the ground floor and sleeping accommodation on the upper floor. They had verandas on both levels and commonly were built on corner sites. Several, such as the early Royal Hotel in Levuka, of around 1860, and

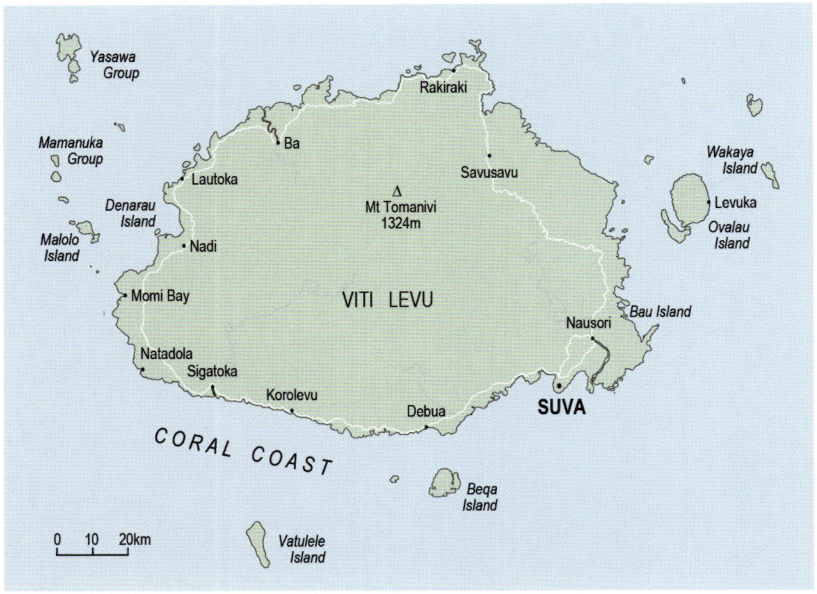

the Club and Melbourne hotels, which opened in Suva in the early 1880s, were known throughout the Pacific. Many of these nineteenth-century hotels continued to operate into the twentieth century. Parts of the original fourteen-room Royal Hotel remain, making the Royal the oldest hotel still in use in the South Pacific.[3]

In the succeeding decades, as Suva continued to grow in size and importance, the demand for first-class accommodation increased. The fine fifty-one-room colonial house of 1907, built by a leading Fijian citizen, Sir Henry Milne Scott, was taken over as the Ocean Hotel, which was deemed one of the finest in the South Pacific.[4] In Suva new hotels were opened and others upgraded or replaced, such as the Pier Hotel of 1882, which was demolished and in 1914 a new building constructed (later the Garrick Hotel). The hotels of Fiji, however, did not rival the Hôtel de la Gare in Noumea until the opening of the Grand Pacific Hotel, Suva, in 1914, which surpassed the Hôtel de la Gare for elegance.

The Grand Pacific Hotel, by the New Zealand firm of Salmond and Vanes, was built by the Union Steam Ship Company to accommodate its trans-Pacific passengers.[5] It was opened on 23 May 1914, a few months before the beginning of World War I. The seventy-five rooms were designed to resemble shipboard staterooms. The 4.5-metre-wide verandas encompassing the building took on the role of promenade decks for strolling and surveying the harbour – even the plumbing resembled that of ships' cabins, with saltwater baths available on request![6] The Grand Pacific was a distinguished two-storeyed building of concrete construction built by the sea on a site previously reclaimed for a park. It is an impressive hotel with well-balanced proportions in the formal colonial manner with a prominent central portico. The hotel had all the spaces expected of a first-class hotel including a billiard room, gentlemen's lounge and smoking room. The grand central atrium, which also served as the ballroom, remains one of the renowned architectural spaces of the South Pacific. The hotel furniture and fittings were of high quality – mostly imported – and at the time of its opening, the interior was described as having fine appointments. The hotel was closed in 1992, yet it has remained an impressive building strongly evocative of the time of its previous glory.[7] The hotel has attained iconic status throughout the South Pacific, and in his 2009 Budget address, Fiji's prime minister, Commodore Frank Bainimarama, announced government support for its restoration. A partnership was formed between the superannuation funds of Fiji and New Guinea and the PNG Lamana Development Group to collaborate on the project, with completion scheduled for April 2014.[8]

Flying to Fiji

World War I and World War II bracketed a quiet time for tourism in the Pacific, and no more so than in Fiji. It was in 1941 that the first Pan Am clipper service flew into Fiji harbour, but shortly afterwards the Japanese struck Pearl Harbor, and all flights were cancelled.[9] After the war tourists again started to seek the sun of Fiji, and the luxury ships of the Matson, Orient and Pacific Lines brought travellers to the islands. The ships were soon joined by seaplanes, and the wartime flying boat base, which was to the west of Suva, initially became the principal point of entry. In 1947 the New Zealand National Airways Corporation (NZNAC) commenced a flying boat service to Fiji, Tonga, Samoa and the Cook Islands, called 'the Coral Route', and Qantas also began flying to Fiji in the late 1940s.[10] The advent of regular public air travel introduced a new dimension to the accessibility of such a remote country. One-time US air force headquarters at Nausori, outside Suva, had been built hurriedly during the war but due to possible flooding, it was later rejected by the Civil Aviation Authority as a long-term international airport.[11] Nadi on the west coast had the airstrip built by New Zealand forces, but road travel between Suva and Nadi was difficult. Even Queens Road along the south coast was in very poor condition, with virtually no facilities on the way. Despite problems of communication, it was decided to upgrade Nadi airport to international standards. The initial tarmac runway at

Nadi was constructed in 1946, and in 1947 the first hotel, the Mocambo Hotel, was built behind the single-storey terminal.[12] After 1952 the hotel was operated by Stuart (Barry) Philp, who had moved to Fiji from Australia in 1949.[13] Philp, a builder and a pioneer entrepreneur who played a significant role in developing Fiji's tourist industry, was to initiate a successive range of new hotels.

In 1950 the apron at Nadi airport was extended so that it could accommodate the new commercial jet aircraft. In 1951 Harold Gatty established Fiji Airways, with flights to the outer islands, and by 1955 shuttle flights were in place between Nadi and Suva to service the international airport.[14] With this upgrade and the introduction of the large jet aircraft in 1958, Nadi replaced Suva as the gateway to the country. International carriers on the Pacific route such as Pan Am, American Airlines, Qantas, BOAC and NZNAC stopped in Nadi in the era before long-haul jet aircraft were put into service. As flight crews changed duty, minimal stopover facilities were built to accommodate them. Tourists then arrived in Nadi, and while transportation by air to Suva was available and roads were slightly improved, a fresh focus for tourism developed in regions with direct access from Nadi airport. Fiji's own airline, Fiji Airways, was acquired by Qantas in 1958, and in 1971 it was renamed Air Pacific. The airline commenced international flights to Tonga in 1950, Australia in 1973 and to New Zealand in 1974, bringing many of the initial visitors to the new Fiji resorts. In 1974 the Fiji Government acquired a controlling interest in the company.[15]

The new air-conditioned Nadi International Airport Terminal building, 1960, was a modern, partly prefabricated structure consisting of three interlocking geometric components: the low rectangular arrivals hall, the elevated departures hall and the long pedestrian access ways that linked the terminal to the aircraft. The building was described as 'one of the most modern in the world', being specifically engineered to service up to three jet airliners at one time.[16] Because of the changed runway layout, the new terminal was sited away from the 'old' Mocambo Hotel, and in 1961 Philp opened the 'new' Mocambo on Namaka Hill, just outside the new airport entrance.

The new Mocambo Hotel was a modern hotel of sixty-five rooms with air conditioning and a swimming pool.[17] The only other hotel in Nadi was the smaller thirty-two-room Skylodge, 1962, operated by the Fiji Resorts Company, both founded by Pan Am pilot Captain George Wilson with other ex-Pan Am staff, including Peter Kyne Slimmer and engineer J P (Paddy) Doyle, who had been brought in to supervise the extensions to the Nadi runway.[18] While building the Mocambo, Philp had been conceiving plans for a major new hotel initiative for a forty-two-hectare site on Yanuca Island on the Coral Coast, eighty kilometres

TOP: Grand Pacific Hotel, Suva, 1914. Salmond and Vanes.
ABOVE: Dining Room. *Courtesy of the National Archives of Fiji.*

PREVIOUS PAGE: Barrack House.

ABOVE: Korolevu Beach Hotel, Viti Levu, 2006. Place Design Group. Proposed Site Master Plan. *Courtesy of Place Design Group.*

RIGHT: Korolevu Beach Hotel, c.1948–49. Advertisement. *South Pacific Travel Trade News.*

OPPOSITE: Beachcomber Hotel, Debua, Viti Levu, 1949. Advertisement. *South Pacific Travel Trade News.*

along Queens Road towards Suva, and he had consulted the Honolulu architects Wimberly and Cook concerning its design.[19] In 1962 Philp sold the Mocambo and the lease of the island site to the Pan Am group and moved further eastwards to establish the Reef Lodge at Korotogo (later the Reef Hotel and later still the Outrigger Lagoon Resort).[20]

As the flow of tourists through Nadi increased, further hotels were built to accommodate the numbers. The major hotels were the Tanoa Hotel, 1966, by Derrick and Derrick, the Gateway Hotel, 1968, by Derrick Dignan & Associates, and the Dominion International Hotel, 1972, by Architects Engineers Partnership under the direction of Murray Cockburn. All of these competed with the new hotels of Suva, notably the Outrigger Hotel, 1966, by Derrick and Derrick, and the Suva Travelodge, 1968.[21] More venturesome was the Tradewinds Hotel, 1968, just west of Lami, ten kilometres south of Suva with easy access to the town. The Tradewinds Hotel, which offered limited resort facilities, was built along and overhanging the edge of the waterfront and overlooked the Bay of Islands. It was designed by Colin Philp and constructed by Barry Philp. Colin was an Australian architect and boat builder and had been a partner in the Tasmanian firm of Philp Leighton Floyd & Beattie before he joined his brother in Fiji in 1963.[22]

The Resorts: From Korolevu to Dere Bay

The principal expansion occurred with the building of vacation 'resorts' in picturesque settings. Initially these were on the Coral Coast with access from both Suva and Nadi, but vacation accommodation also became available on the smaller islands. While some resorts were built on freehold land, most were on land acquired as leasehold property, with ownership remaining with the traditional owners. Fiji pioneered the introduction of holiday 'resorts' in the South Pacific, and apart from temporary setbacks, maintained a sustained pattern of growth and innovation throughout the century. Resort architecture in Fiji developed in a different direction to that of most of the South Pacific, with exclusive, private 'boutique' resorts, and the opening of mega-resorts – 'integrated' resorts – combining hotel and apartment holiday accommodation with residential subdivisions of leasehold land and a wide offering of sporting and cultural facilities.[23]

Along the Coral Coast

The first 'resort' hotel in the South Pacific was the Korolevu Beach Hotel, which opened around 1948–49 on the Coral Coast on the southern shore of Viti Levu, near Sigatoka and halfway between Suva and Nadi.[24] The Korolevu Beach Hotel was built on an outstanding, largely freehold site with a wide sandy beach and

a reef close offshore. It was owned by entrepreneur Hugh Ragg, chairman of Northern Hotels, a company that held a hotel chain in Fiji.[25] The Korolevu Beach Hotel site was laid out by Belt Collins and Associates of Hawaii, who later were to undertake the majority of the resort planning/landscaping in Fiji.[26] In 1953 civil engineer Robert M Belt and planner Walter K Collins founded the Hawaiian firm of Belt Collins to serve the Asia-Pacific region. The firm offered urban and land planning, civil engineering, landscape architecture and environmental consulting within one professional organization. In many ways the Korolevu Beach Hotel was an innovative project for the South Pacific in that it was a first-class resort that provided guests with the opportunity to experience living in vernacular bure dwellings, to enjoy local food and culture, and to participate in marine activities, such as big-game fishing.[27] It was a luxury resort designed to resemble a Fijian village with a main entertainment-dining hall, (called *adi kuila bure*) serving as the social centre for the thirty-five thatched bures spread along the sandy beachfront.[28] The bures had glazed windows, electricity, a telephone and a bathroom.[29] To overcome difficulties of access, Korolevu Air Transport was opened in 1959 by the pioneer pilot Tom French and offered charter flights, freight and mail services. The air service was based at the resort, where a grass airstrip was constructed on the other side of Queens Road.[30]

The Korolevu Beach Hotel was partly burnt down in 1965, but the hotel reopened and continued to operate successfully through to 1983, when two events finally led to its closure. First, a hurricane that year destroyed power lines along the coast and disrupted electricity supply for some months. Second, all the furnishings and fittings disappeared one night following a leaseholding dispute.[31] Thirty years on, the Korolevu site, under new ownership, is planned for redevelopment to a master plan by Place Design Group, Brisbane.[32] In the mid-1980s Belt Collins opened an office on the Gold Coast in Australia, and when the firm was restructured in 2000 to focus on Hawaii and Hong Kong, the regional offices were offered for sale. The Australian planner and managing director of Belt Collins, Australia, Lindsay Thorpe, who had been with Belt Collins since the 1970s, took up the Australian option and founded the successful multi-disciplinary firm of Place Design Group in 2001.[33]

Another hotel of considerable early fame was Philp's 1949 Beachcomber at Debua, which was described as 'a modern ranch-style hotel' that offered local entertainment and water-based sports activities.[34] It acquired some renown in 1952 when it became the location for the Warners Bros film *His Majesty O'Keefe* starring Burt Lancaster.[35] The Beachcomber was acquired by Ragg, probably in 1962, who successfully developed it as a centre for day-trippers from the cruise liners anchored at Suva. There they would witness the Beqa Firewalkers and participate in a *meke*, or island dancing, with a feast of food cooked in the ground.[36] The old Beachcomber burnt down in 1967, to be replaced in 1974 by a further Beachcomber on the same site, as part of the newly developed Pacific Harbour Estate.[37]

The most significant project, which heralded the beginning of the major resorts, was the Fiji Resorts Company's Fijian Hotel on Yanuka Island, 1967.[38] Doyle supervised its construction, and for a period he and Slimmer managed the hotel.[39] The master plan again was by Belt Collins with the buildings by the Hawaiian firm of Wimberly, Whisenand, Allison and Tong. Previously architects for the Hotel Bora Bora, French Polynesia, 1961, and the Pago Pago InterContinental Hotel (Rainmaker), 1966, they later became the most successful resort and hotel architects in the Pacific.[40] The 108-room Fijian Hotel was set in large grounds and was connected by a causeway to Viti Levu. The hotel originally had the use of twenty-one hectares of the forty-one-hectare island, but in 1970 it leased the remainder, and by 1975 a new wing and a second beach-dining complex had been added.[41] The Fijian is a modern three-storeyed hotel-resort similar in type to those designed by the firm for Hawaii. The buildings make some concession to the Fiji location in the roof pitches of the accommodation wings and the steep

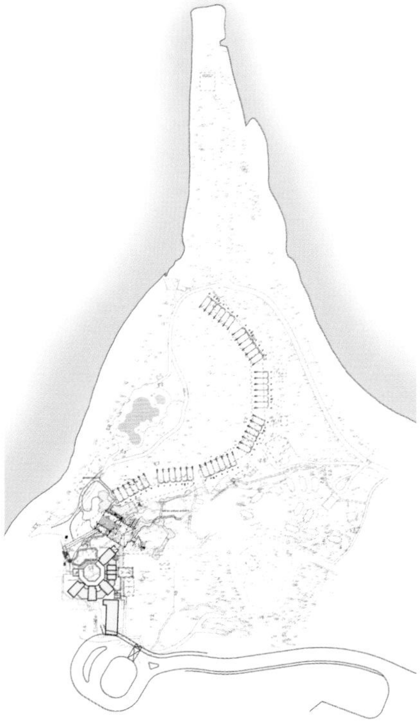

ABOVE: Fijian Hotel, Yanuca Island, 1967. Wimberly, Whisenand, Allison and Tong.
LEFT: Site Plan.

OPPOSITE: Outrigger Reef Fiji Resort, Korotogo, Viti Levu, 2000. Adrian Sofield.

shingled roofs of the central dining and recreational facilities adjacent to the pool. The Fijian was a highly accomplished building that provided the model for similar later tourism ventures in Fiji. Architects Pacific undertook several extensions to the resort with extensive reconstructions in 1996 and 1999. With 436 rooms, the Fijian was the largest hotel in Fiji. After the opening of the Fijian, the Coral Coast became a favoured location for investment, which included a further large hotel, the Warwick, completed in 1979.[42]

By the end of the century numerous hotels had opened along Queens Road. The resorts exhibited differing approaches, from sophisticated contemporary hotels to projects based on the Korolevu model. Among the more ambitious resorts was a 254-room redevelopment, the Outrigger Reef Fiji Resort, 2000, to a concept by Adrian Sofield, on the site of Philp's Reef Hotel, Korotogo.[43] Sofield, a 1970 graduate from the Western Australian Institute of Technology, first went to Fiji in 1976 and worked with the Murray Cockburn Partnership. He opened his own office in 1979, but in the period 1988–2000 again worked with Cockburn and later, while maintaining his single practice, continued an association with that firm.[44] Sofield undertook a wide range of projects but was particularly known for his resort and residential work.[45] At Korotogo the 165 rooms in the four-storeyed principal accommodation wings are built into the steep hillside and step down the slope from Queens Road. They overlook the beach-level amenities (with gardens and pools by Place Design Group), the renovated three-storeyed waterfront block of the original Reef Hotel, the sandy beach and out to the reef beyond. The Outrigger Reef brings together contemporary accommodation with weaving thatched walkways, Fijian-style bures and public facilities of creative, well-crafted designs evolved from local arts and practices. Of particular note is the impressive structure by Sofield for the restaurant, with its high roof and original interior detail. The Outrigger Reef, a highly appropriate solution for its setting, takes full advantage of the contrasting topography and the scenic potential of the site.

Going Offshore

The islands away from the principal places of settlement added a further dimension of romance and remoteness, and with improvements in commercial internal air travel they became more readily accessible. Many resorts, however, remain serviced by charter seaplane flights.

One of Fiji's first outer-island resorts, Castaway Island in the Mamanuca Group, was sufficiently close to Nadi to be reached by catamarans and small seaplanes. Philp was involved in the planning of Castaway Island Resort, which was opened by the Australian Richard (Dick) Smith in 1966.[46] It proved to be an

Outrigger Reef Fiji Resort, Korotogo, Viti Levu, 2000. Adrian Sofield. *Photograph by Ross Eason.*

FAR LEFT: The Point, Vatulele Island Resort, 2002. Architects Pacific. *Courtesy of Architects Pacific.*

LEFT: Raintree Lodge, Viti Levu, 2000. Vitia Architects. Dining Veranda.

ABOVE: Vatulele Island Resort, 1990. Douglas Nelson, Martin Livingston and Adrian Sofield. Entrance. *Courtesy of Vatulele Island Resort.*

important exemplar for the future direction of Fiji's island resorts.[47] Smith was an adventurer who sailed the world in the powerboat *Stardust* then came to Fiji and ran Stardust cruises to the Mamanucas, before buying the lease on picturesque Qalito Island and building Castaway.[48] The resort occupies the whole seventy-hectare island, which is covered with lush tropical vegetation, surrounded by white sand beaches and encircled by coral reefs. The sense of 'getting away' was reinforced by the addition of buildings that followed those of Korolevu in creating the semblance of a Fijian village with spacious, secluded bures. The resort was badly damaged by Hurricane Oscar of 1983 when most of the buildings were partly destroyed, with half of those suffering significant structural damage. The Murray Cockburn Partnership undertook an extensive upgrade that retained the original concept, with sixty-six thatched bures of traditional timber construction plus major extensions to the public facilities, including the boatshed, bar and restaurant.[49] The island was hit by a further hurricane in 1997, and the resort again suffered considerable damage.

By the end of the 1970s, optimism regarding the future of the tourist industry returned, and with government encouragement many new projects with hundreds of accommodation units were initiated. While Viti Levu was the most convenient location, the smaller islands also appeared to hold promise as tourist venues. Among the ambitious schemes was the 1970 700-room resort for Vatulele Island, south of Korolevu, designed by Neville Price of Price Adams Dodd of Auckland, and the 1969 proposal to develop a 600-room resort on the island of Wakaya, east of Ovalau, which was masterplanned by Sydney architect Sam Sloan.[50] While it was reported that 100 bures of the Vatulele project were completed, the Wakaya resort was not realized.[51] But the dreams of the early 1970s were short-lived, and the projected rise in tourist numbers did not occur. The global financial upheaval resulted in significant funding problems and the disbandment of many planned projects, some of which recovered in the boom years of the 1990s; among these were Vatulele and Wakaya, which underwent fresh development as small exclusive resorts.

LEFT: Jean-Michel Cousteau Fiji Islands Resort, Vanua Levu, 1995. Jean-Michel Cousteau.
ABOVE: Main Dining Hall and Pool.

Vatulele ('Ringing Rock') Island Resort opened in 1990 with nineteen guest villas, including The Point, a large luxury two-storeyed unit with private pool, by Architects Pacific, which was completed in 2002. The resort site is under leasehold from the landowners, the Mataqali group, who are partners in the project. The concept of the original owners, Australian film and television personality Henry Crawford and artist Martin Livingston, was for an artistic blend of local ways of building and craft reinterpreted in a contemporary language and adapted to contemporary needs.[52] No large construction equipment was used, and 100 men cleared the site with knives.[53]

The buildings, of timber and stone with colourful ochre walls[54] and crafted roof structures, are of a hybrid style between Fijian and Mexican design, derived from the concept of the Santa Fe style, which Crawford first saw in a publication that included the work of the architect Doug Nelson of, Mainstreet Architects and Planners, Ventura, California.[55] Crawford engaged Nelson to prepare the design concept, and Livingston, Sofield and Crawford worked with Nelson on the resolution of the design.[56] Of particular interest is Livingston's wood carvings throughout the resort.

RIGHT: Namale Fiji Resort and Spa, Savusavu, Vanua Levu, 1995–2005. Vitia Architects. Interior design by Robert Trown Associates, Aspen, Colorado. Entrance to Spa. *Courtesy of Vitia Architects.*
BELOW: Spa. *Courtesy of Vitia Architects.*

In 1994 Jean-Michel Cousteau,[57] who graduated from the Paris School of Architecture in 1964, visited the Fijian-style Na Koro ('my village') Resort on Lesiacevu Point, which is six kilometres from Savusavu on the island of Vanua Levu. When the property became available for sale, he, with interested investors, developed the design of the Jean-Michel Cousteau Fiji Islands Resort, which opened with twenty thatched bures on 22 April, World Environment Day, 1995. Cousteau, who founded the Ocean Futures Society, placed a priority on environmental sustainability, 'to demonstrate that it is possible to be environmentally friendly and financially successful at the same time'.[58] He worked closely in association with the noted marine biologist Richard C Murphy who prepared and implemented the environmental master plan.[59] The resort employs a full-time on-site marine biologist and demonstrates an increasing concern for the natural environment with the introduction of non-invasive mosquito control and a ban on motorized water sports.[60] The buildings are of local timber and thatch, and are designed with fans only, for low-energy usage. The resort, however, has some high-tech equipment, such as video link by which divers can communicate with non-diving guests in the resort, who can view the surrounding underwater environment on a giant video screen.

Raintree Lodge, 2000, and Namale Fiji Resort and Spa, 1995–2005, were designed by Filipe Tauva, who previously had been responsible for the Parliament House of Fiji. Tauva graduated from the University of Auckland, and on his return to Fiji, he joined Architects Pacific where he practised from 1978 to 1987. In 1988 he established his own practice, Vitia Architects, with a policy to design ecologically sustainable buildings that draw 'inspiration from the essence of tropical architecture and the rich, diverse cultures and traditions of the Pacific'.[61] The years following the completion of Parliament House were quiet, and this allowed Tauva to pursue his interest in sustainable planning and traditional building construction, notably the bure, which had been a subject of his research studies at the university. Raintree Lodge, ten kilometres outside of Suva, provided Tauva with an opportunity to apply the techniques he had studied and later applied at Namale. The lodge is a pleasantly informal group of buildings scattered through trees and built partially over a small lake. It operates primarily as a backpacker hostel that sleeps eighty-five,

Likuliku Lagoon Resort, Malolo Island, Mamanuca Group, 2007. Architects Pacific. Master Plan.

OPPOSITE: Likuliku Lagoon Resort, 2007. Architects Pacific. *Courtesy of Architects Pacific.*

Likuliku Lagoon Resort, 2007. Architects Pacific. Guest Suite.

with the choice of dormitory accommodation, bunk rooms and private bure accommodation. Raintree Lodge was developed in accord with a comprehensive ecological design commitment that covers material selection; shading elements, including wide sheltering roofs, screens and timber decks; restrictions on the consumption of power; water supply reticulation; and sophisticated systems of waste disposal. Further, Raintree Lodge was Tauva's first attempt to engineer the bure roof as it was traditionally built. In this means of construction all the rafters are lightweight and of even size, and are supported by the under-purlins, so the structure becomes a lattice and not a truss system. The bure roofs at Namale Fiji Resort and Spa complex, were constructed by Ratu Manoa Rasigatal on this traditional 'membrane' principle, using steam to bend the members.

In the 1990s Tauva was introduced to Anthony (Tony) Robbins, American author, television personality and peak performance coach. At Savusavu Robbins had purchased 212 hectares on a private peninsula facing the Koro Sea to build Namale Fiji Resort and Spa. Tauva's work at Namale, which is primarily of Pacific inspiration with timber construction and thatch for the roofs, extended over a ten-year period.[62] Robbins later decided to develop the resort into a seminar centre as part of his leadership training, and a large gymnasium and spa with subsidiary seminar rooms were constructed. The project is spaciously designed and richly finished, especially the later 930-square-metre spa and sanctuary. The plan of the spa is symmetrical with a geometric spatial organization suggestive of classical precedent. The interior design, by Robert Trown Associates, Aspen, Colorado, is sensuous with scented woods, columns carved with traditional patterns, translucent roof panels, fabric lashings of unconventional colours, and soft light and greenery.[63] The outstanding traditional timberwork and lashings of the spa were designed and executed by Ratu Manoa Rasigatale and his team. While it is a select resort with deluxe appointments, the Namale Fiji Resort and Spa is designed along ecological and structural principles and aims to be a place of learning and the 'complete' responsible resort.

Still Going Offshore

Despite the unpredictable nature of Fiji's future tourist market, ultra-luxurious resorts, primarily by Architects Pacific, continued to be built into the twenty-first century. Likuliku Lagoon Resort, 2007, by Architects Pacific, provides a further example of the increasing awareness of the importance accorded to eco-friendly design. The US$ 21 million resort is ideally located, twenty-five kilometres out of Nadi, on Malolo Island in the Mamanuca Group. Likuliku is a private enterprise scheme with the landholding unit of the Mataqali Ketenamasi owning a direct profit share as shareholders and partners. The project was initiated by Tony Whitten of Ahura Resorts and specifically designed for the high-end tourist market.[64] An Environmental Impact Study and Environmental Management Plan were introduced for the protection of the environment and ecosystems, and ancient sites. This was implemented with site planning by Architects Pacific and landscape design by Belt Collins. Fruit, vegetables and herbs are grown in the resort's hydroponics farm, and in order to preserve sea life, the Paramount Chief of the Mamanucas Ratu Jeremaia Naitaniyalo declared the water surrounding the island a marine sanctuary. The planning of Phase I is uncommon in Fiji as, in addition to thirty-six beachfront and pool pavilions, it has structures built over the lagoon in the manner of the Polynesian resorts, including the arrival building, restaurant and ten bures with bathing pavilions. Because of the shallowness of the water the bures are built well out along the reef drop off and are reached by boat or a very long timber walkway.[65] The resort architecture is an elegant reinterpretation of Melanesian forms, notably the central complex, which is approached from the Masima Island arrival bure along an overwater walkway.

Laucala Island Resort, which opened in 2008, shares a history similar to those of other resorts in Fiji, having been purchased in 1972 by Malcolm Forbes but not developed as a resort until 2003 under the new ownership of Austrian businessman Dietrich Mateschitz.[66] The island, approximately five kilometres long and three kilometres across, is located off the north-east coast of Taveuni, with a private airport reached from Nadi International Airport in forty-five minutes.

TOP: Whispering Tides, Tunuloa Peninsula, Vanua Levu, 2000–2010. Architects Pacific.
ABOVE: Stairway to Chapel. OPPOSITE: Guest Bure.

LEFT: Morais House, Taveuni Estates, Taveuni Island, Fiji. Refurbished 1995. Murray Cockburn Partnership.

OPPOSITE, LEFT: Vale O, Wakaya Club and Spa, Wakaya Island, 1989. Adrian Sofield. OPPOSITE, RIGHT: Deck and Pool. *Photographs by Barbara Kraft.*

The resort, designed by Architects Pacific, is built around an early colonial-style plantation house and offers twenty-five bures and extensive sporting facilities. The traditional-style bures, raised off the ground and perched high on the sides of the hill, are linked by walkways. The programme for the resort embraces the whole island, including the villages, and involves the production of building materials and craftworks, and locally grown livestock and vegetables. The resort aims to be self-sufficient and is supported by a desalination plant and a hydroponics unit.

The ultimate escape is to your own private resort. Whispering Tides, the Bob and Debbie Trette House, also by Architects Pacific, was designed as such a retreat. The complex, on the Tunuloa Peninsula, Vanua Levu, is situated on hilly terrain on an extensive site of sixty hectares that affords splendid views over the Somosomo Strait. It consists of the principal house, five guest bures, a caretaker's house, a jetty and ancillary buildings arranged along the water's edge. The composition is capped by the chapel, standing high on a steep hillock. The large neo-colonial house of 370 square metres, with wide verandas and a steeply pitched roof with exposed timber trusses is luxuriously appointed, with all the furniture, appliances, artwork and decoration being imported from California. The guest bures, also with raised verandas, are of local materials, and the décor of the interiors makes references to traditional Fijian patterns.[67]

Integrated Resorts on the Outer Islands: the 1990s

The dual development of a resort and land subdivision, seen in large resorts on Viti Levu, is also found in the outer islands, as at the Taveuni Estate and some of the other privately owned resorts, such as the Wakaya Club and the Dere Bay project. The Taveuni Estate is on Taveuni Island, the third largest island of the Fijian group, and was subject to a 1978 master plan for the subdivision of freehold land. The property languished until it was purchased in 1995 by new owners and given a substantial revision.[68] This freehold land was once a coconut plantation, and some of the original buildings have been renovated as luxury dwellings, such as the Morais House, refurbished in 2005 by the Murray Cockburn Partnership.

In 1972 Canadian industrialist David Gilmour, who was concurrently engaged in developing his large property at Pacific Harbour, purchased the leasehold to the 890-hectare Wakaya Island and, with the cooperation of 240 Fijians from the local village, worked to protect the natural state of the island. One-third of the land was divided into 100 residential lots for individual private residences and included villas of high quality design and construction, such as Architects Pacific's Robert Corner house, Lewedua, of 1982, and their Hunt and Shorrock Residence, Kelekele, 1985. The resort has shared communal facilities and a nine-hole golf course and is accessed by private aircraft to the resort's landing strip. In 1990 Gilmour opened the exclusive Wakaya Club with ten large villas with garden and ocean views, plus two luxury villas ranging between 223 square metres and 418 square metres. It also includes the 1114-square-metre Vale O ('House in the Clouds'), which was completed in 1989 by Sofield, who also designed the restaurant.[69] Vale O stands on a six-hectare estate with amenities including a rock-rimmed pool with waterfall and Jacuzzi, a night-lit tennis court, a boules court and a gymnasium. As with the other buildings of the resort, Vale O is finished with quality local materials and designs, such as the woven bamboo wall coverings and indigenous Yaka timber flooring. The house comes with its own staff, chef and chauffeur. Vale O was followed in 2010 by the large sumptuous Sena Na Leqa, 'No Worries House', which consists of the spacious master wing with curved ceilings over nine metres high, a nearby guest villa and a thatched luncheon pavilion on the private beach. The concept for the house came from designer Toni Chi, with architectural design by Ronald Evitts Architect and interior design by Kiki Dennis Interiors, both of New York.[70] The exterior space is as generous as that of the interior, with a private thirty-eight-metre pool with an integrated spa pool and an exercise pool in the master wing.

The 303-hectare Dere Bay project, Koro Island, consists of the Dere Bay Resort and Koro Seaview Estates and is a further example of a private enterprise-real estate venture. The Koro Estate of 242 hectares was purchased in 1995 and offered as 450 individual freehold lots, most with forest surroundings and ocean views, and by 2009 more than fifty solar-powered houses had been completed.[71] The estate is located on the north-west tip of the island, which is serviced by a weekly airplane (that lands uphill) and a twice-weekly late-night vehicle ferry connecting to Suva. The Dere Bay development was designed and managed by Elsa and David Miller, operating under the umbrella of Taveuni Development Company.[72] The architect, Elsa Miller, graduated from the University of Sydney in 1974 and

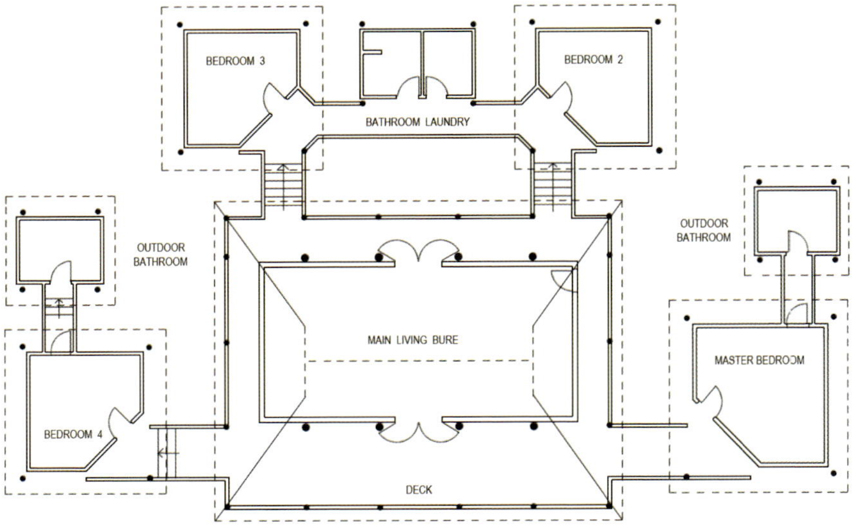

LEFT: Dere Bay Resort, Koro Island, 2003. Elsa Miller. Hollywood Dream Home.
ABOVE: Plan.

acquired landscaping skills in the office of the Sydney architect Bruce Rickard. In 1989 she travelled to Suva and initially worked for Architects Pacific, then in 1995 established her own firm, Tropical Landscapes. While with Architects Pacific, Miller was involved in many significant projects (primarily with landscaping) including the Ryoichi Jinnai Conference Centre, Suva, the South Pacific Commission Headquarters, Noumea, and the Pacific Pavilion at the Seville Expo '92 in Spain.

The Dere Bay Resort, built progressively since 1997, is an intimate group of buildings primarily intended to provide accommodation for potential purchasers of land on the estate. The central lodge, a wide spreading timber building surrounding a central lush tropical courtyard, overlooks the swimming pool, the sandy beach and along the long jetty that reaches out to the deep water beyond. The accommodation consists of three distinctive bures and a nearby three-storeyed villa constructed with timber poles, plus the 2003 boomerang-shaped Miller House with a private landing jetty. The roofs generally are thatched, but the bures are roofed with white corrugated steel. In 2009 the site was extended over water by the addition of two well-crafted bures that terminate the end of each of the long jetties.

On a delightful waterfront site at Dere Bay is the 'Hollywood Dream Home' designed and built by Miller in 2003 for the American reality television series *Under One Roof*.[73] The house was to accommodate five families and was planned with four separate small pavilions with bathing facilities, built around a central open living and dining space. The house was to be completed in seven weeks.[74] The project, which included both the building of the house and the filming of the series, put a strain on local labour and resources due to the isolation of the island. This was an impressive achievement, and the resulting thatched complex makes a pleasing addition to Dere Bay Resort's informal cluster of appealing and appropriate architecture.

While these small exclusive resorts are frequently owner-developed with the personal control of investment, the large mega-resorts require extensive funding and are generally reliant on overseas sources as well as Fiji Government support. This makes them more vulnerable to the impact of international events.

TOP LEFT: Dere Bay Resort, Koro Island, 1997. Elsa Miller. Bure at Night.
TOP RIGHT: Central Lodge and Pool.
ABOVE: Central Lodge Interior.

The Mega-Resorts

'Play in the sun … Frolic in the sea … Laze on the beach … Party to the Island Beat … Dive clear blue seas … Feast like royalty … Move to Fiji time … Romance under the stars … Chase a rainbow…Indulge your fantasies … Live your dreams … Get your passports and escape…' Advertisement, Warwick Hotel

Fiji's large 'integrated' resorts, with the mixed-usage of resort with land subdivisions, are cast in very ambitious programmes in terms of size, quality and amenity, requiring extensive funding with long lead times to maturity and realization. As the tourist industry is a critical factor in Fiji's economy, the Fiji Government has strong motivation to encourage these far-reaching investment projects that are supported at different levels of joint enterprise between government and investor. For the developer, the government's promotion of tourism has resulted in substantial tax relief, the availability of government loans and sometimes direct financing in the project (as in the installation of infrastructure). The integrated resorts are attractive to users as well as investors, as they are presented with the choice of a wide range of accommodation types and levels of involvement, from overnight accommodation in a hotel to long-term ownership. For all groups of guests, the extensive recreational and dining options offered in the facilities of the resort are available and convenient.

These large mixed-use resorts, however, remain highly speculative financial ventures and are particularly susceptible to movement in the global economy. Fiji also has an unstable political history, with the recent succession of coups disrupting the local social and economic conditions of the country.[1] Thus, forecasts for forward tourist numbers are somewhat unreliable, and the future uncertain. To sustain growth over many years, the estates are dependent on the economic survival of the investors, often using amalgamated funding from various sources. As Fiji's custom law retains the custody of most land, long negotiation procedures are sometimes needed to obtain the necessary leases, and that adds another note of unpredictability. Further, the vulnerability of Fiji's coastal land to natural devastation places infrastructure as well as buildings under constant physical threat. Despite these risks, the integrated mega-resorts have remained a preferred pattern for extensive undertakings in Fiji.

The Beginnings: Optimism and Setbacks

In the 1970s the government approved the applications for the release of several large holdings of primarily leasehold land for integrated projects. These included 3025 hectares at Debua for the resort of Pacific Harbour, a 2420-hectare resort was planned for an adjacent resort at Taunovo Bay, 275 hectares for an estate at Denarau Island and 2630 hectares for one at Natadola Bay. Construction commenced at Pacific Harbour and Denarau Island, but it was several decades before they were fully established. The Taunovo Bay and Natadola Bay Resorts did not proceed until the next century.

In 1973 a report on potential sites and recommendations for development was commissioned from Belt Collins and Associates, Harris, Kerr, Forster & Co., Lyon Associates and Wimberly, Whisenand, Allison, Tong and Goo. The report, *Tourism Development Programme for Fiji*, was funded by the United Nations Development Programme and managed by the International Bank for Reconstruction and Development and the Government of Fiji.[2] The brief to the consultants was as follows: 'This Study shall consist of two parts. Part I shall include: [a] the preparation of a master plan for the development of an integrated tourist resort at Natadola on Viti Levu; and [b] a master plan for long-term development of tourism in Fiji, together with recommendations on those areas other than Natadola which should be developed in the first five years, together with specific recommendations concerning the related administrative and institutional arrangements and education

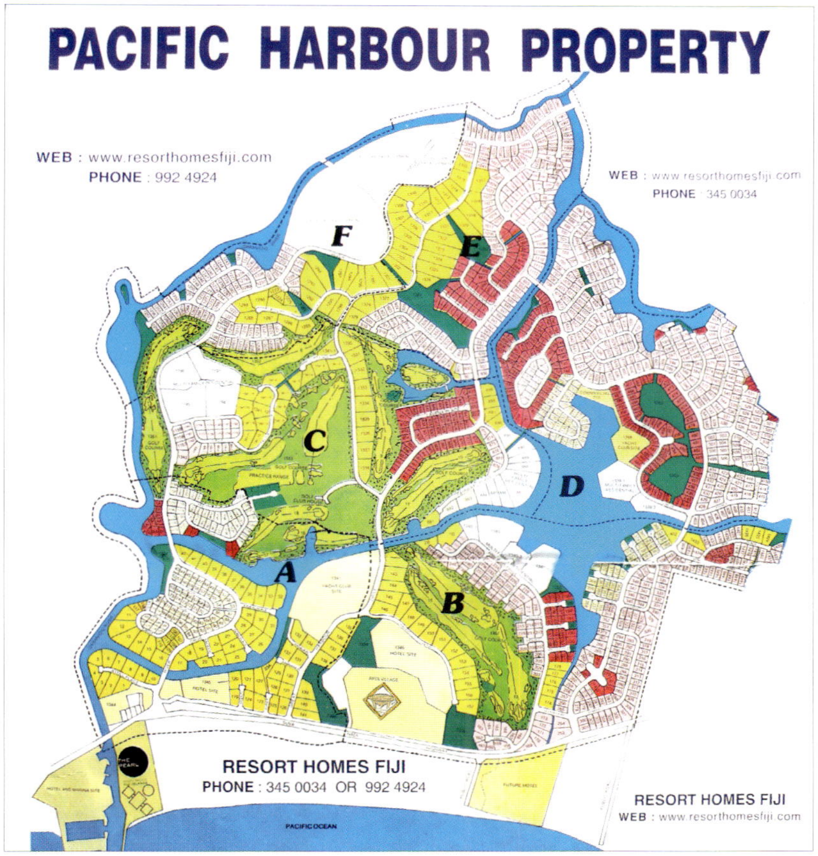

Pacific Harbour Estate, Debua, Viti Levu, Fiji.
Project Planning Associates International. Toronto.
Subdivision Plan of Pacific Harbour Estate, 2007.
Courtesy of Pacific Harbour Estate.

and training programmes. Part II shall include technical studies for the first stage infrastructure works at Natadola and, in less detail, the other areas to be developed in the first five years.'[3]

While the detailed proposals were for integrated resorts on Viti Levu, a further objective of the programme was to encourage a wide distribution of the benefits of tourism throughout Fiji. Hence, smaller islands, including Wakaya and Taveuni, were also examined for their potential, and recommendations were made.

In the early 1970s three world events occurred that caused a realignment of investment interests. First, in 1970 the Boeing 747 airliner was introduced on the Pacific route, and this enabled direct flights to take place between Australia and America, so it was no longer necessary to land at Nadi for refuelling. The second event was the October 1973 oil crisis and third was the 1973–74 stockmarket crash. Just when the Fiji tourist market was set to flourish, these worldwide events were to dampen enthusiasm for new projects.

Pacific Harbour

Fiji's first major scheme combining a hotel and residential estate was the 3025-hectare Pacific Harbour Estate at Debua, which included the site of the old Beachcomber Hotel. Pacific Harbour is a large-scale recreational, residential and resort complex located fifty-six kilometres south-west of Suva. The project was instigated by Australian ex-pilot Pat Samuel with financial backing from Canadians David Gilmour and Peter Munk who, in 1969, had founded the South Pacific Hotel Corporation, which rapidly became one of the largest hotel chains in the Pacific.[4] The 1973 report recommended the development of Pacific Harbour as a satellite town to Suva with a large section of the site retained for residential use. The report also advised that fast connections to the capital would be necessary with improvements to Queens Road, regular use of the airstrip and the introduction of fast boats, such as hydrofoils.[5] The planning of Pacific Harbour was undertaken by Project Planning Associates (International) of Toronto.[6] The master plan proposed five hotels and sited the new Beachcomber, the principal hotel, and the smaller Tropic Sands Hotel on the Beqa Passage seafront, the remainder of the complex including the Lagoon Resort being located on the other side of the Suva–Nadi highway, on what was marshy land.[7] The introduction of canals to drain the water created a forty-hectare lagoon and picturesque meandering canals, now edged by the landscaped lots of a large residential subdivision surrounding an international golf course and backed by green hills. As with Korolevu, the resort had its own airstrip to bring guests by charter plane, principally from Nadi's international terminal.

The new eighty-four-room Beachcomber Hotel, by the Canadian architect Harry B Kohl, was opened in 1972 but not completed until 1974.[8] The hotel, set in generous landscaped grounds, consists of a spacious central area, with foyer, dining rooms and other public spaces under high-pitched thatched roofs. The hotel rooms are located to each side in three-storied contemporary masonry wings with strongly articulated façades divided by raked blade walls between units. The 1974 Southern Pacific Property's company report stated that the overall Pacific Harbour scheme was completed, including the eighteen-hole championship golf course laid out by Robert Trent Jones Jr., and that 'only about 200 of the 1300 house sites remained to be sold'.[9] While the individual villas were designed

ABOVE: Pacific Harbour Estate, Debua. Villa No. 18.

ABOVE RIGHT: Pacific Harbour Cultural Centre. Chief's Bure.

BELOW: Beachcomber Hotel, Pacific Harbour Estate, Debua, 1974. Harry B Khol.

OPPOSITE: Pacific Harbour Cultural Centre, Debua, 1973. Wimberley, Whisenand, Allison, Tong and Goo. Perspective. *Courtesy of Wimberly, Allison, Tong and Goo.*

by various architects, including Kohl, the Mexican architect Luis Favela, and the Australian project developers Pettit and Sevitt, they generally made reference to Fijian building materials and roof forms and blended harmoniously with the location. A number of these houses were offered as short-term accommodation in parallel to that of the hotel. Each had a private swimming pool and four hours of maid service a day. Related are the designs for other buildings that formed part of the complex, such as the 1974 Pacific Harbour Golf Club House by Favela and the restaurant of 1980 by the Murray Cockburn Partnership. The Pacific Harbour Arts Village and Cultural Centre provides the principal shopping and entertainment centre for Pacific Harbour.[10] The 1973 Arts Centre, by Wimberly, Whisenand, Allison, Tong and Goo, consists of a colonial 'town' cluster of boutique shops, restaurants and historic displays.[11] Adjoining is the Pacific Harbour Cultural Centre including a recreated Fijian village built along a path climbing the hillside of the site. The central complex, the built village, lectures, performances, and demonstrations of arts and crafts were planned to present and interpret Fijian culture.

Pacific Harbour was a visionary programme that, in the 1980s, tended to fall by the wayside of Fiji's tourist development. The estate passed through many changes of ownership, and over the years its growth had been affected in part by the rivalry of the new resorts that were closer to Nadi airport, as on Denarau Island, poor financial management, the failure of a building contractor's firm and the slump in the tourist market in Fiji generally.[12] As had occurred elsewhere in the

South Pacific, some funding relief came from Hollywood. The Columbia Studios picture *Anacondas: The Hunt for the Blood Orchid*, which was filmed on-site at Pacific Harbour in 2003, brought major capital into the economy, making possible the revival of the project. In 2004 the Pacific Harbour Estate, under new ownership, was reinvigorated, including a major upgrading of the golf course and an extensive renovation of the Beachcomber Hotel as the Pearl South Pacific Resort and Spa, by the Australian architect Alan Mitchel.[13]

Denarau Island Resort

The Denarau Island Resort, which was to rival and surpass Pacific Harbour as a prime real estate development, was a further key project of the 1973 advisory report for Fiji's plans to build on the country's tourist potential. The original US$ 84 million project was initiated in 1969 by the American developer Dennis McElrath and established in the early 1970s by Jerry Moss from California and the Bishop Corporation from Hawaii. The original concept was to erect retaining walls and reclaim land, build six hotels, 600 residential blocks, a marina and an eighteen-hole golf course to a master plan by Belt Collins and Associates.[14] As at Pacific Harbour, the project was ambitious but, due primarily to location, more realistic in context. What McElrath and Moss basically achieved was site work and the completion of the first of the hotels, the Fiji Regent, which opened in July 1975.[15]

Denarau Island Resort occupies 275 hectares of tropical landscape, immediately adjacent to the town of Nadi and within easy reach of the international airport. The property covers two of the principal islands in Nadi Bay, plus some adjacent mangrove swamps. The islands were joined by fill, and the reclaimed land was utilized as a golf course.[16] The estate includes leading international hotels spaced throughout luxurious gardens, with pools and pavilions lining the shores of the 3.5-kilometre sandy beach along the northern and western sides of the island, together with residential unit sites on sea-front and canal subdivisions. Residents and visitors alike enjoy the gardens, beaches, swimming pools, the Denarau Golf and Racquet Club, which has an eighteen-hole championship golf course and ten tennis courts, and many other shared facilities. The core of the estate is the Marina Port Denarau, the gateway to the Mamanuca and Yasawa Island Groups, with the 2007 maritime, retail and commercial centre at Port Denarau, by ProDesigners (New Zealand), with landscaping by Place Design Group.

Despite a slow beginning and fluctuating markets, Denarau property sold well, and the investment experienced the most successful residential sales in Fiji. Contributing to the success of the project is the independent centralized administrative structure. Denarau Island falls outside the Nadi Town Council boundaries; consequently Denarau Island set up, through its integrated resort structure, a body corporate entity, Denarau Corporation. The company was structured as a quasi-town council, regulating development and carrying out the maintenance functions for the common areas of the resort. New work had to meet exacting standards. The corporation had an approved panel of architects and builders, and those not on the panel had to obtain agreement from the development review committee to proceed. To maintain high standards of landscaping and presentation, architectural plans submitted to the development review committee were required to include a landscaping plan with a nominated planting schedule.[17]

The Fiji Regent Hotel was designed by Black, Pagliuso, Kikuchi and O'Dowd, with landscape design by Belt Collins.[18] Originally from California, Black, Pagliuso, Kikuchi and O'Dowd established a Hawaii branch in 1968.[19] The Fiji Regent Hotel is an impressive establishment with traditional associations, drawing on Fijian construction techniques and imagery, and enriched by the extensive use of local art, handcraft and artefacts. The hotel, standing on a two-hectare site, consists of a large central hall, with a high vaulted roof, opening towards the ocean on to broad terraces and the main swimming pool. The 274 rooms are housed in eight two-storied buildings spread over the site and linked to the central facilities by covered walkways. In 2005–06 the hotel underwent extensive renovation by Architects Pacific[20] consisting of the refurbishment of all rooms and walkways, extensions to the restaurants and terraces, and the addition of a large portico. The new interiors were by Rick Wylie of Chhada Siembieda Australia. Architects Pacific again

worked in collaboration with Belt Collins, planners of the original landscape, in an substantial redesign of the grounds, including extensions to the principal pool.

Not long after the completion of the Fiji Regent Hotel, the decline in world tourism affected Fiji, and the Denarau Island project languished. However, the second hotel on the island, the Sheraton Fiji Resort, by Media Five, was completed in 1988 on a two-hectare site to the west of the Fiji Regent. When Black, Pagliuso, Kikuchi and O'Dowd closed the Hawaii branch in 1972, Tom Pagliuso established Media Five in Honolulu and continued to practise in Fiji.[21] The site planning of the Sheraton Fiji followed the arrangement of the Fiji Regent, with a single-storied central pavilion and seven blocks of two-storied units, but rather than the natural materials and earthy tones of the Fiji Regent, the Sheraton Fiji is an apricot-coloured concrete formal composition that complements the landscape by contrast.

From Vision to Reality

In 1988 interest in Denarau Island was rekindled by Harunori Takahashi of the enterprising Japanese company EIE International Corporation, and the firm of Palffy & Associates of Tokyo prepared a comprehensive master plan for the resort.[22] Takahashi employed Andrew Thompson, one of the South Pacific's best-known hoteliers and tourism specialists, to manage the project.[23] In the first phase of work initiated by Takahashi, US$ 30 million was spent on extensive engineering works,

Fiji Regent Hotel, Denarau Island Resort, Viti Levu, 1975. Black, Pagliuso, Kikuchi and O'Dowd.

OPPOSITE: Denarau Island Resort, Viti Levu. Master Plan. *Courtesy of Denarau Corporation.*

Fiji Regent Hotel, Denarau Island Resort, Viti Levu, 2005. Architects Pacific. Interiors by Chhada Siembieda Australia Refurbished Guest Room.

reclamation, excavation and landfill to create five kilometres of tidal waterways that enhance the site while providing extensive waterfront properties. Over two million cubic metres of earth fill was used to increase the height of the low-lying estate. Further, to provide shelter against cyclones, flooding and tidal surges, a protective wall was built around the island.[24] Design and construction of all site works including marine, tidal canals and landfill as well as water, sewerage and road infrastructure were undertaken by Kramer Engineering Group for construction company Kumagai Gumi, Tokyo. The amenities of the Denarau Golf Club, 1993, were enhanced by the opening in 1999 of the Denarau Golf and Racquet Club by the Murray Cockburn Partnership. The club is an extensive building with a typical high-pitched Fijian roof covered with timber shakes. The structure is of rough-hewn timber posts supporting pairs of projecting timber rafters that, in turn, support the surrounding covered walkways.

In 1996 the Singapore company Tabua Investments, along with Air Pacific and ITT Sheraton,[25] acquired the Denarau Island Estate from EIE International Corporation and placed it under the management of Martin Darveniza, who remained chief executive for the following thirteen years.[26] Its first major project was the Sheraton Denarau Villas, 1999, by Warren and Mahoney from New Zealand. The villas, built on a small site between the Sheraton Fiji and the Fiji Regent, differ from the hotels because while being associated with the Sheraton Fiji, the units were for individual sale. The eighty-two villas were laid out on a different planning arrangement with blocks more formally sited around a central courtyard with an internal watercourse. Dark-stained timber shutters set off the white of the villas, and the effect introduced a note reminiscent of a Mediterranean village. Texture and colour were added by the high-pitched redwood shake roofs of some of the units. Further private residential lots were opened up, and properties of design quality were erected on the estates. Among these was Barrack House, 2003, by Adrian Sofield in partnership again with Martin Livingston. Livingston's hand is clearly evident in the creative timberwork found throughout the house,

LEFT: Sheraton Denarau Villas, Denarau Island Resort, 1999. Warren and Mahoney.

ABOVE: Sheraton Fiji Resort, Denarau Island Resort, 1988. Media Five.

notably the intriguing posts fashioned through the creative reworking of rainforest tree trunks 'as found', and the dramatic structure and *magimagi* binding of the roof trusses (see p. 142)

More Optimism and More Setbacks

Despite considerable variability, tourism continued to grow over the decades, and the country saw the number of hotel rooms increase from 700 in 1965 to 6140 rooms in 2004. Further delays followed the third coup in 2000; however, hotel rooms reached a total of 8837 in 2006.[27] While another collapse occurred following the 2006 coup, *The Fiji Tourism Development Plan 2007–2016* sought to achieve a growth scenario of 1.1 million visitors for 2016 and an increased tourist infrastructure that included 16 000 rooms.[28] To maintain its position as a premier global tourist destination, Fiji needed to ensure enough accommodation, particularly that of luxury standard. The continuing optimism over tourism growth

Barrack House, Denarau Island Resort, 2003.
Adrian Sofield and Martin Livingston.

ABOVE AND ABOVE RIGHT: Taunovo Bay Resort and Spa, Viti Levu, 2006. Grounds Kent Architects. Guest House Entrance.

was reflected in the opening of many new large hotels and the revival of the Taunovo Bay scheme, with a luxury resort, by Grounds Kent from Australia and landscaping by Belt Collins, that opened in 2006. Architects Pacific were also involved in new ventures such as Momi Bay.[29] Yet, in reality, the future of Fiji's tourist industry remained fragile and unpredictable.

Denarau Island Resort Revisited

The optimistic years of the new century led to increased pressure to build tourist accommodation in Fiji. In 2005 Prime Minister Laisenia Qarase said the government expected an increase to more than 700 000 visitors to Fiji by 2010, thus predicting a strong demand for new accommodation.[30] On Denarau Island further residential sites were opened and sold quickly, and in 2005–06 several hotels, apartments and numerous dwellings were added to the estate. Units included the 2005 Golf Terraces Apartments,[31] a forty-four-apartment complex in one three-storied accommodation block following the edge of the golf course, by Ignite from New Zealand with landscape by Place Design Group, and a further Tabua Investments project, the Radisson Beach Resort, 2007, also by Ignite.[32] The Radisson Beach Resort, on four hectares of landscaped gardens, operates within a condominium arrangement. The site plan, again with landscaping by Place Design Group, is uncommon for a tropical resort, with the extensive facilities and two-storied villas clustered together encircling the large central series of artificial lagoons, making up what is described as 'the largest and most spectacular pool area in the South Pacific'.[33] The subsequent first-class hotels, namely the Sofitel Fiji Resort and Spa Denarau Island, 2005, and the Fiji Beach Resort and Spa, managed by Hilton, that

Radisson Beach Resort, Denarau Island Resort, 2007. Ignite. *Photograph by Mike Langford.*

Fiji Beach Resort and Spa, Denarau Island Resort,
Concept Drawing 2005. Group GSA. Site Plan.

Fiji Beach Resort and Spa, Denarau Island Resort,
Concept Drawing 2005. Group GSA. Perspective.

opened, incomplete, in 2006, were to be large establishments. The 249-room Sofitel Fiji Resort and Spa, by Tippett Schrock Architects, Townsville, Australia, with landscaping by the Townsville office of Place Design Group and interiors by Sofield, is a conventional hotel spread over three hectares of landscaped gardens. Conversely, the Fiji Beach Resort and Spa, by the Sydney architects Group GSA, was planned as an extensive resort along a 1.45-kilometre beachfront. The complex was arranged around a series of large open central pavilions with 300 villas scattered along the beach and through tropical gardens. With the global economic downtown of 2008–09 the Fiji Beach Resort and Spa was facing financial difficulties, and while Stage 1 and Stage 2 of the villas had been completed, work on further extensions was deferred.[34] Overall, however, Denarau Island Estate remained the most stable of the large-scale tourist projects in Fiji.

Momi Bay Resort

In 2003, a highly optimistic time regarding the predicted growth of Fiji's tourist market, one of Fiji's largest estates, Momi Bay, estimated to cost in excess of US$ 266 million, was planned for a site thirty-five kilometres south of Nadi. It was to be the first fully public-private partnership, with the developer installing the infrastructure, with costs to be reimbursed by the government at the completion of the work. The 2003 master plan for the 400-hectare site was prepared by Architects Pacific in association with Belt Collins for landscaping. It was a well-integrated project that took advantage of the varying topography, allowing differentiated areas of specific character to be created and opening up desirable views over the bay to the west and north. The master plan for the resort, which was intended to be the most comprehensive in Fiji, included two major hotels, the JW Marriott and the Ritz-Carlton, and the accommodation and social and recreational facilities common to such Fijian projects. The work involved land-forming and fill to create swimming lagoons and artificial islands with beaches, an eighty-berth marina and what were to be the first overwater bures in Fiji.[35] The central buildings, containing the front office and lobby, were set out over the water and were related primarily to the extensively reshaped beach. The 600 residential lots were positioned along the waterfront and around the twenty-seven-hole golf course, designed by Australian

LEFT: Momi Bay Resort, Viti Levu, 2003. Architects Pacific. Bure Under Construction.
BELOW: 2003 Master Plan.

golfer Peter Thomson. A wedding chapel was proposed for a small knoll that terminates the eastern arm of beachside units.

The project was planned to be built in stages, and Architects Pacific were appointed architects for Stage I, which included the JW Marriott Fiji Resort and Spa and the golf clubhouse along with nine holes of the course. The Marriott resort offered beachfront accommodation in seven accommodation blocks with 136 rooms, seventy-eight duplex units and fourteen suites, plus two overwater suites and twenty other overwater single units. The venture, however, ran into difficulties. The circumstances surrounding the 2006 political coup, severe cyclones, the financial collapse in July 2007 of one of the major overseas investors, New Zealand's Bridgecorp Holdings, and the extensive floods in January 2009, resulted in the foreclosure of the project by the major national investor, the Fiji National Provident Fund (FNPF).[36] Work on the site ceased, including that on the Marriot Hotel (initially programmed to be opened in 2005), which was nearing completion. In his 2009 Budget address, delivered on 21 November 2008, Prime Minister Commodore Bainimarama, announced government support for the recommencement of the project in 2009. It was, however, passed into receivership in 2009.[37] The Momi Bay Resort was to be the jewel in the Fijian crown, and in 2012 was again moving, albeit slowly, towards achieving its ambitious objectives.[38]

Natadola Bay

Beginnings in the 1970s

While Natadola Bay had been selected by the government in the 1970s as the prime site for potential development, it was not until over thirty years later that work on the first 350 hectares commenced. Natadola Bay initially had been proposed in the 1960s for an extensive resort complex, but plans were delayed for almost four years while trying to clarify the conflicting landholding claims between the Fijian landowners, the Crown and private freehold owners.[39] The 1973 *Tourism Development Programme for Fiji* had envisaged a scheme of 3000 accommodation units by 1981.[40] The site is only fifty-two kilometres from Nadi, and by 1974 30 per cent of the 2630 hectares of land were already privately held by the Fiji Resorts Company that also owned the Fijian Hotel and the Mocambo Hotel.[41] In 1974 the Fiji Resorts Company was bought

J W Marriott Fiji Resort and Spa, Momi Bay Resort, Viti Levu, 2003. Architects Pacific. Perspective. *Courtesy of Architects Pacific.*

into by a leading investor, the Malaysian Chinese businessman Robert Kuok, who controlled a major interest.[42] Further, the government, which had intended to provide the massive infrastructure, decided to wait for the 1974 *Natadola Bay Report*, a special survey with recommendations on the Natadola Beach area, as specified in the 1973 *Tourism Development Programme for Fiji*. The 1973 Report called for a self-contained town of 20 000 people to be built over fifteen to twenty years, with fifteen hotels, and residential neighbourhoods, schools, two major golf courses, an airport and a museum.[43] It was planned to accommodate 30 000 vacationers per annum by 1977 and nearly 400 000 by 1986.[44] With the global recession of the 1970s, this early project was abandoned.

Natadola Revisited

In the subsequent decades, Natadola Bay, a splendid Coral Coast site with fine beaches and lush vegetation, remained relatively untouched – apart from the Natadola Beach Resort, a small, quality resort of eleven fan-cooled rooms that was opened in 2000. The extensive 1970s Natadola Bay proposal, however, was revitalized with an extensive investment project, principally with funds from Asia Pacific Resort International of Hong Kong. It commenced construction in 2004, and the project was inaugurated on 25 January 2005 as the Natadola Integrated Resort Project. After the 2006 coup Asia Pacific Resort International was discharged and Natadola Bay Resorts Limited, a company formed by the FNPF, was set up to oversee and manage the Natadola development. Following in the footsteps of the 1973 report, the master plan for the resort was completed by the original designers, Belt Collins, and is based on a policy to create a 'natural destination resort'. Fundamental to the agreement was the pledge to create a resort integrated with a viable community for the resident population. The resort is planned as a three-phase integrated project, intended for completion in 2016.

As in the 1970s, the government support of the project, including the cost of the infrastructure, was part of its policy for stability and its drive to boost growth and investment. As stated in Prime Minister Qarase's inauguration speech, 2005: 'Without this level of financial and technical commitment from Government, investment on the scale planned at Natadola cannot take place. We see this as our responsibility. It is one of the roles of Government in our broader partnership with different sectors of the community for lifting living standards and making more jobs. Figuring highly in its platform is the government's argument of the economic benefit the development will bring to the leased land of traditional landholders

InterContinental Fiji Golf Resort and Spa, Natadola Bay Resort, Viti Levu, 2009. DBI Design. Master Plan. *Courtesy of DBI Design.*

InterContinental Fiji Golf Resort and Spa, Natadola Bay Resort, 2009, Landscaping by Place Design Group. Golf Club House by Ignite. *Courtesy of Place Design Group.*

who will receive substantial rental incomes from their land leased out for the resort. They will reap the benefits of employment, and acquire valuable skills from extensive construction, trade and hotel training schemes. There is wide scope for landowner involvement in starting supply and service businesses.'[45]

Phase 1 included the large InterContinental Fiji Golf Resort and Spa located at Natadola's main beach, which was opened in 2009. The design competition was won by DBI Design of the Gold Coast, Australia.[46] The architecture of the resort, with high-pitched shingled roofs, open pavilions with shutters and stone claddings, makes abstract reference to vernacular forms but rephrases them in contemporary terms. The plan for the 16.8 hectare hotel site is organized with the accommodation in two-storey blocks, primarily with twelve units in each, allowing a density that affords reasonable convenience from the 271 rooms to the recreational and dining complexes. These buildings are primarily distributed along vistas paths, including a significant watercourse and a long *Meki* lawn for ceremonial occasions and performances, and the height, density and distribution of the accommodation gives the project an uncommon urban character.[47] The Natadola Bay Resort is a significant project that breaks from the faux South Pacific 'thatched village' models that have characterized Pacific resorts since the Hotel Bora Bora. According to the Natadola Resort Report of 2004: 'Also staged for Phase 1 was a 120-villa luxury resort on Navo Island, a vacation-ownership resort, and an entertainment, cultural and retail centre, and an eighteen-hole championship golf course designed by Fijian International golfer, Vijay Singh, with landscaping by Place Design Group.[48] Phase 2, planned for construction between 2009 and 2012, included two more luxury resorts, villa and apartment residences, a convention centre and a marina. In Phase 3, between 2013 and 2016, it is proposed to develop a further boutique luxury five-star hotel of eighty rooms, and additional residential and villa accommodation, a Spa complex and

ABOVE: InterContinental Fiji Golf Resort and Spa, Natadola Bay Resort, 2009. DBI Design. Wedding Chapel.
RIGHT: Entrance. *Photographs by Ken Seet.*

Thalassotherapy Centre, an equestrian centre, a rugby field and a polo field are also planned.'

In 2009 Fiji was still recovering from the 2006 coup. At Natadola, while the major road and associated infrastructure were in place, the InterContinental Fiji Golf Resort and Spa was operating, the residential subdivisions (by Place Design Group) surrounding the golf course had been completed, and the eighteen-hole golf course (with landscaping by Place Design Group) and the Golf Clubhouse, 2009, by Ignite, were open, little else was happening.[49] Investment in Natadola Resort was revived in 2011, and Fiji Resorts' land parcel, situated to the west of the existing resort, was also awaiting development.[50]

The Natadola project, which has been ongoing since 1970, spans the time from the introduction of the proposals for the first Fijian integrated resort through to the current project and provides a microcosm of the overall rises and falls in the history of the building of large-scale tourist accommodation in Fiji.

Part IV

PLACES OF THE SOUTH PACIFIC

WITHIN THE POLYNESIAN TRIANGLE

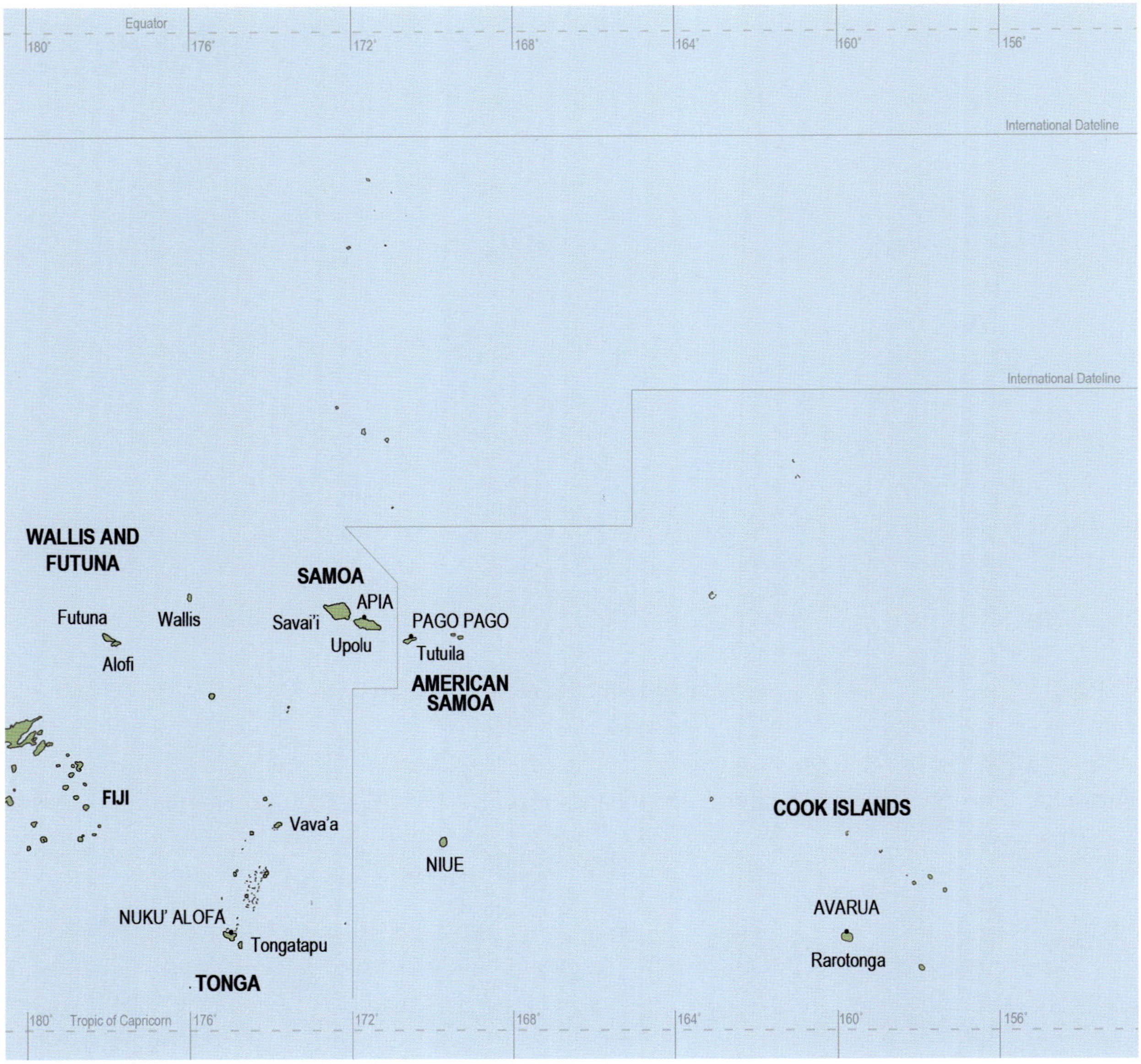
Equator
180°
176°
172°
168°
164°
160°
156°
International Dateline
International Dateline
WALLIS AND FUTUNA
Futuna
Alofi
Wallis
SAMOA
APIA
Savai'i
Upolu
PAGO PAGO
Tutuila
AMERICAN SAMOA
FIJI
Vava'a
NIUE
NUKU' ALOFA
Tongatapu
TONGA
COOK ISLANDS
AVARUA
Rarotonga
Tropic of Capricorn

THE SCATTERED ISLES OF CENTRAL SEAS

Western Polynesia contains a group of English-speaking countries, including Tonga, Samoa, American Samoa, Niue and the Cook Islands. Centrally located within the Polynesian triangle, the islands straddle the International Date Line and stretch eastwards from Fiji towards the archipelagos of French Polynesia. All of the nations are small in size with populations ranging from 1549 in Niue to 186 340 in Samoa. Above Fiji to the east is the French-controlled territory of Wallis and Futuna, population 14 000. Prior to European contact, Polynesia enjoyed historical and cultural homogeneity. Following colonization by the descendants of the Lapita people, the Tonga-Samoa crescent became the centre for the emergence of a coherent Polynesian culture that spread across the Pacific. Over time, differences in the cultures of the eastern and western Polynesians developed, and each country tended to structure somewhat different indigenous chiefly systems, which still play important roles in the societies today. These outer islands of the South Pacific have quite distinct histories of European settlement and differing patterns of growth, with towns primarily concentrated on one or two of the largest islands. Since colonization, the countries have evolved various political structures as independent or semi-independent states. The economies of the countries of western Polynesia – with the exception of American Samoa, which has liberal American support – are reliant on substantial overseas aid programmes and remittances sent home from those who have found employment abroad.

The characteristic building type of the regional vernacular throughout Polynesia is the fale (in French Polynesia, 'fare') that serves as most building types. At its simplest, the traditional fale is a round or oblong building defined by the curved thatched roof, supported on timber posts and commonly open on all sides. More contemporary fales tend to be rectangular in plan. In some instances the high level of transparency is countered by partial enclosure or lightweight hangings. In houses, owners commonly have a cupboard or trunk in which they can store their personal items, but otherwise security is trust and the fact that 'there is always someone around'.[1]

FROM COLONIES TO 'COCONUTS'

7

Colonial Presence: Modern Impact

Europeans first sighted the western Polynesian islands in the early eighteenth century, and by the first decades of the nineteenth century considerable numbers had arrived there. By the late nineteenth century the colonial powers were vying for possession of the region.

Settlement

The Cook Islands

The Cook Islands consists of a group of fifteen small islands in 1.8 million square kilometres of ocean between Tonga and French Polynesia. In 2011 its population was 17 794.[1] The islands were poor in produce and lacked good harbours, so initially they were mainly bypassed by traders. The most significant European settlers in the Cook Islands were the missionaries, who first arrived in 1821. Cannibalism in these islands was known to be particularly rampant, yet the Christian mission led by the London Missionary Society preacher the Reverend John Williams, was successful, and the rate of conversion in the country was rapid. The missionaries established a rigid system of religious control that is still evident in the country today.

Although Britain was exercising its authority through the missionaries, it was not until 1888 that the country was officially declared a British protectorate. In 1901 the islands were annexed to New Zealand, and in 1965 the Cook Islands were granted partial self-government. After sixty-five years of missionary rule, followed by seventy-seven years of colonial rule, the country acquired a certain degree of independence.[2]

With the exception of the buildings for the Church, there are no surviving colonial buildings of note in the Cook Islands. The only town of any size, Avarua, has not experienced the recent development seen in many of the South Pacific capitals.

ABOVE: Fita Fita Barracks, Pago Pago, American Samoa, 1908. *Courtesy of Jean P Heydon Museum, American Samoa: PH138J.*

RIGHT: High Court of American Samoa (previously the Naval Station Administration Building), Pago Pago, 1904.
BELOW: Plan.

PREVIOUS PAGE: Coconuts Beach Club.

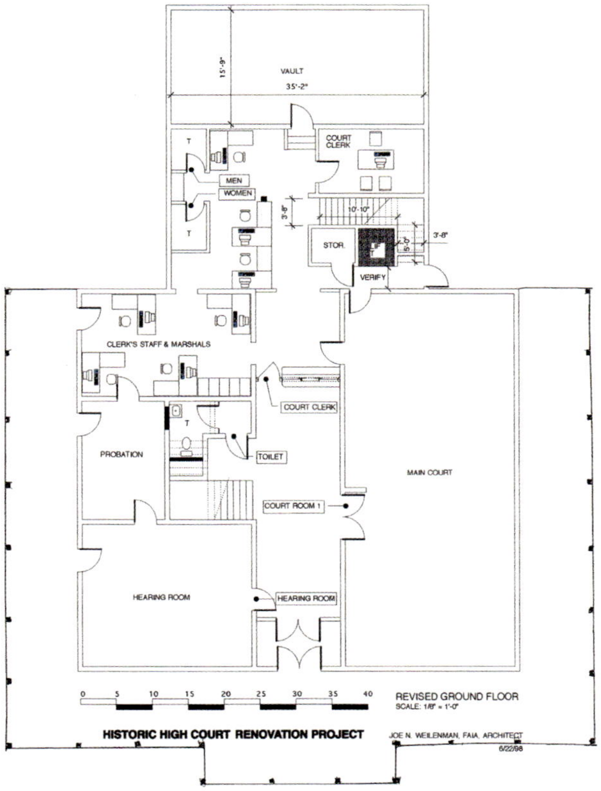

The Samoan Islands

The Samoan Islands were subject to civil wars between 1886 and 1894, resulting in the involvement of the British, American and German governments – the latter supporting one faction while Britain and America supported the other. This led to a confrontation between the three nations in Apia Harbour in 1889, and war was only averted due to a great typhoon that sank six battleships.[3] Subsequently, the 1889 Treaty of Berlin was signed to guarantee the neutrality of the islands by creating a Condominium, whereby responsibility for administration was shared, but further civil war broke out in 1898. The 1899 Tripartite Convention resulted in the division of Samoa, with the United States annexing Eastern Samoa, and Western Samoa (later Samoa) becoming a German colony – British interests being satisfied in Fiji.[4]

American Samoa

American Samoa consists of a spectacular group of volcanic islands, with Pago Pago standing on one of the finest inlets providing protected anchorage in the South Pacific. The country, with a population of 67 242, is much smaller than Samoa.[5] In 1888 America signed a treaty to enable it to establish a naval depot at Pago Pago in exchange for protection against the competing interests of Germany and Great Britain. In 1900 formal annexation took place, and it became an American territory administered by naval governors.[6] The principal US Navy base in the South Pacific was at Tutuila, and during World War II US Naval Station Tutuila was expanded considerably, and the island became a substantial military depot.[7] The closest it came to the war was a minor submarine attack on Pago Pago harbour. More recently the harbour has provided a haven for fishing boats and has operated as wharfage serving a cannery for the large tuna fishing industry in the surrounding regions.[8]

Western Samoa

Western Samoa was nurtured under a benign German administration, but after the start of World War I New Zealand troops invaded Western Samoa, and it became a New Zealand protectorate under a League of Nations mandate. New Zealand did little for Western Samoa, and there was active resistance to its administration. After independence in 1962 Western Samoa generally prospered until the early 1990s, when disease wiped out the export taro crops and two severe cyclones did considerable damage. In 1997 the constitution was amended to change the country's name to Samoa. The Samoan diaspora has been considerable, with around only half of the population still living on the islands.[9] The islanders respect customary values, and Samoa remains the most traditional of the nation states. The people still follow old ways and mores, with community life and social structures centred on the village. Since the late twentieth century gifts from overseas nations of several large public buildings have introduced an unprecedented increase in size, scale and technology into the townscape of Apia. In order to better align itself with its benefactors and major trading partners (China, Australia and New Zealand), Samoa had the International Date Line moved further to the east at midnight on 30 December 2011.[10]

Colonial Heritage

The region is subject to the destructive natural forces that have wrought considerable damage over time. These, plus low levels of maintenance, have meant the survival of few early buildings.

American Samoa

In contrast to Samoa, American Samoa has a structured conservation policy that is determined by the American Samoa Environmental Protection Agency and administered by the State Historic Preservation Officer.[11] Further, because of its relationship with the US Navy, more government buildings were constructed in American Samoa than in Samoa or the Cook Islands, and as they remained under the care of the US Navy until the closure of the naval base in 1951, more have survived there than elsewhere in the region. Important remaining structures in the main street of Pago Pago include the Fita Fita Barracks and the Naval Station Administration

ABOVE: Governor's Residence, 1903. (Overlooking Rainmaker Hotel), Pago Pago. *Sketch by Joe Weilenman.*

BELOW: Court House, Apia, Samoa, 1906. Albert Schaaffhausen. Author's Drawing.

Building.[12] The barracks were built in 1908 for the Fita Fita Guard (and Band) to house the first group of Samoan soldiers in the US Navy.[13] It is a long imposing two-storeyed building of timber construction with an arched masonry colonnade at ground level and an upper-level veranda – originally with a fine geometric balustrade.[14]

The most notable building constructed by the navy is the Naval Station Administration Building, which housed the executive offices of the base and the island government, and now serves as the High Court of American Samoa. The building initially stood on the harbour edge, but because of extensive land reclamation it now fronts the main street. The Administration Building of 1904 was a timber-frame structure with a central staircase and skylight, and a four-column-wide projecting portico. On each level, three-metre-wide verandas with geometric balustrading, as on the Fita Fita Barracks, surrounded the building. In 1998 both the interior and the exterior were subject to a rigorous rehabilitation programme by architect Joe Weilenman and John Enright, the State Historic Preservation Officer. The building was restored to its original design but was subsequently damaged by the tsunami of September 2009, before reopening in June 2011.[15] Also still in use is the naval communication building of 1917, built of concrete block to resist termites and hurricanes.

Overlooking Pago Pago from Togotogo Ridge in the adjoining bayside town of Utulei is the impressive two-storeyed Governor's Residence. The residence was constructed in 1903 in what is described as Tropical Victorian Military style. Samoan workers, under the direction of naval architects, built the timber-frame house, which served as the residence for naval and subsequent civilian governors.[16] The residence can be seen from the town and is an important component of the landscape. The building was in need of care, but recently was restored and reoccupied by the governor. The colonial-style Fagalele Boys' School at Sogi was constructed in 1855 by the London Missionary Society but was destroyed by the cyclone of 1991. South of Pago Pago and still existing but in a poor state of disrepair, is the Atauloma Girls' School, 1899, located high on the hillside overlooking Afao village and bay. The school, also built by the Church, was an architecturally impressive building of two storeys surrounding an internal courtyard and with wide verandas on all sides.[17]

Western Samoa

Administrative, civic and residential buildings were built during German colonization, but they were neglected under New Zealand control, and few are still standing. Unlike American Samoa, there is little protection for historic property in Samoa, and funding is poor. The Court House is one of the few historic structures remaining in

LEFT: Vailima, Mt Vaea, Upulo, Samoa, 1890. Tapa Room. *Courtesy of the Robert Louis Stevenson Museum.*

BELOW: Vailima, 1890.

BOTTOM: Old Hospital, Apia, Samoa, c.1900. Albert Schaaffhausen.

Apia. The building of 1906, by Albert Schaaffhausen, is one of the more innovative colonial works of the South Pacific.[18] While it follows the generic two-storeyed model of the official buildings of the colonies, it deviates from the norm, with a broken gabled-roof form, an eccentric bracketed corner porch, and decorative curving woodwork, with some hints of Art Nouveau. The building was carefully restored in 2007. Schaaffhausen was also the designer of the Old Hospital, a wide spreading timber bungalow that was presented to the people of Samoa by a German benefactor, Dr Gustaf Kunst.[19]

As the home of Robert Louis Stevenson, Vailima is a pilgrimage destination for European visitors to Samoa. Stevenson, who arrived in Samoa in 1889, built the first house on the slopes of Mt Vaea outside Apia in 1890. Australian and New Zealand timbers were used in its construction along with Californian Redwood floorboards. In Stevenson's lifetime the house consisted of two buildings, the larger one built as a platform raised on tall posts supporting enclosed and open living spaces, and some contained spaces on ground level.[20] The more private east wing was built by Stevenson for his mother.

After the death of Stevenson in 1894, Kunst purchased Vailima and 'added another wing to the house making it something of a mansion. Before the final improvements were completed the war of 1899 broke out,' and the 'main building at Vailima was pierced in many places by fragments of exploding shells' fired from British and American ships.[21] Kunst restored and extended the house 'following carefully and exactly the original plans'[22] and 'it was not until about 1903 that Vailima was brought to its present state of perfection'.[23] On Kunst's death the house passed into the ownership of the German Government. The cyclone of 1991 damaged the building, and in 1994, as a part of the celebration of the hundredth anniversary of Stevenson's death, the house was extensively restored and now stands as an imposing complex.[24] Vailima served as the home of the New Zealand High Commissioner and subsequently as the residence of the Samoan Head of State, before being renovated as the Robert Louis Stevenson Museum.[25]

The Towns: the Modern Impact

The mid-Pacific colonial towns were established as focal places for international contact and overseas administration. Hence, they are all on the coast with the principal buildings sited along the harbour. This was specifically relevant for the founding and growth of Pago Pago, with its role as a naval base and fishing port. In contrast to the deep inlet of Pago Pago Harbour, Apia stands on a wide open bay. Throughout much of the South Pacific, the foreshores of the towns have been extended by reef reclamation due to the shortage of sites for expansion, as most existing land is

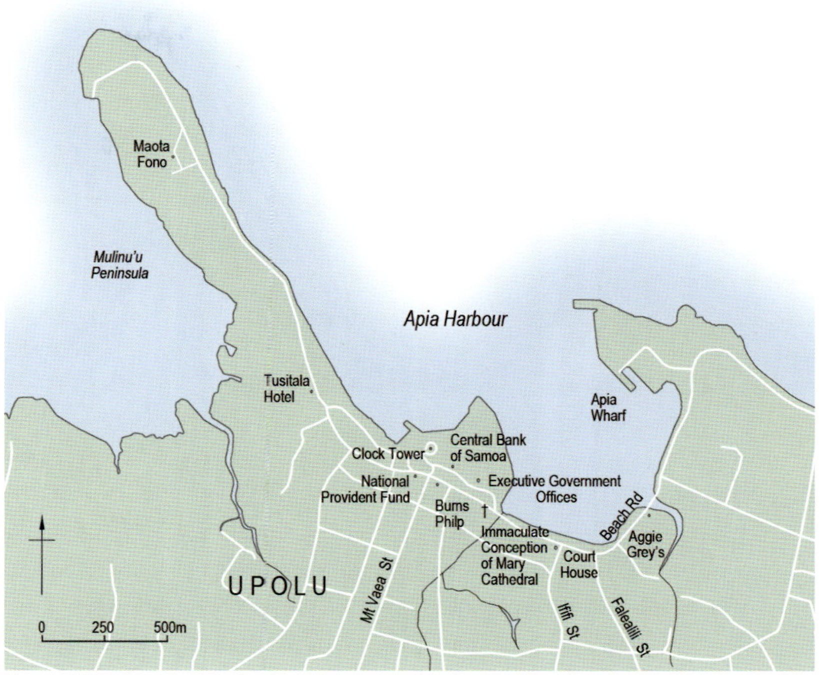

Plan of Apia.

unprocurable due to customary title and in the case of Pago Pago, because of the mountainous nature of the island.[26]

Few tall buildings mar the skylines of the towns of western Polynesia. The towns are small: Avarua with a population of 12 000, Apia 38 000 and Pago Pago 33 000.[27] Until the 1990s they were still sleepy easy-going places with buildings scattered along the waterfront and, in Pago Pago, climbing into the foothills of the protecting slopes behind. While Avarua is little changed the modern world is evident in Apia and to a certain extent in Pago Pago. However, with the transfer of the naval base to Honolulu, the town lost its strategic importance and growth slowed.

Given the small population of the Cook Islands it is not surprising the call for architectural services is low. The Ministry of Infrastructure and Planning in Avarua is responsible for building codes compliance and has undertaken some competent architecture, notably by engineer, land surveyor and planner George Cowan, who was employed as Secretary of the Ministry for sixteen years. Between 1962 and 1966 Ken Mills, an architect from New Zealand, filled the role of Government Architect, but when Mills resigned he was not replaced. Mills was twenty-four when he arrived in 1954 to take up a position as administrator. After leaving the position of Government Architect, Mills worked for a while in Fiji but later returned to the Cook Islands.[28]

TOP LEFT: Executive Government Offices (left), 1993. Chinese Government; Central Bank of Samoa (right), Apia, 1996. G M Meredith and Associates. Project architect: Geoffrey Lentz.

TOP CENTRE: Clock Tower, Apia.

TOP RIGHT: Accident Compensation Board, Apia, 2000. Swan Railley and Clapham and Associates.

CENTRE LEFT: National Provident Fund Building, Apia, 1978. Brian Kirkcaldy.

BOTTOM: Burns Philp Trading Company (now Chan Mow & Co. Ltd.), Apia, 1934.

There are few architects in the Samoan Islands, with most major projects being run by the Apia-based engineering firm of G M Meredith and Associates. George Meredith, who was educated at Canterbury College, New Zealand, engages architects from Australia and New Zealand when required for specific projects. The longest-standing architect in American Samoa is the American Joe Weilenman, who came to the islands in 1984 and worked initially for the government.[29] He later established his own practice, and since then has undertaken a considerable amount of work in Pago Pago. As there are no civil engineers in American Samoa, apart from those in Public Works, Weilenman primarily designs with engineers from Apia. The building codes for Samoa are based on the New Zealand code for earthquakes and the Fiji code for cyclones, while the building and electrical codes of American Samoa follow those of the United States.

Urban Development of Apia

Apia first grew along the seafront, Beach Road, then expanded south along Mt Vaea Street and the shopping streets Ififi and Falealili. Apia's central marker, the Clock Tower, was built as a memorial to those who fell serving in World War I and stands by the waterfront at the intersection of Beach Road and Mt Vaea Street. Another landmark on Beach Road was the impressive Roman Catholic Immaculate Conception of Mary Cathedral, 1905, with its glistening white façade that served as the beacon of the city for returning seamen.[30] The surroundings of the clock tower have always housed focal buildings, such as the arcaded store of the 1934 Burns Philp Trading Company and later the Samoa National Provident Fund Building, with its ground floor a bustling retail zone. The twin pavilions of the Samoa National Provident Fund Building, 1978, by architect Brian Kirkcaldy, stand on a corner site on Beach Road facing the clock tower.[31] It is an arresting building with a deeply modelled concrete frame and strongly expressed horizontal divisions between floors. While relatively large, its impact is reduced due to its division into two parts, and the compatible roof height, and deep, red cornices that relate to the red roof of the Burns Philp Building. With white walls and strong-red ground floor columns matching the roof, the building adds a certain festive note to this principal intersection.

Subsequent to the destruction caused by the severe cyclones of 1990 and 1991, the Samoa Government acquired two new buildings to house the growing bureaucracy. In 1993 the existing urban morphology of Apia Harbour was interrupted by the erection of the Executive Government Offices, a large seven-storeyed building that was a gift from the Chinese Government.[32] As is customary with such gifts, the design, materials and much of the labour were sent from China.[33] The Executive Government Offices are sited in a prominent position near the clock tower on the harbour side of Beach Road. The site is on land that was reclaimed in the 1960s over a coral reef buried by dredging. The visually heavy concrete building consists of angled building blocks related through the regimented order of the deeply recessed windows that establish a strong repetitive pattern across the façades. The size and sobriety of the offices are countered on the rooftop by a fale, designed as a two-storeyed building with a VIP meeting room on the lower level and plant rooms in the upper.

In 1996 the construction of the Central Bank of Samoa on the site adjacent to the government offices further divorced the town from the bay. The building was designed by Geoffrey Lentz from Australia, engaged by G M Meredith and Associates, and constructed by Fletcher Construction.[34] There is some further reference to the fale in the bank with its curved plan, curved roof and the gesture of the surrounding colonnade. This is an unconventional building that derives much of its unusual appearance from solutions arrived at by careful consideration of the climatic conditions. The bank is divided into differentiated parts – the offices and a fully glazed zone of major spaces set back and capped by a distinctive 'flying' quadrant roof. Pale green-and-cream panels clad the western end, but on the northern face the colonnade is interrupted and appropriate deep-set overhangs substituted. With its complex, articulated form and conspicuous use of glazing, the bank provides a marked contrast to the solidity and uniformity of the adjacent executive offices. A related colonnade with deep setbacks also occurs in the severe horizontal American Samoa Executive Government Offices, Pago Pago, 1990, also by G M Meredith and Associates but designed by architect Garry Jones from Australia.

A fourth large office building in Apia, the Accident Compensation Board Offices, by Swan Railley Clapham and Associates from New Zealand, was completed in 2000. This aluminium-clad concrete building is less prominent than the buildings of the 1990s, being of five floors and set into the streetscape on Beach Road. On the outskirts of the town the New Zealand firm of ProDesigners Architects, with a long history of architecture for the South Pacific, added further multi-level buildings to Apia, including the streamlined SamoaTel Exchange and Headquarters Building (in association with Tinai, Gordon and Associates), 2004.

The towns of western Polynesia underwent differing rates of change through the second half of the twentieth century. While some modern buildings now line the streets of Avarua, the town has retained much of its earlier size and scale. Recent years have seen the addition to Pago Pago of multi-storeyed blocks, such as the Centenary Building, 2000, by Mark Liveley, but it is the profile of Apia that has been altered most dramatically, notably through the developments of the 1990s on the reclaimed land along Beach Road.

'Staying Over': from Sadie's to Fales

'That sea I loved, and once or twice
I touched at Isles of Paradise'. Robert Louis Stevenson

Robert Louis Stevenson was but one of many Europeans who, in the nineteenth and twentieth centuries, sought paradise in the South Pacific and fell under its seductive spell. The islands of western Polynesia were not feted as remote havens of escape and romance in art and literature as were those of French Polynesia, yet they attracted the venturesome.

Deutschen Handels und Plantagen Gesellschaft Headquarters Building, Upulo, Apia, Samoa 1913. Albert Schaaffhausen. *Courtesy of the Museum of Samoa.*

The Samoan Islands

The first hotel of note in the Samoan Islands was the 1887 two-storeyed International Hotel, Apia, which burnt down early in the twentieth century. This was followed by the Apia Hotel, established in 1913 in the vacated Deutschen Handels und Plantagen Gesellschaft headquarters building of the German Trading and Plantation Company.[1] In 1913, to meet the needs of its overseas staff, the DHPG had built an imposing building among tropical gardens on the shores of Apia Harbour.[2] The building had two projecting corner bays and a central porch, with the arched colonnade of the lower loggia supporting wide upper-floor verandas. It became known locally as the Casino, but shortly after its opening the country was invaded by New Zealand forces, and when the Germans were expelled the building was converted into the Apia Hotel. At various times a few adventurous women tried to manage it but were unsuccessful until in 1940, Mary, the sister of famous hotelier Aggie Grey, took up the lease. She ran it as a 140-room hotel until the end of World War II under the name of the Casino Hotel.[3] During the war it provided accommodation for the American General Price. The hotel was demolished and replaced by the Tusitala Hotel, which opened in 1974.

While comparatively modest, two other hotels of the first half of the century became a part of local and international folklore due to their association with two women: Sadie Thompson and Aggie Grey. The building that houses the Sadie Thompson Inn and Sadie's Restaurant was built in 1903 as the house of the Meredith family, merchants and traders from Pago Pago. It was later renovated as a hotel and became a South Pacific meeting place, notably for American travellers due to American control of the colony. Somerset Maugham stayed there in 1916 and became acquainted with the 'fallen woman' Sadie Thompson and made the hotel the setting of his famous short story *Sadie Thompson*. The name of Sadie Thompson and the hotel were spread through later plays and movies such as *Sadie Thompson* (1928), *Rain* (1932), *Dirty Girtie* (1946) and *Miss Sadie Thompson* (1954).[4] The hotel, lacking the pretensions of the Casino Hotel and the South Pacific's other famous early hotels, was a simple two-storeyed timber-framed building with front verandas on both levels, built on what was then the water's edge.[5] By 1928 the hotel had been extended and upgraded and was operating under the name of the Haleck Hotel – later to be renamed Sadie Thompson Inn.[6] After being refurbished many times over several decades, the Sadie Thompson Inn remains in operation with the most recent renovation being by Weilenman. The

upper-level verandas were enclosed with the exception of those of the eastern wing, which gives some impression of the character of the original hotel.

The story of Aggie Grey and her hotel is also colourful. Aggie Grey's stood on the waterfront in Apia, and became known to travellers, principally those from New Zealand, due to its colonial connections and the relative proximity to Auckland, from where produce and building materials for Samoa were obtained. There are conflicting stories about the beginning of Aggie Grey's commercial interests, but it would seem that she opened a 'bar' in 1935 and expanded the business during World War II, selling hamburgers and coffee to American soldiers. She soon realized the opportunities offered by the war years and in 1944 established her first hotel in a building formerly occupied by the British Club, which stood on the waterfront on Beach Road on a site adjacent to Aggie's father's pharmacy shop. She leased the building from a Mr Heatherington who had returned to New Zealand and subsequently bought it from him.[7] The British Club was built of Kauri timbers (probably shipped to Samoa as ballast), which had been salvaged following the International Hotel fire. The original Aggie Grey's hotel was a one-storeyed timber-framed and clad building set in spacious gardens and overlooking the bay. Aggie extended the hotel with a second level, which increased the accommodation to twenty rooms. The investment was successful due, in part, to the accommodation required for the filming in 1952 of *Return to Paradise*, starring Gary Cooper and Roberta Haines, and in the same year, the commencement of TEAL's (Tasman Empire Airways Limited)

ABOVE: Sadie Thompson Inn, Pago Pago, Tutuila, American Samoa.

LEFT: Haleck Inn in 1928 (later Sadie Thompson Inn). *Courtesy of the Jean P Heydon Museum, American Samoa.*

BELOW: Aggie Grey's Hotel (left), 1987. Fletcher Construction; Protestant Church (right), 1958. Apia.

Tusitala Hotel, Apia, 1974. Derrick, Dignan, Retchford and Sofarnos.

OPPOSITE: Moana Sands Beachfront Hotel, Rarotonga, Cook Islands, 1974. Swan Railley and Associates.

Pacific Resort, Muri Beach, Rarotonga, 1987.

Rainmaker Hotel in 2003, Pago Pago, 1966. Wimberly, Whisenand, Allison and Tong.

Coral Route three-day package flight from Fiji.[8] The present-day neo-colonial Aggie Grey's hotel, which stands fronting the bay on Beach Road was erected as a design-and-build project by Fletcher Construction in 1987.[9]

The New Era

In the 1960s, with the introduction of the large jet aircraft, Pan Am extended its interest in the Pacific by becoming involved in a series of hotels as a part of its expansion plan.[10] The second of these was the Hotel Pago Pago InterContinental (Rainmaker), 1966, which stands on a promontory directly below the governor's residence at Utulei on the outskirts of Pago Pago. The hotel was built by the American Samoan Development Corporation alongside a picturesque beach on a 2.75-hectare site with tropical gardens, adjacent to the earlier Rainmaker Hotel. Named after the mountain across the bay, the original Rainmaker Hotel had been a twelve-room nurses' quarters built by the US Navy during World War II.[11] The Hotel InterContinental that followed the Hotel Bora Bora, French Polynesia, was the second major South Pacific hotel designed by Wimberly, Whisenand, Allison and Tong.[12] In 1973 the InterContinental lease was taken over for twenty years by Americana Hotels, and the hotel was extended and the name changed to the Rainmaker. Further additions occurred, notably one by Wimberly, Whisenand, Allison, Tong, and Goo with Fletcher Construction in 1980.[13]

The experience gained through building the Hotel Bora Bora is evident in the Rainmaker Hotel. The accommodation consisted of 225 rooms in beach fales and four two-storeyed pavilions adjacent to open terraces, aligned to allowed tropical winds to flow across the entire hotel complex.[14] For these, the arched-roof fale form was extended into long shingle-roofed curved arcs with three early blocks following the beachfront and a series of distinctive buildings with public facilities at the end of the promontory. The result is a picturesque composition of evocative forms arranged along a spit of land projecting into the harbour. At its peak the Rainmaker Hotel provided a high standard of accommodation and hosted a number of prominent international guests. It operated as a successful hotel until the mid-1990s, but by the end of the century the hotel had been neglected and fell into disrepair. It was later revived by Weilenman and two refurbished wings, leased to the owners of the Sadie Thompson Inn, were opened under the name of Sadie's by the Sea.

The local vernacular also forms the underlying concept for the Tusitala Hotel, Apia, built for the Western Samoan Government on the former Casino Hotel site.[15] (Tusitala, 'story teller', the local name given to Robert Louis Stevenson). The hotel, by Derrick, Dignan, Retchford and Sofarnos of Suva, has accommodation of 100 rooms in two-storeyed connected blocks, with the public areas laid out to resemble a Samoan village. The public rooms have high convex roofs constructed by local craftsmen using

FAR LEFT: Stevenson's at Manase, Savai'i. Interior showing Tapa.

LEFT: Coconuts Beach Club, Upolu. Fale Mural.

BELOW: Holiday Fale, Savai'i.

Asi toa wood bound with handwoven sennit and roofed with shingles. The hotel demonstrates a different approach to those of the firm's previous hotels for the South Pacific, which tended not to draw on local precedent. The addition of a new block by Architects Pacific, Suva, was completed in 1992. After the building of the Tusitala Hotel, no major hotels were built in the Samoan Islands until 2003. In 1984 there had been a proposal to build the Royal Samoan Hotel on a large swamp landfill off the coast at Taumesina, but the venture failed financially, despite the 1984 Royal Samoan Hotel Act, which provided taxation relief and other concessions to the Royal Samoan Hotel Corporation.[16]

The new hotels of the early twenty-first century included the Tradewinds Hotel, American Samoa, 2003, a pink three-storeyed building in a pseudo-colonial style, by Kenneth B Harris of Utah, America, and the extensive Aggie Grey's Lagoon Beach Resort and Spa, 2005, a joint venture between Aggie Grey's Limited, the Samoa Government and other private investors. The resort is set on a site of eighty-nine hectares, which includes an international standard golf course. The accommodation is housed in six separate buildings, each containing twenty-four rooms over two levels, three to each side of the central facilities block.[17] The design was by Robert Railley of Swan Railley and Associates, New Zealand.

The Cook Islands

By the 1960s tourism had become an important source of income for the small Cook Islands, which attract more tourists on a per capita basis than any other Pacific nation.[18] Most are accommodated on the largest island, Rarotonga, which is ringed with small-to-medium resorts generally comprised of informally sited bungalows. Typical are the Rarotongan Beach Resort, 1977, and the smaller, exclusive 1987 Pacific Resort, Muri Beach, on East Coast Road. One exception to the norm is the accomplished Moana Sands Beachfront Hotel, which is situated on the south coast of Rarotonga on one of the finest snorkelling beaches. The hotel, by Railley, was opened in 1974 and extended in stages, with a third floor added in 2002.[19] In marked contrast to the faux-vernacular character of most resorts at the time, the Moana Sands Hotel is a white building of modern design with verandas across the front overlooking the sea.

RIGHT: Coconuts Beach Club, Upolu. Beach Cottage.
BELOW: Overwater Units.

The only major undertaking in the Cook Islands has been the government-owned project the Sheraton Cook Island Resort, with 200 rooms, which commenced construction on the south coast of Rarotonga in 1990. The Italian source of finance ceased in 1992, and the Italian contractors returned to Italy, leaving the hotel incomplete. More recently, the hotel was bought by the New Zealand Tepaki Group, and the new resort was to be called the Captain Cook Lagoon Resort, by Peddle Thorp & Montgomery Architects, but again delays overtook progress.[20] Ultimately, this attempt to revive the scheme also failed.[21]

The Small Resorts of the Western Polynesian Pacific

Both the Cook Islands and Samoan people have been cautious about investing heavily in large resorts and have indicated that they do not wish to see dramatic changes to their current relaxed lifestyle.[22] The fact that little land is available has also contributed to the slow growth of tourist facilities. Small fale beach resorts, however, have been built and run by people of the islands, notably on the coast of Rarotonga and on the island of Savai'i, Samoa. Samoa has for some years successfully pursued a policy of building tourist low-key beach fales run by Samoans, which ensures that earnings remain with those providing the service. Almost exclusively these were arranged with central facilities and a distribution of small fales, mostly with thatched roofs, commonly laid over corrugated steel sheeting. These resorts, of simple design and construction, some overwater, have a relaxed ambience and range from buildings exhibiting sophisticated restraint to basic shelters. Interiors and exterior elements, such as doors, window frames and eaves, are often decorated with imaginative mural designs from local women and craftsmen. Creative ideas can transform a modest shack, as seen in the *siapo* (tapa) ceilings at Stevenson's at Manase on Savai'i, the murals and delicate inlaid timber work of the early cottages at Coconuts Beach Club on Upolu, and the individually crafted beach fales from the 1992 design by Robert Ross, Los Angeles (see p. 180).

While tourism is an important industry for the small islands of western Polynesia, they generally do not attract, and the resorts do not accommodate, large numbers of visitors. Rather, the tourist focus is on small-scale ventures of local rather than international ownership. However, some of the most well-known early hotels in the South Pacific were built in this region.

THE KINGDOM OF TONGA 8

Nuku'alofa: Beyond Vuna Road

The Tonga archipelago, which lies 800 kilometres to the south of Samoa and just west of the International Date Line, consists primarily of the island of Tongatapu and the island groups of Ha'apai and Vava'u. There are 169 islands in all, of which only thirty-six are inhabited. The islands are prone to destructive hurricanes and earthquakes. Polynesians and a small number of Melanesians make up 92 per cent of the population of 103 000 – the remainder consisting of other islanders, Chinese and approximately 300 Europeans.[1] The highest point above sea level on Tongatapu is only about sixty-five metres high, and most of the island is flat and low-lying, which creates substantial difficulties in providing an adequate sewage system.[2] There are large populations of Tongans living abroad, and the numbers are increasing. Tonga has a small export trade, mainly in agricultural goods, but it is principally dependent on external aid and funds sent by the Tongan families living overseas. Recently, AusAID, the European Union, Japan and China have made significant contributions to the economy.

On Tongatapu more substantial buildings have mostly displaced the vernacular Tongan fale of coconut thatched roof and reed or coconut frond walls. These were followed by fales with timber walls, sometimes with tile or flattened-kerosene tin roofs, or, later, possibly corrugated-steel sheets. By the 1980s few lived in traditional housing, rather, they favoured a modified form of fale or house based on foreign styles but of local manufacture, usually of concrete block. The more affluent imported houses, some luxurious. In the twenty-first century concrete block became the most common material due to its resistance to hurricanes and ease of manufacture. Due to the devastation caused by Hurricane Waka in 2001, the government assumed responsibility for building many low-cost standard 'hurricane houses', with 470 of them constructed on the outer islands in 2003 alone.[3]

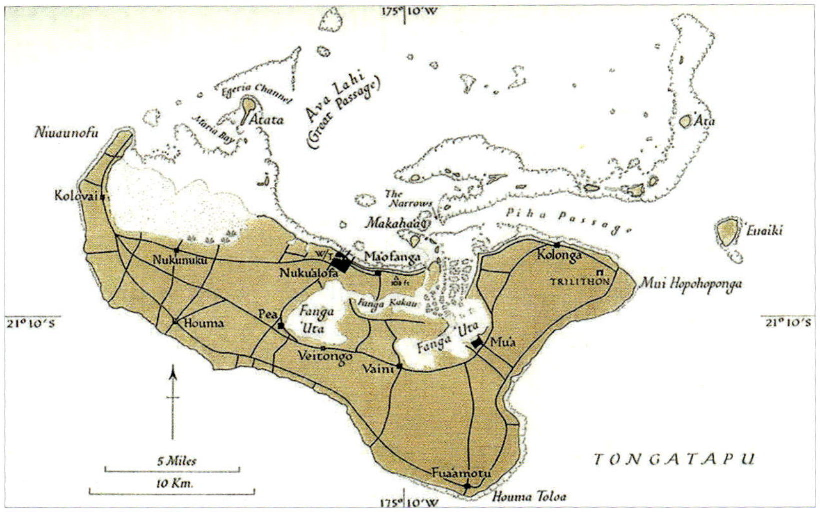

Tongatapu: Roads and Principal Settlements, 1932. *Courtesy of the University of Texas Libraries, The University of Texas at Austin.*

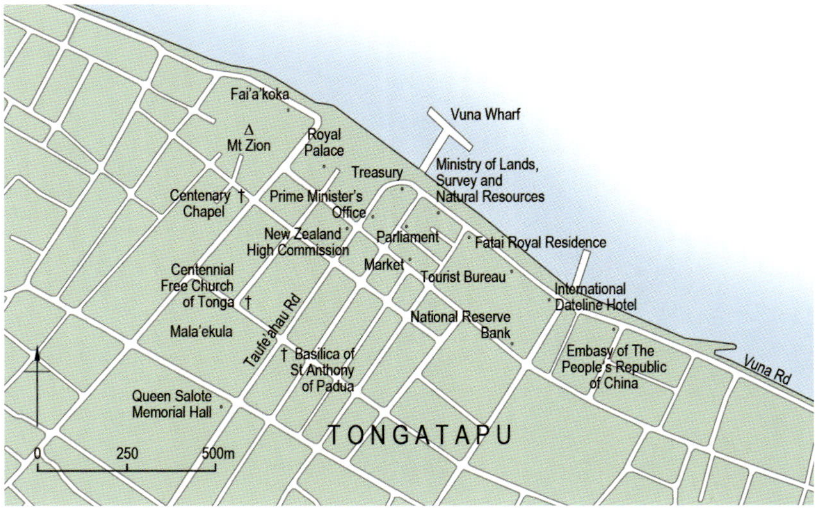

Plan of Nuku'alofa.

PREVIOUS PAGE: Moulton Memorial Chapel.

From Britain and Her Colonies

The first Europeans to visit the islands arrived in the seventeenth century. Many noteworthy expeditions followed, including one led by Samuel Wallis in 1767 and another by James Cook in 1774, who called them the Friendly Islands. The Tonga archipelago was united into a Polynesian kingdom in 1845, and while Tonga is the only South Pacific country never to have been formally colonized, it was deeply influenced by a colonial power, Britain, with whom an association was firmly established by the first ruler of the Kingdom of Tonga, Taufa'ahau I. Taufa'ahau I had converted to the Wesleyan religion and in 1845 declared himself King George Tupou I (after King George IV, whom he greatly admired).[4] King George Tupou adopted the etiquette, dress and architecture of the British Court, and in 1850 enacted a new legal code based on English Common Law, with considerable advice the Wesleyan missionaries and the Chief Justice of New Zealand.[5] These ties with Britain were strengthened by the arrival of the Reverend Shirley Baker, a Wesleyan minister who became the king's personal advisor and eventually prime minister. Together they drew up Tonga's first formal constitution. Before he fell into disfavour and was expelled from the country in 1890, Baker managed to have treaties signed between Tonga, Germany and the United States guaranteeing Tonga's independence. Britain then stepped in and exerted influence at the highest levels of government, eventually signing a Treaty of Friendship with Tonga in 1900. The treaty retained the monarchy but led to the establishment of what was virtually a protectorate, which lasted until 1970.[6] This relationship with Britain had a significant impact on the preferred designs and the production of the buildings of the kingdom.

The British influence on the architecture of Tonga was strengthened by the importation in the nineteenth and twentieth centuries of prefabricated timber buildings from the colonies of Australia and New Zealand. Conspicuous among these are the picturesque Victorian fantasy of the Kauri timber red-and-white Royal Palace, imported from New Zealand and erected in 1865–67, and the Parliament Building, made from prefabricated parts, again from New Zealand, and assembled in its present central position in 1894.[7] In addition, most houses of any substance were imported, including the 1871 President's House for the Free Wesleyan Church, a fine two-storeyed colonial house constructed from a design and materials from Australia,[8] and Fai-'a-koka, a spreading colonial-style bungalow built on the waterfront in the 1880s.[9] Fai-'a-koka has verandas enclosed with lattice sidings and characteristic timber shutters angled for shade and to catch the cooling updraft

Timber-sided Fale, Nuku'alofa, Tongatapu.

from the sea. Also of note is the house for Motekiai Halaholo, which was probably imported from Australia via Fiji in around 1880.[10] This property, which has a central stair and a wide veranda typically protected by windows and propped timber panels, was acquired by the government and leased to the British Government in 1901. The building became the residence of the British High Commissioner until the appointment was terminated in 2007.[11]

European origins are also evident in Tonga's most significant government building of the early twentieth century, the Prime Minister's Office built in brick in 1900 in Nuku'alofa's main street. An uncommon two-level portico with a tall red peak roof makes this otherwise conservative colonial building a notable landmark for the town. The building was extended in 1904, and the tower had to be rebuilt after damage from the 1977 earthquake. To the south of the old building stands a 1986 extension, by Lloyd Evans of South Pacific Architecture Network, that provides an office for the Minister of Foreign Affairs and Defence and a cabinet conference room.[12] Nearby, opposite Vuna Wharf, is the only other notable civic building of the early century, the 1928 Treasury Building. It has a stark neo-Georgian façade with a deep pediment supported by simplified Tuscan columns arranged in pairs and singly across the façade. The Treasury Building initially housed the Post Office and the Customs Office.[13]

The Town of Nuku'alofa

Early Development

Nuku'alofa was founded in 1829 by the Wesleyan missionaries who established their central mission on the north coast of Tongatapu, and when George Tupou I became king he made it his capital. The Royal Palace, which faces the extensive grassed parade grounds, dominates the waterfront. The palace formed a focal point for the young town, which first expanded with port and

Royal Palace, Nuku'alofa, 1865. *Courtesy of the Royal Palace Archives.*

business facilities stretching along the seafront (now Vuna Road) with a major seawall along the foreshore.[14] In 1906 Vuna Wharf was built. The town also grew inland along the commercial street of Taufa'ahau Road, which leads to a further focal point for the town: Mala'ekula, the large park-like space that contains the Royal Tombs. While the Royal Tombs tend to be based on European-style royal tombs, the customary Tongan burial ground is festooned with hanging ceremonial tivaevae (bright, multi-coloured appliquéd quilts used symbolically and given as gifts) marking some graves, and patterned by the imaginative use of on-end beer bottles defining and decorating those of the less affluent. In the second half of the century most of Tonga's important buildings were erected around the perimeter of the green area of the Mala'ekula: the Basilica of St Anthony of Padua, 1980, the Centenary Church of the Free Church of Tonga, 1983, and Queen Sālote Memorial Hall, 1996. Built in the near vicinity was Tupou College for boys, the oldest secondary school in the South Pacific, having been founded in 1866 under the charge of its principal the Reverend Dr James Moulton from Australia. Also nearby were Queen Sālote College for girls, 1923, the Free Wesleyan Centenary Church, 1952, and the Free Wesleyan Administrative Centre, 2000.[15]

Early growth was slow, but by 1931 Nuku'alofa had a population of 4000, and in 2006 its population was estimated to be in excess of 40 000.[16] Today, 73 per cent of Tonga's population live on Tongatapu and 14 per cent on Vava'u – of the total population only 23 per cent live in urban areas. The US military landed in Tonga in May 1940 with a task force of over 7800 men, more than doubling the population of Nuku'alofa.[17] In the short period before their withdrawal in February 1943, the Americans built a new wharf, constructed or repaired over 161 kilometres of roads and undertook extensive sanitation and pest-eradication programmes. When the Americans moved forward, New Zealand forces were garrisoned in Tonga.[18] Before 1970 Tonga's main link with the world was through

TOP LEFT: Parliament Building, Nuku'alofa, 1894.

BOTTOM LEFT: Prime Minister's Office, Nuku'alofa, 1900.

TOP CENTRE: Motekiai Halaholo, Nuku'alofa, 1880. Entrance Portico.

TOP RIGHT: Treasury Building, Nuku'alofa, 1928.

BOTTOM RIGHT: Fai-'a-koka, Nuku'alofa, 1880s.

LEFT: Royal Tombs, Mala'ekuva, Nuku'alofa.

ABOVE: Graveyard, Tongatapu.

OPPOSITE: Graveyard, Nuku'alofa. Ceremonial Tivaevae.

the Union Steam Ship Company from New Zealand, which visited the islands once a month.[19] The establishment of other international connections with Tonga was slow, but the situation was somewhat relieved in 1950 when Fiji Airways commenced flying to Fua'amotu International Airport, which had been built during the war by the New Zealanders.[20] Today Tonga is serviced by several international airlines.[21]

Vuna Road: The International Dateline Hotel

The first post-war building to make an impact on the town was the International Dateline Hotel. Prior to the building of the hotel, the only accommodation was the Beach House guesthouse, a large single-storeyed bungalow built prior to World War II, which had catered for Tonga's visitors since the loss of the few small hotels remaining from the beginning of the century.[22] The International Dateline Hotel, by the Fiji firm of Derrick Dignan & Associates, was built in 1966 for the Tongan Government to accommodate guests attending the coronation festivities of King Taufa'ahau Tupou IV. The International Dateline Hotel was a significant building for Tonga in that it heralded a new era in the kingdom's history.[23] The original hotel was a long three-storey building of fifty-four rooms. Among later alterations was a western wing completed in 2003, increasing the accommodation to 125 guest rooms.[24] There are now many resorts and hotels around the coast and a number of smaller hotels in Nuku'alofa, including the twenty-two-room Little Italy Hotel, which was built on Vuna Road in 2008. The town of Neiafu claims the only other early hotel of note in the country, the Port of Refuge Hotel, Vava'u, which first opened in 1972.[25] The Port of Refuge consists of a series of single-storeyed units that step in wings down the hillside overlooking the bay.[26]

Vuna Road continued to be developed with the addition of the Ministry of Lands, Survey and Natural Resources, 1977, the new Tourist Bureau, 1978, the Australian High Commissioner's Residence, 1982, the rebuilding of the Cathedral of the Immaculate Conception of Mary, 1992, and the central Talamahu Market, 1995. The Ministry of Lands, Survey and Natural Resources, by the Ministry of Works Government Architect, is a long two-storeyed building of competent design with verandas on both levels and projecting mullions denoting the structural bays and establishing a regular tempo along the façade. The building, however, makes little concession to its location among the buildings of Nuku'alofa's seafront. The original tourist bureau was damaged beyond repair by the 1977 earthquake, and a new building was commissioned, which, on the king's directive, was to be

TEVITA V. HAVEA

seen as representative of Tongan traditions and skills. The building, conceived by Saia Katoa, a 'celebrated Tongan house builder'[27] and financed by the Australian Government, was built in two sections: a rectangular office and work area and an oval fale-form reception area with a shingled roof supported by Koka posts. This room faithfully follows Tongan custom with local building materials used, including young bamboo, which is used extensively. As is conventional in Tongan building practice, no nails were used in the construction of the building. The binding and tying of the timbers with plaited coconut husk fibre are skilfully executed with the fibres woven to form pictures that include stars, the Norfolk pines that stand in front of the palace and an ancient pattern known as Tokotoko, characterized by a row of reclining triangles. The interior is decorated, with the walls and ceiling covered by patterned woven pandanus mats and tapa cloth. Tapa is one of the principal and most widespread art forms of the South Pacific and consists of highly decorative geometric or natural designs painted on bark that comes mainly from the breadfruit or paper mulberry tree (*Broussonetia papyrifera*). Tapa is principally made by the women of the Samoan Islands, Tonga, Fiji, and Wallis and Futuna. The making and decorating of tapa is one of the most celebrated crafts of Tonga.

In the rebuilding of Nuku'alofa after the 1977 earthquake, the high commissions of Australia and New Zealand added several new buildings to the town. Among these was the Australian High Commissioner's Residence on Vuna Road, by the firm of Philip Cox and Partners from Australia, completed in 1981. The residence, which is set in large tropical gardens, resembles a rural Australian house, being a single-storeyed building with wide verandas and a galvanized-steel roof. In contrast, Craig Craig and Moller's 1978 New Zealand High Commission in the centre of town is a two-storeyed building with a central courtyard. It was constructed of concrete columns and floors, walls sheeted with shiplap weatherboard cladding and profile metal roofing. Timber, including Rimu, is used extensively in the interior with Radiata Pine laminated perimeter beams.[28] The commission, with broad roofs and attached upper-level verandas wrapped in white lattice screening, makes a distinctive urban statement and provides a lively contrasting contribution to the streetscape of Taufa'ahau Road.

The Later Architects of Tonga

Although there are some Tongan architects working and living in Tonga who were trained in Papua New Guinea, Hawaii, New Zealand or Australia, they are primarily employed by the Ministry of Works Department and rarely undertake private commissions. Prominent among those who received their architectural training at the Papua New Guinea University of Technology were George Moala[29] and Leveni 'Aho, who subsequently attended the University of New South Wales.

OPPOSITE, LEFT: International Dateline Hotel, Nuku'alofa, 1966. Derrick Dignan & Associates.

OPPOSITE, RIGHT: Ministry of Lands, Survey and Natural Resources, Nuku'alofa, 1977. Government Architect.

TOP LEFT: New Zealand High Commission, Nuku'alofa, 1978. Craig Craig and Moller.

TOP RIGHT: Port of Refuge Hotel, Neiafu, Vava'u, 1972.

LEFT: Australian High Commissioner's House, Nuku'alofa, 1982. Philip Cox and Partners.

Tonga Development Bank, Nuku'alofa, Stage 1, Rounds Lee and Partners, 1983; Stage 2, Jaimi Associates, 1992.

The most successful architectural firm that operated in Tonga was Jaimi Associates.[30] The Fiji firm of John Rounds, Lee and Partners commenced practice in Tonga in the 1970s. When Rounds retired in 1982, Lee continued to practise in Tonga, and in 1984 Lee and Jaimi established the Tongan branch of Lee Associates, becoming Jaimi Associates in 1990. Jaimi left Tonga in 1993 but subsequently opened a small branch office in 1994. Consequently, some projects (for example, the Tonga Development Bank) were started by Rounds Lee and Partners and were completed by one of the subsequent related firms.[31] Among the projects on Tongatapu were the National Indoor Stadium at 'Atele, 1994, buildings for the University of the South Pacific, the Tonga Development Bank, (Stage 1 by John Rounds 1983 and Stage 2 by Jaimi, 1992), the Cathedral of the Immaculate Conception of Mary, 1992,[32] the National Reserve Bank of Tonga, 1994, Queen Sālote Memorial Hall, 1996, the new Fatai Royal Residence, 1996, the Free Wesleyan Administrative Centre, 2000, and buildings for the Seventh-Day Adventist Church. The National Indoor Stadium is an atypical large concrete building, while the university projects are characteristic of the firm's later work, in consisting of small-scaled buildings scattered through generous landscaping.

The Tonga Development Bank is sheltered under a raking single-pitch steel roof extending down over two levels and, uncommon for Tonga, exhibits robust post-and-beam construction. It is a pleasant well-scaled building that has an appropriate relationship to its setting in the town. The National Reserve Bank of Tonga, 1994, with five floors, is the tallest building in Nuku'alofa and a conspicuous element in the town. While the bank is a conventional concrete-framed office building, it achieves some character from the projecting entry canopy, the glass-block external wall to the staircase, the expressed external round red columns on the front façade, plus the continuous projecting panels over the bands of horizontal windows to the various floors.

After the death of Queen Sālote in 1965, the Tongan people determined on the building of the Queen Sālote Memorial Hall, to be funded by her subjects both in Tonga and overseas. The funds proved inadequate, and the project was later financed by the Tongan Government and the Republic of China. Constructed on

ABOVE: Queen Sālote Memorial Hall, Nuku'alofa, 1996. Jaimi Associates. Ceiling Detail.
RIGHT: Entrance.

the edge of the main downtown area and completed in 1996, the Queen Sālote Memorial Hall is one of the chief landmarks of Nuku'alofa. The hall is mostly used for large audiences and for special functions, but it also serves as the venue for the opening of parliament by the king. The building form comes from the play of the geometry of three arched volumes. The main hall, which seats 4000, is fronted by the lower roof of the entry hall, with the composition balanced by the third volume to the rear, located along the cross axis to the halls. The projecting rectilinear entry porch provides a satisfactory counterpoint to the form of the rest of the composition. The lines of the main building were generated by the curved laminated roof beams from New Zealand and emphasized by other lighter roof timbers that create geometric patterns in the interior. The Fatai Royal Residence, which occupies a prominent position on the seafront on Vuna Road, was originally constructed in 1953 and extended in 1959. The 1996 redesign by Jaimi Associates is a balanced composition consisting of two bungalows with generous verandas linked by a connecting wing across the front, defining a large courtyard to the rear. Marking the entry is the pyramidal roof of the centrally located, freestanding porte-cochère.

Further International Investment

The conspicuous presence in central Nuku'alofa of the Embassy and Residence of the People's Republic of China is indicative of the growing interest of Asian nations in Tonga and the South Pacific generally. The Embassy, by Swan Railley Clapham and Associates, is a two-building complex within a large compound. The original concept was by the project architect Leveni 'Aho, and initially the building was constructed for the Republic of China, but before it was completed in November 1998 it was handed over to the People's Republic of China subsequent to Tonga's

Fatai Royal Residence, Nuku'alofa, 1996.
Jaimi Associates.

OPPOSITE: Tonga National Cultural Centre,
Nuku'alofa, 1998. Japanese Government.

Embassy and Residence of the People's Republic
of China, Nuku'alofa, 1998. Swan Railley
Clapham and Associates.

recognition of that country.[33] The embassy combines modern and traditional elements, with evident Chinese influence in the choice of the white walls and grey slate roof tiles, the roof form, and the treatment and assembly of the principal timbers. Asian countries have contributed widely to the increased number of buildings in Tongatapu, and such international partners substantially influence the body politic as well as the built environment. Besides the Queen Sālote Memorial Hall, Asian-aided projects include the large complex of individual structures that make up the 1988 Tonga National Cultural Centre, which was financed by Japan and built by Japanese workmen, and the Talamahu Market, 1995, funded by the government and the Asian Development Bank (ADB).[34] The Chinese Government also provided funds for the new high school and also assisted with the planning and reconstruction of the central business district following the riots of 2006.[35] In addition, the ADB has joined AusAID to assist in establishing a new urban planning unit in Tonga.[36]

The Ministry of Health Building, 2004, by James Cubitt Architects, Brisbane, also was an AusAID project constructed adjacent to Vaiola Hospital on the outskirts of Nuku'alofa.[37] The building was designed for passive climatic control and to be capable of being built by local contractors using local labour.[38] The ministry is of two storeys: public matters are dealt with on the lower floor, which is constructed of locally made concrete blocks, while the upper floor is restricted to senior ministry staff and is constructed of corrugated sheet metal, visually differentiating the two functions. Large overhangs provide shade around the building with external sunscreens to the lower level for additional control of sun penetration. The same principles had previously been employed for Cubitt's Laboratory Building, Laucala Campus (USP), Suva, 1997.[39]

While there has been considerable rebuilding since the 1977 earthquake, Nuku'alofa remains a casual, relatively low-rise town spreading out along the north coast of Tongatapu, and apart from the banks and government buildings, the architecture retains an informal character. Little disturbed the town's peace until the uprising of the 2006 Pro-Democracy Movement when a substantial amount of the downtown was burned.[40] With legislative changes facilitating a shift towards a more inclusive democratic structure, Tonga's political status is more stable. However, the decreasing population, and the kingdom's reliance on outside funding, pose an unpredictable future for Tonga and its architecture.

Kings and Clerics

The history of the Protestant Church in Tonga has been determined by the relations between the Tongan Royal Family and the powerful Wesleyan Church, while the dedication of a long line of French Marist priests has ensured the continuing presence of the Catholic minority. The first missionaries to arrive in the islands were members of the London Missionary Society, who landed in 1797, but withdrew shortly thereafter as they received a hostile reception. A further group of Wesleyan missionaries arrived in 1822 but they too failed.[1] Subsequently, in 1826 two further Wesleyan missionaries were sent from Tahiti and were followed by others in 1828. They stayed, and the church became the most powerful religious body in Tonga, claiming 40 per cent of the population. The first Roman Catholic priest to serve in Tonga took up his mission in 1842. By then, the Wesleyans had converted much of the population, and today there is a small but significant Catholic congregation.[2]

The Church of Jesus Christ of Latter-Day Saints (Mormons) and the Seventh-Day Adventist Church were well established in Tonga before World War II. The first Mormon missionaries came to Tonga from Samoa in 1891 but withdrew in 1897 after only six people joined the Church. In 1907 they returned and stayed.[3] The Mormon church now claims 16.8 per cent of the Tongan population, maintaining Tonga as the country with the highest percentage of Mormons in the world.[4] The Mormon chapels and those of the Seventh-Day Adventists are generally conservative and based on standard designs. The large complex of the 1983 Temple of Liahona outside Nuku'alofa, is of conventional design that conforms to the established form and layout typical of other Pacific temples by the American architect Emil B Fetzer.

The Wesleyan Churches

Most of the Protestant denominations of Tonga are offshoots of the Wesleyan Mission. King George Tupou I had a disagreement with the Australian Wesleyan Mission and with the rebel Wesleyan missionary Reverend Shirley Baker, led the founding in 1885 of the breakaway church, the Free Church of Tonga.[5] In 1924 Queen Sālote Tupou III brought the Wesleyan and the Free Church together, founding the Free Wesleyan Church of Tonga, with 30000 adherents. It remains the official church of the royal family. Not all were in agreement with the amalgamation, and a number of the congregation remained independent, hence the Wesleyan Church of Tonga and the Free Church of Tonga both continue to have followers. Despite Baker's expulsion from the kingdom in 1890, he returned to the Ha'apai Islands in 1898, built a small house there and somewhat unlawfully founded the Anglican Church.[6] The present Anglican Church in Nuku'alofa, which resembles an English village church, was built in 1929–30 and has no connection with Baker, who died in 1903 at Ha'apai.[7]

The Church Fale

As in much of the South Pacific, architects rarely have been involved in the design of any but the most important religious buildings, and most churches, even major edifices, have been principally built by volunteer labour. Unlike most Christian churches of the Pacific, which did not adapt the vernacular forms to church buildings, the Protestant denominations of Tonga turned to the fale form as an appropriate precedent to house the Christian service. The church fale usually is raised and enclosed with glass doors that can be opened for ventilation, ease of access and to allow for large congregations to gather outside on the surrounding verandas. The first Wesleyan church in Nuku'alofa was a fale known as Zion with a shingle roof and the addition of a bell tower, which may have been initiated by Baker in 1871.[8] Influential on further church projects has been the fale form of the Sia'atoutai Theological College Chapel, c. 1910, which provides a convincing example of the satisfactory blending of Christianity and regional practice.[9] The building originally may have been the chapel for Tupou College, which stood

Sia'atoutai Chapel, Sia'atoutai, Tongatapu, Tonga, c. 1910.

Moulton Memorial Chapel, Tupou College, Tongatapu, 1986. Lloyd Evans and George Moala.

Free Wesleyan Church, Pelehake, Tongatapu, 1989. George Moala.

adjacent to the site later occupied by the Free Wesleyan Centenary Church. In 1948 Tupou College moved to another location, and in 1950 the Reverend Rodger Page visited Tonga from Sydney to supervise the moving of an old fale church that was on the Centenary Chapel site, so that the new church could be built.[10] In the same design family, but on a much larger scale, is the Moulton Memorial Chapel of Tupou College, 1986, by Lloyd Evans of Pacific Architects with George Moala.[11] This impressive fale combines traditional Tongan construction with New Zealand timber technology and accommodates more than 1000 people seated on the floor. The roof of the oval-shaped chapel was built primarily from laminated Douglas fir arches splayed on an angle of 16 degrees to form a diamond pattern. 'The arches are 437 mm by 188 mm and support the 51.6-metre-long by 20.4-metre-wide building and contribute to its lateral stability, providing an interesting alternative to the standard arch configuration.'[12] All work was undertaken by local craftsmen with the binding of the structural lashings being executed by the college students. The workers were trained by Tamari, a chief from Niutoua, notably for the intricate task of attaching the *pule'oto* (cowry) shells to the roof timbers in decorative patterns, which give a rich and shimmering quality to the ceiling (see p. 194).[13]

Directly inspired by the Sia'atoutai Theological College Chapel is the eclectic Free Wesleyan Church at Pelehake, by Moala, completed in 1989. The church plan breaks from the conventional solution of an attached flat-roofed veranda surrounding the fale. Rather, the walls are set back from the perimeter, thus providing exterior space under the fale roof. The church adheres to traditional building practices, including binding instead of nailing, but in this instance combines circular painted steel beams with fine timbers obtained from Samoa. The striking geometric patterns of the coconut fibre bindings of this church, designed and executed by the minister and members of the congregation, are particularly distinctive and of fine quality. Balancing the oval plan and horizontal lines of the church building is the arresting verticality of a nearby rocket-shaped bell and water tower.

The fale form has given Tonga many of its distinctive churches in the villages. Representative of these is the Free Wesleyan Church at Kolovai, 1976, which stands on the site of the 1869 church, built to celebrate the nearby landing of the early missionary John Thomas.[14] The fine structure of the large roof is graphically expressed in the ceiling as a series of dark ribs radiating out from the central ridgeline and patterned against the white ceiling. Typically, the interior is bright

LEFT: Church of Jesus Christ of Latter-Day Saints Temple, Liahona, Tongatapu, 1983. Emil B Fetzer.

BELOW: Free Wesleyan Church, Pelehake, Tongatapu, 1989. George Moala. Detail of Bindings.
BOTTOM: Interior.

Free Wesleyan Church, Sangato, Tongatapu.

Free Wesleyan Church, Ha'ateiho, Tongatapu. Architect: Tavi.

Free Wesleyan Church, Kolavai, Tongatapu, 1976.

with a band of clerestory windows and operable glass doors on all sides of the periphery leading to an encompassing porch.

Tongan villages abound with imaginative, often brightly painted churches, such as the fine red-and-white clapboard Free Church of Tonga at Lavengatonga and the brightly striped 'rainbow' doorway of the Free Wesleyan Church at Sangato. Unique is the Free Church of Tonga at Ha'ateiho, by Tavi from Denmark. The first introduction to the church is the remarkable porch with coloured-glass walls, capped by a three-tier stepped roof. The ambience engendered in the porch is carried into the nave where, again, the walls are liberally filled with coloured glass, which gives off a soft glowing light creating a mystical atmosphere.

The City Churches

The central Nuku'alofa edifices of the Free Wesleyan Centenary Church (the Centenary Chapel), 1952, and the Centennial Church of the Free Church of Tonga, 1985, are of quite a different ilk – both being heavy masonry buildings. The Centenary Chapel, a large church with a seating capacity of 2000, has been described as 'the product of royal piety and high post-war copra prices'.[15] The church is of brick construction with a wide central portico, a nave opening up with glass doors to each side, and one offset western tower with a low-pitched roof. The architect was W C Brown from Sydney working with a local foreman, Amini Fonua. Many materials were donated by church members and, apart from some specialized tradesmen, the church was built by voluntary labour over a period of two years.[16] The Centennial Church of the Free Church of Tonga, by Keio Thompson, stands facing the royal tombs. The church commemorates the centenary of the founding of the Free Church of Tonga. It is an imposing concrete and coral stone neo-Gothic building with flying buttresses over the side aisles. The church has three red-roofed spires rising from the towers that flank the southern entry and one over the crossing. The large circular window in the southern façade, with a contemporary design of triangular blue, green and purple glass panels, is exceptional for Tonga.

The Catholic Churches

The buildings of the Catholic Church in Tonga – with one major exception, the Basilica of St Anthony of Padua – adhere to established form and iconography. Typical is the traditional stone Church of St Michael's at Lapaha.[17] Built in 1894, the Lapaha church has a wide western tower fronting across the nave of the church, and the church

FAR LEFT: Church of the Sacred Heart of Jesus, Houma, Tongatapu, 1939–40. Father George Callet.
LEFT: Pilaster Detail.

BELOW: Church of St Michael's, Lapaha, Tongatapu, 1894.

walls are heavily buttressed to increase its earthquake resistance. This church is the oldest surviving Roman Catholic stone church on Tongatapu. It was damaged by the earthquake of 1977 but has since been repaired. The 1992 Cathedral of the Immaculate Conception of Mary stands on Vuna Road. The first Catholic cathedral was a wooden fale on the site, which was destroyed by hurricane in 1877.[18] A new cathedral was built using coral stone hewn from the reef at low tide and floated to the shore on the incoming tide. That cathedral was blessed in 1877 and stood until rendered unsafe by the 1977 earthquake. The new 1992 building now standing on the site is a twin-tower cathedral, ostensibly a reconstruction of the earlier building, but evidences considerable differences, notably in the massing and unconventional proportions. Stones from the old building were used in the reconstruction by being split and treated as a veneer on the new walls.[19] The idiosyncratic cathedral, with a disproportionate relationship of height to width and length, creates the impression that the building is sinking into the ground. This strange lowering of the proportional height of the church and the towers suggests a possible shortage of appropriate material. The high intersecting roof forms of the nave and transepts are constructed of elegant steel beams tied with fine sloping cross members, finished to allow light to penetrate along the ridge. The ceiling is lined with honey-coloured boarding that gives the interior a warm reflected light. The roof makes an evident reference to local fale forms, successfully presenting a subtle hybrid of two building traditions.

Father George Callet

The strength of the tie to European precedence is demonstrated to an extraordinary degree by the concrete Church of the Sacred Heart of Jesus at

FAR LEFT: Free Wesleyan Centenary Church, Nuku'alofa, 1952. W C Brown.

LEFT: Centennial Church of the Free Church of Tonga, Nuku'alofa, 1985. Keio Thompson.

BELOW: Cathedral of the Immaculate Conception of Mary, Nuku'alofa, 1992. John Rounds Lee and Partners and Lee and Associates.

PALŌKIA SANGATO SOSEFO
KO E
TANGATA NGĀUE

ABOVE: Church of St Joseph the Worker, Neiafu, 1962, Father George Callet and Father Lionel Roy, (original church 1935. Father Albert Kerrmann).

OPPOSITE: Church of St Joseph the Worker, Neiafu, Vava'u, 1932. Father Albert Kerrmann, (Façade and towers restored1962, Father George Callet and Father Lionel Roy).

Houma, built between 1939 and 1940 by a remarkable figure, Father George Callet.[20] An intrepid French missionary, Father Callet was born in Lyon in 1909 and took up his post in Tonga in 1937, where he continued to work until his death in 1995. Callet, who had no formal training in design or construction, became a dedicated builder of churches, presbyteries and missions. It appears he had an innate ability to work with people and engender communal pride. None of the building was carried out by paid construction workers, 'in every case it was Father Callet empowering the people.'[21] This makes even more extraordinary the building of the church at Houma, complete with concrete pilasters, with formed capitals in the Ionic order. It is difficult to determine how this unlikely construction was realized, but it is possible that a master craftsman carved the moulds for the capitals from timber.

Among Callet's many building efforts, two particular interventions are of primary significance. The first was his role in the rebuilding of the Church of St Joseph the Worker, Neiafu, and second, his contribution to the building of the Basilica of St Anthony of Padua, Nuku'alofa. Standing high and overlooking the Port of Refuge, the Church of St Joseph is a fine example of Catholic colonial architecture. The building is very well sited and is approached by a commanding set of broad stairs. The splendid white façade steps up and culminates in the high central clock tower, which, with its dominant form, serves as a landmark from the sea. The original church, by Monsignor Albert Kerrmann, was built in 1932, consecrated by the French Bishop Blanc in 1946[22] and enlarged between 1940 and 1949.[23] The priest at the time of its extension was Monsignor Ke ekolio Kailao, who was stationed at Neiafu between 1940 and 1958.[24] The façade and its tower are the only part of the original building that remains, the rest having been destroyed by the 1961 hurricane that blew the roof into the harbour. In 1962 Callet and Father Lionel Roy, a priest who arrived in Tonga from Canada in 1946, were sent to rebuild the cathedral.[25] While Callet is commonly credited with the new design, Roy, who had studied building engineering and was a competent quantity surveyor, draftsman and builder, presumably would have assumed responsibility for the more practical aspects of building. The new nave, of concrete construction, is an impressive achievement with its height, light colours and abundance of natural light.

In the 1970s Callet was serving in Nuku'alofa and was the initiator and driving force behind the building of the remarkable Basilica of St Anthony of Padua. 'A church of the age of remittances and low copra prices', it was consecrated in 1980 by the bishop of Tonga in the presence of King Tupou IV.[26] While architectural accreditation is given to Basilino Hafoka, a Tongan-born architect living and working in New Zealand, Callet, named on the foundation stone as parish priest and building supervisor, is commonly acknowledged as the source of the ideas and construction ingenuity.[27] 'The building was scheduled to commence on 9 May 1977 and in order to prepare the property twenty young workers were asked to come on Anzac Day, 25 April. More than 400 workers arrived – men, women and youths, bringing with them food and flower necklaces. Not only was the ground cleared but a good part of the foundations were dug that day.'[28]

The basilica, which is raised over office space and public rooms, such as a meeting hall and the library, is approached by two imposing stairs that lead to the projecting porch with gently arced rafters supporting the white corrugated-steel roof sheets. The rising movement established in the stairway and porch roof continues in the principal roof over the body of the church, which also curves up to the central cone that caps the building. The interior is lit with a red glow through the cupola and from the dormer windows around the circumference of the rotunda. The impressive space, defined by the radiating timbers of the roof, culminates 30.5 metres above the pavement. The building, with an interior diameter of 36.5 metres, is of concrete

CENTRE: Basilica of St Anthony of Padua, Nuku'alofa, 1980. Basilino Hafoka and Father George Callet. West Elevation.
TOP RIGHT: Glazed Apex of Spire. OPPOSITE: Elevated Entrance Porch.

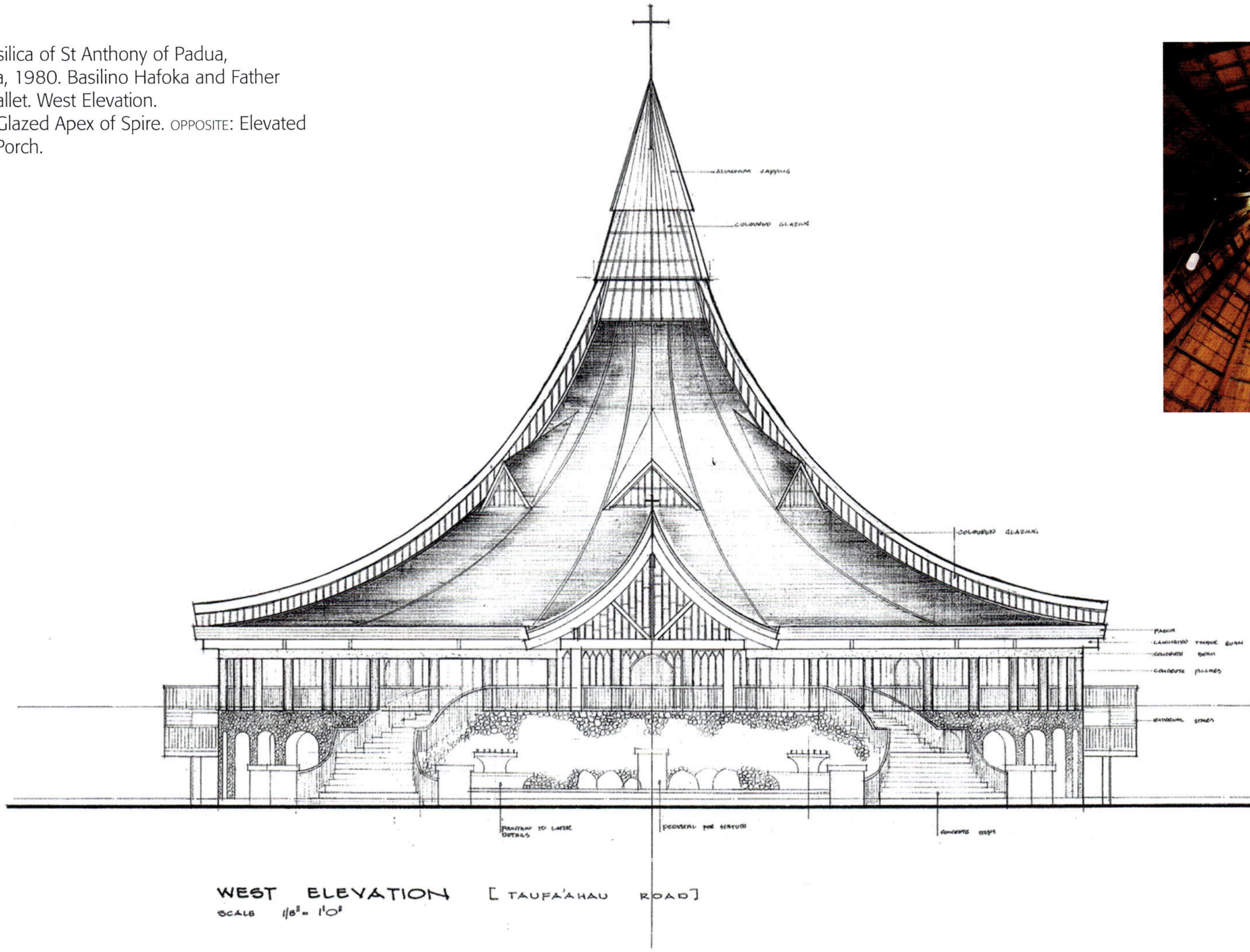

construction and the roof, formed by large curved laminated beams from New Zealand, was erected without cranes. Again, voluntary help from the congregation made the work possible. The greatest challenge faced was the problem of how to lift the large beams into position in the roof without a crane. The tools deployed were manpower, two old winches and two Casuarina trees lifted to prop the beams into position and hold them while they were fixed into place. These trees were later carved to make the lectern and statues for the church.[29] The basilica is also rich with mats, notably the coconut sennit mats that cover the roof joints, hangings and bindings, all produced by the local women. Outstanding are the women's design and craftsmanship in the encrusted shell patterns on the beams of the library and conference rooms. With its centralized plan, accentuated by its curved lines and the upward sweep of its space, the basilica severs ties with the conventional past.

Tonga's churches include the colourful buildings in the villages, the impressive Moulton Memorial Chapel of Tupou College and the remarkable accomplishments of Father George Callet, who notably contributed to the Church of St Joseph the Worker at Neiafu, with arguably the most beautiful façade in the South Pacific, and to the Basilica of St Anthony of Padua, the creation of which is one of the most original achievements of the architecture of the South Pacific.

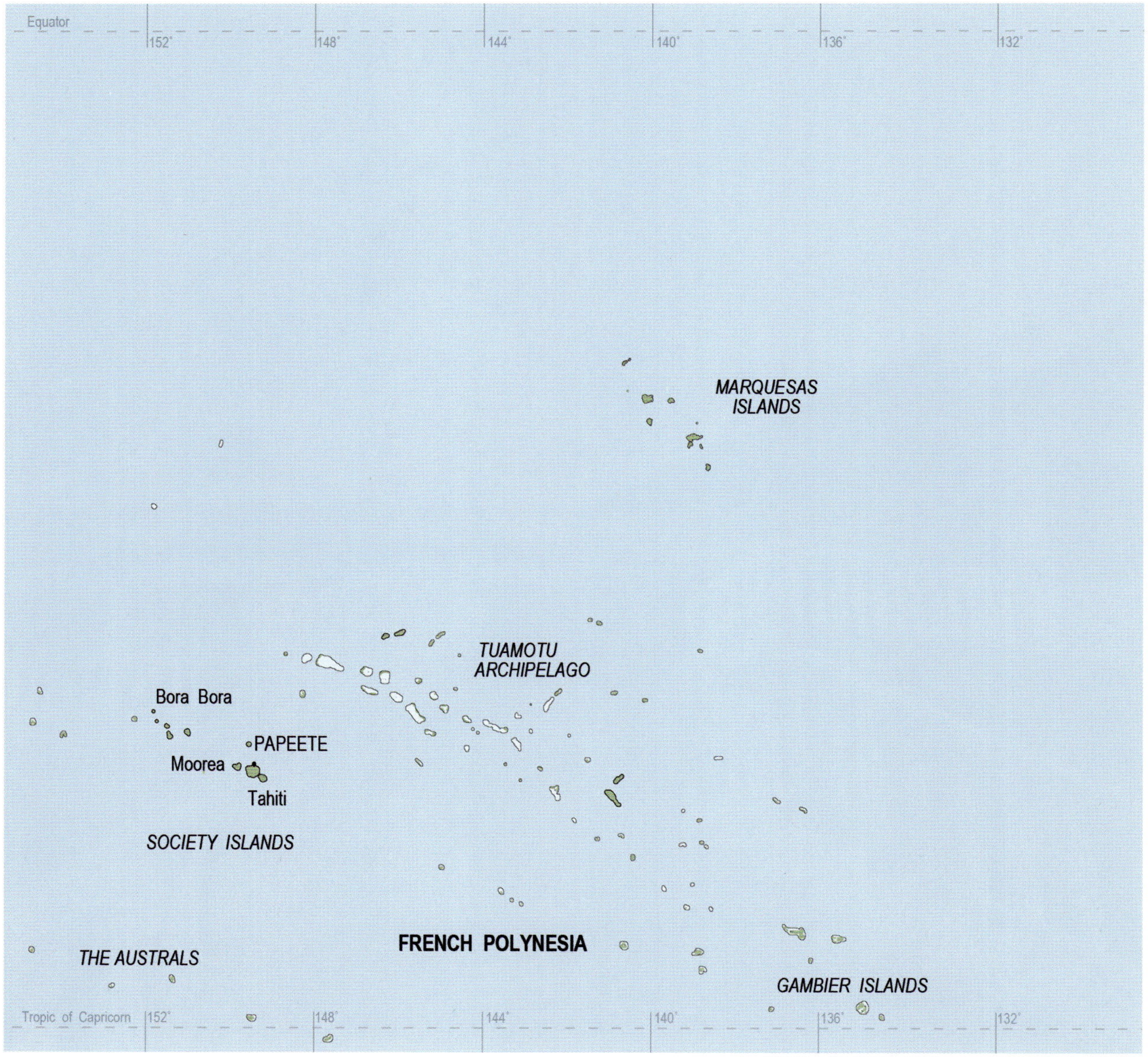
Equator
152°
148°
144°
140°
136°
132°
MARQUESAS ISLANDS
TUAMOTU ARCHIPELAGO
Bora Bora
PAPEETE
Moorea
Tahiti
SOCIETY ISLANDS
FRENCH POLYNESIA
THE AUSTRALS
GAMBIER ISLANDS
Tropic of Capricorn
152°
148°
144°
140°
136°
132°

FRENCH POLYNESIA TO THE EAST

French Polynesia, with its 118 small dispersed islands, is distant from any large landmass, being central to the immense waters of the South Pacific. Due to the vast distances, the first settlement in east Polynesia was not until around 1025 AD, when migrant groups, sailing from Samoa in huge double-hulled travelling canoes crossed the 3000 kilometres of open ocean and initiated the rapid spread of eastern Polynesian colonization.[1] Beginning in the late eighteenth century, Tahiti became a main port of call for European travellers, as word had spread subsequent to the reports of the French navigator Louis de Bougainville and James Cook as to its abundance. Tahiti, ruled by Queen Pomare Vahine IV from 1827 to 1877, came under the influence of the London Missionary Society and the British Government, before France established Tahiti as its own protectorate in 1847 following the Tahitian-French war.[2] French authority was not easily accepted over the Leeward Islands, and at the end of the nineteenth century, fortifications were built around Papeete in the struggle to preserve the small village.[3] In 1880 Tahiti became a colony, and France annexed four island groups and created the establishment Français de l'Océanie (EPO), a name which it held until it was changed to French Polynesia in 1957. French-appointed governors administered the colony during this time.

The shelling of Papeete by German warships in 1914 led 1000 volunteers to serve in World War I, and during World War II the colony declared its support for the Free French. In 1946 in recognition of services rendered in the war, the colony was granted the status of an overseas territory and was provided with an elected territorial assembly and two seats in the French Parliament. In 1958 a referendum was held, with the people voting for a continued French alliance.[4] In 2003 the status of French Polynesia was changed to an overseas collectivity of France (*collectivités d'outre-mer* or COM).

TAHITI: THE POLYNESIAN MYTH

9

Eden: After Eden

'Yet the myth still endures today, expressing not what is the South Pacific but what people in other parts of the world wish it to be. Like Cook, Banks and Bougainville, most of us carry our own Pacific Islands with us.' Steven Roger Fischer

The vision of the South Pacific as an idyllic setting, as described in the colourful reports of Bougainville who arrived in Tahiti in 1768, has endured through to the present time.[1] From that early European visit the seeds of the perception of Polynesia as a utopia were sown. The image of Tahiti as an Eden continued to flourish, becoming more and more legendary as the centuries passed. Today, Eden may be lost but the myth remains and paradise returns in the 'hyper-real' gated communities of the large resorts. While Polynesia covers a vast number of far-flung islands, it is French Polynesia (notably the islands of Tahiti, Moorea and Bora Bora) that continues to hold the strongest romantic appeal. No other Pacific islands carry the same sense of the exotic, and French Polynesia's great physical beauty continues to sustain the myth of the Garden of Eden.

The Paradise Myth

The stories of the eighteenth-century explorers told of the self-sustaining islands, inhabited by handsome brown youths and voluptuous welcoming females living and loving in thatched fares, dancing to drums, swimming in sparkling blue seas, and eating the plentiful fruit and fish. Bougainville described seductive 'Venus-like women' with 'the celestial forms of that goddess', while the more reserved Cook wrote in his diary that he was 'shocked by indecent dancing and lewd singing of the women'.[2] French Polynesia's appeal also lay in its remoteness – a distant place promising relaxation and escape, and more accessible seashores as compared to some other South Pacific

ABOVE: Aerial view of Bora Bora Island, French Polynesia. *Courtesy of Getty Images. Photograph by Chad Ehlers.*

PREVIOUS PAGE: Maeva Beach Hotel.

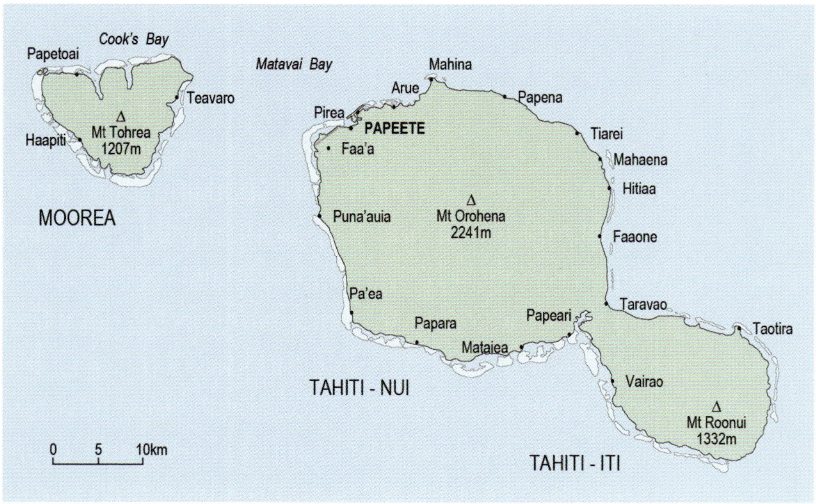

islands.[3] Its dramatic scenery – the most spectacular to be found in the Pacific and some of the most enthralling in the world – provides a setting for an attainable dreamland and promises a fantasy life of delight. Such readings of the South Pacific attracted writers and painters. Artists came: the French painters, Paul Gauguin, who lived there from 1891 to 1893, and Henri Matisse, who visited Papeete in the 1930s. The paintings celebrated the beauty, notably of women, and gave further credence to the tales of the seductive primitivism of Tahiti. The male was admired as an enviable figure of innate nobility, free of the influences of civilization. The writers came: the English soldier-poet Rupert Brooke visited Tahiti in 1913 'to hunt for lost Gauguins' and the English playwright and novelist Somerset Maugham arrived in 1916.[4] Further word of Tahiti reached the western world in 1935 with the release of the early film *Mutiny on the Bounty* with Clark Gable as Christian and Charles Laughton as Bligh.[5] The epic was followed in 1937 by the first version of *Hurricane*, starring the glamorous Dorothy Lamour.[6] So the stage of Shangri-La had been set early in the century.

le Rêve – The Daydream

But World War II and the subsequent increased contact with the outside world brought changes to the islands that rapidly eroded the fabled Polynesian way of

THIS PAGE: Robinson House, Paea, Tahiti, 1934. William Robinson.

FAR LEFT: Hotel Stuart, Papeete, Tahiti, 1923. *Courtesy of Jean-Louis Saquet*.

TOP CENTRE: Hôtel de France, Papeete, Tahiti, 1905. *Courtesy of the French Polynesia Archives.*

TOP RIGHT: Hotel Young (Blue Lagoon), Papeete, Tahiti, 1930. *Courtesy of Jean-Louis Saquet.*

LEFT: Tiare Hotel, Papeete, Tahiti, 1905. *Courtesy of the French Polynesia Archives.*

life. To a marked extent, the reality became not a self-sustaining community but a country dependent on French support. While Papeete stands on a fine harbour, it grew into a city far from a vernacular utopia, and the roads on major islands, especially Tahiti, became highways of moving vehicles. Rather than picking fresh fruit from the tree and taking fish from the sea, imported canned food stands on the shelves of the supermarkets. The missionaries covered the sensuous female body, and while French Polynesia is less sexually restrictive than the neighbouring mid-Pacific countries, with 54 per cent of the islanders being strict Protestants, free love is far from the norm. The French testing of nuclear explosives from 1966 onwards destroyed forever the innocence of the islands.

Today, the major source of income for the French Polynesian economy is tourism. Even the tourist office refers to the cliché of Tahitian life: 'Live under an eternal sun, the feet in the water – *le rêve* ['the daydream – the illusion']'.[7] The tourists come for the idyllic once-in-a-lifetime experience promised in the myth and the tourist brochure, so, the myth has to be sustained to keep the islands viable. Thus the tourist industry is dependent on not only the provision of accommodation but also on the recreation of the lost Eden. To do this, it needs investors and developers, and designers and builders. Until recently, most of the investors were from overseas, and therefore much revenue left the island, however, the tourist industry not only brings in capital but also, directly and indirectly, provides work for a high proportion of islanders – both in the building and service industries. At the same time an increase in tourism, as found elsewhere, can create its own problems of overuse, pollution and visual degradation.

Passage to Paradise

Sailing to Paradise

The period before 1950, when transportation to Tahiti by air was not readily available, was the era of the passenger liners bringing travellers primarily from America and Europe – notably the wealthy, writers, playboys and second sons of European gentry.[8] While the name Tahiti conjured up visions of adventure in the South Seas, for most paradise was a little bit of America or Europe amidst

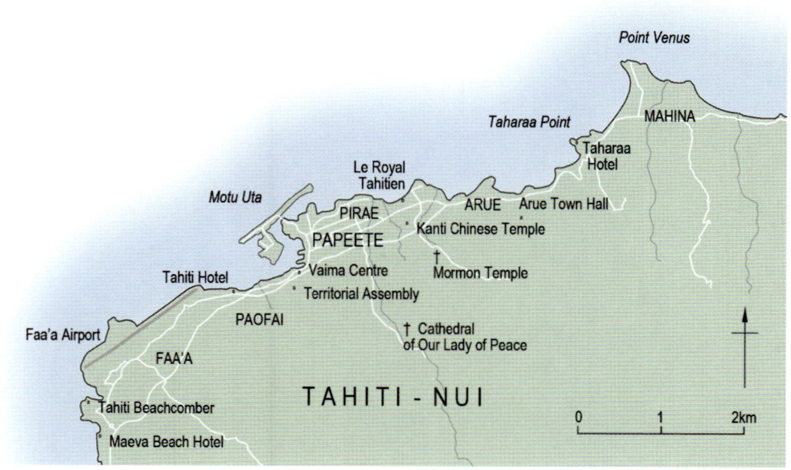

ABOVE: Map of Papeete and Adjacent Development, Tahiti, French Polynesia.

LEFT: Tiki Figures.

the foreign exotica in this isolated spot. A small handful of travellers were looking for an alternate way of life, and a few of these made Tahiti their home. Notable among them was the American philanthropist William Albert Robinson, a naval architect who, in 1929, stopped for eight months in Tahiti during his voyage around the world on a ten-tonne ketch, *The Svaap*. On his return to Tahiti in 1934, he built a house at Paea that combines a Western understanding of design with a notable sensitivity to the Tahitian milieu.[9] Robinson built the house himself with help from four local villagers, and he sourced the wood for the main posts – Tamanu wood (*Calophyllum inophyllum)* – from the nearby hillside. It was built on a 31-hectare old coconut plantation next to a lagoon, 32 kilometres out of Papeete.[10] The house consists of a wide central fare with a handsome thatched roof supported by an elegant black minimal frame and linked by open walkways through lush gardens with ponds to smaller special-use fares. Like the vernacular fare, the sides of the house are not enclosed, rather, they are shielded by light woven screening and colourful tropical planting. Rattan furniture, and wall and floor mats contribute to the alluring ambience. Robinson's close understanding and appreciation of the rich possibilities inherent in local ways of living in Tahiti have imbued this house with a lasting beauty and a sense of belonging.

The most famous of the hotels of the South Pacific in the early twentieth century were the 1860 Royal Hotel in Levuka, Fiji, Noumea's 1905 Hôtel de la Gare, the 1914 Grand Pacific Hotel in Suva and the Casino Hotel in Apia, also of 1914. In this period travellers to the islands were mostly accommodated in private homes, modest guesthouses and small hotels, such as Papeete's 1905 hotels, the Tiare Hotel and the Hôtel de France. Later were the Hotel Tahiti on rue Jeanne d'Arc and the Te Puna Bel Air at Puna'auia, with forty-eight modern motel-style rooms and twenty-eight thatched bungalows, that was one of the few owned and operated by a Tahitian family.[11] The Tiare[12] attained some fame when Somerset Maugham stayed there after he arrived in Tahiti in 1916 and wrote his novel on the life of Paul Gauguin, *The Moon and Sixpence.* The hotel, which was run by 'a buxom woman, Lovaina Chapman', was 'a picturesque bungalow with a surrounding veranda, in a garden abundant with flowers'.[13] In contrast, the Hôtel de France was a two-storeyed building with a veranda across the upper level, standing on rue de Rivoli, a main street of the town.[14]

In French Polynesia tourism initially was concentrated on the island of Tahiti. The first of the noted hotels was the Hotel Stuart, built opposite the seafront in 1923, and it remained the leading hotel of French Polynesia up to the 1960s. The Hotel Stuart was built by Virginie Ernestine Pignon and her husband David Arthur

Stuart, initially to house an American film crew, and it was written that it had 'an air of tropical refinement with covered balconies and a columnar façade.[15] The hotel consisted of four floors of masonry construction with cement balusters, the moulds for which had been ordered from America. The Hotel Stuart attracted notoriety in the 1930s when Matisse lived there for three months in Room 14 and upset the landlord by using his wife as a model for a painting he did on one of the windows.[16] The hotel was demolished and re-interpreted in 1984 by Rodolphe Weinmann, who designed a six-floor version of the hotel for the Bank of Polynesia.[17]

The Hotel Young (later The Blue Lagoon) and the Chez Rivnac were built and owned by Milos Rivnac, a Czechoslovakian who arrived in Tahiti in 1926 at the age of forty-one.[18] The Hotel Young, which was constructed on the outskirts of Papeete at Taunoa, consisted of wooden buildings, partly of two floors, supported on planks on wooden piers. 'The accommodation is provided in bungalows with running water, which for the most part were built half on dry land and the other half over the water on pylons'.[19] It offered a lesser standard of accommodation to that of the Hotel Stuart but was described as being 'well situated and of modern comfortable design'.[20] Tahiti has a shortage of flat land as the mountains commonly rise straight out of the sea, and there is some precedence for 'overwater' living on the northern islands where the homes of fishermen often are built over the lagoon. Chez Rivnac was on a far more remote site at Fisherman's Point in the vicinity of Puna'auia on the west coast of Tahiti. The hotel sought to give the tourist an 'authentic' Tahitian experience and offered beachside fares resembling those of the local people.[21] Rivnac married a Tahitian woman, Terière Gooding, who ran the hotels, and the original features and local influence evident in these establishments might well be due to her input. The Hotel Aimeo, built at Cook's Bay on the island of Moorea in the 1930s is the oldest continuously running hotel in French Polynesia. The Aimeo, with a two-storeyed building of twenty rooms, plus a restaurant and five bungalows standing over the water, was built by Mrs Winklestroeter and was taken over by the 'Bali Hai Boys' in 1982.[22]

Flying to Paradise: The First Airline Era

World War II and the opening up of air travel heralded a new era for French Polynesia. The arrival of the American soldiers in 1942 for Operation Bobcat and the building of the Bora Bora 2000-metre airstrip brought about significant shifts in the history of the islands. Although the Americans were only on Bora Bora for a very short time (the base was closed in 1946), the life of the islands was influenced by their presence.[23] Yet Operation Bobcat remains only physically evident in the airstrip, Farepiti wharf and some surviving coastal defence guns. Due

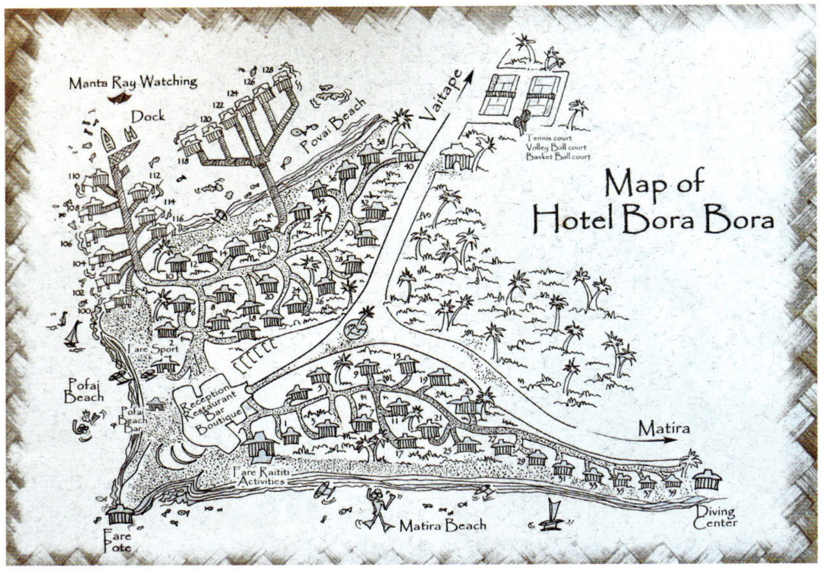

to the very mountainous terrain of Bora Bora, the airstrip was located on an islet (or motu) of the coral strip that encircles the island, forming its lagoon. The Bora Bora airstrip allowed mail to be delivered by air, and passenger travel commenced with the first Paris–Tahiti flights in 1950. The national airline, Air Tahiti, commenced services in 1950, but before the building of the airport at Faa'a in 1961, tourist traffic to Tahiti continued to be almost exclusively transported by passenger liners, with fifty-five ships stopping in Papeete in 1958. As the visitors on the ships were accommodated on board, there was little call for hotels.

The Period of American Investment 1960 – Early 1970s

Bora Bora means 'first born'. Americans called the island 'The Pearl of the Pacific', and reports on the beauty of the islands and the people taken back to America by the troops brought further fame. Among these military personnel was author James A Michener, who wrote *Tales of the South Pacific* in the New Hebrides; however, on visiting Moorea he said that the scene was exactly as he had in mind when he 'invented' Bali Hai. Later, on seeing Bora Bora he described it as 'the Bali Hai of the spirit', saying, 'there can be no other island more perfect than this.'[24]

Of much importance to the growth of tourism was the cult of the Pacific that flowered as the 'Tiki' fashion in the 1950s and 1960s, notably in America.[25] The Tiki craze introduced Pacific designs, patterns, materials, motifs, food and drinks

OPPOSITE: Hotel Bora Bora, Bora Bora. 1961. Wimberly and Cook. *Brochure: Courtesy of Hotel Bora Bora.*
FAR LEFT: Aerial showing Povai Beach Overwater Bungalows. *Courtesy of Getty Images. Photograph by Holger Leue.*
LEFT: Overwater Bungalows with Mt Otemanu in background. *Courtesy of Getty Images. Photograph by Jean-Bernard Carillet.*

for a wide range of goods from milk jugs to restaurants.[26] While Hawaii, which had become the fiftieth state in 1959, was the most readily available source for Polynesian motifs and materials, the widespread promotion and popularity of Pacific design boosted the perception of other Pacific islands as desirable locations. On 1 October 1971 a grand opening was held at Disneyland, California, for The Polynesian, a hotel of 492 rooms by Welton Becket and Associates of Santa Monica. The publicity promised 'a tropical island adventure'. Guests were accommodated in eight longhouses spread out over a sixteen-hectare site facing a sandy beach edging a lagoon. The Tahitian-themed architecture was reinforced by the landscaping, décor, entertainment and food, to provide the Disneyland setting for a 'South Seas vacation'.[27] In addition, with the exception of Hawaii, French Polynesia is the closest of the islands to America and its armed forces had opened up a direct passage through the airstrip at Bora Bora. It was therefore predictable that the initial interest in overseas visitors and investment would come from America.

Hotel Bora Bora

Given the location of the airstrip and the beauty of Bora Bora it is not surprising that the first major hotel of French Polynesia was built there. As the island is remote, even from Tahiti, Bora Bora also had the advantage of sustaining the romantic myth of the Pacific. While the Korolevu Beach Hotel, Fiji, 1948–49, was the first resort in the South Pacific to pioneer first-class accommodation in traditional-styled buildings, the Hotel Bora Bora, 1961, financed with American money, was the first international hotel in the South Pacific to do so. The hotel, designed by Wimberly and Cook (with Prévot as local associate architect), is situated on Point Raititi at the south-west end of the island, where fine beaches edge accessible reefs teeming with colourful fish. The hotel was built by local tradesmen utilizing Polynesian building techniques.[28] In 1961 craftsmen were readily available to build with bamboo, pandanus and coconut using regional means of joining, weaving and binding, and the hotel and subsequent resorts provided the opportunity for training the next generation, thus keeping these traditions and skills alive. Decorative arts are also celebrated in such items as the shell chandeliers, and other resorts followed the Hotel Bora Bora example in displaying many fine local craft works, such as the woven-straw lampshades of the Royal Papeete Hotel and the exceptional shell curtains and chandeliers of the Moorea Beachcomber.

The Hotel Bora Bora consisted of a central building complex on the upper level, with guest fares arranged in lush gardens at the level of the beaches below and six overwater units, complete with floating platforms giving easy access to the water, built along a jetty stretching out from Povai Beach.[29] The hotel was enlarged in 1965 and again in 1968, with nine additional overwater bungalows

TOP: Hotel Bora Bora, 1961. Wimberly and Cook. Aerial showing Povai Beach Overwater Bungalows. *Courtesy of Getty Images. Photograph by Hauke Dressler.*
ABOVE LEFT: Shell Chandelier.

ABOVE RIGHT: Moorea Beachcomber Resort, Moorea. Shell Curtains.

edging Point Raititi, and with a later extension to the restaurant by Jean-Hugues Tricard who in 1973 had founded a practice with his Tahitian architect wife, Rosalie, whom he had met while they were studying at university in Paris.[30] The central complex, dominated by the spectacular view of Mount Otemanu, looked down to the small cove of Povai Beach, with the gazebo Fare Pate on the point. The major spaces were generous and mostly unenclosed, as in the lobby where the simple roof was supported by crossed rafters, while, in the main dining space an upward-branching construction of ribs radiated out from the central post and held the roof. The use of plant materials, rich decorative bindings and island décor contributed to the regional character. The accommodation units that fanned back along Povai Beach to the north-west and along Matira Beach to the south were reached by paths of black volcanic rock that passed through lush vegetation. The fares were of timber construction with thatched roofs and high woven pandanus ceilings. The Hotel Bora Bora intentionally developed the novel overwater concept, taking advantage of the cooling effect and allowing the guests to have a close view of the fish life through glass panels in the floor. The building contractor Gerald Garnier (a Tahitian living in Rarotonga) was responsible for many of the innovative design ideas of the hotel – including the fish-viewing glass floors, as he had noticed that fish gathered in the shade under jetties and piers.[31] Given the low tidal swings of French Polynesian seas and the shortage of flat land on the islands and motus, overwater bungalows were logical in the amenity they offered. The picturesque Hotel Bora Bora retained its aura and was considered the leading hotel of French Polynesia, and ranked among the world's best hotels, until its closure in 2008. It has since been undergoing reconstruction by Aman Resorts.[32]

With the 1961 opening of Faa'a International Airport, Papeete, attention shifted to Tahiti. The only other major hotel built on Bora Bora, until the period of growth at the end of the century, was the Hotel Marara Beach.[33] The Hotel Marara Beach, which followed a similar Polynesian theme, was specifically built in 1978 by film director Dino de Laurentiis to house the actors and film crew for the making of the second version of the film *Hurricane*.[34]

After Faa'a International Airport

The second production of the *Mutiny on the Bounty*, starring Marlon Brando as Christian and Trevor Howard as Bligh, filmed on Tahiti and Moorea in 1961–62, brought further fame and publicity to the islands. An entire village at Mahina was restored for the film set.[35] Tourist facilities were greatly improved with added amenities, such as the new Tourist Bureau by Regaud and Prévot on the waterfront in central Papeete, and the Oliver Bréaud International Golf Course, laid out in

1970 by the American Bob Baldock. The Clubhouse, 1978, by Claude Pottier, is a well-balanced composition of two open/semi-open fares with tall curved shingled roofs opening to a wide terrace and pool.

The first new Tahitian hotel to be built after the Faa'a airport opened was the 1960 colonial-style Hotel Tahiti, with over 100 units and located between Papeete and Faa'a. The forty-room Royal Tahitien Hotel, built east of the city in1962, was the first of the new-generation hotels on the island of Tahiti specifically designed for the American market. It was constructed by owner Mr Wong at Pirae on the north coast, not far from Papeete, on the site of a previous 1940s hotel. The bungalows of the original hotel were demolished by the new owner, but the dining room on the water's edge remained. The two-storey accommodation wings with textured masonry blade walls between units are contemporary in style and face inward towards the central garden. From a raised stone podium, the hotel overlooks a black sand beach that is used by the local people and not readily accessible from the hotel – a divorce of the two worlds. The pool at the Royal Tahitien is discreetly placed adjacent to the accommodation wings. In later hotels, the pool became the central focus of the amenities. As with the early hotels, the Royal Tahitien sought to provide American standards in an enclave from which the local events and scenery could be visited but which offered a return to 'America' and Americans, as desired.

The increased availability of air travel, plus the buoyant economy, together with Governor Sicurani's conscious policy to promote and assist investment in tourist facilities opened the door to the expansion of hotel investments. Air Tahiti was running hydroplane services to the outer islands with regular flights to Moorea, where they opened the large resort of Club Med in 1963 on the north coast of the island. Also on the north coast of Moorea was the 1962 Hotel Bali Hai, built by the American adventurers Hugh Kelley, 'Muk' McCallum and Jay Carlisle (known as the Bali Hai Boys), who designed and developed several sites in French Polynesia over a period of more than twenty years.[36] The Bali Hai Boys had given up their positions in America and went to Polynesia to grow vanilla; however, not long after their arrival, the vanilla market failed. In 1961 they turned their interests to buying the Mateahani Hotel with four rooms and four bungalows, which a Tahitian politician had started to construct, and they extended this as the Hotel Bali Hai.[37] Kelley assumed the role of architect and supervised the construction of ten new bungalows and the renovation of others. The bungalows, which were elevated off the ground with the bathrooms below, were inspired by the nearby 1927 Kellan House, which was raised on posts. The first bungalows were primitive as the developers were inexperienced and short of money, and had to improvise the construction: 'We would take one piece of steel and then put a pipe over it and fill it with cement and put a tie beam in place then build the frame

TOP: Royal Tahitien Hotel, Pirae, Tahiti, 1962.

ABOVE: Oliver Bréaud International Golf Course, Papara, Tahiti, 1978. Claude Pottier.

in timber and use pandanus for the roof and walls.'[38] The primitiveness appealed to American Tiki taste, and with the building design and the form of hosting especially attuned to the American group-tour market, the project was a success. Following the Hotel Bali Hai, they bought and extended two other resorts on the islands of Raiatea and Huahine. In 1967 they introduced six overwater bungalows at Raiatea, and in 1968–69, after ascertaining that they would stand up to local storm conditions, built further overwater bungalows at Moorea Bali Hai.[39] Huahine Bali Hai opened in 1973 with similar bungalows located out over the lagoon and around the pool and beach. When they acquired the 1930s Hotel Aimeo, they extended the existing accommodation and added tennis courts, a pool and a bar, together with further beachfront units, as the Club Bali Hai.

The major airlines followed their previous 1966 investments in the Hôtel Chateau Royal (UTA), New Caledonia, and the Rainmaker InterContinental (Pan Am), American Samoa, with the first major international hotels on the island of Tahiti, which were also the two largest hotels in the Pacific: the Tahara'a Hotel (Pan Am) and Maeva Beach Hotel (UTA).[40] In the same year UTA financed another international hotel, Le Lagon, Vanuatu. The Tahara'a Hotel at Matavai Bay, 1969, was built in a dramatic setting high up on a hillside named One Tree Hill by Cook and overlooks a black sand beach on the north coast.[41] The architects were the now-expanded firm of Wimberly, Whisenand, Allison and Tong again in association with Prévot. The major hall, with its dominant thatched roof built in the form of a Polynesian war canoe, stands behind the pools

Cook's Bay Resort, Moorea, 1985.

OPPOSITE: Maeva Beach Hotel, Faa'a, Tahiti, 1969. Carcoub and Bruner Architects.

Tahara'a Hotel, Matavai Bay, Tahiti, 1969. Wimberly, Whisenand, Allison and Tong.

at the top of the hill. The 204 rooms are aligned on ten levels in a striking stepped design across the slope in descending terraces. As with the Royal Tahitien Hotel, there is no direct connection to the beach, although a funicular was planned but never built. Here, the central pools provide the focus for the hotel. The Tahara'a attempted to provide the best of both worlds, with the combination of modern architecture in the accommodation terraces and a rich Polynesian setting in the principal building, colourful planting and an extensive collection of Polynesian art and craft.[42] The Maeva Beach Hotel, also of 1969, on the north-west coast of Tahiti, is an accomplished transitional building that was the first of the large resorts to open out and generously spread over large gardens with exotic planting and a pool leading to the sea beyond. The wide beach is readily accessed from the gardens and is used by local people and guests alike. The hotel was designed by the young French architect Oliver C Carcoub, winner of the 1953 Prix de Rome, from the firm of Carcoub and Bruner Architects.[43] As with the Tahara'a, the Maeva Beach consists of two sections but is of a very different character, with a reserved foyer and elegant lounges, restaurants and piano bars. The central reception building of contemporary design with concrete construction, rendered pink walls and a shingled roof is in marked contrast to the mass of the accommodation wing, which is modelled after the eleven-step pyramid marae of Mahaiatea.[44] A regional character is added to the building by the abstract Tahitian-inspired design of the timber balustrades to the balconies, which creates a shifting op art effect (see p. 220). The Maeva Beach Hotel was one of the earliest accomplished attempts in Tahiti to create a sophisticated modern building that at the same time acknowledged and celebrated the difference of location.

Among the last of the major developments of the 1960s and 1970s were the Moorea Lagoon Hotel, 1970, and the Travelodge, 1974. The entrepreneur Howard Picard built the Moorea Lagoon Hotel, designed by the Hawaiian architect George Logue, in the traditional Tahitian thatched bungalow style. Logue was well known in the Pacific, having completed several Hawaiian resorts and the Hawaii Pavilion at the New York World's Fair.[45] Architect Alain Parker, also from Hawaii, designed a hotel of over 200 units for the American company Travelodge at Tata'a Point near the airport at Faa'a (it became the Tahiti Beachcomber in 1979).[46] This was the largest project undertaken by Travelodge in the Pacific, and most of the materials were imported, including specially made wooden shingles from Canada and America.

As happened elsewhere in the South Pacific, the late 1970s and 1980s were quieter times in the French Polynesian tourist industry, and few major resorts were built as investment was directed to upgrading and extending the existing hotels rather than opening new ones. The exceptions were two resorts on Moorea: the 1985 Cook's Bay Resort, in a mock colonial style, and the 1987 Grand Hotel (later the Moorea Beachcomber), which was designed by the French architect Fenelon in 1987.[47] By the end of 1987 Tahiti had a total of 2890 rooms in luxury hotels.[48] The tourists were still predominately American, though by 1985 the market had diversified, with Americans making up 50 per cent, Europeans 20 per cent, and the remainder made up by Australians, Japanese and South Americans.[49] The pre-war low-scale developments evidenced a laid-back charm and character that lent weight to the legend of Tahiti as the undiscovered Eden of the South Seas. In the first half of the century relatively small hotels were built on the island of Tahiti to accommodate the tourists who came by sea, among them, writers and painters seeking the beauty and pristine quality of the islands. After 1950 regular air travel and international investment changed the nature of the Tahitian experience. The spectacular growth in tourist numbers that were predicted following the completion of the airstrip at Faa'a did not eventuate in the 1960s. Tourist numbers, however, did increase, and by the end of the decade, international hotels had been built on Bora Bora and Tahiti.

Beyond Eden!

'Why do we have to invent Eden, to live submerged in the nostalgia of a lost paradise, to make up utopias, propose a future for ourselves?' Julio Cortazar

In 1970 Belt Collins and Associates, Harris, Kerr, Forster and Company and Lyon Associates produced a master plan for tourist development in French Polynesia.[1] The optimistic report made several assumptions about growth in tourism that did not materialize: 'increased air access and hotel accommodation, development of the Japanese market, establishment of duty-free shopping and competitive pricing',[2] and there was little new building until the mid-1990s. The situation changed radically, however, towards the turn of the twenty-first century, and French Polynesia, primarily catering for a luxury market, emerged as a major world tourist destination, with the building of hotels that were bigger, more extravagant and increasingly 'Polynesian'. From 1995 French Polynesia attracted a growing number of tourists, and the number of hotel rooms increased from 4070 in 1995 to 6135 in 2004.[3] In 2008, around 200 000 tourists visited the country, but by 2011 the number had declined to 162 776, reflecting the effects of the global financial crisis, with tourists from North America still making up almost 40 per cent.[4] The popularity of French Polynesia can be credited to a marked extent to the architecture of the exclusive resorts, generally in secluded locations of outstanding physical beauty. This is augmented by its central-Pacific location readily reached by non-stop flights from both sides of the Pacific, and the safety and security due to French control.[5] A revival in the popularity of cruise ships – many of them based in Papeete – increased visits to French Polynesia. The government continued to support tourism as part of its plan to increase economic independence; however, the fiscal policy favours the large hotel chains and disadvantages older hotels, such as the Tahara'a and the Cook's Bay Hotel, Moorea. Others, such as the Hotel Tahiti, Bali Hai Moorea and Moorea Lagoon, were taken over by financial groups and extended. Only the Hotel Bora Bora managed to retain its original name.

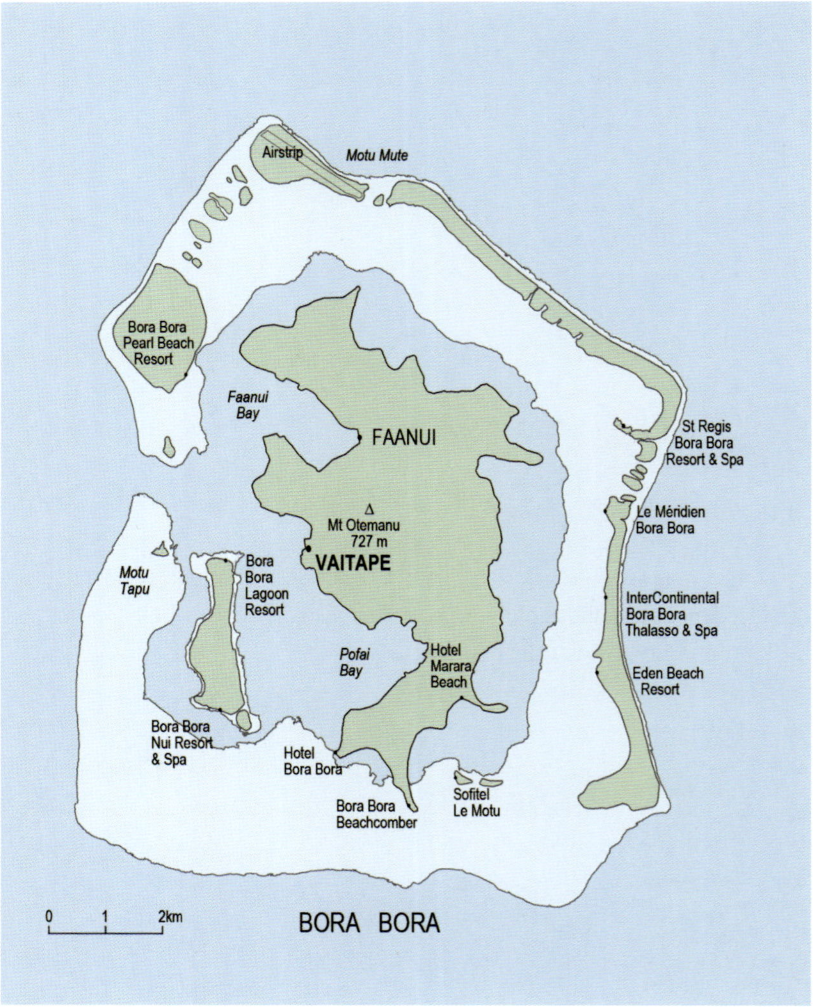

There are major differences that distinguish the new resorts from their predecessors. First, rather than employing overseas firms to design these large projects, local architects received the commissions. There were also changes in the investment pattern. While in America in the 1980s and 1990s there was a revival of the Tiki movement of the 1960s (described as post-Polynesian Pop), American funds no longer provided the major finance for development in the islands. American interests continued, however, primarily through the involvement of the large hotel chains. In the late 1980s and 1990s the Japanese were spreading their investments throughout the world, and there was some interest in the tourist industry in French Polynesia. Further, local developers such as Air Tahiti, Louis Wane and Richard Bailey played significant roles in the next stage of French Polynesian tourist development.[6] While the motus of Bora Bora had Robinson Crusoe appeal, the less visited of the Society Islands could be seen as even more primitive and remote – further from the everyday world and the cares of reality – but with every possible modern comfort.

The new resorts ushered in high-profile seductive publicity centred again on the Polynesian dream with images of beautiful girls, joyous couples, colourful fish and romantic thatched fares with Polynesian décor. 'Overwater' continued to figure highly in the promotional material, with overwater bungalows, restaurants, check-ins and even swimming pools. Coffee tables with lift-up lids to assist in fish feeding became desirable additions. Helipads and Jacuzzis, along with fitness centres, mini-golf and wedding chapels joined the other attractions. Fan cooling gave way to air conditioning. These are opulent resorts of high international standing.

The resorts followed the theme pattern established earlier with central buildings of 'Tahitian' character and accommodation provided in individual bungalows in gardens, on the beaches and overwater, though proportionally, the number of overwater bungalows increased considerably. From the earlier bungalows of quite modest dimensions, those of the more recent resorts have expanded in size with two or three bedrooms with matching ensuites and a choice of indoor sitting areas and outdoor spaces, as each new hotel attempts to out-do the previous one. There was also a major shift in construction techniques as in most resorts milled and dressed timbers and modern jointing techniques replaced the local hewn timbers and traditional binding practices. While the designs are intended to represent Polynesian buildings, rarely are there attempts at authenticity, with some 'Polynesian' bungalows being ordered prefabricated from New Zealand and synthetic pandanus being used for thatching.[7] Moreover, 'Polynesian' bungalows are proving popular in other parts of the world, with architect Jean-Hugues Tricard and others preparing designs for resorts as far as Bahrain, and Angkor in Cambodia.[8]

Vaitape Wharf Redevelopment, Bora Bora, 2003.
Tropical Architecture. Competition Scheme.

Bora Bora

As the number of tourists continued to increase, many more facilities and hotels were built to accommodate their needs. Papeete's Faa'a International Airport conveniently serves Bora Bora, where a new terminal building had been built in 1975. However, Tropical Architecture, the practice established by Pierre Lacombe in 1990, was commissioned to build a further terminal more in keeping with Bora Bora's image and increasing status as a tourist centre. The open, high-roofed group of buildings in timber introduces a restrained Polynesian theme and provides an appropriate transition across its shared roles of both air and sea terminal. The wharf at Vaitape, the island's principal town, serves as the main square and is the entry point for boats from the airport. The five-hectare Vaitape wharf site was the subject of a 2003 competition to greatly increase the quality of tourist and local facilities, including the construction of a new town hall, post office, police station,

Le Méridien Bora Bora, Bora Bora. Jean Hugues Tricard, 1998, View to Mt Otemanu.

Le Méridien Tahiti, Puna'auia, 1998. Jean-Hugues Tricard. *Courtesy of Le Méridien Tahiti.*

OPPOSITE: Tahiti Beachcomber, Faa'a, Tahiti, 1992. Jean-Hugues Tricard. Pool and view towards Moorea.

tourist office and shops, and the Radio Bora Bora building. The buildings were to be of local character, built of wood and with roofs thatched with pandanus. Three schemes were considered from the studios of Tricard, Lacombe and a further French Polynesian architect, David Chauvin. Lacombe was successful with a design that accommodates the community activities in a series of small units located in a landscape of water and parks. The looseness of the site planning was balanced and controlled by the strongly axial, symmetrical composition of the central group of buildings, which culminates in the partially overwater town hall. As of 2012, several buildings and the new and extended harbour had been constructed.

The island of Bora Bora has been subjected to further intensive building on the surrounding rim of the motus with numerous overwater buildings projecting into the lagoon altering the visual qualities of this beautiful island. These resorts offer prime venues for escapism, as the guest can fly to the motu, be ferried across the lagoon to the resort and back again without contact even with Bora Bora Island. The location on the motus also opens up the view of the spectacular silhouette of Mount Otemanu ('Mountain of the Birds') standing at 727 metres.

The 1990s

In the 1990s Tricard was commissioned to design the Bora Bora Lagoon Resort, 1993, Le Méridien Tahiti and Le Méridien Bora Bora, both of 1998. Prior to this, he had undertaken several extensions to major hotels, including the Tahara'a in 1988 and the Tahiti Beachcomber in 1992 – where he designed the overwater Lotus Restaurant and a striking extension to the freshwater pool consisting of a large saltwater on-sand pool with bar. The seventy-seven-unit Bora Bora Lagoon Resort, the first major venture on the Bora Bora motus, was built in a coconut grove on a sand spit located on the point of Motu Toopua, a small island to the west of the Bora Bora lagoon. Tricard followed this with Le Méridien Tahiti, built on the site of the old Chez Rivnac on the coast near Puna'auia. The 151-room hotel is an imposing building of two and three-storeyed wings under dramatic shingled roofs that together make for an interesting overlapping image. The buildings are arranged in relation to the pool and look out across the lagoon to Moorea.[9] Le Méridien Tahiti is a relatively formal building with major conference facilities including a 500-seat theatre, and a 400-seat conference room.[10] In marked contrast is Le

LEFT: Le Méridien Bora Bora, Bora Bora, 1998. Jean-Hugues Tricard.

ABOVE: Le Méridien Bora Bora, 1998. Jean-Hugues Tricard. Fish Viewing Glass Floor in Overwater Bungalow.

Méridien Bora Bora, which is a Polynesian-style resort spread over the large site on the northern point of Motu Piti Aau. Le Méridien Bora Bora sought to emulate the vision of the lost Tahitian paradise and, with its lavish simulacrum of an imagined Shangri-La, it ushered in the large exotic 'stage-set' resorts of the new century.[11] The resort is built on and around an artificially formed sand beach and a contained lagoon stocked with fish (and also baby turtles of the Turtle Care Breeding Centre) with which the guests can swim.[12] The picturesque complex – with the vista across the lagoon extending to Mt Otemanu – consists of reception areas and restaurants, some standing in the lagoon, all housed under various pitched thatched roofs suggestive of a romanticized South Pacific village. The major spaces are contained in open-sided structures with complex decorative roof formations. The 100 bungalows of the resort have pyramidal roofs, and eighty-three of them, with large glass viewing floors, are arranged along two branching piers out over the lagoon. The interiors, by Didier Le Port from France, are in a restrained Polynesian mode with burnished hardwood, louvered windows, pandanus-lined ceilings and earth-toned fabrics.

Local Investment

Overseas money continued to be invested in Polynesian resorts, including that of the Japanese which was primarily directed towards the purchase and upgrading of existing hotels.[13] In the 1990s, however, opportunities were also available for local developers to participate in tourism. Air Tahiti extended the network of resorts beyond the earlier targeted islands of Tahiti, Moorea and Bora Bora, on which all major resorts had been built. In this they were following in the footsteps of Pan Am and UTA in the 1960s, by building their own hotels and at the same time boosting air traffic. Air Tahiti built several small resorts on the outer islands as the Pearl

Giant Tiki, Moorea Pearl Beach Resort, Moorea.

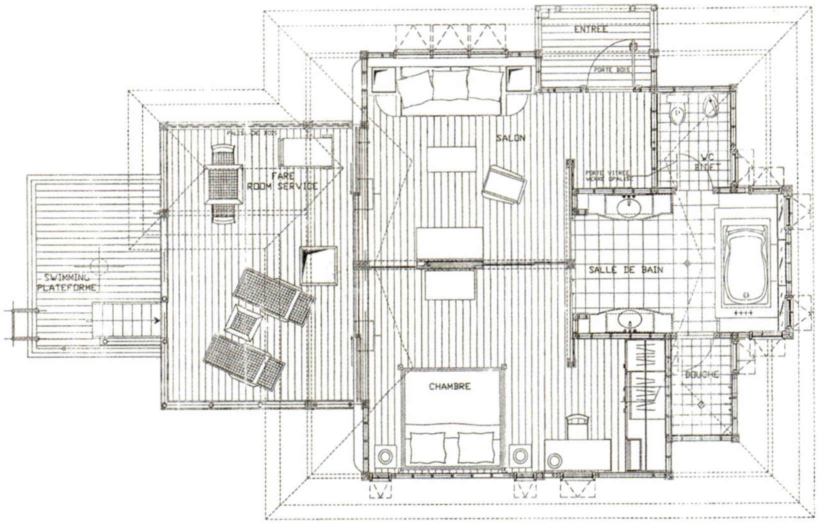

ABOVE LEFT: Moorea Pearl Beach Resort, Moorea, 2002. Tropical Architecture.

ABOVE RIGHT: Bora Bora Nui Resort, Bora Bora, 2003. Tropical Architecture. Plan of Bungalow.
LEFT: Hotel Brochure. *Courtesy of the Bora Bora Nui Hilton Hotel.*

Beach chain.[14] Pierre-Jean Picart designed several of these projects including the Pearl Beach Resort, Manihi,1995, the Bora Bora Pearl Beach Resort, 1998, and the Taha'a Pearl Beach Resort and Spa, 2002. He had studied at Toulouse University and then came to French Polynesia in the 1980s to complete his military service. He worked in Tricard's office for ten years on many hotel designs including the Bora Bora Lagoon Resort, 1993, and renovations and extensions to several hotels during the 1980s and 1990s, including the Tahara'a Hotel and the Moorea and Tahiti Beachcomber Hotels.[15] Picart's description of the team working on the Tahara'a Hotel gives some insight into the international nature of these large developments: 'we had a project manager from Hong Kong, an interior designer from Australia, a landscape architect from Hawaii and another from Los Angeles, and I was French so I had to learn to speak with them in English.'[16]

In 2002 Picart undertook a 'US$ 1 million enhancement programme' for a Japanese client on the Bora Bora Lagoon Resort, which included major artworks by the celebrated Tahitian artist Garrick Yrondi for the reception area and an extensive addition of new landscaping. Picart's hotels are typical of the luxurious quality resorts of this period. They are based on the Polynesian theme with bungalows and open fares, but the elegant timber work and quality crafted interiors offer an elite version of the vernacular. The Taha'a Pearl Beach Resort and Spa, built in 2002 on the western Motu Tautau of Taha'a Island, is a small resort that demonstrates Picart's intention to create a distinctive environment.[17] The resort's forty-eight overwater suites and twelve beach suites, each of more than a 100 square metres, face east across the lagoon to the island of Taha'a with views of Bora Bora on the ocean side. The restaurant is raised off the ground and is constructed within some large trees,

FAR LEFT: Taha'a Pearl Beach Resort and Spa, Motu Tautau, Taha'a Island, 2002. Pierre-Jean Picart. Entrance. LEFT: Dining Room. BELOW: Aerial. *Photographs by Eric Saillet.*

St Regis Bora Bora Resort and Spa, Motu Tofari, 2006. Tropical Architecture. Overwater Villas. *Courtesy of St Regis Bora Bora Resort and Spa.*

St Regis Bora Bora Resort and Spa, Motu Tofari, 2006. Tropical Architecture. Premier Overwater Villas. *Courtesy of St Regis Bora Bora Resort and Spa.*

St Regis Bora Bora Resort and Spa, Motu Tofari, 2006. Tropical Architecture. Royal Spa. *Courtesy of St Regis Bora Bora Resort and Spa.*

allowing views to the gardens and water below. Local craft artefacts, weavings and sculptures, all of a high standard, are generously displayed and contribute to the unique atmosphere of the major spaces, such as the dining room. The rocks and timbers are specially selected pieces from Taha'a; light shades are of local plant material, and the roofs are of pandanus. The principal building is the central focus of the site and from it paths lead to the spa, pool and tennis courts, to bungalows along the beaches and become branching piers serving the overwater bungalows and the arrival dock.

Lacombe, who had designed the Sofitel la Ora Resort on Moorea, 1992, and the Sofitel Le Motu, Bora Bora, 1998, was invited by Air Tahiti to design Moorea Pearl Beach Resort, 2002, the site of the original Bali Hai Hotel. As with Picart's architecture, the buildings are refined but with gleaming tiles and modern construction, dressed details and carved octagonal columns of rich timbers. The sloping site with public buildings on various levels leading up from the beach, called for a more structured circulation system that is organized in relation to a central covered walkway.

Beyond Eden

The local black pearl industry, which became the second largest money earning industry (after tourism) in French Polynesia, boomed and further funds were available for investment. Local entrepreneurs such as Chinese-Tahitian Louis Wane became involved in resort development.[18] Wane initially invested in the 1998–99 redevelopments of the Hotel Tahiti at Faa'a as the Sheraton Tahiti Hotel, and the Moorea Lagoon Hotel as the Sheraton Moorea Lagoon Resort and Spa, both to designs by Philippe Grandou of Eurl D'Architecture 'iihi', Papeete.[19] In the new century Wane further invested in large resort design and commissioned Lacombe to design two luxury hotels on the Bora Bora motus with the intention of attracting wealthy American clients: the Bora Bora Nui Resort and Spa, 2003, and the St Regis Bora Bora Resort and Spa, 2006.

In these hotels, intended to 'create the "dream" of Polynesia'[20] the 'resort' enters another dimension in terms of opulence, space, and facilities. The Bora Bora Nui was a large development on a seven-hectare site with 200 units distributed over the water, beach and terraced hillside. The landscaping, with hundreds of planted coconut palms, was overseen by Lulu Wane, the Tahitian wife of Louis Wane.[21] The Bora Bora Nui boasted several records, including the first overwater check-in, the first full-treatment spa and the 900-square-metre swimming pool being the largest in the Bora Bora group. The bungalows are large, often with several bedrooms and a variety of sitting areas.[22] Lulu Wane also directed the designs of the interiors, which are visually heavier and more elaborate than in most 'Tahitian' hotels, due to the combination of custom-ordered mahogany furniture from Bali with the lighter furniture made of rattan and local timbers.

Even more extravagant in terms of opulence, space and setting is Lacombe's design for the 2006 St Regis Bora Bora Resort and Spa Bora Bora, with a cost of US$ 1 million per villa.[23] The resort, built on eighteen hectares on Motu Tofari, features a man-made saltwater lagoon and a constructed 'hoa' inlet replenished with rich nutrients to attract and sustain fish life.[24] The 101 villas are equipped with every luxury, some with private overwater Jacuzzis or swimming pools. The 743-square-metre Royal Estate, located on a secluded swimming beach, also offers swimming in its luxurious private pool. These late luxury Polynesian resorts are distinctive in the South Pacific in the beauty and remoteness of their settings on Bora Bora, their exotic presentation of the illusion of the Tahitian legend and the unequalled sumptuousness of their architecture.

Redressing the Cost of 'Paradise': Ecotourism and the Environment

Throughout the Pacific, alternatives to the paradise enclaves are offered by small resorts such as the Matira Beach Hotel on Bora Bora, and Pension Motu Iti on Moorea, sometimes of only two or three fares, built and run by local individuals or groups. These are commonly of simple design and constructed of readily available materials.

While the environmental problems faced by the large resorts in French Polynesia are serious and wide-ranging, leadership in these regards, on a modest scale is to be found in some of the smaller establishments, as in the 2001 Eden Beach Resort, by architect Xavier Lebigre, on the motu adjacent to Le Méridien Bora Bora.[25] Eden Beach is a resort of twelve individual bungalows arranged along the waterfront. All power is produced on-site, principally by solar panels, and water comes from bores while rainwater is collected for the swimming pool.[26] Each unit has a back-up gas cylinder to provide hot water on non-sunny days. The resort also has flower and vegetable gardens, a waste treatment plant and a desalination plant.[27] Waste is processed by a Bio-Disk waste-water treatment system, and the perimeter of the site has been chemically treated to ward off mosquitoes.

Significant steps towards environmentally sound tourist resorts were taken in those owned and operated by Richard Bailey, a dual-passport American-Tahitian who studied at Stanford and Harvard before coming to Tahiti in 1986. At the end of the 1990s he bought and upgraded the Beachcomber Tahiti, Moorea and Bora Bora as the InterContinental resorts. Bailey, who works in collaboration with the Ministry of the Environment to develop programmes for saving the natural environment, is a dedicated conservationist who employs a fulltime marine

ABOVE: Matira Beach Hotel, Bora Bora. Beachside Bungalow.

BELOW: Pension Motu Iti, Moorea. Bathing Pavilion.

LEFT: Eden Beach Resort (Hotel Le Jardin d'Eden), Bora Bora, 2001. Xavier Lebigre. Preliminary Drawings. *Courtesy of the architect.*

OPPOSITE, LEFT: InterContinental Bora Bora Resort Thalasso and Spa, 2006. Philippe Grandou. *Courtesy of the InterContinental Hotels French Polynesia. Photograph by Pierre Lesage.*

OPPOSITE, RIGHT: The Brando, Tetiaroa Island, 2014. Pierre-Jean Picart. Photomontage.

biologist and veterinarian to study and care for the ecosystems of his resorts. Bailey's InterContinental Bora Bora Thalasso Spa, 2006, designed by Grandou, aspires to 'nurture complete harmony between mind, spirit and nature' with a design that gives 'ecotourism, escape and wellness a whole new dimension'.[28] The luxurious 'Polynesian' resort of eighty 100-square-metre overwater villas was built at a cost of US$ 70 million. Here, the design goes one step further with glass-top coffee tables that are also illuminated at night to attract fish. The air conditioning system throughout the resort operates on deep-drawn seawater, whereby fresh seawater to cool the air is siphoned from a depth of 800 metres. The water is also used in the Thalassotherapy and Balneotherapy centre.

Interestingly, Dr Zbigniew Bromberek makes the point that the overwater bungalows 'take advantage of the moderating impact of the ocean on the resort's microclimate, as they are elevated and fully exposed to cooling winds and breezes, and their lightweight structures quickly lose heat gained during the day. Built to a design greatly influenced by the traditional Polynesian hut with high cathedral ceilings, thatched roofs, thin walls woven with pandanus leaves, the bungalows are superbly suited for the climate. Unfortunately, the vast majority of holidaymakers staying at the resort prefer to trust the air-conditioning systems provided in each bungalow rather than its ingenious design. This makes resort operations prohibitively expensive since their design is inappropriate for air conditioning.' It is this cost that Bailey's InterContinental Bora Bora Thalasso Spa, 2006, has ingeniously managed to elude.[29] Bailey's next project was the design and construction of a hotel called The Brando on the atoll of Tetiaroa. Marlon Brando married the leading lady, Tarita Teriipia, in the film *Mutiny on the*

Bounty and in 1966 leased part of Tetiaroa and built a modest resort of twelve fares of local timber construction with thatched roofs and basic furnishings.[30] In 1971 he invited the American architect Bernard Judge to join him as master planner, and they worked together over the following two years.[31] Tetiaroa is an exceptionally beautiful, unspoiled atoll with thirteen motus encircling the lagoon and is legendary as a former island retreat of the royal family of the Pomare dynasty.

Subsequently, Bailey worked together on the current project with Brando for three years before Brando's death, and with The Brando, Bailey is playing 'a part in his legacy by bringing one of his dreams to fruition.' Eight of Brando's children are acting as developers for the resort, which plans to open in 2014.[32] To fulfil their joint vision for an 'environmentally enlightened project', the resort is planned to disturb the eco-system as little as possible, to be unobtrusive and blend with the natural environment through form and materials, and to use the latest renewable energy technologies including the deep-seawater air-conditioning system previously employed for the InterContinental Bora Bora project. Before determining the location of the airstrip and the siting and extent of the development, the archaeological department of the Tahiti and its Islands Museum conducted research into the past use of the atoll, and it was also subject to extensive studies to ensure that the project would not disturb the flora and fauna. Dedicated sanctuaries were declared, such as the sea turtle hatching grounds and Motu Tahuna Iti, which provides a home to thousands of rare indigenous seabirds. Bailey's project has the potential to set a benchmark for future eco-sustainable architecture in the Pacific.

The resort history of French Polynesia has been conditioned by various responses to the Tahitian paradise fable and has followed an evolutionary process. First moving from the enclave of the Hotel Stuart, which provided a haven from which to venture forth and explore the exotic surroundings, through various phases until the full circle is turned and the gated community of the hotel, rather than being a little bit of France or America in the alien land, now provides a ritualized enactment of a sumptuous Polynesian world that appropriates the Tahitian myth and offers it up in a scene 'beyond Eden'. But 'there's no such thing as revisiting paradise. Step into it for a peek and you've already altered it in unknowable ways for an unforeseeable future.'[33]

Until recently, the environmental impact of these and other highly populated enclaves has not been given adequate consideration, but today examples of responsible eco-design are appearing.

Part V

FAITH ACROSS THE SOUTHERN OCEAN

PLACES OF WORSHIP 10

Temples, Shrines, Mosques and Churches

With the exception of Fiji, which is ethnically Melanesian yet geographically on the edge of the mid-Pacific, the people of the central seas are predominantly Polynesian. Christianity is a fundamental influence, establishing social mores as well as religious practices. The missions had both negative and positive effects. While the arrival of the Europeans brought diseases, and the missions tried to put a stop to local religious practices, nudity and other aspects of traditional life, they also provided centres of learning and education, and health-care facilities. In many instances they were the first to record the various Polynesian and Melanesian languages and hence provide a documented source of culture and history for the islands and their people.

While a very high percentage of the population is Christian, other religions have built temples, shrines and mosques. As would be expected, the Hindu places of worship are primarily found in Fiji and range from small shrines commonly found in villages and along roadsides to large complexes of several buildings arranged in relation to courtyards. Typical of the wayside shrines is the colourful Shree Laxmi Narayan, Suva, and the Shiri Vishnu Temple, just outside Nadi – both of rude local design and construction but decorated with imaginative sculptures and paintings by village artists. The oldest, largest and most celebrated Hindu temple in Fiji is the brilliantly ornamented Sri Siva Subramaniya Swami Temple, Nadi, 1994, by V Ganapati Sthapati of Madras with Manikam Achari Palaniswami, the resident architect. The temple, enclosed by a perimeter wall, is an impressive complex of individual temple buildings and related spaces. The original Subramaniya Swami Temple of Nadi was founded by Ramaswami Pillai in 1913 on land leased from native Fijians.[1]

LEFT: Shree Laxmi Narayan Temple, Suva, Viti Levu, Fiji.

RIGHT (ALL IMAGES): Shiri Vishnu Temple, Nadi.

OPPOSITE: Sri Siva Subramaniya Swami Temple, Nadi, 1994. V Ganapati Sthapati with Manikam Achari Palaniswami.

PREVIOUS PAGE: Temple at Paofai. After the Service.

The Dudley Memorial Church, Suva, 1934, constructed by a builder named Bidesi, is an uncommon hybrid of Christian and Hindu forms. The church was built by Indian Christians in memory of Australian missionary Hannah Dudley, who came to Fiji in the early twentieth century and was revered mostly for her care of Indian orphans.[2] Mosques, such as the Masjid Noor on Bau Street, Suva, 1980, and the mosque at Flagstaff, both by Denis Biggs and Associates, tend to be more austere buildings that are given prominence by the customary simple domes and minarets. In contrast to this sobriety is the exuberant pink elephant-bedecked bell tower of the Muslim Masimasi Primary School.

Chinese religions and the Hare Krishna and Baha'i faiths also have their adherents. Large Chinese temples such as the Kanti Chinese Temple at Mamao in Papeete are uncommon in the mid-Pacific. The original timber Kanti temple, built in 1876 by the first Chinese in Tahiti, was destroyed by fire in 1981. A much larger new temple was designed along traditional lines by the Taiwanese architect Patrick Siu

TOP: Kanti Chinese Temple, Mamao, Papeete, French Polynesia, 1985. Patrick Siu.

ABOVE LEFT: Masimasi Primary School, Viti Levu, Fiji. Bell Tower.

ABOVE RIGHT: Sri Krishna Kaliya Temple, Lautoka, Fiji, 1976. Murray Cockburn Partnership.

RIGHT: Baha'i House of Worship, Tiapapata, Samoa, 1984. Hossein Amanat.

OPPOSITE, ABOVE: Masjid Noor, Suva, Fiji, 1980. Denis Biggs.

OPPOSITE, BELOW: Dudley Memorial Church, Suva, 1934.

and built in 1985 with donations from the community. The Hare Krishna Sri Krishna Kaliya Temple at Lautoka, Fiji, 1976, by Murray Cockburn Partnership, is an austere symmetrical building with a perimeter of blade walls supporting a flat roof. Raised above ancillary spaces located below, it is approached by a wide imposing central stairway. The interior is light and spacious with arched double doors down each side.

The 1984 Baha'i House of Worship at Tiapapata in the highlands of Upolu, Samoa, by architect Hossein Amanat, is the only building of the followers in the South Pacific.[3] The temple is picturesquely sited at the end of an axis passing through large flowering gardens. The building consists of a deeply indented podium containing the nine-sided body of the temple, which is roofed with an 'opening lotus' form of concrete shell construction. The serene interior is lit from the glass walls on all sides and through the divisions between the shells of the roof, giving a cool even light. The Baha'i House of Worship, Tiapapata, is among the most engaging buildings of the South Pacific.

In the Wake of the Missionaries

The establishment and spread of Christianity in the Polynesian islands was to a large measure determined by the parts played by several Catholic missionaries, such as Peter Chanel in Futuna, and the pivotal role of Reverend John Williams of the London Missionary Society (LMS) in the spread of the Protestant religion. Williams has been described as 'a Leonardo da Vinci, a man with rare gifts'. He was only twenty-one years old when he arrived in Tahiti in 1817. 'He learnt Tahitian, Rarotongan and Samoan like child's play, and translated the Bible into the latter two languages: he was in turn carpenter, joiner, boat-builder, sailor, schoolteacher, preacher, lawgiver, farmer and mason.'[1] In 1839 Williams was killed by islanders on the beach at Erromango, New Hebrides.[2] Much of the preaching in the Pacific was done by trainees, notably Tahitian, so the Christian message was also spread in the Pacific through them, contributing considerably to the success of the religion.

The Seventh-Day Adventist Church and the Church of Jesus Christ of Latter-Day Saints have long histories of ministering in the Pacific, and in recent times their numbers have been increasing significantly – particularly those of the Mormons, who have a policy of education and financial support for students.[3] While as

LEFT: Church of Jesus Christ of Latter-Day Saints Temple, Papeete, Tahiti, French Polynesia, 1983. Emil B Fetzer and local associate Pierre-Jean Picart.

OPPOSITE: Church of Jesus Christ of Latter-Day Saints Chapel, Lami, Viti Levu, Fiji, 2005. Fraser Clark.

elsewhere, the Seventh-Day Adventist churches generally are of unassuming character and follow the planning and appearance of the standard models, there are rare exceptions. One such is the 1995 Seventh-Day Adventist Church, Avarua, Cook Islands, by the Ministry of Works, which consists of twin linked octagonal pavilions with tented 'carousel' roofs, referring to the form of the tents in which the congregation lives for assemblies once a year.[4] In addition to the 1983 Liahona Temple of Tonga, the American architect Emil B Fetzer, with the Mormon Church architects, was also responsible for those of Apia, Samoa and Papeete, Tahiti[5] – both also built in 1983.[6] The temple at Apia, burnt down on 9 July 2003 while being refurbished, was rebuilt in 2005, and the Angel Moroni statue that survived the fire reclaimed its place atop the spire of the new temple. Architects Pacific, in collaboration with the Church architects, were the designers for a fourth temple, constructed in Suva, Fiji, in 2000. The temples of the Mormons in the South Pacific adhere to the single spire model and often are related to campus-like complexes with classrooms, libraries and other educational buildings. Generally, the meeting chapels are uniformly white and of traditional appearance, such as the 2005 Chapel at Lami, by Fraser Clark, designed following a vocabulary sent by the church from New Zealand.

Pastors, Priests and Precedence

Several events of significance occurred in the history of the Christian churches in the South Pacific. These included: first, the events within the Wesleyan Church of Tonga and the remarkable role played by Father George Callet in the building of the Catholic churches that set Tonga apart from the mainstream of church architecture in the region; second, the survival of the early coral stone churches of the Cook Islands; third, the loyalty to the Gothic tradition in major religious edifices (French Polynesia being the exception); fourth, the clinging to an established stereotype in the Protestant churches of French Polynesia; and fifth, the uniqueness of the extraordinary churches of Wallis and Futuna, which places them outside the main tenets of church design.

The conspicuous presence of the churches dominates the built landscape of many of the islands, where often colourful and inventive churches are found on the roadsides and as the centres of life in towns and villages. Such a concentration of places of worship can be seen in Samoa, where there are over sixty churches along the road between the airport and Apia.[7] The churches range from conservative buildings, such as the Church of the Immaculate Conception, Lepua, American Samoa, 1928–31, and the Apia Protestant Church, Samoa, 1958, to eccentric designs as shown in the 1991 Congregational Christian Church of American Samoa (the Calvary Church) at Pava'ia'i, by local structural engineer Asiata Taeao. In addition, mission churches have been built on outer islands since the beginning of the century, notably in Fiji, with one of the finest being the Wairiki Catholic Mission, Taveuni, 1907, which overlooks the Somosomo Strait. Its attractive interior with pastel shading, shining mauve floor and patterned walls, roofed by a handsome beam ceiling and lit through stained-glass windows, which reportedly came from

OPPOSITE, ABOVE: Congregational Christian Church of American Samoa, Pava'ia'i, American Samoa, 1991. Engineer: Asiata Taeao.

OPPOSITE, BELOW: Mission Church of St Francis Xavier, Navuibutu, Fiji, 1917. Mural by Jean Charlot, 1962–63.

ABOVE: Wairiki Catholic Mission, Taveuni, Fiji, 1907.

LEFT: Protestant Church, Apia, Samoa, 1958.

France. In 1917 a Catholic mission was established at Naiserelagi village outside Rakiraki on a hill overlooking Viti Levu Bay. The Mission Church of St Francis Xavier, built of soapstone carved from the top of the hill, is conventional but of interest due to the triptych altar panel 'Black Christ and Worshippers' painted in 1962–63 by Jean Charlot.

The Coral Churches of the Cook Islands

The survival of the original LMS coral stone churches of the Cook Islands is unusual when one considers the absence of a history of building conservation in the South Pacific. This is explained in part by the fact that the churches were built of stone and the Cook Islands are not as subject to earthquakes as most of the Pacific – although they do suffer from occasional severe cyclones.[8] Furthermore, while churches in the South Pacific commonly fall into disrepair or are abandoned or demolished in order to build a new one, this is not so in the Cook Islands where few churches have been built in the twentieth century. Rather, the early churches have been continually maintained and renovated and now are a part of the evolving twenty-first-century architecture of the islands. For example, the early church at Titikaveka, 1835, was updated, restructured and reconditioned in 1865, 1884, 1955 and 1986.[9]

Williams was a critical figure in the founding of the LMS in the Cook Islands in 1821 and in the subsequent building of the early churches. The church remained under LMS authority until 1965 and was then formally renamed the Cook Islands Christian Church (CICC) in 1968. Williams landed in 1821 on the island of Aitutaki on his way from Tahiti to Australia and on sailing, left in charge of the mission Papeiha and Vahapata, converted Polynesians from the Society Islands.[10] He returned two years later to find all the islanders converted to Christianity. In 1823 he sailed to Rarotonga, which he later 'claimed he had discovered'.[11] The first coral stone church was built in 1828 at Arutanga on Aitutaki, by Papeiha and Vahapata, and Williams' direct heritage in the Cook Islands can be seen in five churches on Rarotonga and two on the outer islands, which are among the oldest surviving in the South Pacific. Williams and his Polynesian teachers created the churches with the help of traditional builders, *tufuga fai*. The craftsmen adapted the means of construction to which they were accustomed to meet the needs of the Christian church.

The Rarotonga churches were erected in the villages of Titikaveka, Avarua, Arorangi, Ngatangiia and Matavera. The first of these was the engaging church at Titikaveka, which was erected in 1835 but not consecrated until 1841. The church was built to a square plan to symbolize the equality of all in its presence.[12] The

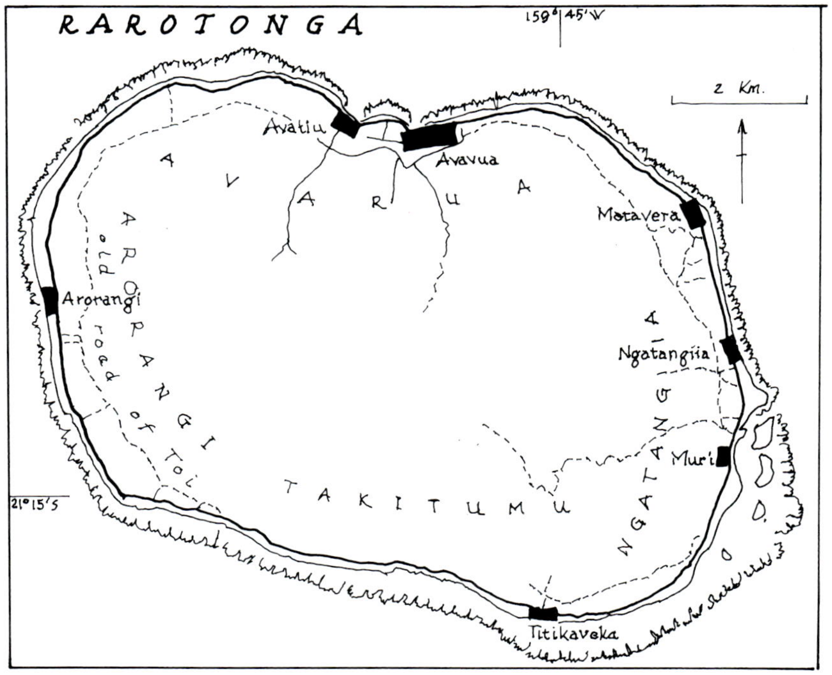

ABOVE: Plan of Rarotonga Roads and Settlements, Cook Islands. *Redrawn from map provided courtesy of the University of Texas Libraries, the University of Texas at Austin.*

LEFT: Cook Islands Christian Church, Arorangi, Rarotonga, 1849. Aaron Buzacott.

church at Titikaveka – one of three established by Williams – was built by recent converts, and the construction was supervised by Cunningham, an English planter-builder.[13] The coral blocks used in the wall construction, some a metre deep, were cut from the nearby beach at low tide and transported to the site on rafts, with the smaller blocks passed from hand to hand. Behind the severe limestone façade is the delightful interior with an irregular structure of posts and beams, and elegant timber circles forming roof trusses – all painted bright blue.[14] The church initially had three gabled pandanus woven roofs but, as they leaked at the junctions, an early pastor replaced them with the current single-gabled roof.[15] The timber posts and roof beams came from the mountains in Titikaveka and Arorangi, and these were soaked in mud for preservation purposes and to make the wood bitter so

ABOVE: Cook Island Christian Church, Titikaveka, Rarotonga, 1835. Roof Framing Detail.
TOP RIGHT: Front Façade.

ABOVE: Cook Islands Christian Church, Matavera, Rarotonga, 1853.

that borers would not attack it.[16] The original timber flooring, joinery and windows came from England.[17] Much of the appeal of the Titikaveka church is in the very evident amateurism and inventiveness of its construction. Spacings are uneven, timber sizes varied, and column capitals are of single rectangular blocks of timber – no two being of the same size or shape.

The second stone church on Rarotonga, that of Arorangi, 1849, on the west coast became the focal point for the first missionary-built settlement, which was intended to serve as a model for future villages. This coastal community was founded by the missionary Reverend Aaron Buzacott, who arrived in the Cook Islands in 1828.[18] The straightforward rectangular form of the Arorangi church, 1849, encloses one of the most delightful interiors in the Cook Islands. A flat ceiling covers the sanctuary, the side aisles and the balcony, and provides the counterpoint to the startling blue-and-white folded-plate ceiling canopy, supported on wooden columns, that rises over the central nave, creating a sense of shelter and containment. The dark stained-timber pews contrast with the lighter tones of the balcony with its pierced white balustrade infill. The third coral stone church, the romantic church at Matavera, 1853, is of similar form and construction.[19] Buzacott also built the 1853 church at Avarua, which measures 19.5 metres long with a width of 12 metres and a gallery on three sides, seating 1000 people.[20] It is a remarkably strong church of heavy sculptural massing expressive of its limestone construction of walls 80 centimetres thick, a large square tower at the western end and several thick buttresses. Buzacott also built the nearby Takamoa Bible School, Avarua, 1837, establishing the oldest theological college in the South Pacific.[21] Also surviving is the Avarua Sunday School Hall of 1845, rescued from ruinous condition, restored and converted into a part of the Beachcomber Gallery by David Raggs in 1992.[22]

Cook Islands Christian Church, Avarua, Rarotonga, 1853.

Congregational Christian Church, Sapapali'i, Savai'i Island, Samoa, 2006. *Photograph by © Paul Kennedy, Lonely Planet Images.*

Pastors and Precedence

The Christian symbolism and authority inherent in the form and space of the Gothic serves as precedent for many major edifices for the Protestant church in the mid-Pacific. An exception is the Holy Trinity Cathedral of the Diocese of Polynesia, Suva, which was built over a period of twenty-five years in two distinct stages and of two different architectural styles. The striking two-tier apse and choir of the first stage, by C H Nettleton, 1952, contrasts with the 1974 nave extension by Derrick Dignan & Associates, which is relatively simple and modern with a low heavy beamed timber ceiling.

The impressive Siona Chapel was built in 1900 by the LMS to celebrate the landing of Williams in 1832 in the Polynesian town of Leone, the ancient capital of Tutuila. It was built on the site of the original church, which was the first in what is now American Samoa.[23] It is a handsome building with square twin western towers, an uncommon raised semi-circular balcony over the entry porch and a richly decorated interior with fine carvings and stained glass. A Polynesian gesture is made by the circular fale standing to the side in front of the edifice. This church was followed by the large Congregational Christian Church of American Samoa (*O Le Ki O Le Malo O Le Lagi* – Key to the Kingdom of Heaven) on a site next to the high court in central Pago Pago. It commenced in 1935, but World War II interrupted construction and the building was not completed until 1949.[24] The church, which bears similarities to the Leone Siona Chapel, is of a traditional composition with a wide five-bay arcaded porch extending across the façade. The Pago Pago church was renovated over a two-year period, being completed in 1994.[25]

A further church dedicated to John Williams was built at Sapapali'i on the island of Savai'i in Samoa, where he landed in 1830. The first church on the site was completed in 1909. In 1930, to mark the centenary of the landing, a new church was built on the same foundations. It was renovated in 1955 and 1980, and a third new church was built and dedicated in 2006. The 1930s church was set high on a podium and approached by a grand staircase of two flights. It was of distinctive design with a scalloped façade between two decorative towers capped by a pierced balustrade. The present church, now named Mataniu Feagai Ma Le Ata, is of equal interest with handsome geometric towers with the tiers defined by projecting horizontal bands and capped by a raised cupola on columns, which makes an allusion to the centralized fale.[26]

ABOVE: Siona Chapel, Leone, American Samoa, 1900.

BELOW: Holy Trinity Cathedral, Suva, Fiji, 1952. C H Nettleton.

RIGHT: Congregational Christian Church of American Samoa, Pago Pago, American Samoa, 1949.

Hats and Hymns

Priests and Precedence

The architectural efforts of the Catholic minority have been primarily concentrated on the building of cathedrals and churches in the major towns. The Cathedral of the Immaculate Conception of Mary (the Mulivai Catholic Cathedral), Apia – one of the finest cathedrals in the South Pacific – was demolished in 2011 due to structural failure following severe cyclones and an earthquake.[1] Construction commenced on the old building in 1884; it was dedicated in 1905 and restored in 1999.[2] The cathedral was an imposing building of traditional twin tower, triple-portal design with further portals to the side aisles facing the sea in downtown Apia. The north-east façade was composed of plain white, rendered geometric forms that terminated in the crenulations of the tall towers. The plainness of the façade was relieved by the subtle use of pale-blue colouration of both the niches in the buttresses (containing statues of saints) and on the image of Virgin Mary and Child on the apex of the front gable of the roof. The light and spacious interior was enclosed overhead by the arresting barrel vault and the half-cupola over the apse, each of which was shaped by flat planes. This space was enhanced by the use of white and the blue of the façade that appeared again in the nave, used with the same level of restraint. The Sacred Heart Cathedral, Suva, is also based on the conventional planning for major Catholic churches, with a cruciform plan with a nave, transepts and twin western towers. There were three principal periods of construction. The original 1902 building was under the direction of Father Anthelme Rosier. The handsome towers were added in 1939 by Father Pierre Boudier, and in 1993–94 Jaimi Associates undertook the construction of the sanctuary and major upgrading.[3]

While the principal Catholic churches are to be found in the towns, some significant buildings were built outside the town centres, such as the traditional Catholic Church of the Immaculate Conception, Lepua, American Samoa, on which construction commenced in 1929.[4] This is a heavy stone building with a central

OPPOSITE, ABOVE: Sacred Heart Cathedral, Suva, Fiji, 1939. Father Pierre Boudier.
OPPOSITE, BELOW: Apse. 1993–94. Jaimi Associates.

LEFT: Church of the Immaculate Conception, Lepua, American Samoa, 1929.

FAR LEFT: Cathedral of the Immaculate Conception, Apia, Samoa, 1905.
BELOW: Interior.

OPPOSITE: Church of the Holy Family, Haapiti, Moorea, French Polynesia, 1891.

FAR LEFT: Catholic Cathedral dedicated to the Holy Family, Pago Pago, American Samoa, 1995. Nerad Otto/Mazanek.

LEFT: Catholic Church, Taravao, Tahiti, French Polynesia, 1956. Father Albert.

square western tower. The white interior is lighter, with the nave covered by a timber barrel vault and defined by semi-circular arches and supported on slim square columns.[5] Also related through the French Gothic tradition is the Catholic church at Taravao, in the south of Tahiti, the second most important Catholic centre in the country after Papeete. The church, completed in 1956, was designed and supervised by the resident priest, Father Albert from France.[6] While conforming to type in its overall form, the church is quite distinct in detail, with vertical piers stressing the height of the towers, which are terminated by decorative incised cappings with a crenulated lacy band forming the transition to the sky. The deep central porch is unconventional, with its strange mask-like façade supported by three columns and set forward from the towers.

The Catholic Church of the Holy Family, Moorea, built in 1891 and renovated in 1991, is a striking composition with a central porch flanked by severe tall towers that are relieved by the incised decorative pattern of the attics. The planar, white rendered walls are highlighted by the strong deep red of the roofs, the decoration of the porch and the frames within the small windows and uncommon roof attics, making this one of the most striking churches in French Polynesia. The church stands on a site outside the town of Haapiti on the west coast of Moorea, and when first built it was the main Catholic church on Moorea. In 1995 a new Catholic cathedral dedicated to the Holy Family was constructed on the outskirts of Pago Pago. The cathedral was designed by Nerad-Mazanek Architects from Clarendon Hills, Illinois, with Otto Nerad as project architect.[7] It is true to the conventional basilican model, apart from the vaulted light scoops that illuminate the eastern end. The cathedral has a seating capacity of 940 but can be extended to 1400 persons. The pews were constructed by the Cathedral carpenter using Fijian Mahogany, and the stained glass windows were created by local artist Sven Ortquist.[8]

The Catholic Cathedral of St Joseph, Avarua, Cook Islands, was constructed in 1994. The cathedral rejects the basilican composition in favour of an octagonal plan with a surrounding colonnade. While the centralized plan form is unusual, there is precedence in the octagonal Papetoai Temple, Moorea, which was originally erected in 1822 by the LMS but totally reconstructed at the end of the nineteenth century.[9] The cathedral is a modern concrete building with a sheet-metal roof supported by timber beams from New Zealand. It was designed by Jaimi Associates and built by the Public Works Department.[10] St Joseph's is related to the firm's work in Fiji, notably by the centralized plan seen in two churches of Jaimi Associates: St Peter Chanel Chapel, Pacific Regional Seminary, Suva, and the fan-shaped plan of Our Lady of Assumption, Lomary.

Break from Precedence – French Polynesia

A further major Catholic church of the mid-Pacific to break with precedence was the arresting Cathedral of Our Lady of Peace (*Cathedrale Maria no te au Papeete*), erected outside Papeete in 1978 in order to accommodate large congregations, as the 1875 Cathedral of the Immaculate Conception at Papeete had become too small.[11] The new cathedral by BIRO and Jean-Jacques Fernier from Paris holds 800 seated in chairs or 2000 sitting on the floor.[12] Steel space-framed trusses resting on large rugged concrete footings support the wide tent roof that encloses a dramatic uninterrupted space. The roof slopes down almost to the ground in a series of overlapping horizontal sheets clad in dark-brown shingles that subtly turn up at the eaves and overhang the footing, producing a serrated silhouette. A full glass wall behind the altar and a decorative glazed central slit in the front façade light this impressive space. A glazed ridge allows further light into the nave from above, dramatically linking these openings. The Cathedral of Our Lady of Peace is among the most original examples of church architecture in the South Pacific. While not directly derivative of the vernacular, it subtly acknowledges the significance of the roof in form, size and material, to produce a large meaningful building rooted in the Pacific tradition. The 1995 Church of St Etienne at Puna'auia on the west coast of Tahiti relates to the precedence of the cathedral. The Church of St Etienne, by Jean-Hugues Tricard, is akin to the cathedral through the deep, shingled tented roof, but the roof at Puna'auia is divided into stepped units along the nave that form roof lights.[13] The light entering through both the roof and the splendid stained glass wall evenly illuminates the interior. Large embroidered wall hangings depicting the Stations of the Cross by Paul Ieiva line the walls.

Another model, one with a single central western tower with belfry, was adopted for the majority of the churches of French Polynesia. This became virtually standardized for the Protestant churches but also appears in Catholic examples. The design was first established in the modest Cathedral of the Immaculate Conception, Papeete, built by Bishop Florentin-Étienne Jaussen in 1875, who set the plan dimensions and the height of the belfry for future buildings.[14] Typical of the successive Catholic churches is the pink and ochre of St Michel's Church at Papara, originally built in 1899. The present St Michel's of 1989 has some uncommon features, including a stepped bell tower and a wide portal with five arched doors. The Church of the Sacred Heart, Arue, 1996, just east of Papeete, was built on the site of the first church (consecrated in 1882) and its successors. Tricard enhanced this small church with a decorative pieced pediment over the projecting porch, to contrast with the austere, planar quality of the rest of the façade. Arue is also a celebrated site for the Protestants, as it

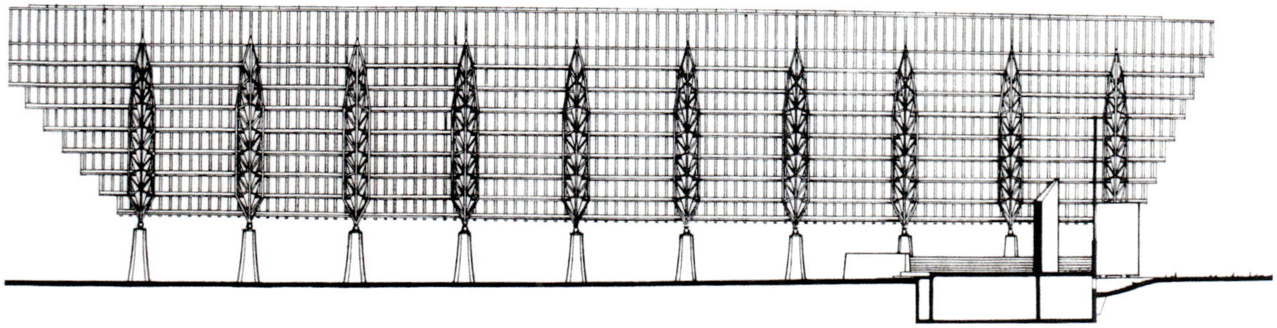

LEFT: Cathedral of Our Lady of Peace, Papeete, French Polynesia, 1978. BIRO and Jean-Jacques Fernier. Section.
BELOW: Exterior.

OPPOSITE, LEFT: Cathedral of St Joseph, Avarua, Rarotonga, Cook Islands, 1994. Jaimi Associates.

OPPOSITE, RIGHT: Octagonal Temple, Papetoai, Moorea, French Polynesia, 1822 (rebuilt at end of the nineteenth century).

LEFT: Church of St Etienne, Puna'auia, Tahiti, French Polynesia, 1995. Jean-Hugues Tricard.
BELOW LEFT: Stepped Roof Lights. BELOW RIGHT: Stained Glass Window.

was at nearby Papaoa that King Pomare I was baptized in 1819 in a specially built 200-metre-long chapel.[15]

Towers, Spires and Steeples

After Williams landed in Tahiti in 1817 he travelled in the Society Islands and founded Uturoa, the future capital of the Leeward Islands, before leaving for the Cook Islands and Samoa.[16] While not in Tahiti for long, he had a marked influence on the life of the Tahitian Protestants. Little remains of the early Protestant churches due to the problems common elsewhere of consistent damage caused by natural forces or termite attack and demolition of churches in order to make way for a newer and frequently larger version – an act seen as a powerful expression of faith.[17] As a result, most of the standing churches were built after 1980.

Church of the Sacred Heart, Arue, Tahiti, French Polynesia, 1996. Jean-Hugues Tricard.

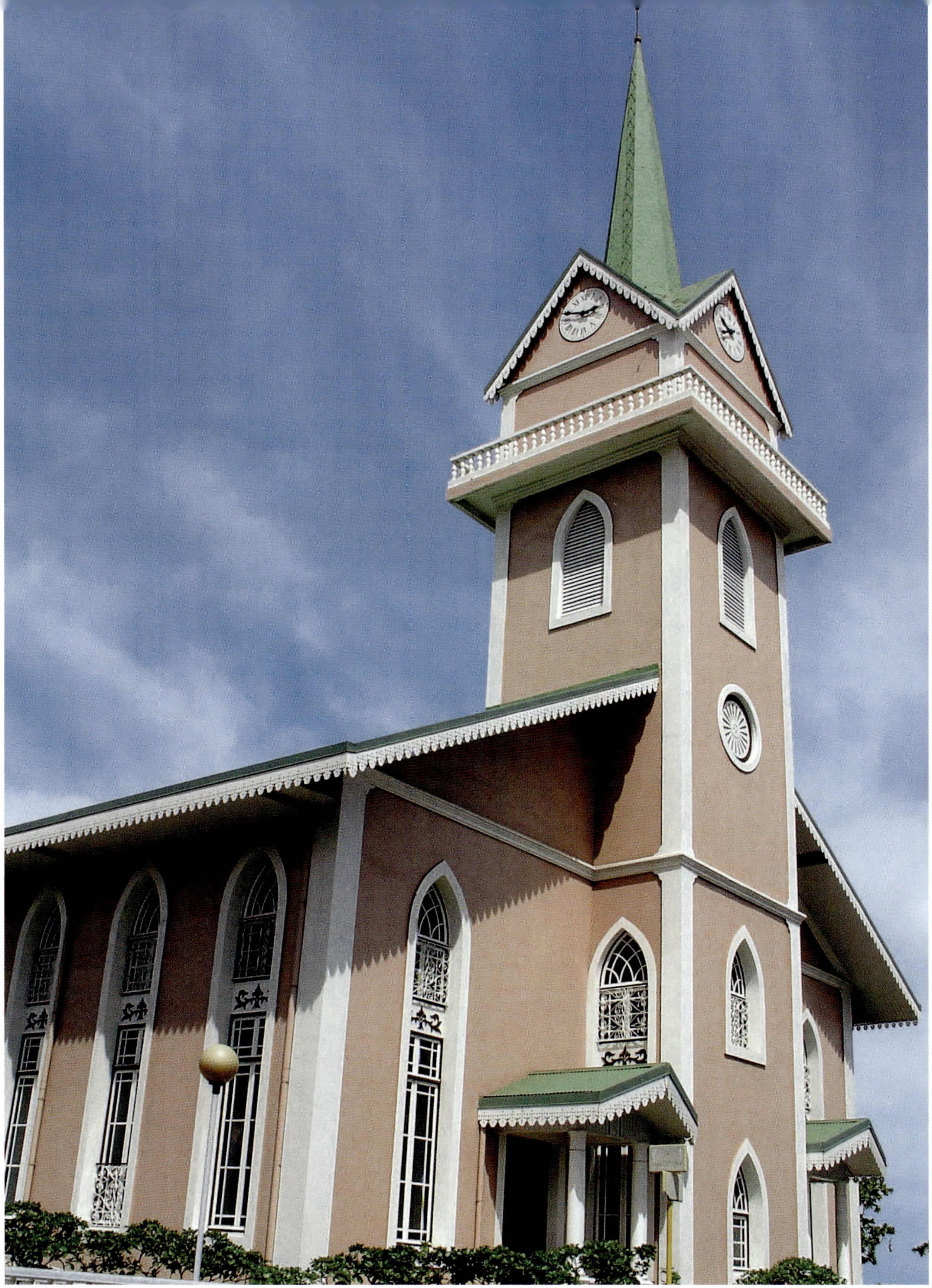

LEFT: Temple at Paofai, Papeete, Tahiti, 1980. Rodolphe Weinmann.

OPPOSITE, LEFT: Temple at Taunoa, Tahiti, French Polynesia, 1986. Rodolphe Weinmann.
OPPOSITE, RIGHT: Interior.

The Evangelical Church of French Polynesia Temple at Paofai, Papeete, was the mother church of the LMS in French Polynesia (since 1963, the Church of Tahiti) was built on land that was allocated by Queen Pomare Vahine IV at the site where Williams landed. The original church was founded by the missionary George Pritchard who came to Papeete in 1824.[18] The Paofai church established a model with the single central bell tower that became the norm. Its interior laid down a standard plan with a central pulpit with its back to the belltower and the altar in front. The front pews are set back behind a real or understood barrier, the *purupiti,* separating the congregation from the protruding chancel (see p. 246). Balconies are common on one or three sides. A parish community hall for meetings and informal gatherings, the *fare putuputuraa* is generally found near to the church. Successive churches have been built on the Paofai site. The present Paofai Temple, designed by Weinmann, completed in 1980, is based on the early precedent but also established one of its own with the design of the façades and tower. Weinmann's Paofai Temple presents a fanciful image with its pink walls, white trim and lacy details edging the main roof and those of the twin porches on front and side, its tall lancet windows with the delicate geometric pattern of the clear lead light glass, and its clock tower capped by four triangular pediments and terminated by a slim pointed spire. Weinmann followed Paofai with the temples at Taunoa, 1986, Papara, 1997, and Pirae, 1997, which are in accord with the composition and character of the temple at Paofai.

The impressive Temple at Taunoa, 1986, with its pastel colours and white trims, and its steeple of a 'witch's hat' spire on top of a stepped tower, belongs to the same family but differs in having the tower off-centre and a grand porch substituted at the west end. The temple, at forty-five metres long, eighteen metres wide and twenty-seven metres to the top of the clock tower, is the largest in French Polynesia. The interior is conventional but is more decorative than is common, with rich timbers used in the construction of the deep balcony and for the furnishings of the chancel. For the Temple at Papara, 1997, Weinmann returned to the central tower model but set it well back to allow for an uncommonly wide

LEFT: Temple at Papara, Tahiti, French Polynesia, 1997. Rodolphe Weinmann.

OPPOSITE, LEFT: Temple at Faauni, Bora Bora, French Polynesia, 1987–88.

OPPOSITE, RIGHT: Temple of Ebene Ezera, Vaitape, Bora Bora, French Polynesia, 1938 (remodelled in1996).

porch supporting an overhead balcony. While the colours of the Papara temple are stronger, it remains in the world of fantasy with its elaborate white balustrades and lacy bargeboards. The large shed-like *fare putuputuraa* stands across the street from the church. Churches on this model have continued to be built on the smaller islands of French Polynesia. Typical are the 1938 (renovated and remodelled 1995–96) Temple of Ebene Ezera at Vaitape, Bora Bora, which is a simple yet refined building with a belfry tower that is topped with a red hat with splayed brim, and the more rural church at Faanui, also on Bora Bora, 1987, which stands at the head of the bay and has a timber barrel-vaulted nave and a tall steeple with a grey pointed spire on the tower. Both provide landmarks for those travelling on the only route to Vaitape: the sea.[19]

The consistency of the designs of these churches is expressive of the strict controlling tenets of the Protestant denominations. Further, it could be attributed to, in part, the conservative nature of the religion, whereas the Catholic building programme in this region is more adventurous. Because of the constant destruction of the buildings, most of these churches were built over a short more recent time span, which explains their fresh and new appearance. Their similarities are also attributable to the fact they were primarily built to the designs of one architect.

Faith and Fantasy: The Later Churches of Wallis and Futuna

The French overseas territory of Wallis and Futuna lies approximately midway between Fiji and Samoa, with 230 kilometres separating Wallis from Futuna and Alofi, which lie to the south-west. They are small islands: Wallis is the emerged summit of an underwater volcano, while Futuna and Alofi (the Horn Archipelago), formed by geological upheaval caused by the movement of the Pacific plate, are of relatively steep mountainous terrain.[1] There are devastating cyclones, such as those of 1907 and 1986, and Futuna is near a flaw in the Oceanic plate. The last major earthquake occurred in 1993, and stone churches, chapels and missions were destroyed. Settlement is almost entirely restricted to the coastal borders of the main islands, while Alofi, lacking adequate fresh water, is uninhabited but reputed to support 10 000 pigs.[2] Sixty-seven per cent of the population live on Wallis, the largest of the islands, on the east coast of which lies Mata-Utu, the capital of the territory.[3]

Futuna was first sighted by Dutch navigators in 1616, but it was not until 1767 that Samuel Wallis from England anchored off Wallis and sent a landing party ashore for fresh water. After 1820, the islands served, in a minor way, as whaling stations and as a base for beachcombers, deserters, mutineers and those shipwrecked.[4] A Marist ship anchored at Futuna in 1801, and in 1837 a Marist mission was established, which, within three decades had converted the islands into one united Catholic church under the leadership of Father Pierre Bataillon on Wallis and Father Peter Chanel on Futuna.[5] In 1836 Protestant catechists from Tonga landed on Wallis but were killed.[6] By 1845 Wesleyan missionaries had settled on Wallis, but they met with opposition from the Roman Catholic missionaries and departed.[7] In 1887 the islands were declared a French protectorate, and in 1961 they were united as one country and granted the status of an overseas territory of France with

Vernacular Fale, Wallis.

a territorial assembly and representatives on both the French National Assembly and the French Senate. Virtually all residents have French nationality. Wallis and Futuna are ruled under customary law by three kings but in other matters by France. While there is a self-sufficient economy comprised of subsistence agriculture and some production of copra, handicrafts, fishing and lumber, for major expenditure the country is still dependent on French economic assistance. Up to the 1940s the territory was isolated and maintained its traditional culture. Major contact with the outside world came on a single day in 1942 with the arrival of 2000 US troops who set up a front-line base on Wallis, but the islands were never engaged in warfare.[8] The Americans built a road network and two airports on Wallis – one of which today is the principal airport of Hihifo.[9] The first civil air transport began at Hihifo in 1956, but Futuna remained untouched throughout the war, and general access by air did not reach it until 1969.[10]

The islands are remote, and while modern technology has recently arrived on Wallis, it is less evident on Futuna. By the mid-1990s Wallis had 100 kilometres of road with 16 kilometres paved, while Futuna still had few paved roads. The territory is not on the normal routes across the Pacific, and telephone and radio only reached Wallis in 1975. In 1992 a hospital was built on Futuna, and by 1993 there was a public school on each of the islands.[11] By 2000 the territory had regular contact with the outside world, satisfactory services, and educational, medical and communication facilities. Round-ended fales serve most village needs, and apart from the churches, there are few buildings of any size or distinction. The birth rate is high, with an average of seven to eight children per couple, and several generations usually live together.[12] The roof of the traditional fale is constructed with four central posts made from breadfruit trees supporting a coconut tree frame roof covered with pandanus leaves. Today, while many fales are built with concrete poles and sometimes iron roofing, the vernacular form is still followed. The fale fono at Vaisei, Futuna, shows a high standard of the craft of construction, with wooden columns and beams lashed together by sennit of coconut fibre.

It is estimated that there are approximately 20 000 Wallisians and Futunians living in New Caledonia, while the total resident population of Wallis and Futuna combined is only 13 256.[13] Emigration commenced mainly between 1969 and 1976 when New Caledonia's nickel industry prospered and additional jobs were created.[14] The local people are 98 per cent Polynesian, but each of the islands has a distinct society, with the Wallisians' way of life deriving from Tongan culture and that of the Futunians' from Samoa. The fortifications of the archaeological sites of Talietumu and Tonga Toto evidence the Tongan dominance of Wallis during its occupation in the fifteenth century. The population is almost entirely Catholic – a unique occurrence in the South Pacific. The control of the Church over the islands is universal, and its governance has been described as 'missionary colonization'.[15]

Buildings of Faith

The religious fervour of the people is given expression in what is the most distinctive and creative collection of churches to be found anywhere in the South Pacific.[16] The nineteenth century saw the construction of some imposing stone churches: 'In all Oceania the four churches of Wallis (Mu'a, Mata-Utu, Hihifo and Lano) are spoken of as a wonder.'[17] While the destruction wrought by cyclones and earthquakes would have resulted in considerable loss of churches, it does not fully explain the minimal evidence of significant twentieth-century building construction on the islands until the end of the century and the widespread outbreak of activity in church building in the 1990s. The initiative for the construction and reconstruction of the new churches 'seems to come more from the parishioners (elders and village chiefs) than from the priests themselves'.[18] These churches are mainly located in the coastal villages, but even remote uninhabited isles have small chapels and shrines. The number, size, and construction of these new Catholic churches are impressive, especially considering the small population and the

Fale Fono Vaisei, Futuna. Roof Detail.

isolation of the islands. Even with unpaid labour the cost of building the edifices would have been considerable. One can only assume the expense would have to have been borne by the Church or France – perhaps aided after 1970 by money sent from families in New Caledonia and foreign donations following the various earthquake damage reports.

As Wallis and Futuna do not share the same geological and cultural contexts, architectural expression and the use of buildings materials differ. Since Wallis is of volcanic origin, volcanic stone is readily available, while in Futuna, formed by a rising of the ocean plates, coral stone and also concrete block are the most common materials. The churches follow the established plan and massing of Christian churches elsewhere, but beyond that they exhibit remarkably individual and arresting arrangements, colours and textures. Outstanding features of the churches include the handsome patterning of the stonework on Wallis, the exuberance of forms and details on Futuna and the profuse refined decoration of the interiors on both islands. Idiosyncratic arrangements of some type are found in most of the churches, such as the spiral external stair of the 2001 Church of St Michael, Mala'e, Futuna, the arresting four-tier 'pagoda' tower at the Church of St Peter and St Paul, Vaitupu, Wallis, 2003, and the extraordinary horned façade and 'walking' porch of the Chapel of St John the Baptist, Vailala. In all cases the churches were designed, constructed and decorated by the people of the islands, often over a very short time with virtually no sophisticated tools. Further, given the isolation of the islands, most of the inventiveness of the architecture had to have come from within the cultures and through the French priests and after 1976, from local priests trained in Fiji.[19]

Precedent

As significant early churches had been built on Wallis, models existed on the island for the late twentieth-century churches, notable among these are the monumentality of the cathedral at Mata-Utu, Our Lady of Good Hope; the form and use of materials of the Church of St Joseph at Mu'a (Mala'efo'ou),[20] and the diverse imagery in the decoration of both the Church of St Joseph and the mission church of St Maria Immaculate at Lano. Father Pierre Bataillon was responsible for the founding of the Church of St Joseph at Mu'a in 1840, the first church to be established in Wallis and Futuna, and the building of the modest timber church at Mata-Utu in 1849. The Church of St Joseph took ten years to build, and for a long time was the only major monument in the islands.[21] The Mu'a church is a severe building externally, with a distinctive central clock tower. As became customary for most Wallis churches, it was built of ordered black volcanic stone marked by a strong chequered pattern by the white mortar joints, found inside and out. The large black-on-white spot pattern to the soffits of the galleries are conspicuous features of the interior. The glory of the church was the kaleidoscope of colour from the floor rugs, and abstract and pictorial patterns covering walls, columns and vaults. The church suffered damage at the beginning of this century and much of the decoration has been lost. Parts of the present church have been built with a reinforced concrete frame. Father Bataillon was buried in the church of St Joseph in 1877.

In 1854–56 the timber church of Father Bataillon at Mata-Utu was replaced by the church of Father Meriais, which was constructed of hand-cut blue volcanic stone.[22] As evidenced in an early watercolour, in 1885 the towers were not yet built and the adjacent palace was still a timber building, but by 1886 the two towers and spires that dominate the lagoon had been constructed.[23] In 1950 Father

TOP: Chapel of St John the Baptist, Vailala, Wallis.

ABOVE: Church of St Michael, Mala'e, Futuna, 2001. Staircase.

RIGHT: Church of St Peter and St Paul, Vaitupu, Wallis, 2003.

Petelo Hamale restored the towers and conceived and realized the current façade with the royal insignia, the Maltese Cross. The church was completed in 1959 and consecrated as the Cathedral of our Lady of Good Hope.[24] The dominant edifice of the cathedral stands next to the new Royal Palace, a large but restrained stone building of two floors with a surrounding upper veranda.[25] It replaced the timber palace built by Bataillon in 1876 and 'appears to have been built at the same time as the new towers on the cathedral'.[26] The cathedral and palace face towards the lagoon over the large green that is the centre of communal activities for the people of Mata-Utu, including sports such as the Polynesian version of cricket, *kiliriti*, with more than forty people on the field at one time.

ABOVE LEFT: Church of St Joseph, Mu'a, Wallis, founded in 1840 (partially rebuilt in the twentieth century).
TOP RIGHT: Interior in 1999. *Courtesy of Tony Wheeler.*

ABOVE RIGHT: New Royal Palace, Mata'Utu, Wallis, 1886. (Replaced the 1876 Palace of Father Bataillon.)

OPPOSITE: Cathedral of Our Lady of Good Hope, Mata-Utu, Wallis, 1854–56 (Towers 1886, Façade 1950, completed 1959).

Some of the finest tapa drawings of the island are to be seen in the Mission Church of St Maria Immaculate, which was established in 1840 though parts of the current mission church were built in 1889–90.[27] The mission is a large complex, 'a true collegiate structure, with a vast sanctuary, perfectly suited to pontifical ceremonies, a choir with fifty places for our other pupils, two sacristies, and two lateral chapels surmounted with graceful turrets'.[28] The interior walls and ceiling are adorned with sensitively laid-out and executed random patterns, biblical scenes, happenings of daily life and tapa sea images showing boats, shells and fish in the lagoon.

The Later Churches

Wallis

The precedent established by the churches of the nineteenth century is clear in the later churches of Wallis, such as those at Fuga'uvea and Halalo. The tower of the Church of the Sacred Heart, Fuga'uvea, 1991, is the most dramatic of those of the churches of Wallis. The church is of concrete construction, but the stone work on the walls is distinctive with the usual dark volcanic basalt stone artistically enlivened with rosettes of coloured stones. However, the most spectacular is the tall circular tower, consisting of six diminishing towers on top of each other, resembling an extended telescope. The tower rises in front of the wide spreading body of the church, which has an uncommon shallow sloping roof and a flat ceiling over the nave.

The persistent use of traditional building techniques and the skills evident in the patterning of the older interiors is evident in the Church of Joan of Arc, Halalo, Wallis, which was designed and built by local builders in 1996–2000. This is a quality building, exhibiting a variation in the use of basalt, with a random arrangement giving a mottled pattern to the walls. The stonework is given further interest by small decorative motifs at key points of the building. Slim pink columns, decorated with delicately patterned white bands, provide contrast to the dominant black-and-white walls and enliven the interior. The outstanding artistic creations of this church are to be seen, however, in the ceiling covered with the splendid tapa patterns worked by the women of the village.

Futuna

Futuna does not have a monumental building tradition as Wallis does, and while the churches of Wallis are somewhat severe and imposing, those of Futuna are light and fanciful. Peter Chanel, who was to have a profound and lasting impact on the islanders, was assassinated on Futuna on 28 April 1841.[29]

OPPOSITE, ABOVE AND BELOW: Mission Church of St Mary Immaculate, Lano, Wallis. Wall tapa.

LEFT: Church of the Sacred Heart, Fuga'uvea, Wallis, 1991.
ABOVE: Detail.

LEFT: Church of Joan of Arc, Halalo, Wallis, 1996-2000. Interior showing Tapa-lined Ceiling.
ABOVE: Exterior.

OPPOSITE, LEFT: Basilica of St Peter Chanel, Poi, Futuna, 1986.
OPPOSITE, RIGHT: Apse.

The first of the new generation of Futunian churches, the white Basilica of St Peter Chanel at Poi, built to commemorate the life of the saint, was erected in 1986 near the place of the assassination.[30] Earlier churches on the site had been destroyed – in 1907 'the hurricane blew with such terrific violence that a large stone church with walls 0.7m thick was blown to atoms. The convent and church were also absolutely destroyed.'[31] There was a further devastating cyclone (Raja) in 1986 and an earthquake in 1993. The present basilica is a very large church reputed to seat over 1000 worshippers, which may seem excessive given the small size of the local population. Large attendances, however, are common on feast days on the islands – 'On feast days these churches, vast as they are, are too small; as the whole population assists at the offices – at the close of the Jubilee, at Mu'a, we gave communion to 1050 persons; in the other parishes there was the same affluence'.[32] The interior of the church at Poi is an exceptional

space defined by the simple but highly effective use of repetitive rectangular coloured-glass clerestory windows. The windows, in three rows, pattern the wall behind the altar with single rows banding the clerestory zone and edging and defining the walls of the nave and side aisles. The church is decorated throughout with brown-and-white tapa. The exterior is also a striking composition, presenting a façade bedecked by a lower colonnade of pale-blue columns capped by a white tower, and with pale-green decorative columns and trim that step up in multiple tiers culminating in a spire topped by a cross. The Chapel of St Peter Chanel, 1994, which houses the relics of St Peter Chanel, stands adjacent to the basilica on the site of the assassination. The octagonal chapel, of traditional timber construction with a central post and coconut fibre rope bindings, replaced its predecessors on the site.

Facing the sea further along the coast is the delightful Chapel at Tamana, which contains the tomb of Musumusu. The king, Niuliki, feared his friend

OPPOSITE: Chapel, Tamana, Futuna.
LEFT: Altar Tapa. BELOW: Interior.

ABOVE: Chapel, Point Oneliki, Futuna, 2000.

OPPOSITE: Church of Our Lady of Seven Sorrows, Ono, Futuna, 1995.
FAR LEFT: Interior. LEFT: Figurative carvings.

the missionary Peter Chanel as a rival and ordered his son-in-law to kill him. Subsequent to the murder, Musumusu became deeply repentant and prayed for forgiveness, but shortly afterwards he fell ill of a 'languishing sickness' and died as a penitent in 1845.[33] The white exterior of the chapel presents a light-hearted, even frivolous, confection of whimsical decoration, and the delightful interior is festooned with brightly coloured tassels, flowers and tapa hangings, most notably the large fale tapa over the altar. Behind the chapel stands the thatched roof fale that serves as a meeting house. Such small chapels are found in many places and are usually carefully sited, as with the open-sided Chapel at Point Oneliki, 2000, which stands on the black rocks of the headland.

The contrasting scale and extraordinary juxtaposition of the churches and fales of the villages of Futuna is illustrated by the Church of Our Lady of Seven Sorrows, of the village of Ono. This large church of concrete and concrete block, highly decorated with blue-and-white trim, was built in 1995. The artists of Wallis and Futuna are noted for their woodcarving (commonly executed today using a chainsaw) and the church at Ono contains a remarkable example of this work with carved figures of men leaning out from the sidewalls of the nave, each with an outstretched arm supporting the elaborately carved beams of the ceiling.

The most spectacular of the churches of Wallis and Futuna is the three-towered Disneyland creation of the Church of St Joseph at Sau Sau, the religious precinct of Nuku village in the kingdom of Sigave, Futuna. The fanciful white octagonal towers with black decorative banding are topped by a circular colonnaded upper tier and capped with pointed red 'witch's hat' roofs, giving a whimsical character to the church. The first church on the site built by R P Junillon in 1878 was destroyed by earthquake.[34] The next church was also destroyed by earthquake in the 1930s, and the subsequent church, the predecessor to the

ABOVE: Community Fale, Futuna.

OPPOSITE: Church of St Joseph, Sau Sau, Futuna, 1995.

present church, was devastated by the severe earthquake of 1993. In a remarkably short time the new church was built and decorated by the people of Sigave and consecrated in 1995 in time for the ordination of the third Futunian priest, Father Pierre Joane Fatutata.[35]

After the building of the Basilica of St Peter Chanel in 1986, there was a period that witnessed the construction of many new churches throughout the islands. While the need for new churches on Futuna is evident, and limited overseas aid and finance was available to assist the country rebuild after the natural disasters at the end of the twentieth century, these factors do not explain why so many large churches were built on Wallis. Given the size of the islands and the small populations, the number, size and seating capacity of the churches is extraordinary. There are no other large buildings on these islands, and the appearance of these churches in the small-scale villages is dramatic. But most impressive is the originality of the designs and the glory of the decoration of the interiors.

Part VI

VOICES OF THE SOUTH PACIFIC

'D'où venons nous? Que sommes nous? Où allons nous?'

Wearied by the corrupting influences of Western civilization, in 1891 Gauguin sailed to Tahiti. This symbolic masterpiece from his last years in the islands depicts Tahitian life in the states of birth, adulthood and 'after', and presents the culmination of his thoughts on existence with the metaphysical questions posed by the painting, *Where do we come from? What are we? Where are we going?*

Gauguin's metaphysical uncertainties, embodied in this 1897–98 depiction of the elemental nature of everyday life in Tahiti, might well have been transposed to the physical realm to portray the reality of the uncertainties of the shifting contexts and mores that the people of countries of the South Pacific were subjected to at that time – compelled to change by colonial administrations, persuaded by the bible through the missionaries and touched by the varying tides of European civilization that arrived on their shores.

Throughout the South Pacific expressions of identity emerge naturally in the differing vernacular buildings of each region. With the arrival from Europe of people of contrasting geographic and cultural backgrounds, a further set of values and needs, and therefore building practices, was introduced. The traditional cultural heritage of the Pacific Islanders is largely ephemeral (often something to be performed and experienced), with material forms of cultural expression, such as artefacts and buildings, predominantly fashioned from a range of types of organic materials that tend to have short lives in a tropical environment.[1] The European legacy of solid, lasting constructions, that today constitutes a major part of the urban fabric of Oceania, is far from ephemeral, and offers a different concept and medium for the representation of culture and country.

D'où Venons Nous? Que Sommes Nous? Où Allons Nous?, Paul Gauguin, 1897–98. *Photograph © 2014, Museum of Fine Arts Boston.*

In the second half of the twentieth century many countries entered the post-colonial stage of their development and have been exploring forms and insignia, both vernacular and European, for the construction of emblematic buildings to reflect the socio-political order and to house the government bodies and tribal councils, and cultural objects. The Parliament buildings of Fiji, Papua New Guinea and the Samoan Islands, take as their starting point vernacular building forms, such as the *bure kalou* in Fiji, the *haus tambaran* in Papua New Guinea, and the *fale fono* in Samoa. On the other hand, some countries, notably those with French ties, have wished to proclaim their European connection. Representations of place and culture by other artistic means, such as craft, dance, music and drama, provide fascinating glimpses of the very diverse natures of the people and their traditions and customs. The challenge of representing place and identity in the concrete form of architecture, however, has been made more problematic with much of the funding coming from outside sources, and commissions for designing national buildings often being awarded to architects foreign to the land and its people, but this does not necessarily preclude a distinctive meaningful architecture to stand for both people and place.

A MATTER OF PERSPECTIVE 11

View from the West: Ambiguous Answers

The Solomon Islands gained independence in 1978 and Vanuatu in 1980. New Caledonia presents a different situation, with the political upheaval of the 1980s and its current status as a special territorial collectivity of France. Since 2008 the intergovernmental organization known as the Melanesian Spearhead Group (MSG) has provided a meeting point for the Melanesian people.

The distribution of the traditional architecture of the islands along the Coral Sea is typical of the great South Pacific area in general. As would be expected in the less developed countries the building practices of the past remain more evident, as can be see in the Solomon Islands where, due to the wide dispersal of the islands, the local culture has been disturbed only in a limited number of places. Buildings in different regions respond directly to the local conditions and materials, bringing about distinct variations, for example in the high 'stilt' buildings of New Manra beach on the south-west coast of Ghizo Island, Solomon Islands. Vanuatu consists of a scattered series of islands, with the persistence of some customary ways of living on the outer islands, but only a small distribution of traditional villages on the principal island of Efate. Pitched roofs sloping down to the ground are typical of vernacular houses of these islands that are so subject to tropical cyclones. Yet the lightweight tradition of building persists in most settlements, and the church and the kava house rival the principal focal role of the meeting house. New Caledonia presents a special case, as it retains examples of a rich surviving local architectural tradition. Notable are the several *grandes cases* (built as chief's houses and meeting houses) still in existence on the outer islands, particularly on the Loyalty Islands.[1] The timbers of the *grandes cases* are

ABOVE LEFT: Meeting House, We, Lifou, New Caledonia. ABOVE RIGHT: Wall Detail.

PREVIOUS PAGE: South Pacific Commission Headquarters.

customarily richly carved, primarily as standing, though recumbent, figures occasionally appear as beams. Among the important *cases* on Lifou are those at Hnathalo and Jokin, both initially built in the nineteenth century. The ritualistic building of ceremonial houses was banned in the later nineteenth century, as it was feared that the gathering of so many chiefs could lead to political unrest.[2] The *grandes cases* on Grande Terre rose to heights of up to eighteen metres, usually constructed by binding two or three tree trunks together to make a central post – but only one of this type survives: the thirteen-metre-high *Grande Case de Petit Couli*, Sarraméa, built in the nineteenth century.[3] While the thatched hut is still widely built as a living unit, the traditional ceremonial buildings call for highly developed skills and training, now mostly to be found only in the elderly.[4]

Politics/Practice/Parliaments

The Solomon Islands

After self-government was declared for the Solomon Islands, the Legislative Council met in the High Court Building, 1963, a modest single-storeyed building designed as a circular main court chamber with wings radiating outwards. The design was probably by an architect by the name of Wassum from Switzerland (who was senior architect up to 1963 when Jock Stevenson arrived), with construction supervised by Alfred Munday from England, who became the assistant architect to Stevenson.[5] But, as with many of the Pacific countries, after independence ambitious projects were proposed for future national buildings, and in 1989–90 the Chief Architect of Public

LEFT: *Grande Case*, Hnathalo, Lifou.

BELOW: *Grande Case de Petit Couli*,
Sarraméa, Grand Terre, New Caledonia.

Works John Coombes commenced design on two major projects: the State House, to be occupied by the Governor-General, and the new Parliament House.

The high commissioners had occupied Government House, on the beach side of Mendana Avenue, from as early as 1963. In the 1960s Stevenson worked on changes to this building in association with architects Warren and Mahoney from New Zealand. Following independence in 1978, it was decided to build a new State House on West Kola'a Ridge. John Coombes' sketch design for the State House was for a very ambitious proposal with two principal buildings of widely differing designs: the residence being a square building with a central courtyard and the chancery consisting of two long wings of administrative and reception rooms crossed in an 'X' formation. Coombes left the Solomon Islands in 1992, and a subsequent competition was held for the design but the work did not proceed.

Coombes' design for Parliament House was equally imposing with a site plan related to that of the State House. The building consists of a commanding central structure linked by walkways to two flanking buildings enfolding central courtyards. The major parliament building was a centralized, regular, twelve-sided design with the apex of the building rising up above the roof planes to give the building a crowned effect. The centralized design is uncommon in the buildings of the Solomon Islands, which are usually laid out on a rectangular plan. The present Parliament House, 1993, which stands in a dominant position overlooking the low-scale shopping street in Honiara, was not built to Coombes' design. Parliament House was funded by the US Government to commemorate the fiftieth anniversary of the US landings on Guadalcanal, and it was decided it would be more beneficial to pass the project responsibility to the design arm of the Seabees (that is, the Construction Battalion of the US Navy) in association with the engineering firm of Martin and Chuck.[6] The building contract was won by the Japanese company of Kitano Construction on a successful tender bid.[7] The adjacent subsidiary buildings were not built at the time, but the Parliamentary Offices, a gift from the Taiwan Government, were completed in 2012 to a design by Pacific Architects.

The American modifications to the central Parliament House have resulted in a visually heavier building on a concrete podium, made even more assertive

by protruding concrete stairs. The unfamiliar nature of the design is made more explicit by the proximal location of the traditional thatched meeting hall.[8] However, the interior – notably the parliamentary chamber – designed by a naval architect in Hawaii, is impressive in its spatial quality, decorative surface treatment and the high standard of workmanship.[9] Noteworthy aspects include the seven-pointed Elven or Faerie Star at the top of the dome, the lively black-and-white bands of figures around the dome, the geometric patterns on the wall panels and the banding of the balconies on the mezzanine level that encircle the chamber.[10] The coloured fibreglass panel inserts of the dome, which are primarily of Melanesian inspiration, were cut to a computer program in Australia and then fitted in place.[11] This black-and-white patterning is well balanced by the colour and

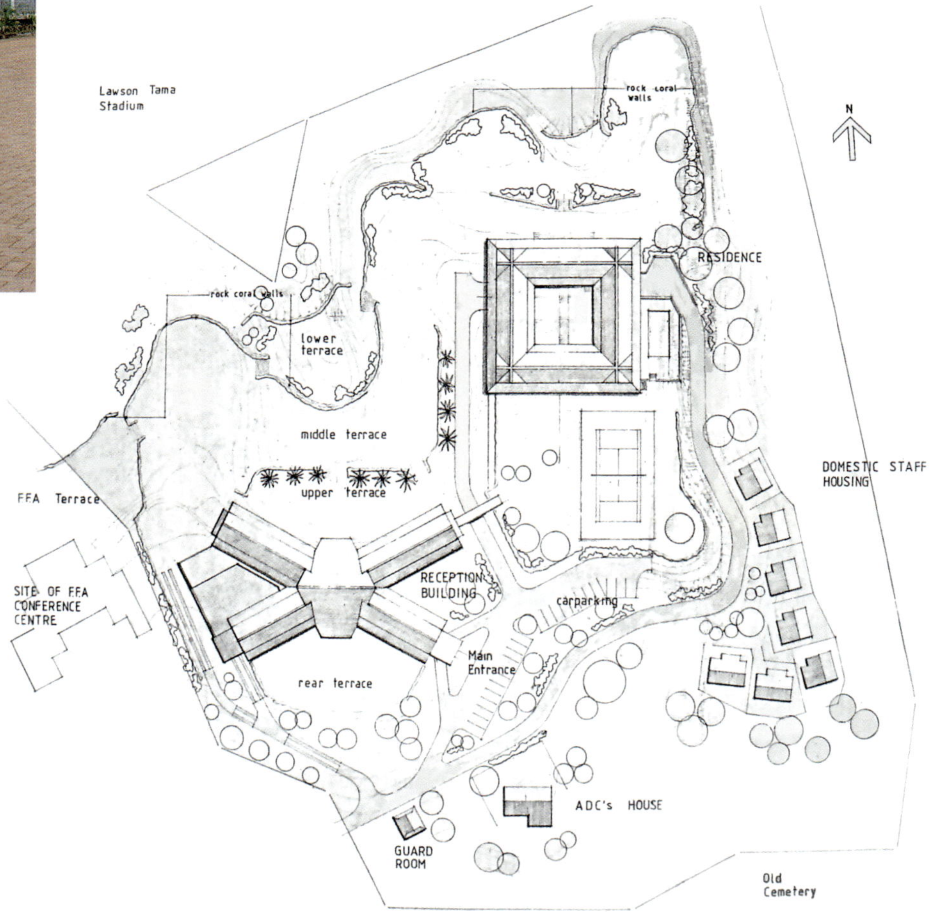

ABOVE: High Court, Honiara, Solomon Islands, 1963. M Wassum.

RIGHT: Proposed State House, Honiara, 1990. John Coombes. Site Plan.

OPPOSITE, LEFT: Solomon Islands Parliament House, Honiara, 1993. Construction Battalion of the US Navy in association with the engineering firm of Martin and Chuck. Parliamentary Chamber. OPPOSITE, RIGHT: Frigatebird Door Detail.

design of the subdued rose-and-white marble floor, and by the rich timber of the furnishings. Notable also are the handsome doors to the chamber with frigatebird door handles and shield-patterned panels. In all, the chamber of the Parliament House of the Solomon Islands contains one of the most accomplished interior spaces in the South Pacific.

Vanuatu

From its hillside position facing the bay, the bold geometric forms of the Parliament House of the Republic of Vanuatu, 1992, brings a new scale and massing to the morphology of Port Vila. Vanuatu is reliant, in part, on overseas funding, and the building was a gift from the Chinese Government. Designed in China,

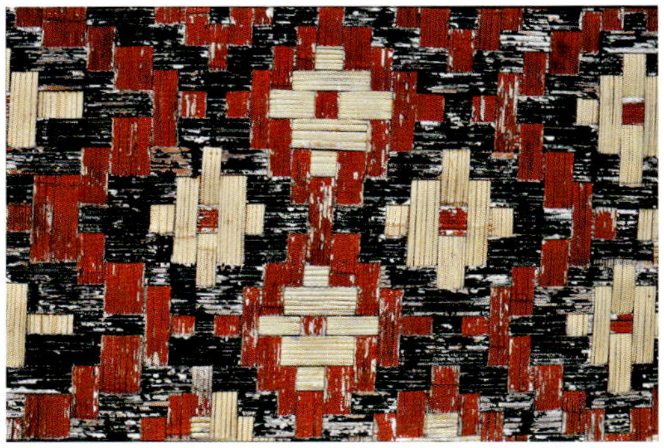

FAR LEFT: Nakamal Meeting House for Chiefs, Port Vila, Vanuatu. Interior.
LEFT: Detail of Wall Weaving. BELOW: Exterior Façade.

LEFT: Vanuatu Parliament, 1992. Chinese Government. Exterior.
ABOVE: Parliamentary Chamber. *Courtesy of the Parliament of Vanuatu.*

it was primarily built with Chinese materials by Chinese workers.[12] The Chinese followed this gesture with the gift of the Secretariat Building for MSG, built in Port Vila in 2008. In such projects, funding and responsibility ceases with the completion of the building, and in Vanuatu, as with many of the Pacific countries, maintenance of these new large buildings is problematic. The Parliament House is symmetrical about a central axis with a progression of spaces leading towards to the parliamentary chamber. The thatched entry portico opens into a large block of administrative wings surrounding a courtyard. In the centre of the courtyard stands a thatched hall covering a circular platform, which is used for ceremonial purposes by the Council of Chiefs. This is followed by the chamber, which is a large cream concrete and timber building of bold forms with planar walls that are incised by the clean-cut rectangular openings of the windows and verandas. Fittingly, the parliamentary complex is dominated by the red steel hipped roofs atop the central chamber and the administration blocks, which largely determine its character. In addition to the thatched entry and meeting hall, a further concession to Pacific culture can be seen in the protruding ornamental ridgepoles. In their gesture to the country, the Chinese Government has given Vanuatu an impressive landmark building for their parliament – but this has not been a culture of landmarks.

A marked contrast is found in the design for a group of cultural buildings facing Parliament House across rue Dartois. The group consists of the Nakamal (the meeting house of the chiefs), the Vanuatu Cultural Centre, housing the National Museum and National Film and Sound Unit, 1995, and the Centre of the Vanuatu National Council of Women, 1998, all arranged around an extensive open-air dance and spectacle area. The Nakamal is an excellent example of the traditional construction and form of important Vanuatu buildings, being rectangular in plan with a timber structure supporting a pitched roof. In the dark interior the

FAR LEFT: Vanuatu Cultural Centre, Port Vila, 1995. François Raulet, Frigatebird Ridge Beam Detail.
BELOW: Exterior.

LEFT: A-frame Indigenous Hut, Vanuatu.

French High Commission, Noumea, New Caledonia,1996. François Raulet. *Courtesy of Haut Commissariat de La République Nouvelle-Calédonie*.

Congress Office Building, Noumea, 1974.

walls sparkle with multiple specks of light entering through the delicate enclosures of woven cane. Externally, the walls are brightly decorated with coloured paints picking up on the various patterns created by the weaving. The modest Council of Women stands adjacent to the cultural centre.

The 1994 international competition for the design for the Vanuatu Cultural Centre was won by the New Caledonian architect François Raulet, who, in 1979, had designed a large hall in New Caledonia as a centre for the coming together of the Wallisian and Futunian people.[13] Its roof, supported by laminated timber beams, was decorated by the Wallisian and Futunian communities with frescoes of cultural themes inspired by tapas. Michael Heffernan, who had been selected by the Australian High Commission to submit a scheme for the cultural centre, was placed second in the competition with an interesting proposal for a group consisting of a central building with a strong axial geometric form within a complex of small pyramidal pavilions, chosen for their better cyclone resistance.

Raulet's Vanuatu Cultural Centre follows the design of the village hut, rather than the more ceremonial form of the chiefs' meeting house. The centre, with a rectangular building sheltering under a large pitched roof low to the ground, follows customary building forms that are comprehensible to the local builders. The timber A-frame of the indigenous huts is translated into steel in an expressed structure with exposed trusses in the large spaces of the exhibition halls, and boasts an artistically carved ridge beam depicting the frigatebird, a symbol of creativity and culture.

Because of the size of the building, external large-diameter PVC tubes substitute for the traditional external tie-down poles of the hut to secure the clip-lock steel roof sheets against cyclones. As a further gesture to local construction, the portico is roofed with thatch. The familiar, affordable cultural centre is comfortably at home in Vanuatu with its straightforward design that successfully reinterprets local custom.

New Caledonia

New Caledonia has a unique status within the French republic and the symbolic building of government is the revivalist French High Commission in Noumea, which stands on the site of the demolished Government House of 1865. The very large grounds contain other subsidiary office buildings and the Residency. The

Loyalty Islands Provincial Government Offices,
Lifou, New Caledonia, 1990. Patrick Frére.

venue of the elected body, the Congress of New Caledonia, which is currently in the process of assuming increasing responsibility for many aspects of the country's government, is a special-purpose congress hall, built in 1966 by the engineering firm Pierre Gomez. The administration is housed nearby in an unremarkable 1974 office building with a glazed façade on rue Sébastopol.[14] Outside of Noumea, some recognition of the Kanak culture found expression in civic buildings, as in the 1990 Loyalty Islands Provincial Government Offices, We, Lifou, by Patrick Frére.

In 1989, immediately after the Matignon Accords, a competition was held for a new building to serve the French High Commission and to symbolize the presence of France in the country. François Raulet won the competition with a building based on the design of the old Government House. A conserved stone archway bridges the principal axis of the forecourt, which is reached by monumental curving stone stairs to each side of the arch. The High Commission, completed in 1996, is a neo-Palladian building with a symmetrical façade and a prominent colonnaded entry porch. The richly decorated interior, by Gérard Colson, continues the formality of the façade. With its romantic, neoclassical spirit, the High Commission carries forward the traditional imagery, and consequent messages, of colonial architecture in the Pacific.

On the other hand, two of the major South Pacific buildings that most successfully respond to indigenous culture in a meaningful way have been built in Noumea, and as with the Parliament Houses of the Solomon Islands and Vanuatu, the architects for these buildings were from outside the country. The first was the South Pacific Commission Headquarters (SPC), 1995, by Architects Pacific, Fiji, and the second, the Jean-Marie Tjibaou Cultural Centre, by Renzo Piano Workshop, Italy, which was inaugurated in 1998.

In 1992 an international competition was held for the design of the South Pacific Commission Headquarters (SPC) (after 1997 the Secretariat of the Pacific Community), Noumea, intended to be representative of the various island states of the Pacific and serve as a meeting house. The headquarters were to be built at Anse Vata next to the site of the wartime Pentagon, which had been deployed as a temporary home for the SPC after the Americans left Noumea. The winning scheme, by Architects Pacific, imbued with Pacific metaphors, is akin in spirit to earlier buildings the firm designed for the South Pacific Bureau for Economic Co-operation, Suva. The headquarters is a very large complex consisting of quite diverse buildings accommodating mixed functions. These include a conference chamber, library, meeting rooms and office accommodation wings that are linked in various ways by aerial walkways around a series of seemingly unstructured main spaces. The site planning, however, is subtly organized, as the remarkable Micronesian ancient navigation charts of the Marshall Islands were studied to establish an underlying order for the design of the site. The conference chamber is the most symbolic section of the campus, with its structure and form following creative Pacific practices. Its striking 'upturned-canoe' roof bridges a moat that lies both inside and outside the eastern wall, reflecting shimmering light into the chamber and creating an evocative building calling to mind visions of the waters of the Pacific Ocean. The principal eastern wall consists of stitched coconut wood panels assembled using traditional canoe-building techniques, while large operable vertical louvers of white *masi* (tapa cloth) control the light entering from the south. The SPC headquarters is a significant building that creates a contemporary statement, poetically enriched by architectural allusions to the nature of the commission and the location of the building in the Pacific (see p. 292).

The Jean-Marie Tjibaou Cultural Centre provides one of the memorable architectural images of the late twentieth century. The building is a remarkable achievement in that it demonstrates the harmony possible between international technology and the culture of specific place. One outcome of the Matignon Accords was a proposal to conduct an international competition for the design of such a centre. The competition was held in 1991, with Renzo Piano awarded the commission.

LEFT: South Pacific Commission Headquarters, Noumea, 1995. Architects Pacific. Site Plan.
ABOVE: Conference Chamber.

Piano's cultural centre is a politically balanced, Mitterrand-commissioned complex bridging Kanak civilization and the continuing French presence.[15] The cultural centre was a gift from France, built in restitution for the 1989 assassination of Jean-Marie Tjibaou, the leader of the Kanak and Socialist National Liberation Front. The centre was built to showcase Kanak culture, to honour the contribution of Tjibaou to that culture, and to acknowledge and celebrate the Kanak people.

Construction of the centre commenced in 1993 on an eight-hectare site on the Tina Peninsula ten kilometres out of Noumea. It is a large complex of 8000 square metres arranged traditionally as three 'villages' and planted places, linked by a 235-metre walkway along the peninsula ridgeline, which is defined by the dramatic conical forms derived from the traditional *case*, such as the *Grande Case de Petit Couli*. These are ventilated through their double-layered 'skins' and modified in response to the climatic conditions of the site, turning their backs to the windy ocean side and opening up to the tranquil waters of the lagoon. The low buildings of the complex are located on the sheltered lagoon side of this passage. The planting of numerous forest trees, such as the tall narrow pines of the islands *(Araucaria columnaris)* furthers the identity of the building with place. The centre is furnished throughout with state-of-the-art technical aids and draws on international materials and technology – the *case* are of laminated timber construction clad externally by Iroko wood from Africa and prefabricated in France.

ABOVE: Jean-Marie Tjibaou Cultural Centre, Noumea, 1998. Renzo Piano Workshop. Iroko Wood *Case* Construction.
OPPOSITE ABOVE: Site Plan

LEFT: South Pacific Commission Headquarters, Noumea, 1995. Architects Pacific. Conference Chamber. Moat Detail.
OPPOSITE, BELOW: Conference Chamber.

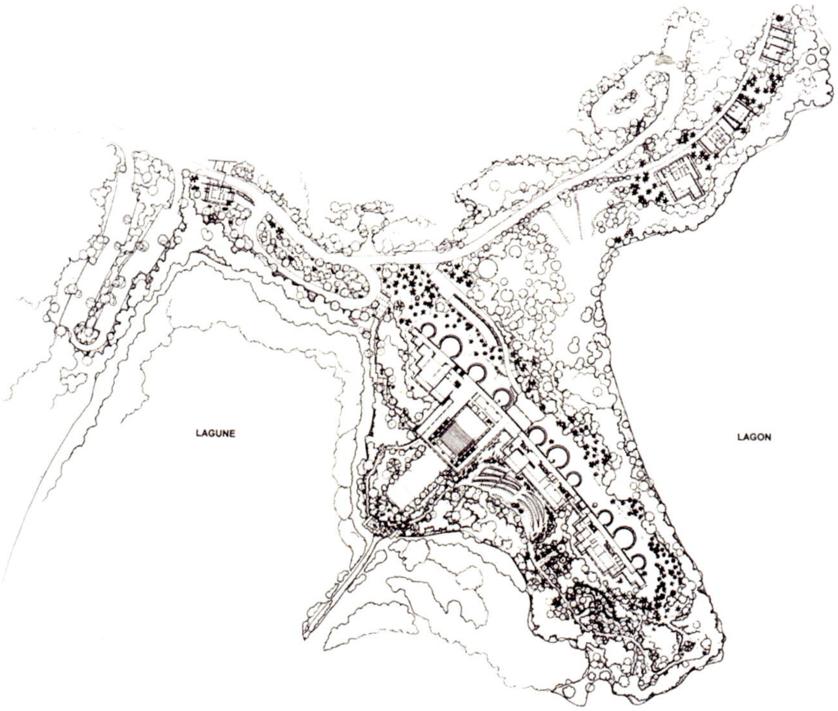

The technology testifies to how reinterpreted old materials and building practices can work positively with the new. The centre combines ultra-high-tech systems with simple, proven natural climatic control and demonstrates that a sustainable architecture can emerge that is not technologically obsessive but retains beauty and the emotive qualities of architecture as part of a sustainable whole. The centre's role is one of instruction, and the building itself and its libraries, media rooms, art galleries, theatres and gardens tell of the culture and native trees and food crops and present a rich, accessible fund of experience and information for both local families and visitors from other places in an engaging environment.

The Tjibaou Cultural Centre is the result of a highly conscientious cultural and ecological research programme. Piano developed his ideas in consultation with the Kanak people in collaboration with Alban Bensa, the noted anthropologist on the South Pacific, and through observation over many days on the site.[16] The building is remarkable in its response to the political issues that conditioned its beginning and its commitment to the way forward for Kanak life in the contemporary world.

As a further outcome of the Noumea Accord, a competition was held in 2009 for a complex to house the Customary Senate, to be located on a site adjacent to the sea at Nouville. The design competition called for a building to be constructed to 'represent Kanak culture as a totality' and was won by the Noumea firm ARCA 2 – Bernard Quinne architect. As the senate would become a symbol representing Melanesia, the concept was based on the premise that it would reflect the values of Melanesian culture, for example, its attachment to the land, respect for elders and the customary way of doing things. The centre brings together two departments that had been housed separately – the Senate Department and the Department of Administration. The site plan is arranged in an orthogonal axial composition of low pitched buildings, bounding a long landscaped court that centres on the circular senate building, designed in the form of a 14.5-metre-high *case*.[17]

This spectrum of representative building reflects the marked differences in the economic and political structures of the diverse countries. With the exception of Raulet in Noumea, the architects of the major buildings came from outside the country of the buildings' genesis. In the Solomon Islands and Vanuatu the desire for representation of the nations' pride in self-governance was met with donated overseas funding, resulting in a shift from the familiar to the unfamiliar. The architecture of New Caledonia with French control and relative financial independence derived from a different world. The national architecture reflects the disparities in the circumstances of countries in the South Pacific and projects images of, not necessarily their fundamental natures, but of their current state of affairs.

ABOVE: Proposed Kanak Senate, Noumea, New Caledonia. ARCA2, Competition-winning Scheme.

RIGHT AND OPPOSITE: Jean-Marie Tjibaou Cultural Centre, Noumea, 1998, Renzo Piano Workshop. Aerial View. *Courtesy of Renzo Piano Workshop.* BELOW: Section. OPPOSITE: Laminated Timber *Case* Shell Construction.

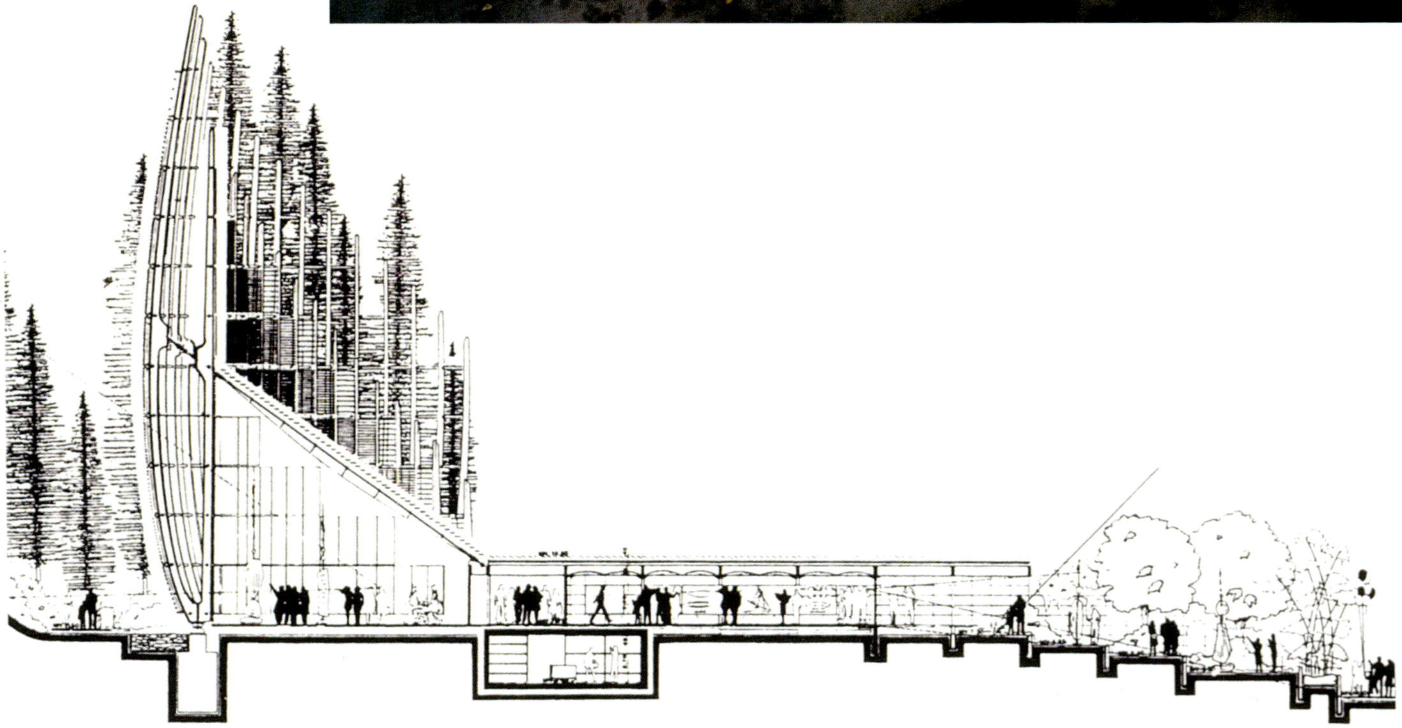

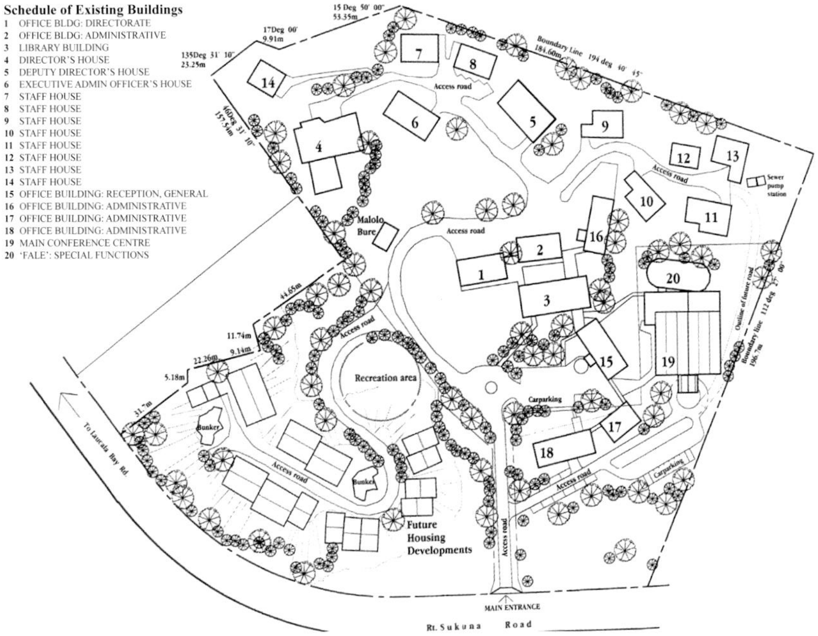

The Pacific Image of Fiji

Given the ethnic structure of Fiji, which consists primarily of indigenous Fijians and Indo-Fijians, the representative buildings are challenged to give a suitable reflection of the nation's dual values, societies and ambitions. For the most part, the expression of Indian and Melanesian cultures has remained distinctive. Buildings celebrating Indian identity are mostly those of a religious nature. In contrast, logically adhering to Pacific prototypes are the buildings that are supportive of various tourist interests and the ceremonial buildings of the Fijian chiefly class. The cultural references of Parliament House also primarily relate to Pacific precedent. In addition, Fiji is home to the buildings of the Pacific Islands Forum Secretariat, serving as a meeting house and representative of the nations of the Pacific.

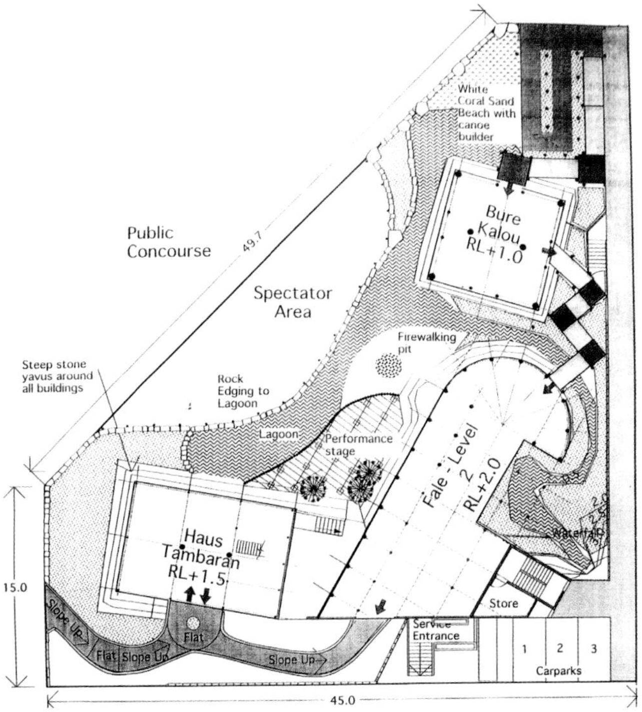

Representing the Pacific

Stuart Huggett of Architects Pacific Design Partnership (later Architects Pacific) provided early examples of the successful deployment of lessons from local traditions to the making of a Pacific architecture within a contemporary milieu. In this context Huggett's early buildings were matched in the South Pacific only by those by Michel Prévot in Tahiti. The first work of note was the 1976 headquarters for the newly formed South Pacific Bureau for Economic Co-operation (SPEC) in Muanikau, Suva. The complex was to represent not just Fiji but also the South Pacific in general. After 2000, SPEC came to include all of the Pacific and was renamed the Pacific Islands Forum Secretariat. The original 1976 development, of concrete block construction with timber verandas, consisted of a Conference Centre and accompanying buildings for office and residential use.[1] The complex is sensitively related to the topography and the existing mature tropical landscape. The focus of the composition is the *rara* (the entry court) with a very large vaivai tree,[2] which gives shade and protection to the main reception area, around which the offices are grouped.[3] The principal building, the Conference Centre, with its steep, triple-

OPPOSITE, ABOVE: South Pacific Bureau for Economic Co-operation, Suva, Fiji, Architects Pacific. Site Plan of 1997.

OPPOSITE, BELOW: Pacific Village, Seville Universal Exposition, Seville, Spain, 1992. Architects Pacific. Site Plan.

LEFT: Conference Centre, South Pacific Bureau for Economic Co-operation, Suva, Fiji, 1976. Architects Pacific. Gable.

pitched roof, oversailing gables and eaves typical of indigenous Pacific buildings, and a painted Sepik River artwork in the gable end facing the *rara*, was a demonstrative modern work reflecting the Pacific context.[4] The two and three-storeyed office blocks relate to the terrain and are protected by deep overhangs and exterior access verandas. Architects Pacific also designed several major extensions of office and residential accommodation to the complex, especially in the 1980s and early 1990s.[5] The SPEC campus was an aid project from the New Zealand Government that specified that the buildings should reflect the indigenous culture and make use of local materials and components where possible.[6] Further, the architects worked to stringent joinery specifications to minimize the use of materials. The roofs were intended to have timber shakes, but, with the exception of the Conference Centre roof, they were erected with corrugated steel sheets. Further, they are all naturally ventilated, again with the exception of the Conference Centre, which was enclosed for privacy considerations. Architects Pacific's SPC Headquarters, Noumea, followed this in 1992.

The 1991 limited competition for the Ryoichi Jinnai Conference Centre, also to be built at Muanikau adjacent to existing SPEC buildings, was won by Architects Pacific.[7] The 1994 Conference Centre consists of a sizeable building with several meeting rooms and an adjacent special function space with a finely crafted structure based on the Samoan fale. The centre was intended to be air-conditioned, but this was not installed due to the favourable performance of the building under natural cooling systems.[8] As with the earlier buildings of the Pacific Islands Forum Secretariat, the Ryoichi Jinnai Conference Centre demonstrates a way of achieving a unique contemporary architecture with a Pacific identity.

At the same time, Architects Pacific, which had designed the Pacific Village for the World Expo '88 in Brisbane, was invited to design the Pacific Village project that would represent the Pacific at the 1992 Seville Universal Exposition. The exhibition was extensive and presented a range of iconic vernacular building types from across the Pacific that were prefabricated in Fiji using modern and traditional methods and erected in Seville. Thirty Fijians worked on building the village, which

BELOW: Ryoichi Jinnai Conference Centre, South Pacific Bureau for Economic Co-operation, Suva, 1994. Architects Pacific. Special Function Fale. Elevation.
RIGHT: Roof Structure. Detail.

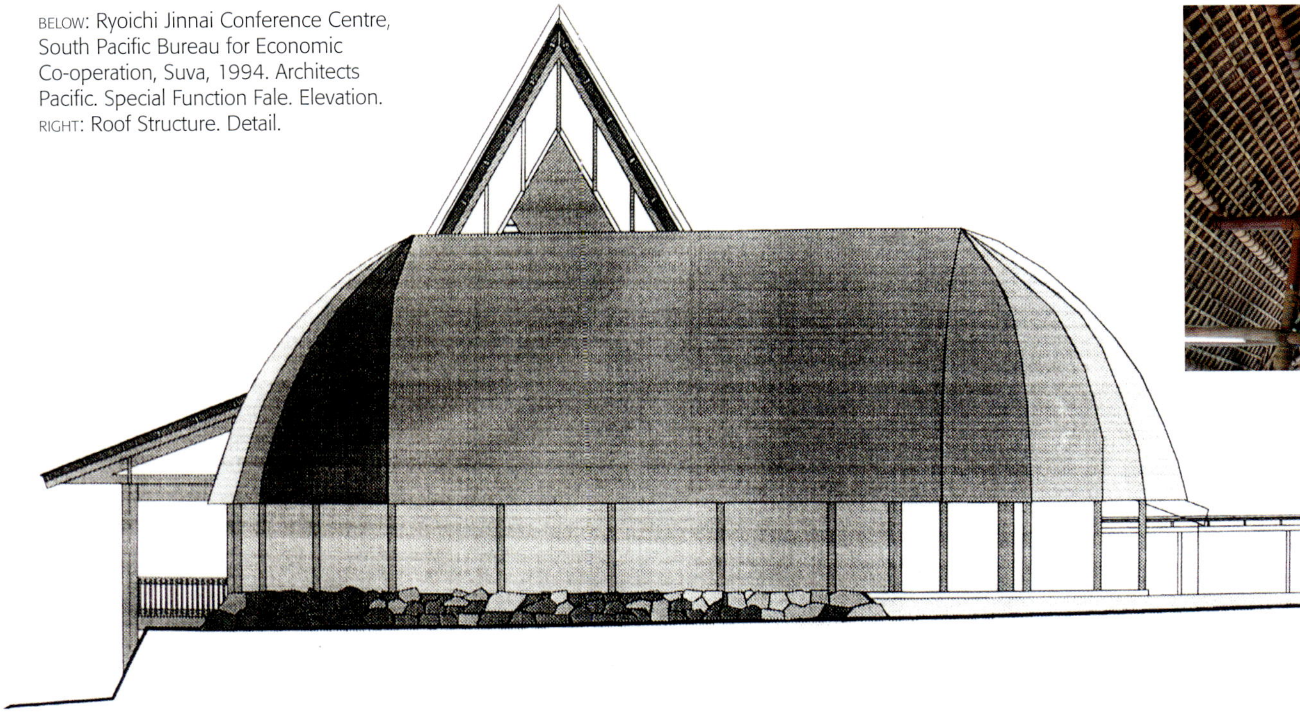

was accidentally burnt down three days before the Expo opened.[9] Architects Pacific also was appointed to design the Pacific Village at Expo 2000 Hanover, and the Pacific Pavilion at the 2010 World Expo, Shanghai.

The 1995 competition for a National Centre for Culture and the Arts, sponsored by the Fiji Museum, was a significant initiative. The centre was later developed into the Oceania Centre for Arts, Culture and Pacific Studies (OCAC) and was built on the Laucala Campus of the University of the South Pacific. The centre was established in 1997 as a special project of the university council to foster cultural conservation and development. Under the founding director, the Tongan-born social anthropologist and author Epeli Hau'ofa, the centre aimed to encourage an Oceanic cultural identity that was transcendent of national interests and identity.[10] Jaimi Associates won the competition for the building with a scheme combining inside and outside spaces appropriate for the display of the diverse arts and crafts of this vast region. In particular, the building sought to reflect principles of Oceanic spatial organization for an environment that would be culturally familiar to the artists involved. 'This explains the differences that anyone can see between the spatial layout and organization of the OCAC and the rest of the Laucala Campus'.[11]

Representing the Pacific Heritage of Fiji

Tourism

Up until the post-war period Fiji's villages had changed little since European settlement. The colonial architecture stood aloof and drew its logic and imagery from Britain. With the revival of tourism in the 1950s came recognition of the desirability of attracting visitors to an 'exotic' Pacific accommodation experience. Following the success of Korolevu, the first of such ventures, the building of pseudo-Fijian resorts soon became widespread. They promoted an idealized image of Melanesian Fiji, and traditional crafts have been kept alive through their patronage. By the 1970s tourism had become an important industry in Fiji. Private industry promoted Melanesian culture, and government funds were made available to encourage and display Fijian work and traditions.[12] The 1974 Pacific Cultural Centre at the Pacific Harbour Resort included a recreated village, to both educate and entertain the visitors. In the same year Architects Pacific designed a rare example of a traditional *bure kalou* on Orchid Island, south of Suva, as a part of the attractions of the Orchid Island Botanical Garden.[13] Lived-in villages also capitalized on tourist interest, and in places such as Navala in the Nausori highlands of Viti Levu, self-imposed restrictions on building forms and materials were introduced in order to maintain an authentic look. Such restrictions included the use of only local materials, with a ban on corrugated steel that was favoured in most villages because of its low cost, ease of erection, strength and durability.

Buildings for the Great Chiefs

In 1985 Architects Pacific was invited by the chiefs of Fiji to be architects for the Chiefly Mausoleum on the Island of Bau, the Sau-Tabu, the spiritual heart of Fiji as the burial place of the *vunivalu*, the supreme tribal chiefs. The mausoleum was to formally house the bones of the chiefs, to be lifted from the soil of Bau.[14] The mausoleum is located within a ceremonial area on the top of the hill that crowns this small island. The building consists of two principal sections: the underground tunnels and lower chamber with the burial vaults, and the upper chamber of the *bure kalou*, which stands on a rock-faced platform, the *lavu*, and dominates the skyline. The clients requested a concrete building, and this has been finished with patterned-marble facings to the concrete block walls inside and out, slate floors and a steep lightweight

RIGHT: Bure Kalou, Orchid Island, Viti Levu, Fiji, 1974. Architects Pacific.

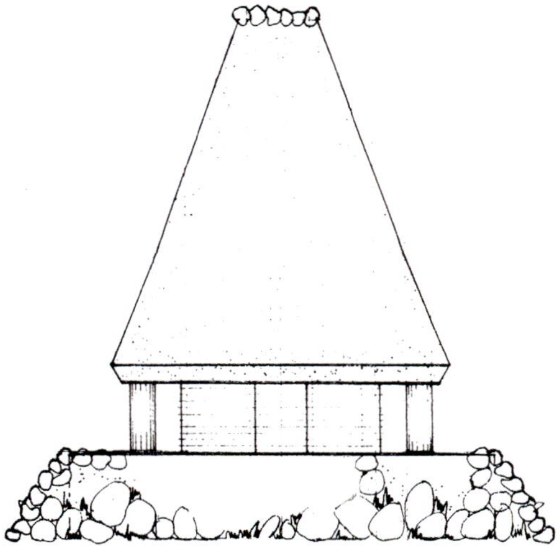

BELOW: Bau Mausoleum, Bau Island, Fiji, 1985. Architects Pacific. Elevation.

Great Council of Chiefs Meeting House and William Cross Memorial Hall, Somosomo, Taveuni Island, Fiji, 1985. Lee Associates.

concrete roof with an exposed aggregate finish. Architects Pacific also designed a large meeting house for the village, located on a lower level of the island.

The most important political buildings in Fiji are Parliament House, which represents the nation, and the Great Chiefs' Meeting Houses, which, as well as their functional roles, are symbolic of the interests of indigenous people. The buildings for the Great Chiefs' Meeting House, Suva, and Parliament House in Suva were both commissioned by new governments succeeding political coups. The Great Council of Chiefs (*Bose Levu Vakaturaga*) was established in 1876 to advise the governors with regard to policy on indigenous affairs. Under the 1997 constitution the Great Council, consisting of fifty-six members, was authorized to appoint fourteen out of thirty-two members of the Senate, with the right to appoint the president and vice president of Fiji.

The Great Council of Chiefs' Meeting House, the Domain, Suva, was the subject of a competition held in 2005, with the commission being awarded to Jaimi Associates. Jaimi, for Lee Associates, had previously designed a meeting house for the Great Chiefs on the island of Taveuni. The Somosomo Meeting House and the William Cross Memorial Hall, both completed in 1985, stand together on a large flat, grassed site. These unassuming buildings are among Jaimi's most successful projects in his search for a contemporary Pacific architecture and appear at home in the setting of the islands. The buildings share a similar pallet of soft browns in the timbers and the spreading steel roofs, with variation in plan and form as related to their functions. The low pitch of the Memorial Hall's entry portico is strikingly countered by the steep 'Fijian' roof and spreading wings of beams over the singular centre-aisle plan of the nave. In contrast, the Meeting House is a restful non-directional building with a row of clerestory window lights above the uncommon flat-roofed surrounding verandas.

The Great Council of Chiefs' Meeting House, Suva, was completed in 2008 for a cost of US$ 10.5 million.[15] The plan of the complex is clearly organized, with the Legislative Chamber (*Vale ni Bose Lawa*) flanked by the Secretariat and the members lounge, to which it is linked by walkways, with a well-located portico serving both the main hall and the lounge. The raised ceremonial court of the *rara* is defined on three sides by the main hall, the north wing building, which contains the conference centre and offices, and the south wing building of offices. These long wings are regular, three-storeyed buildings with sheet-metal roofs and wide verandas that provide a frame for the main hall that stands on the raised stone platform of the *lava* on the central axis. The hall is a reserved building, making subtle reference to traditional Fijian architecture in the form of its shingled roof and the gable projection of the iconic *loru*, which protrude beyond the heavy timbers of the ridge of the roof construction and ornament each end.[16] Louvers enclose the covered surrounding walkway. The complex is ceremonially contained by a 3.5-metre-high wall faced with rough rock and incorporates the earlier War Memorial and restored Veivueti House War Museum. In March 2012 the prime

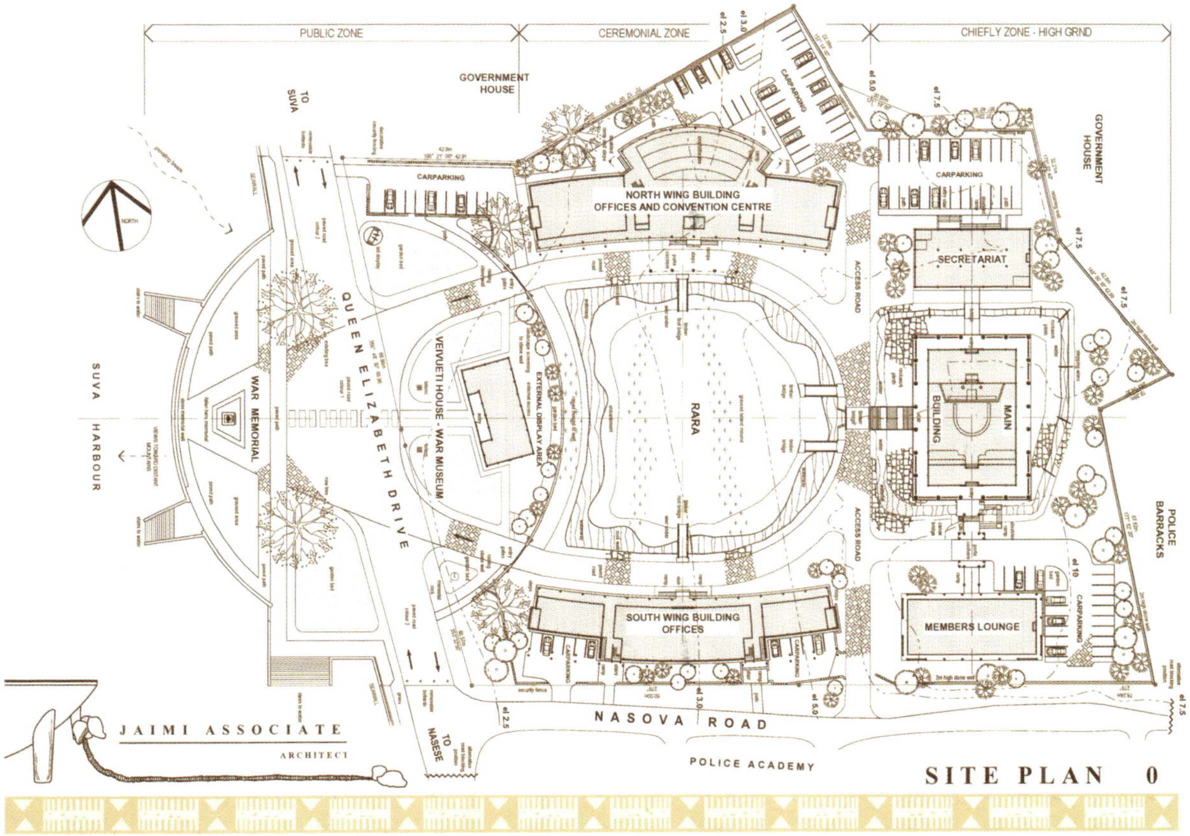

minister, Commodore Frank Bainimarama, abolished the Council, and the building currently is known simply as the Meeting House (*Vale ni Bose*).[17]

Representing the Nation

Ensuing from the coups of May and September of 1987, and the subsequent 7 October declaration of Fiji as a republic, the Fiji Government determined to erect a Parliament House to replace the Administration Building in which it customarily met. This originally was to be a temporary building, but later funds were provided for a permanent Parliament House.[18] It was specifically requested that the building be 'Fijian' in character.[19] The shifting political structure of Fiji at that time meant there were changing demands for the new parliament building, and the projected two-year programme became five years. The original project was for a much larger complex that was to be built in two stages, and the total drawings, including working

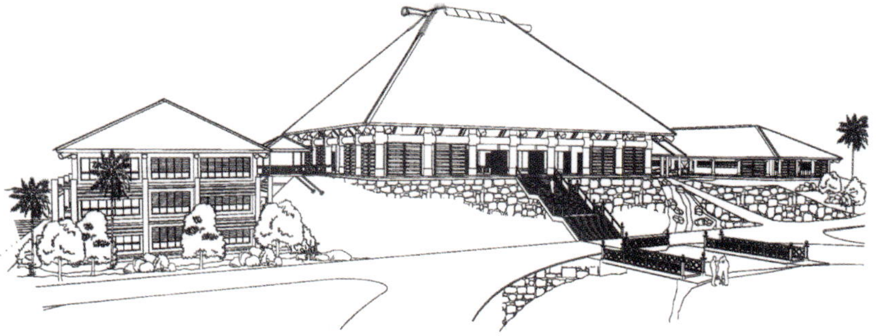

TOP: Great Council of Chiefs' Meeting House, Suva, 2008. Jaimi Associates. Site Plan.
ABOVE: Perspective.

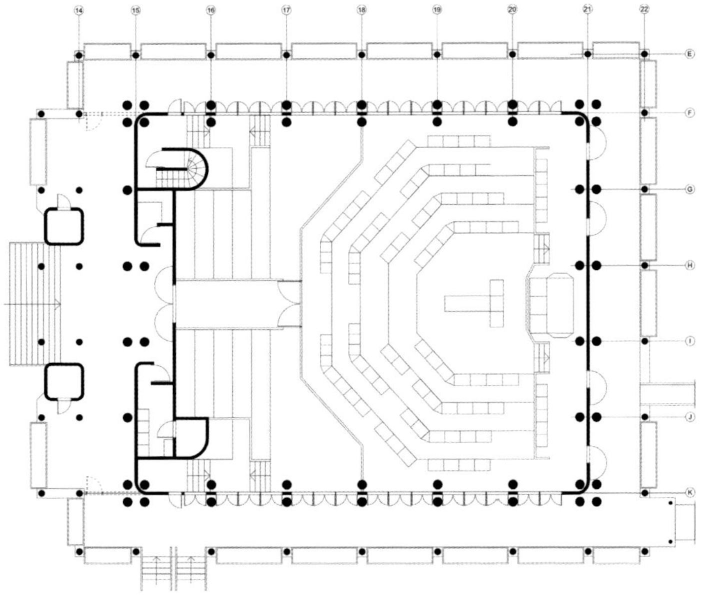

Parliament of Fiji
Vale ni Bose Lawa – Chamber Floor Plan

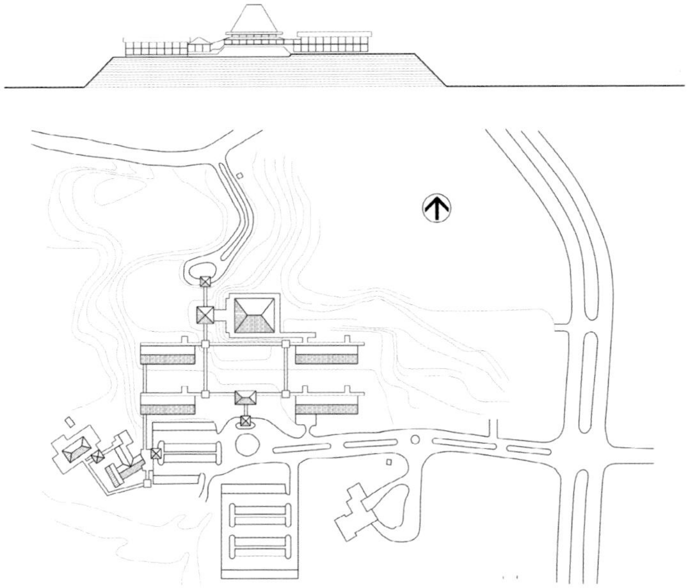

Parliament of Fiji
Master Plan and Elevation

drawings, were completed but only Stage 1 was built. Filipe Tauva of Vitia Architects, with Government Architect Tony Sansom as project director, designed the Parliament House, which opened in July 1992.[20] When the decision was made to build, the Fiji Parliament consulted Sansom. However, following the coup of 1987, many architects had left Fiji, and there were inadequate in-house staff members to undertake the project and he advised the Permanent Secretary that it could not be done within the government office. This posed a problem as, in addition major firms such as Architects Pacific and the Murray Cockburn Partnership had also temporarily left Fiji. With a short-term building originally in mind, Sansom approached the Fijian architect, Filipe Tauva. Tauva managed to assemble staff, and when the brief was determined for a permanent building and the site selected, he continued with the commission.[21] Tauva was seen as an appropriate architect because, in addition to his abilities and experience as a partner in Architects Pacific, he was concerned with issues that Sansom deemed to be of importance for the new Parliament House.

With its celebration of Fijian traditions, the Parliament House encapsulated the government's policy and provided a further milestone towards the evolution of Fijian architecture. The underlying concept was based on the model of the Fijian village, but, with the exception of the *Vale ni Bose Lawa* housing the main Legislative Chamber, the buildings are not overtly 'Fijian'. The five buildings of the complex are arranged around three interconnected courtyards with the principal chamber centrally located and appropriately linked to the less significant buildings by open verandas and covered walkways, which are not only suitable for the climate but also give the complex a tropical ambience. As is found throughout the rest of South Pacific, Fijian architecture is a 'roof' architecture, concerned with shelter from the sun and the rain, and the orange roof forms extend the imagery and make for visual cohesion within the parliamentary complex.

The Parliamentary Chamber is based on the *bure kalou*, with the dominant shingle-clad steeply pitched roof denoting its status. The rising terrain allowed for its placement on an elevated site at the apex of the composition, and the site planning and landscaping reinforce this focus. The chamber is elevated on a stone podium, as with the traditional *rara*, so that it overlooks and symbolically links the sea to one side and the land to the other. On the middle level of the site are four two-storeyed administrative support services buildings, the parliamentarian offices and general committee rooms. The lower level holds social and recreational

OPPOSITE, LEFT: Parliament House of Fiji, Suva, 1992. Vitia Architects. Plan of Parliamentary Chamber.

OPPOSITE, RIGHT: Elevation and Site Plan. ABOVE LEFT: Exterior. ABOVE RIGHT: Speaker's Chair.

facilities and housing for parliamentary staff. The construction of the main buildings is of concrete or pole frames, timber trusses and shingle roofing. Tropic pine was not only chosen to maximize local resources to help the economy, but also by necessity because of the trade bans in place following the coup. Fiji's noted hardwoods are used only on the floors. The high roof of the major chamber creates a dramatic interior with round concrete columns that refer to structural timber poles. The chamber is simply finished with wood-carved furniture, *lalawa magimagi* (decorative sennet binding), mat weaving and hanging pennants of *masi* (bark cloth) and *lalawa masi* (tapa cloth).

With its central location among the Pacific nations and its position at the crossroads of the Melanesian, Micronesian and Polynesian cultures, Fiji is well placed to serve as a meeting place for the disparate political and cultural worlds of the Pacific, which are sympathetically represented in the 'Pacific' buildings. The indigenous architecture of Fiji is kept alive both through the preservation and revival of traditional works and in recent symbolic buildings, while the challenge to represent the distinctiveness of its dual ethnicity remains. Concurrently, there is evolving a discernable contemporary architectural culture also drawing on Melanesian precedent.

Speaking for the Central Isles

The countries of western Polynesia have inherited different political structures primarily of European derivation, and questions of identity and its expression are diverse. Tonga is unique in being the only independent ruling monarchy in the South Pacific. Samoa and Tuvalu are the only fully independent post-colonial countries. American Samoa remains an overseas territory of the United States, the Cook Islands are self-governing in free association with New Zealand[1] and Wallis and Futuna is an overseas territory of France.[2] The Cook Islands Parliament occupies a low timber building of 1974, that served as accommodation for New Zealanders who came to work on the construction of the airport, and the Tongan Parliament continues to meet in a nineteenth-century single-room timber building. Following constitutional reforms in 2010, King George Tupou V handed over power to a democratically elected government. In order to house the functions that support the monarch in a democracy, such as the Privy Council, the Lord Chamberlain and the Government Archives, the 1867 palace was tripled in size. Swan Railley Architects added symmetrical office wings to each side of the original building, replicating the details of the early palace. To the rear, corner towers emulate the original central tower (but are smaller) and symbolize the sharing of power with the people.

New representative buildings based on the fale as the most clearly identified symbol of local culture were commissioned for the parliaments of Samoa and American Samoa. Traditional building techniques are still deployed for some buildings in the villages and in the construction of special works, notably large meeting halls, such as the greeting fale at Pago Pago International Airport, 1992, and the Great Hall of the National University of Samoa, Apia, which was built as a part of the upgrading of the university, with a 1997 grant from Japan. With its large and impressive space and bold structure of robust timber members, the university fale is one of the most notable among those of the South Pacific. Although of more

ABOVE: Parliament of the Cook Islands, Avarua, Rarotonga, Cook Islands, 1974. New Zealand Government.

LEFT: Parliament House, Nuku'alofa, Tonga, 1894.

Great Hall Fale, National University of Samoa,
Apia, Samoa, 1997.

Great Hall Fale, National University of Samoa,
Apia, 1997.

modest size, the airport fale also is of fine design with a particularly high quality of craftsmanship in the handling of the smaller timber members of the roof.

The Legislative Assembly Building of the Maota Fono, Ti-Afau, Apia, by the Ministry of Works Department of Samoa, was opened in 1972.[3] A *fono* is a governing council – be it of a village or country – hence *fale fono* or, in the case of Parliament House, Maota Fono. Initially, the building was funded by the government then, later, New Zealand assisted in the financing. The assembly building is part of a convincing composition of four buildings and a flagpole standing on the extensive *malae* – the others being the old *fono* building, the administrative wing and the thatched fale committee hall of 1998 sited at the rear of Parliament House. Traditionally, in Samoa the most important fale in the village is the round *Fale Talimatu*, which serves as a meeting house. The old *fono* building followed tradition in being a round open-sided building with a thatched roof, which was replaced with a steel roof in 1975.[4] The parliamentary complex stands on the Mulinu'u peninsula, the site of the old ceremonial capital, and the presence of the old *fale fono* led to the selection of the location for the Parliament House. Parliament met there for several years before the completion of the new building. When the ceiling of the new Maota Fono collapsed in 1990, Parliament temporarily moved back into the old *fono*.[5]

The Maota Fono Building (*Maoto o Luafatasaga Kalapu* – named after the first Speaker) is a circular building with a heavy projecting overhang and a domed concrete roof clad with welded polyurethane sheets.[6] Standing on the green field of the *malae* and backed by mountains, the very simplicity and singularity of the building impart an iconic status. Security would seem not to be a concern as the striking red chamber is simply enclosed with transparent glazed walls with operable doors.[7] Even more convincing than the composition of forms is the way the 1972 complex captures a sense of historical continuity and accord with the way of life of the people. This became even more evident with the contrast resulting from the gifts from the Chinese Government of the imposing neoclassical US$ 15 million Court House, constructed along the western edge of the *malae* in 2010 and, on the eastern edge, the equally dominant four-storeyed Parliamentary Office Complex of 2012.[8]

The Maota Fono complex in Pago Pago is the meeting chamber of the Legislature of American Samoa. The original home of the *fono* was across the *malae* in a former naval barracks. That building burned down in 1970, and in 1973 the *fono* moved into its new buildings, by American firm Roe and McIndoe, which were planned as 'a tribute to traditional Samoan architecture'.[9] While of related form, the American Samoan Parliament House contrasts with that of Samoa, in

Parliament House (Maoto Fono), Apia, Samoa, 1972. Department of Public Works Samoa, in association with Joseph Snearly and T E Smith McNaught.

Old *Fono* Building, Apia.

being on a main street of the town and composed as a group of buildings with a central circular chamber flanked by two long curved fales for the offices and meeting rooms.

In 1989, rather than build a new Parliament House, the Prime Minister of the Cook Islands determined to erect a large culture centre as a *marae* for the people. The resulting Sir Geoffrey Henry National Culture Centre, Rarotonga, which opened in 1992, was a large and ambitious project comprising the National Museum, the Conservatory and National Archives, the National Library, the National Auditorium and offices for the Ministry of Cultural Development.[10] The concept for the centre came from Jackson Teece Chesterman Willis of Sydney. Development and construction was by Mainline Brown Construction (Pacific) Ltd. with David Muir of the Sydney firm continuing as supervising architect.[11] The impressive complex consists of three simple but distinctive buildings based on forms familiar in local building practice but subtly translated into two-storeyed pastel-coloured 'sheds' sheltered by deep shading roofs, 'configured as Canoe Vaila with outriggers'.[12] The pavilions of the museum and library stand parallel facing the road and enclose a large central palm garden courtyard organized in relation to a central axis that passes through a portico and frames the sweeping shapes of the auditorium at the end of the axis. The Culture Centre responds positively to the language of local buildings but is inventive in its use of that language to make a contemporary statement of considerable presence. Adjacent to the Culture Centre is the Te Fuinga o Niva Hospitality Centre offering accommodation for visitors. The hospitality centre is visually arresting, primarily due to its distinctive decorative appearance, especially the uncommon white filigree balustrades and roof trim.

Until recent years decisions regarding the housing of Parliament in western Polynesia were generally but of local concern, and the new public buildings provide a marked contrast to the parliament buildings of Vanuatu and the Solomon Islands. The colourful Cultural Centre of the Cook Islands celebrates the people in its gestures and its cultural amenities, and the simple old timber buildings of the Cook Islands and Tongan Parliaments and the *fonos* of the Samoan Islands Parliament are reflective of the people they represent – but the Pacific is changing.

TOP LEFT: Legislative Assembly (Maoto Fono), Pago Pago, American Samoa, 1973. Roe and McIndoe. Model. *Courtesy of the Jean P Heydon Museum, American Samoa, PH147A.*

TOP RIGHT: Te Fuinga o Niva Hospitality Centre, Avarua, Rarotonga, Cook Islands.

LEFT: Sir Geoffrey Henry National Culture Centre, Avarua, Rarotonga, Cook Islands, 1992. Jackson Teece Chesterman Willis. Project architect: David Muir.

Ideology and Identity: French Polynesia

French Polynesia is singular in the Pacific in that it was the first country to break from the architectural styles of European historic precedent for its public buildings, but it was also the only country in the Pacific to return to them at the end of the twentieth century. Michel Prévot commented, 'Power makes the architecture',[1] and the evidence that rulers can determine the architectural expression of public buildings is clearly demonstrated in French Polynesia. There, buildings based on local practice, directed by Jean Charles Sicurani in the 1960s, stand in contrast to the revivalist architecture built after 1990 during the periods of power of Gaston Flosse.

The Sicurani Years 1965–69

During the transformative years of the late 1950s and 1960s, Governor Sicurani played a major role in the political shifts within the country and its relationship to France. To Sicurani, the new political structure and the moves towards independence needed to be reflected in an architecture that was modern and, considering 80 per cent of the people were Polynesian, expressive of their culture. He hoped to further this through a major public buildings programme. He was a strong and caring governor, and with his vision to raise the status of the islanders, he was ahead of his time. Official government recognition of the Polynesian people did not occur until 1983 with the proclamation of Tahitian as an official language alongside French.[2] Sicurani was a friend of President de Gaulle, and the visit of de Gaulle to Papeete in 1966 gave further recognition to the country, along with support to the representative building programme. The Sicurani buildings were the antithesis of the preceding French colonial architecture, being unassertive, mostly timber structures that were at home in the local milieu. The funds were available, and he was fortunate to have the talents of the architect Michel Prévot. The relationship between client and architect was one of mutual respect. Because of his close association with Sicurani, Prévot did not make formal drawings but worked on tracing paper that has since dried out and disintegrated. Consequently, there are no drawings available of Prévot's public buildings.[3]

In 1955, when Prévot gave up his position as architect and urbanist for the government and established his own practice, the only private practising architect was Ivan Chabana, who had arrived in Tahiti from France in 1932 with the intention of staying for six months as a tourist. He stayed for forty-two years.[4] In 1942 Chabana was arrested as a supporter of Marshal Pétain, but by 1948 he had been reinstated as a member of the Order of Architects. Chabana, who was primarily involved in Papeete designing basic houses using local materials, moved to Tiarei on the east coast in 1973.[5] In 1960 another young architect from France, Christian Regaud, joined Prévot, to form the firm of Regaud and Prévot – a practice that lasted thirty years.[6] Regaud had left France on a sailing boat to avoid the call-up for national service for the war in Algeria.[7] On arrival in Tahiti he decided to stay. He reported to the authorities and spent his first two years with the navy sounding passages and performing such related tasks in French Polynesian waters to complete his mandatory national service requirements.

The first of the new-generation buildings was the Gauguin Museum, by Claude Bach with Rodolphe Weinmann. René Dessirier was responsible for the interiors and the displays, and later worked with Weinmann on several projects.[8] The museum is located outside Papeari on the south coast of Tahiti, adjacent to the Botanic Gardens that were founded by the American Harrison Smith in 1919.[9] Construction commenced in 1963, and the building was completed in 1964 and inaugurated in 1965.[10] The historian Father Patrick O'Reilly is credited with the inspiration for the realization of the project, which was supported with funding provided by the French Fondation Singer-Polignac towards 'enriching a centre of art history for the cultural capital that France hopes to develop in the Pacific.'[11] The gallery, which houses a varied collection of material relating to Gauguin's life

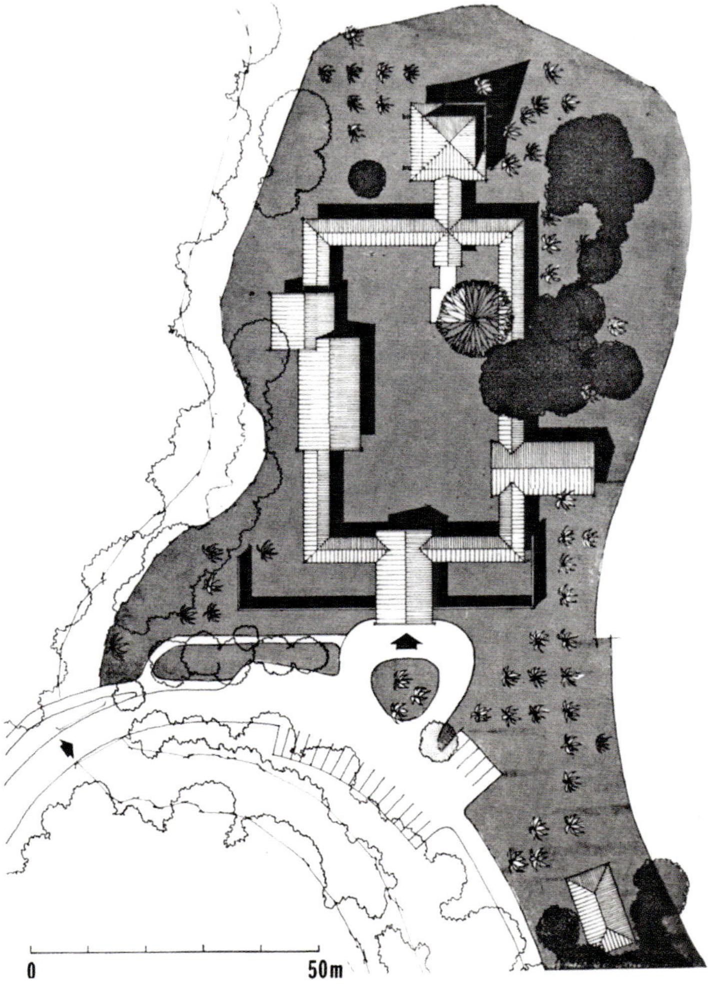

LEFT, ABOVE: Gauguin Museum, Papeari, Tahiti, French Polynesia, 1965. Claude Bach and Rodolphe Weinmann. Site Plan. *Courtesy of Polignac-Signor.*
LEFT, BELOW: Exhibition Building.

and art, is laid out in a large tropical 137-hectare garden as a collection of units in accord with the scale of the vernacular buildings.[12]

The five single-storeyed buildings of masonry walls and pitched roofs, with dramatic white crossed fascias, were constructed by Tahitian labour using customary materials and building practices. The long site edges the ocean with the buildings, facing in towards a central courtyard lawn spaced out in an orderly manner along all sides of a rectangular plan and linked by a covered ambulatory. The overall composition of the site evidences a balance of local custom and European planning with the composition culminating in the high-roofed conservatory, which faces the entrance along the longitudinal axis. Despite the discipline of the planning, the buildings relate comfortably to, and are compatible with, the lush tropical setting. This was a landmark complex, for while it celebrated a French artist, the buildings and Gauguin's art and artefacts exhibited within were steeped in Polynesian history. The museum also provided a much-needed cultural venue for the increasing number of visitors to Tahiti, who were attracted by the new flight schedules and hotels. This is a significant work, providing precedence for architecture to follow. While the museum was already in construction when Sicurani arrived in Tahiti, he was interested in its progress and attended the opening.[13] Bach's planning demonstrated the possibility for a modern yet appropriate Polynesian architecture that he, Sicurani, sought for his subsequent public building programme. It also provided a model for attaining a small scale and local identity in large projects, characteristic of the later designs by Prévot.[14]

Prévot and the Sicurani Vision

In the centre of Papeete the old nineteenth-century buildings, such as the Governor's Palace and the Queen's Palace, which had been in use as a government building since 1903, were in a state of decay and needed to be replaced.[15] They were demolished in 1966, making possible the erection of the new Governor's Residence on the site of the previous Governor's Palace and the Territorial Assembly Building on the Queen's Palace site.[16] The proposed demolition of the Queen's

FAR LEFT: Queen's Palace, Papeete, Tahiti, 1883. *Courtesy of the French Polynesia Archives.*

LEFT: Governor's Palace, Papeete. *Courtesy of Jean-Louis Saquet.*

OPPOSITE, TOP LEFT: Auditorium, Youth Club and Cultural Centre, Papeete, 1973. Christian Regaud and Michel Prévot.

OPPOSITE, TOP RIGHT: Governor's Residence, Papeete, 1966. Christian Regaud and Michel Prévot.

OPPOSITE, BOTTOM LEFT: Territorial Assembly Building, Papeete, 1968. Christian Regaud and Michel Prévot.
OPPOSITE, BOTTOM RIGHT: Chamber Interior.

Palace met with some opposition, and the building was measured and recorded, but the documentation has been lost.[17] Regaud and Prévot were asked to design both buildings together with the Tourist Bureau on the Papeete waterfront and the modern Courts of Justice on Avenue Bruat.

The Assembly Building (*La Fara Manihini*), 1968, was commissioned by Sicurani to be in accord with his political ideology regarding the idea of the rebirth of the Tahitian: 'this country needs to have an image of place, and the image has to be of a fresh and new political institution.'[18] The building is entered through a large open-sided community hall that serves as a gathering space for exhibitions, for parties and as an antechamber to the forty-nine-seat Assembly Chamber.[19] Flanking wings of meeting rooms, offices and other ancillary spaces wrap around the remaining sides of the hall. The architecture resists borrowing of form and materials, but gains a sense of authenticity through the application of principles fundamental to the local practice. The various spaces that make up the complex are on one level and sheltered under a large folded-plate concrete roof, broken only by the raised roof of the Conference Room and the high-pitched roof of the oval Assembly Chamber. The structure is characterized by post-and-beam construction for, as Prévot says, 'the local architecture is post and beam – they did not invent the truss, or corbel. I tried to apply that on this big scale.'[20] This is evident in the many supporting columns throughout the building, the effect of which is especially striking in the meeting hall and the oval Assembly Chamber. Two large concrete posts support a steel twenty-three-metre beam that holds up the typical big roof of Tahitian architecture, here with a curved silhouette to relate to the oval chamber below.

The chamber is a dramatic space lit by large clerestory windows filling the irregular spaces between the hovering roof and the walls. While not overtly Polynesian, the space, with warm natural wood throughout and a high-pitched roof patterned by the expressed lines of the ribs of its structure, captures the scale and character of an important Pacific ceremonial meeting hall. Timber shingles cover the high roofs and that of the folded portico roof, and the projecting steel ridge beam makes token reference to Tahitian buildings of importance. While unmistakably a building of prestige and presence, the Territorial Assembly has an informality that encourages familiarity. Known locally as 'the Place of the People',[21] the Territorial Assembly became the village gathering hall: 'The local people … have lived in it happily for a long time celebrating and enjoying flower exhibitions, dancing.'[22]

The Governor's Residence, 1966, is of a similar ilk to the Assembly Building, in being an unassertive yet distinctive building with arresting roof forms. The house was built in timber over two months in order to be completed in time for de Gaulle's visit in 1966.[23] The highly original folded roof, with ridge-to-ground projecting A-frame gables (five to the front and three each side), are clad in redwood shingles and strongly delineated with white fascia boards. While the building is distinctively modern, the profile is strangely suggestive of rows of high-roofed huts. With this division of the large roof (and therefore the building) and the insertion of balconies to the attic rooms on the upper floor, the scale is reduced to one appropriate for residential use. To further the conservation and promotion of Polynesian culture, Sicurani proposed two major complexes: the Youth Club and Cultural Centre, Papeete, 1973, and the Museum of Tahiti and Its Islands, Puna'auia, 1977.[24] Regaud

and Prévot were appointed architects for the projects. In both, the strategy of multiple small-scale units was adopted as appropriate for local building practice and custom. Funds were made available by the French Government for the Cultural Centre on the condition that it was designed in France. This was agreed, and the funds were provided. When, however, the drawings arrived for a building in the crisp white modern style, Sicurani rejected them and told Prévot to send the drawings back to France and to redesign the Cultural Centre.[25] The site fronts the Papeete harbour on what was once low swampland. Here, rather than the rectangular planning of the Gauguin Museum, a loose clustered grouping is adopted with the buildings forming irregular garden courtyards. The amenities of the centre, such as the library and local crafts hall, are attuned to the needs and interests of young people and of the general community and are accommodated in one-storeyed buildings of simple geometric forms of various sizes arranged as single or multiple units. Like the Assembly Building, the major building, the Auditorium, is covered by a vast sheltering roof that is supported on concrete piers independent of the walls, allowing natural ventilation of the interior.[26] The roof consists of overlapping pitched planes stepping back at graded heights to create clerestory spaces between. The entry vestibule also is sheltered by sloping folded planes.

The opening of the Museum of Tahiti and Its Islands occurred in the year that French Polynesia achieved the status of a semi-autonomous territory of the French Republic. The legacy of Sicurani's ideology is evident in the nature of the complex. The four-hectare site on the oceanfront outside Pura'auia on the west coast allowed for a more spacious arrangement than was afforded by the inner-city site of the Cultural Centre. Again, the buildings take the form of connected one-storey pavilions with walkways and gardens between, but here, in contrast to the informal design of the buildings of the Cultural Centre, they are arranged around a central rectangular courtyard. Also, the pavilions of the museum assume a Mediterranean flavour with red-tiled roofs and white painted masonry walls.

Fundamentally, these buildings of Prévot were political gestures. They mark an important step in the history of the architecture of the South Pacific. For the first time it was deemed appropriate to represent the culture and traditions of the Pacific people in national and cultural buildings. The vision and direction came from Governor Sicurani, and Prévot gives him full credit, seeing himself more as an implementer than an instigator.

The Flosse Years 1984–2005

With the change of political status in 1977 to partial autonomy, the high commissioner replaced the governor, and in the government, led by a vice-

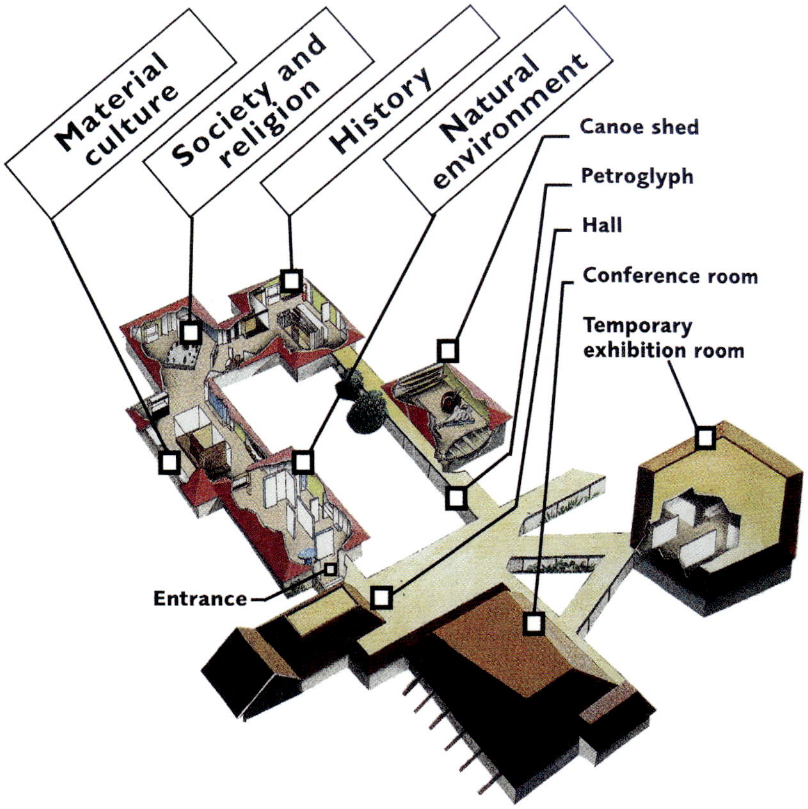

president (the president after autonomy in 1984), a group of new local leaders emerged.[27] The most powerful of these was Gaston Flosse, who was of mixed French and Tahitian descent.[28] He was a close friend of Jacques Chirac and became president of the government in 1984, the same year Chirac was elected president of France.[29] This association was most fruitful for French Polynesia, both politically and economically. Nuclear testing and the accompanying prosperity continued until 1996. Further, funding from the political parties in France was generous as French Polynesia held two seats in the Chamber of Deputies that were swinging seats that could well determine the results in close debates. Hence, even after the income-generating nuclear task force was withdrawn, funds for building continued to be available.[30] In 1972 the French Government expanded the system of municipal government throughout France and the Pacific. Six new communes, in addition to Papeete, were established in the Papeete urban area.[31] This resulted in the construction of new town halls (*mairie*) or the upgrading of existing buildings, as at Arue Town Hall, where, in 1978, the council acquired the decorative 1892 residence of the Austrian Ambassador

OPPOSITE: Museum of Tahiti and Its Islands, Tahiti, 1977. Christian Regaud and Michel Prévot. Axonometric Drawing. *Courtesy of the Museum of Tahiti and Its Islands.*
RIGHT: Entrance Portico.

Victor Raouix.[32] New ancillary buildings, including the police station, were built in on the grounds in the same architectural language. This political building activity culminated in the historicist edifices constructed for Gaston Flosse at the turn of the century.

Faa'a Town Hall, 1989, is an exception among the European eclecticism that characterizes the public buildings of the later part of the century. The driving force behind the building was Mayor Oscar Manutahi Temaru, the territory's leading independence advocate and, with the design and construction undertaken by local builders, it was a further polemical statement.[33] This Polynesian building consists of a gathering of individual units around the council chamber, directly connected or linked by covered walkways. The timber buildings are well crafted, with meeting rooms and the oval council chamber – roofed with elegant structures of fine timber members delineated in white – creating delicate tracery in contrast to the dark natural timbers, the patterns of the bindings and the richly painted brown tapa wall hangings. The 1992 Puna'auia Town Hall, by Tricard, is a strangely hybrid building that was based on the Gold Coast Council Chambers in Australia, which the mayor had seen at a political meeting.[34] The commission was determined by competition and Tricard travelled to the Gold Coast to see the chambers. His winning design included aspects of that building, notably the high-roofed atrium with tiered galleries edged by planter boxes and capped by a triangular-shaped glass clerestory along the ridge. Off this large atrium space opens a number of function rooms, including a wedding chapel, which was designed with operable louvered walls and furnished with Tahitian furniture and artworks.[35]

Political Agendas and Architecture after 1900

The 1990s ushered in a political agenda with a progressive image for French Polynesia. To the political leaders, notably Flosse, the modest regional imagery of the Sicurani-era public buildings was retrogressive and parochial, and an embarrassment to the emerging French Polynesia.[36] Instead they sought to demonstrate that French Polynesia was a country not of uncultured islanders, but one of international standing by conveying a sense of European sophistication through architecture.[37]

The 1990 Papeete Town Hall, by Weinmann, was the first major building to revert to historicist revival examples. Here, at the mayor's request, the previous Queen's Palace was selected as the model for the new building. The small colonial buildings of the convent and town hall were demolished to make available a large site in central Papeete, and construction commenced in 1988.[38] As the palace drawings had been lost, Weinmann had to work from photographs for his design.[39] The new Town Hall is a translation of the language of the early timber prefabricated building into a masonry structure with salmon rendered walls and white trim, capped by a handsome roof of red tiles. The design replicates the general arrangement of the palace, with two tiers of verandas and French doors and decorative features, such as the turned balustrades, and an enlarged roof lantern, and with the addition of a clock. To achieve a stronger presence and to accommodate the processes of city government, the simple design of the palace was transformed by an increase in overall scale, the extension of the front façade, the addition of attic windows in the roof and a central porch reached by a prominent flight of steps. These transformations gave rise to an elaborate building of quite different character to that of the earlier reserved Queen's Palace.

In 2001 Tricard designed the 'Plantation-style' Pirae Town Hall for Flosse, who was also mayor of Pirae.[40] This again was a competition, with Flosse requesting a building like that in *Gone with the Wind*.[41] This building, with a cost exceeding US$ 12.8 million, is a grandiose building, especially as Pirae, with a population of 15 000, is an unexceptional commune on the outskirts of Papeete.[42] The Town Hall stands in a two-hectare park, and the long neoclassical façade of the building, with its colonnade of an order of seven-metre-high Tuscan columns and a projecting two-storeyed pedimented porch, dominates its suburban surroundings. The sixty-eight silicone, fibreglass and acrylic columns of the building were formed in France.[43] A patterned roof in two tones of red enlivened with multiple attic windows crowns the white walls broken up by windows decoratively framed by shutters. It is evident that the façade received the most design care and expense while the interior spaces, apart from the entry stair hall, are surprising narrow, with rooms served by an internal corridor and some ancillary structures to the rear.

During Flosse's 1991–2004 presidential term a competition was held for the design of the precinct of the Presidential Palace in Papeete, as 'French Polynesia required a place in line with its aspirations and its influence in the South Pacific.'[44] Pierre Lacombe, Tropical Architecture, was appointed architect, and the complex was completed in 2000 at a cost of US$ 37 million.[45] The site, at the upper end of Avenue Bruat, was previously that of the 1886 Quartier Broche, the French army barracks, a fine two-storeyed nineteenth-century building.[46] The barracks were in the style of 'Gallieni', so-named after the Marshal, who promoted this style of architecture throughout the French colonial empire.[47] The Quartier Broche 'occupies central page in the history of France' and was deemed of such importance, it was decided that in order to preserve its memory the barracks would be demolished and 'reborn' in the new palace, 'the first institution that pays respect and reflects a dynamic Polynesia'.[48]

The Presidential Precinct occupies a city block and is arranged around four sides of a large planted courtyard. The surrounding streets are presented with strongly

OPPOSITE, TOP LEFT: Town Hall, Papeete, Tahiti, 1990. Rodolphe Weinmann. OPPOSITE, TOP RIGHT: Town Hall, Pirae, Tahiti, 1989. Jean-Hugues Tricard.

OPPOSITE, BOTTOM LEFT: Town Hall, Arue, Tahiti, refurbished 1978. (Austrian Ambassador's residence 1892.)

OPPOSITE, BOTTOM RIGHT: Ministry of Economic, Social and Cultural Affairs, Papeete, Tahiti, 1859. Refurbished 1990.

ABOVE: Town Hall, Puna'auia, Tahiti, 1989, Jean-Hugues Tricard. Wedding Chapel.

LEFT: Town Hall, Faa'a, Tahiti, 1989. Ceiling Detail.

Quartier Broche Military Barracks, Papeete, Tahiti, 1886. *Courtesy of Jean-Louis Saquet.*

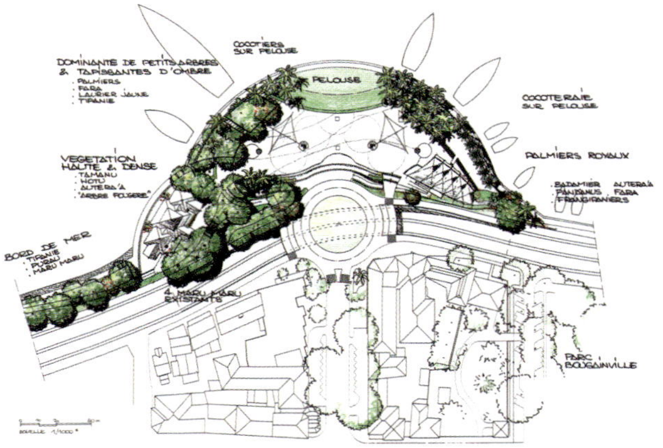

Place Jacques Chirac, Papeete, Tahiti. Tropical Architecture. Plan: competition proposal, 1989.

defining walls that are interrupted by the formal entrance gate on Avenue Bruat.[49] The palace, described as being in the Directoire style, fronts the principal gate across the central axis of the courtyard, with the cross axis linking the conference room and the grand dining hall.[50] Supporting functions are housed in wings that define the remaining sides of the courtyard. While the court is crossed with formal axial paths, these were reserved for the use of the president and his guests only. Colonnaded arcades fronting the perimeter buildings provided the main circulation route around the palace.[51] The design for the palace, with its round-headed arches and light metal framing to the verandas, was based on the historical precedent of the Quartier Broche. While the module and round arches of the barracks are carried into the palace design, there is little resemblance between the austere and restrained barracks and the decorative façade of the palace. Whereas the barracks were strongly modelled with a deeply shadowed colonnade, the Palace façade has shallow modelling and is patterned with the intricate lineal details of the arched multi-panelled French doors, the lace-like fascias, the decorative balustrades and the ornate steel and glass portico.

The interior of the building surpasses the exterior in terms of sumptuous historical eclecticism. Various richly decorated high-ceilinged reception rooms with furnishings, fabrics and carpets imported from France flank the central hall, with its rich, red carpet and grand helical stair, *l'escalier d'honneur*, leading up to the office of the president.[52] The major reception and meeting rooms are themed around different historical French periods: the foyer and the reception hall are in the Empire style, the press room is in the Colonial style and the cabinet room is in Louis XVI style.[53] Exceptions are the salon and the grand dining hall, which seats 300, as these pay deference to local culture through decorative features such as wall and roof coverings of typical local woven materials, and a collection of splendid tapa tapestries provided by the Royal House of Tonga.[54] Throughout the building the imported French furniture and furnishings are luxurious with ornate mirrors, chandeliers, rich curtains and carpets, including Aubusson weavings. On the upper level, the president's office and suite are similarly presented, and the office boasts an original mirror from the Palace of Versailles.[55]

Avenue Bruat

Flosse's ambitions for the emerging Papeete extended to the urban scale, with proposed imposing improvements to Avenue Bruat, the wide formal street of Papeete, which runs for 500 metres at right angles to the harbour and culminates in a park on the waterfront. There are three major components of the scheme: the Presidential Palace, the transformation of Avenue Bruat by lining it with buildings with neoclassical façades and a greatly enlarged harbour-side concourse and park – originally Place General de Gaulle but renamed Place Jacques Chirac. The changes to the avenue commenced with the palace and the restoration in 1990 of the handsome early military storehouse, the Maison du Conseil, 1859, situated opposite the palace at the top of the avenue, as the offices for the Ministry for Economic, Social and Cultural Affairs, 1990, and a derivative government building

ABOVE: Presidential Palace, Papeete, Tahiti, 2000.
Tropical Architecture. Exterior.
RIGHT: l'escalier d'honneur.

built on the adjoining site. The waterside project, half funded by France and supervised by France's EGT, the authority for large public works,[56] was intended to be a new centre for Papeete and an entrance point for private yachts and cruisers bringing tourists. For this it was planned that 50 000 square metres of the waterfront would be reclaimed for the construction of a large underground parking lot and to accommodate parks, restaurants and various tourist and cultural attractions.[57] It was later decided to move the site further north, and a competition was held in 2004 for a new passenger terminal on Boulevard Pomare, which was won by Tropical Architecture. Place Jacques Chirac was laid out as public park.

The representation through the language of the public buildings as to what French Polynesia is, should be or aspires to be, swung through extremes of political ideologies during the second part of the twentieth century.[58] The platform of French Governor Sicurani was that the country was a Polynesian nation and that its identity should be protected and celebrated, and this is reflected in the public buildings programmed under his tenure. The presence of the CEP, with the accompanying influx of money and French personnel, brought about political and economic shifts that over time changed that perspective of the country. The historicist architecture commissioned after political autonomy spoke of the French side of the dual identity and set the stage for a new vision for French Polynesia.

OUT OF DIFFERENCE

The new architecture of Oceania is emerging out of difference. This difference is acted out against the enduring background of the greatest of oceans – the Pacific – a world of extremes.

Over the recent centuries vast change has invaded this southern realm. Geographically, the island lands of the South Pacific are remote and alone, yet at this time they are inexorably linked with the rest of the world by fast travel and communication networks – demanding an extreme shift for consciousness and culture.

Difference lies in the ethnic and cultural groups who now inhabit the Pacific – physically, politically, socially and artistically – with extremes between the architecture born of the Pacific and that of northern climes.

This unique 'Pacific Oceanscape' is in the process of redefining itself in contemporary terms. Adventure and innovation will be needed for a positive, forward-looking architecture that will celebrate the contrasts, even contradictions, which are the essence of this place today. In this context 'traditional' dress is far too limiting, and another's clothes will not fit at all – for the new Oceania, the garments will need to be bespoke. This, then, is the challenge for those architects who seek to refashion architecture in response to both people and place.

There is no conclusion to this book. It is just one snapshot from a possible series taken across the buildings within the evolving milieu of the people of the South Pacific, inhabiting one of the most volatile environments on earth and living in a most volatile time …

*'To return to tradition is a myth; I strive to repeat this.
It's a myth. No People has ever done so.
In the quest for identity, you must look forwards, never backwards.
It's a matter of constant redefinition.'*

Jean-Marie Tjibaou

ENDNOTES

TITLE PAGE

p. 3 Robert Louis Stevenson, *In the South Seas,* Charles Scribner's Sons, New York, 1896.

THE OCEAN OF ISLANDS

p. 4 'Our Sea of Islands' (poem), in Epeli Hau'ofa, *We Are The Ocean: Selected Works*, University of Hawai'i Press, Honolulu, 2008.

p. 5 William Somerset Maugham, *The Trembling of a Leaf: Little Stories of the South Sea Islands*, George H Doran Company, 1921.

'A JOURNEY OF A THOUSAND MILES ...
... BEGINS WITH A SINGLE STEP'

p. 6 Chinese philosopher Laozi, (c. 551 BC–479 BC) in the *Tao Te Ching.*

1 Jennifer Taylor, 'Oceania: Australia, New Zealand, Papua New Guinea and the smaller islands of the South Pacific' in Banister Fletcher, *A History of Architecture*, 19th edn., Butterworths, London, 1987, (20th edn., Butterworths, London, 1996.)

2 For this reason and because we lacked the expertise and the time to deal with such an extensive subject on a broad geographic canvas, specific studies on vernacular architecture are not presented in this work.

3 Jennifer Taylor and William Lim (eds.), 'Oceania', in Kenneth Frampton, *World Architecture 1900–2000: A Critical Mosaic, Southeast Asia and Oceania, Vol. 10*, Springer Wein, New York, 1999.

4 'Oceania', *The Columbia Encyclopedia*, Columbia University Press, New York.

5 The database includes over 600 buildings, more than 8000 photographs and 70 taped interviews.

PART I THE WORLD OF OCEANIA

MAR DEL SUR: THE SOUTHERN SEA

p. 13 'The Ocean in Us' (poem), in Epeli Hau'ofa, *We Are The Ocean: Selected Works*, University of Hawai'i Press, Honolulu, 2008.

1 'Vasco Núñez de Balboa' (Discovery of the Pacific), Encyclopaedia Britannica, viewed on 16 March 2011 at <http://www.britannica.com/EBchecked/topic/49909/Vasco-Nunez-de-Balboa/576/Discovery-of-the-Pacific>.

2 'Volcanoes and the Theory of Plate Tectonics', in Stephen R Brantley, *Volcanoes of the United States*, p. 6, U.S. Geological Survey, viewed on 30 April 2011 at <http://pubs.usgs.gov/gip/volcus/page06.html#theory>.

3 'The New Zealand Meteorological Service classifies tropical cyclones as having winds ranging between 62 to 117 km/hr, and hurricanes as those in which winds exceed 117 km/hr.' John R Campbell, *Dealing with Disaster: Hurricane Response in Fiji*, Government of Fiji, Suva, 1984, p. 8. In the South Pacific, however, the terms are used in accord with local convention rather than according to wind speed, and this book follows regional practice.

4 Steven R Fischer, *A History of the Pacific Isles*, Palgrave, MacMillan, Basingstoke, 2002, p. xvi.

5 Central Intelligence Agency, 'Tuvalu', CIA World Factbook, viewed on 5 February 2011 at <https://www.cia.gov/library/publications/the-world-factbook/geos/tv.html>.

6 Central Intelligence Agency, 'Pitcairn Islands', CIA World Factbook, viewed on 29 April 2011 at <https://www.cia.gov/library/publications/the-world-factbook/geos/pc.html>.

7 For an account of Oceanic languages see Andrew Pawley and Malcolm Ross, 'Chapter 3. The Prehistory of Oceanic Languages: A Current View', in Peter Bellwood, James J Fox and Darrell Tryon (eds.), *The Austronesians: Historical and Comparative Perspectives*, Department of Anthropology, Research School of Pacific and Asian Studies, Australian National University, Canberra 1995, pp. 43–68, viewed at <http://epress.anu.edu.au/>.

8 See 'The First Islanders', in Fischer, pp. 1–22, for a comprehensive discussion of the early migrations.

9 Wilmshurst JM, et al., 'High-precision radiocarbon dating shows recent and rapid initial human colonization of East Polynesia', *Proceedings of the National Academy of Sciences of the United States of America*, Vol. 108, No. 5, 2011, pp. 1815–1820.

10 Fischer, p. 19.

11 Fischer, Introduction, p. xix.

12 Fischer, Introduction, p. xv.

13 'The European Trespass', in Fischer, pp. 81–119, namely Balboa in 1510, Magellan in 1521, Mendana in 1568, Quiros in 1606, Tasman in 1642, Wallis in 1764 and Cook in 1769.

14 Brij V Lal and Kate Fortune (eds.), *The Pacific Islands: An Encyclopedia*, University of Hawai'i Press, Honolulu, 2000, p. 248.

15 'Role and Structure', Secretariat of the South Pacific Commission, viewed on 6 February 2011 at < http://www.spc.int/en/about-spc/role-and-structure.html>.

16 The Members are the Republic of Fiji, the Independent State of Papua New Guinea, the Solomon Islands, the Republic of Vanuatu and the Front de Libération Nationale Kanak et Socialiste (FLNKS) of New Caledonia. Department of Foreign Affairs and Trade, 'Vanuatu Country Brief', viewed on 7 August 2011 at <http://www.dfat.gov.au/geo/vanuatu/vanuatu_brief.html>.

17 South Pacific Commission, 2010 Pocket Statistical Summary, viewed on 5 February 2011 at <http://www.spc.int/prism/>.

18 South Pacific Commission, 2010, Statistical Summary.

19 'Summary', in Australian Government in consultation with regional experts and practioners, *Pacific 2020: Challenges and Opportunities for Growth* (ISBN: 1920861742), Commonwealth of Australia, Canberra, 2006, p. 1.

20 South Pacific Commission, 2010, Statistical Summary.

21 Australian Government, Table 4.1, p. 35.

22 Susan Windybank, 'The China Syndrome', *Policy Magazine*, Winter 2005, viewed on 2 September 2008 at <http://www.cis.org.au/publications/policy-magazine/article/1987>.

23 In traditional structures the builder of the roof may be a different person to the builder of what is underneath, which is deemed as of little consequence, and in many cultures a building may be but a supported roof.

PART II IN TRANSITION: SETTLEMENTS IN THE SOUTH PACIFIC

Chapter 1: Two Towns

Port de France: Noumea

1 See Peter H Raven, 'Plate Tectonics and Southern Hemisphere Biogeography', in Kai Larsen and Lauritz B Holm-Nielsen (eds.), *Tropical Botany*, Academic Press, London, 1980, pp. 3–24.

2 Territorial collectivity (*sui generis collectivity*) of France since 1998. Central Intelligence Agency, 'New Caledonia' (Government), CIA World Factbook, viewed on 14 April 2012 at <https://www.cia.gov/library/publications/the-world-factbook/geos/nc.html>.

3 Australian Government, Department of Foreign Affairs and Trade, 'New Caledonia Briefing Note' (Evolving Status), viewed on 27 July 2011 at <http://www.dfat.gov.au/geo/new_caledonia/new_caledonia_brief.html>.

4 Christophe Sand, *Lapita: The Pottery Collection from the Site at Foué*, New Caledonia, Archaeology Department: Territorial Museums and Heritage Service, Noumea, 1999.

5 New Caledonia remained a convict settlement until 1897.

6 Institut de la Statistique et des Études Économique (ISEE), Images de la population de la Nouvelle-Caledonie/Principaux resultats du recensement 1996. The ethnicity question was removed from the 2004 Census. See ISEE, viewed on 15 May 2012 at <http://www.isee.nc/>.

7 Brij V Lal and Kate Fortune (eds.), *The Pacific Islands: An Encyclopedia*, University of Hawai'i Press, Honolulu, 2000, p. 226.

8 Christian Jost, 'Environmental Constraints and Issues in the French Pacific Territories', in Christian Jost (ed.), *The French-Speaking Pacific: Population, Environment and Development Issues,* Geopacifique Association, Boombana Publications, Mount Nebo, 1998, p. 73.

9 *Les Bâtisseurs: architecture à Nouméa de 1853 à 1940, Exposition juin 1996/juin 1997*, Ville de Nouméa, Musée Archives, Multipress, Noumea, 1996, p. 9.

10 Plan No. 2, 'Plan de Port-de-France en 1858', in *Les Bâtisseurs: architecture à Nouméa de 1853 à 1940*, p. 13.

11 'Place of the Coconuts', because of the numerous coconut palms that grew there.

12 See Plan No. 60 in *Les Bâtisseurs*, 1904, p. 94, for expanded town plan.

13 These are well documented in *Les Bâtisseurs.*

14 The building was destroyed by fire in 1988. It has been rebuilt and operates as the City of Noumea Museum.

15 Today New Caledonia's prison is located there.

16 'Melanesians made up 51 per cent of the population in 1956, but this proportion had declined to 46 per cent by 1969, and to 42 per cent by 1976', Stephen Henningham, *France and the South Pacific: A Contemporary History,* South Seas Books, University of Hawai'i Press, Honolulu, 1992, p. 63.

17 Jean-Pierre Doumenge, 'New Caledonia from the Human Angle', in Jost (ed.), p. 120.

18 'The authorities in the early 1970s hastily developed several low-cost housing settlements (Tindu at Ducos; Pierre Lenquette at Montravel). High-rise buildings mushroomed, first at the entrance to the peninsula (St Quentin) then on the hills above Rivière Salée and at Magenta. The city centre and the Latin Quarter were re-modelled. A new town rose from the ground (or more exactly from reclaimed swamp) at Rivière Salée.' Doumenge in Jost (ed.), p. 126.

19 Correspondence, André Maikovsky, July 2009. Marien, with architects Eugène Beaudouin and Urbain Cassan, designed Tour Maine Montparnasse, Paris, 1972, which, at 210 metres, was then the tallest building in Europe. Emporis, 'Tour Montparnasse', World Buildings, viewed on 17 March 2010 at <http://www.emporis.com/application/?nav=building&lng=3&id=110509>.

20 Correspondence, Maikovsky, July 2009. See also *Varangue*, No. 21, August 2010, p. 65.

21 See *South Pacific Travel Trade News (SPTTN)*, Breckell & Nicholls Ltd, June 1968, p. 33, for a report on the building of the terminal. The *SPTTN* journal was produced by Breckell & Nicholls Ltd. between 1965–74 in Auckland and then subsequently by Thompson Publications in Chippendale, New South Wales, and has proved invaluable in documenting part of this research. Copies were consulted at the NSW State Library.

22 'Woods Bagot wins urban design project for New Caledonia'. *Australian Design Review*, viewed on 8 April 2012 at <http://www.australiandesignreview.com/news/1860-woods-bagot-winds-urban-design-project-for-new-caledonia>.

23 Correspondence, Domenic Alvaro, Woods Bagot, 24 July 2013.

'Water from a Basket': Papeete 1950–70

1 A French Government and military research centre for testing nuclear weapons was established in the Pacific following France granting independence to Algeria in 1962, where earlier nuclear testing had taken place. Forty-two bombs were exploded on Mururoa Atoll alone. Stephen Henningham, *France and the South Pacific: A Contemporary History*, South Seas Books, University of Hawai'i Press, Honolulu, 1992, p. 127.

2 Myth has it that in 'the olden days' Tahitians used to draw crystal-clear water by lowering gourds placed in baskets into the stream that crossed the Pomare Estate. This daily activity gave rise to the name of 'water basket' for the town. The name is used in Robert F Kay, *Hidden Tahiti*, Ulysses Press, Berkeley, California, 2001, p. 102.

3 Thomas Brinkhoff, 'French Polynesia', City Population, viewed on 24

February 2012 at <http://www.citypopulation.de/FrPolynesia.html>.

4 The American Embassy, 1940, stood next to the Hotel Stuart.

5 Christian Gleizal (ed.), *Encyclopédie de la Polynésie*, Vol. 9 Vivre en Polynésie 2, C Gleizal/Multipress, Tahiti, 1986–88, p. 52. Also recorded is a Chinese migration in the first quarter of the twentieth century, mostly from the south-west province of Kwantung. *Institut Statistique de Polynésie Française* (ISPF), viewed on 24 May 2006 at <http://www.ispf.pf>.

6 ISPF.

7 In 1946 'the island is almost cut off from the world, mail spends several months arriving by boat and only the telegraph provides communication.' Adolphe Sylvain, Sylvain website (website recording the life and photographs of Sylvain), viewed on 26 April 2006 at <http:/www.vaea.biz/photos/adolphe-sylvain.php>.

8 Arnauld de Castillon de Saint-Victor, *Tahiti et l'Avion,* Société des Océanistes, Dossier 18, Paris, 1974, p. 18. The Bataillon du Pacifique of 300 Polynesian volunteer soldiers went to Africa to fight the Germans in 1940. *La Présidence de la Polynésie Française* (pamphlet), Papeete, Tahiti, 2000.

9 Outside of Papeete there was no electricity.

10 A photographic study of Papeete by Sylvain in 1950 testifies to the deplorable state of the town. See also Patrick O'Reilly and Raoul Teissier, 'Auzelle, Robert (1913)', in *Tahitiens: Répertoire Biographique de la Polynésie Française*, Publications de la Société des Océanistes No. 36, Musée de l'homme, Paris, 1975, p. 27.

11 O'Reilly and Teissier, p. 27.

12 Ibid.

13 Ibid.

14 Bengt Danielsson and Marie-Thérèse Danielsson (produced by Christian Gleizal), *Papeete 1818–1990*, C Gleizal/Cobalt – Mairie de Papeete, Papeete, c. 1990, p. 183.

15 Jeanine Tehani Sylvain, 'A Life of Joy', Adolphe Sylvain website, viewed on 26 April 2006 at <http:/www.vaea.biz/photos/adolphe-sylvain.php>.

16 O'Reilly and Teissier, p. 27.

17 Ibid.

18 O'Reilly and Teissier, 'Prévot, Michel (1925)', p. 471.

19 Ibid.

20 Conversation, Michel Prévot, architect, Papeete, 2004.

21 Bach was born in Metz (Moselle), a town that was populated by both German and French citizens. O'Reilly and Teissier, 'Bach, Claude' (1929)', p. 29.

22 SETIL: La Caisse des Dépôts et Consignations et la Société d'Équipement de Tahiti et des Îles. Initially and essentially a French Government department responsible for major works and infrastructure planning and development. Currently it is a joint Tahitian-French company responsible for managing the airports in French Polynesia.

23 Gleizal, Vol. 9, p. 77.

24 Authors O'Reilly and Teissier recorded his marriage as being 17 September 1963 and his arrival in Tahiti the same month. Apparently Claude was interested in neo-Polynesian designs and 'finding a modern expression for old Polynesian art forms'. O'Reilly and Teissier, 'Weinmann, Rodolphe (1936)', p. 602.

25 'Liste de References Professionnelles, Rodolphe Weinmann, Architecte', unpublished manuscript, 5 pp. undated. Weinmann retired to Germany in 2004. Material provided by his office in 2005.

26 Danielsson and Danielsson, p. 156.

27 Henningham, p. 127.

28 Paul Le Bourdiec, Gérard Mottet, François Merceron, 'Islands, Communities and Economics of French Polynesia', in Christian Jost (ed.), *The French-Speaking Pacific*, Boombana Publications, Mont Nebo, Australia, 1998, pp. 157–158.

29 O'Reilly and Teissier, 'Bach, Claude (1929)', p. 29.

30 O'Reilly and Teissier, 'Jean Sicurani (1919)', pp. 519–521. Sicurani was a Caucasian born in Algeria in 1915. He graduated in law and served in Indochina (1945–54) and Africa (1955–60). Before coming to Polynesia he was high commissioner to the Republic of Sudan (1959–60).

31 Starring Marlon Brando as Christian and Trevor Howard as Bligh. The first version was not filmed in Tahiti.

32 Papeete first hosted the Pacific Games in 1971.

33 Investment realized during Sicurani's term of office: 'For example; Equipment Administrative: office of the government and the territorial administration, palace for Territorial assembly, Customs house, captain of the ports office. Education, Social and socio-economic: Television station, school at Uturoa, Technical school at Pirea, House for Youth Papeete at Pirea, House of Culture at Pirea, Olympic swimming pool, Olympic stadium at Pirae, City at Tipaerui, renovation of the city of Fautaua, hospital at Mamao, and building allotments. Equipment Economic: New ports at Papeete, industrial zone at Fare Ute, oil works, market at Pirea, Bank of Tahiti, renovation of the commercial centre of Papeete, enlargement of the route into the centre of the island, school of agriculture, aggrandisement of the airport, landing strips at Moorea, Tubbuai, Nuku Hiva, focussing on projects for aerodromes at Huahine, Manihi, and Maupiti.' O'Reilly and Teissier, 'Sicurani, Jean (1915)', p. 520.

34 O'Reilly and Teissier, 'Bach, Claude (1929)', p. 29.

35 Now named the Olivier Bréaud International Golf Course.

36 'Large hotels were built (Tahara'a, Maeva, Royal Papeete, Travel Lodge), the Club Mediterranean was established at Moorea, Taha'a and Rangiroa, while the numerous reception rooms and accommodations for ODT, conference rooms, golf course at Mataiea, centre of tourism at Vaitape and Pueu, Museum of Discovery at Point Venus, commemorative columns for Bougainville at Hitia and restoration of the Tomb of Pomare, management of the Viewpoint at Fare Rau Ape, restoration of a number of Marae, Port de Plaisance at Puna'auia, refurbishing of the hippodrome at Pirae and a Club Nautical at Arue.' O'Reilly and Teissier, 'Sicurani, Jean (1915)', p. 520.

37 ISPF.

38 Gilles Blanchet, 'What Development after the CEP', in Jost, p. 228.

39 O'Reilly and Teissier, 'Sicurani, Jean (1915)', pp. 520–521.

Chapter 2: Builders and Buildings

Early 'Architects' of New Caledonia: 1900–1980

1 'Les architects-voyer', in *Les Bâtisseurs: architecture à Nouméa de 1853 à 1940*, Exposition juin 1996/juin 1997, Ville de Nouméa, Musée Archives, Noumea, 1996, p. 84.

2 Conversation, Gabriel Cayrol, architect, Noumea, 2003, in which he recounted his return to Noumea by flying boat via Sydney after studying architecture in Paris.

3 'L'église Saint-Jean-Baptiste', *Les Bâtisseurs*, pp. 74–75.

4 The original 1878 church was destroyed by cyclone, rebuilt, and again destroyed by cyclone in 1913, and yet again in 1932.

5 Bernheim Library, 'Practical Information', viewed on 1 May 2011 at <http://www.bernheim.nc/distribution.asp?page=information/vihi.asp&inter=0&num=1&parcours=information/pahi.asp>.

6 Christophe Augias, 'La Bibliothèque Bernheim', *Correspondances-Océaniennes*, Vol. 2, October 2003, pp. 7–8, and Philippe Godard and Luc Chevalier, *Le Mémorial Calédonien, Tome 3, 1900–1919*, Editions d'Art Calédoniennes, Noumea, 1980, pp. 65–67.

7 Archives, Museum of the City of Noumea. See also Orso Filippi and Bernard Fustec, *Le Mémorial de Nouméa, 1859–1999, à travers 140 ans d'histoire du conseil municipal,* Editions Planète Mémo, 1999, Noumea, p. 239. The name of the designer has not been determined.

8 Luc Chevalier, *Nouméa de l'an 1954 a l'an 2000*, Les Editions Cagou, Noumea, 1998, p. 35. The hotel was described as follows: 'The architecture, in the style of the nineteenth century, is a harmonious half wood and brick structure. The symmetrical composition of plan and façade, cast iron railings, wooden latticework all comes together in an ensemble of great allure. The bedrooms are spacious and the public rooms are decorated with fine artworks, the dining room is very large and decorated with numerous mirrors. The ensemble oozes voluptuousness and is finished off with a superb garden of flowers and shrubbery.' Quoted from Laurent Esnault, *'Sunday Morning'*. As cited in Filippi and Fustec, p. 239.

9 Taragnat bought thirteen hectares of land in 1867 on which he planned to build a mansion and a chapel. He completed the design but died in 1878 before building commenced. The design was carried through to completion by his wife. The house was restored in 2010. Chateau Hagen, Province Sud, New Caledonia, viewed on 17 March 2010 at <http://www.province-sud.nc/culture/patrimoine/bati/noumea/chateau-hagen>.

10 Province Sud, 'Maison Célières', New Caledonia, viewed on 17 March 2010 at <http://www.province-sud.nc/culture/patrimoine/bati/noumea/maison-celieres>.

11 The house is occupied by the Délégation Française auprès de la Communauté du Pacifique.

12 See 'John Higginson' in Brij V Lal and Kate Fortune, *The Pacific Islands: An Encyclopedia*, University of Hawai'i Press, Honolulu, 2000, pp. 219–220 for a brief account of Higginson's life. Born in 1839, he died in 1904.

13 *Varangue*, No. 10, June 1999, p. 11. Among the goods imported were construction materials, tiles, metal sheets with Wunderlich profiles, and complete structures.

14 Province Sud, *Direction de la culture, de la jeunesse et des sport*. File No. 1284-03, Archives, New Caledonia.

15 File No. 1438, Archives, Museum of the City of Noumea.

16 Conversation, Cayrol, Noumea, 2003, who knew M Ritter. The authors have been unable to find further information on this builder.

17 Archives, Museum of the City of Noumea. Conversation, Cayrol, Noumea, 2003. One of the houses is named Maison La Potinière. They were originally owned by the Mary family.

18 Conversation, Cayrol, Noumea, 2003. Derquennes was a draftsman, but he called himself an architect.

19 Dominique Bayol, Véronique Defrance and Anny Levanqué, *Coup de Coeur pour le béton. l'architecture moderne à Nouméa 1930–1970.* Mairie de Nouméa, Noumea, 2009, p. 37.

20 File No. 1438, Archives, Museum of the City of Noumea. Also material supplied by Sylvie Fardeau, Heritage Guide Association, Noumea, 2003. Currently, some Bottcher houses are in a poor state of repair.

21 Archives, Museum of the City of Noumea. Also, information provided by Professor Jules Guiart, who married Calimbre's daughter and occupies the house. Identification of the architect was not possible. The house is situated at 2 rue de Sébastopol.

22 Kermit Holt, 'Noumea: Squalid War Base now a Charming City', *Chicago Tribune*, 14 August 1967, p. C9. Holt was stationed in Noumea during World War II.

23 For information on the American presence in Noumea see Philippe Godard and Luc Chevalier, pp. 173–180. See also Lacourrège, Gérard and Pierre Alibert, *La Présence américaine en Nouvelle-Calédonie, 1944–1945*, Two volumes, l'Atelier D'Art Graphique, Noumea, 1981. See also Henri Daly, *La Guerre du Pacifique 1941–1945: Nouvelle-Calédonie: porte-avions américain dan les mers du sud*, Société d'Études Historiques de la Nouvelle-Calédonie, Noumea, 2002.

24 It was lost in a fire in 1970.

25 The Anse Vata Clinic huts have since been demolished.

26 Information provided by Isabelle Ohlen (4th Vice President of Congress), Noumea, 2003, who was then the president of the Association Racines. Her family occupies the house. The authors are grateful to Isabelle and her cousin, Kathya Ohlen, for their generous time, extensive advice and assistance with the history of early buildings in New Caledonia.

27 Godard and Chevalier, p. 35. See also Archives, Museum of the City of Noumea.

28 Conversation, Cayrol, Noumea, 2003.

29 Information on Raighasse derived from the following sources: Patrick O'Reilly, *Calédoniens: Répertoire bio-bibliographique de la Nouvelle-Calédonie,* Société des Océanistes, Musée de l'homme, Paris 16e, 1953, p. 332; Godard and Chevalier, Tome 5, pp. 387–388; Conversation, Cayrol, Noumea, 2003.

30 Celebratory plaque attached to the church states Monsignor Bresson made the vow on 25 January 1942: The first sod was turned in August 1949, and the first mass was held in May 1953.

See also Godard and Chevalier, Tome 5, pp. 388–389.
31 The mezzanine was built in by Cayrol 1992–93, alteration 1995. A subtle detail can be seen in the angled wall panels of Cayrol's extension that allow in shaded light to the interior wall surfaces.
32 Conversation, Cayrol, Noumea, 2003.
33 O'Reilly, p. 311.
34 O'Reilly, p. 311. See also Godard and Chevalier, Tome 5, pp. 284–285.
35 Jacqueline Julien, *Let me guide you in Nouméa*, Editions Grain de sable, Noumea, 1999, p. 79.
36 In 2003 it served as an entertainment centre.
37 Three new sports venues were built for the Pacific Games: the sports stadium by Rampal, the swimming pool by Cayrol and the interior sports hall by Raighasse. Godard and Chevalier, Tome 6, pp. 241–245.
38 O'Reilly, p. 332.
39 Conversation, Cayrol, Noumea, 2003. O'Reilly credits Rampal with the design, so it is possible that he made a significant contribution. See O'Reilly, p. 332. See also Godard and Chevalier, Tome 5, pp. 387–388.
40 The wife of the client, Betty Narwa, also was from Australia and possibly knew Douglas Snelling. The authors are grateful to Davina Jackson, a scholar of Snelling's work, for her assistance with Snelling's background and for identifying these houses.
41 State Library of New South Wales, 'Manuscripts, oral history pictures' (catalogue), viewed on 7 June 2012 at <http://acms.sl.nsw.gov.au/item/itemDetailPaged.aspx?itemID=395089>.
42 Gabriel Cayrol died in 2012.
43 Information regarding Cayrol's career was provided by the architect.
44 This building has been radically altered by heavy infilling columns, walls and a corrugated-steel roof.
45 The Hôtel Château Royal was rendered obsolete by new resorts and demolished 2005.
46 *Varangue,* No. 13, July 2002, pp. 24–25.

PART III PLACES OF THE SOUTH PACIFIC: DOWN THE CORAL SEA TO FIJI

ISLAND LANDS OF WESTERN WATERS

1 An interesting discussion of Polynesia can be found in 'The Center of the Triangle', 'The Apex of the Triangle' and 'The Base of the Triangle', in Peter H Buck, *Vikings of the Sunrise*, Frederick A Stokes Company, New York, 1938.
2 Bislama is a developed form of Pidgin English and is an official language in Vanuatu.
3 Secretariat of the Pacific Community, 'Mid-2010 Population Estimate', 2010 Pocket Statistical Summary (ISSN 1021-7436), SPC, Noumea, New Caledonia.

Chapter 3: Diverse Identities

Building the New Noumea

1 The important 1998 Noumea Accord pledged the recognition of Kanak culture and the gradual increase in independence of New Caledonia from the French state.
2 Conversation, Daniel Leroux, architect, Noumea, 2003.
3 Porcheron's great-grandfather was the first mayor of Noumea. Conversation, Willy Porcheron, architect, Noumea, 2003.
4 Conversation, Porcheron, Noumea, 2003.
5 Conversation, François Raulet, architect, Noumea, 2003. See also 'Lifou' (liste des maires successifs) at (French version) <http://fr.wikipedia.org/wiki/Lifou>.
6 The building was renovated by architect Alain-Jean Formis. *Varangue*, No. 16, August 2005, p. 138. *Varangue* is the journal of the New Caledonian Order of Architects and has been published annually since 1990. It is the only regular architectural journal in the South Pacific. The Fiji Association of Architects published a journal (*Fiji Architect*) for a short period between 1975–77.
7 The building has since been considerably altered.
8 New Caledonia is the only country in the region to have building height controls.
9 Information obtained from the working drawings viewed at the Noumea Town Hall by the authors in 2003.
10 Correspondence, Christophe Augias, chief librarian, Bernheim Library, 4 May 2010. See also *Varangue*, No. 16, August 2005, p. 145.
11 Conversation, Raulet, Noumea, 2003.
12 *Varangue*, No. 19, August 2008, p. 46.
13 Ibid.
14 The building was subject to a major extension carried out by Archipel (a firm formed by Raulet in partnership with Olliver Dalla Vecchia) in 2008–09. *Varangue,* No. 19, August 2008, p. 29.
15 A second stage, by Raulet, was added in 2004.
16 *Varangue,* No. 19, August 2008, p. 78 indicates that in 2007 Philippe Flagel completed extensions to the university, including a library, an amphitheatre and a university restaurant.
17 McWilliam Consulting Engineers, and Socalmo (Noumea) and Kamois Membrane Structures, Brisbane. Information from Raulet's brochure of works.
18 Information from architect's brochure.
19 Conversation, Raulet, Noumea, 2003 and 2004. Raulet retired in 2010.
20 Conversation, Leroux, Noumea, 2003. *Varangue,* No. 16, August 2005, p. 96 indicates that the original building was called 'Ma Maison' and was built between 1900 and 1902 by M Werquin.
21 Conversation, Agnes Gabet-Jézéquel, architect, Noumea, 2004. See also *Varangue,* No. 17, July 2006, pp. 126–127 for a brief portrait of her.
22 See Luc Chevalier, *Nouméa de l'an 1854 à l'an 2000*, Les Editions du Cagou, Agence Calédonienne de Diffusion, Noumea, 1998, p. 129.
23 *Varangue,* No. 22, August 2011, p. 28.
24 There had been substantial technical problems to overcome in providing the seawater that fills the thirty-six tanks housing the exhibits, at the correct temperature, adequately filtered and oxygenated. See 'US$ 17M Noumea Aquarium Finally Opens', *The Pacific Tradewinds Quarterly*, Oct/Nov/Dec/ 2007, Vol. 15, No 4, p. 11, viewed on 29 August 2013 at <http://sparce.evac.ou.edu/newsletter/2007Q4.pdf>.
25 Formis, site architect, see 'Plongée dans l'aquarium de Nouméa', *Varangue*, No. 16, August 2005, pp. 200–202. Alain-Jean Formis died in 2009, see Françoise Raulet, 'Obituary', *Varangue*, No. 20, October 2009, p. 17.
26 *Varangue*, No. 19, August 2008, p. 55.
27 Correspondence, Chambre et Vibert, architects, Paris, January 2011.
28 Institut de la Statistique et des Études Économiques (ISEE), New Caledonia, 1996 Census, viewed on 19 May 2010 at <http://www.isee.nc/anglais/home.html> (This is the most recent material available on ethnic distribution).
29 Secretariat of the Pacific Community, 2010 Pocket Statistical Summary, SPC, viewed on 17 May 2011 at <http://www.spc.int/sdp/>.
30 The roof and balustrades have since been repainted beige.
31 Roland Osmont died in 2010. See Jocelyn Picot, 'Obituary', *Varangue*, No. 21, August 2010, pp. 18–19.
32 Cayrol's son Jean-Gabriel joined him in his practice in 1998.
33 *Varangue,* No. 12, June 2001, pp. 89–91.
34 Porcheron has spent considerable time on the Gold Coast in Australia, and this composition is akin to developments found there. *Varangue,* No. 20, October 2009, pp. 160–163 carries an interview with Porcheron on his approach to architecture.

The Solomon Islands: Guadalcanal And After

1 National Library of Australia, 'German Colonies in the Pacific', viewed on 5 June 2012 at <http://www.nla.gov.au/selected-library-collections/german-colonies-in-the-pacific>.
2 U.S. Department of State, 'Background Notes/Country Fact Sheets' –Solomon Islands, viewed on 7 April 2012 at <http://www.state.gov/r/pa/ei/bgn/2799.htm>.
3 U.S. Department of State Background Note – Solomon Islands.
4 *South Pacific Travel Trade News (SPTTN)*, April 1974, p. 15.
5 Seven thousand Americans and 21 000 Japanese lost their lives. U.S. Department of State Background Note: Solomon Islands.
6 It was named Henderson Airport by the Americans after Major Lofton Henderson, a marine flyer killed at Midway. The runway length is 2.04 kilometres. It is now called Honiara International Airport.
7 Brij V Lal and Kate Fortune (eds.), *The Pacific Islands: An Encyclopedia*, University of Hawai'i Press, Honolulu, 2000, pp. 609–610.
8 The Japanese fish cannery was closed, and approximately one half of all jobs in the timber industry were lost.
9 Regional Assistance Mission to Solomon Islands report, viewed on 17 June 2007 at <http://www.ramsi.org/>.
10 The hotel was rebuilt, with extensions in 2007. Correspondence, Don Boykin, architect, Honiara, 2007.
11 Conversation, Aubrey Zeke, architect, Honiara, 2005.
12 'I have never heard of anyone being knocked back.' Conversation, Boykin, Honiara, 2005.
13 Information on projects built by Fletcher Construction provided by John Mulholland, Fletcher's manager for the Solomon Islands, notably from the records of Fletcher Kwaimani. The authors gratefully acknowledge assistance provided by Fletcher Construction (John Walls, information officer) in making available throughout the South Pacific its building records.
14 Fletcher Construction send their drawings out of the country to have the engineering designed, primarily by Kramer Engineering Group, elsewhere. Conversation, John Mulholland, Honiara, 2005. Boykin states, 'I do my own engineering. So far I have been fortunate in that every time I submit something, it seems to get passed without questioning.' Conversation, Boykin, Honiara, 2005.
15 According to Ken Grossmith, Murray-North also had an architect working with them during an active time of building in Honiara in the late 1980s and mid-1990s. Conversation, Ken Grossmith, Honiara, 2005.
16 Correspondence, Murray Cockburn, architect, May 2008.
17 Ancher, Mortlock and Woolley also built the radio station at Port Vila, Vanuatu, 1980.
18 Data from Fletcher Construction.
19 The work also included dormitories for the Solomon Islands College of Higher Education and three elevated houses on the same site, 1988, and the Anda'ua Secondary School, 1991. Data supplied by Fletcher Construction.
20 Osborne Van Gana graduated from the Papua New Guinea University of Technology in 1989 and subsequently became the Director of Architecture and Building at the Ministry of Infrastructure and Development. Conversation, Osborne Van Gana, Port Vila, 2005.
21 Other Melanesian architects, such as Laloma Pabulu, who worked with various practices including that of Cockburn, are engaged with other firms. Correspondence, Cockburn, 2007.
22 Stevenson graduated in architecture in Glasgow in 1962. He had previously served ten years as Government Architect in Nigeria until 1962. In Honiara he had one other qualified architect on staff, Alfred Munday from England, who was mainly employed on housing. Correspondence, Charles Stevenson, architect, 8 April 2008.
23 Conversation, Stevenson, Brisbane, 2008.
24 Grossmith graduated from the University of Auckland in 1987, and Don Boykin received a Bachelor of Arts degree (Architecture/Interior Design) from San Francisco State University in 1968. Also in the office at this time was an American architect, Ed Hackett, and an Australian architect, Charlie Boyle.
25 After Kayhan Khadem returned to Auckland he established the practice of Professional Designers, now ProDesigners Architects.
26 Information concerning Ken Grossmith has been provided by the

architect, Honiara, 2005, also correspondence (email), 12 August 2009.

27 Pacific Architects was initially founded by Charlie Boyle before he returned to Australia for further studies. Conversation, Grossmith, Honiara, 2005.

28 Conversation, Grossmith, Honiara, 2005.

29 Ibid.

30 The Parliament House is discussed further in Chapter 11.

31 Fact Rover, 'Solomon Islands People', Newspapers Online: US and World Media and Facts, viewed on 6 July 2011 at <http://www.factrover.com/people/Solomon_Islands_people.html>.

32 'This was actually done from my office but I had little to do with it. A New Zealand architect, Noel McKernan, was brought in by the Catholic Church; he came to me for local knowledge, and we got on well, so it was arranged that he take over my house/office and look after my business while my family and I went on leave to New Zealand.' Correspondence, Stevenson, March 2008.

33 The authors have been unable to determine the architect of the church. It was most probably a designer brought in by the Church – possibly from New Zealand.

34 The town has been regenerated since the destruction that was wrought by the 2007 tsunami. The Ghizo tsunami of April 2007 was caused by an earthquake of 8.1 on the Richter scale, 45 kilometres to the south-east of the island of Ghizo. It caused major destruction, killing fifty-three people and leaving thousands homeless.

35 These are similar to the sites at Iron Bottom Sound in the bay to the north-west of Honiara.

Vanuatu: The Amiable Isles

1 Happy Planet Index, New Economics Foundation, viewed on 2 September 2008 at <http://www.happyplanetindex.org/data>.

2 *Vanuatu Daily Post*, 21 June 2007 and New Economic Foundation.

3 Blackbirding refers to the forced recruitment of labour in the Pacific Islands – a form of kidnapping and slave trading. See Brij V Lal and Kate Fortune (eds.), *The Pacific Islands: An Encyclopedia*, University of Hawai'i Press, Honolulu, 2000, p. 208.

4 Keith Woodward, 'Historical Note', pp. 16–23, in Brian J Bresnihan and Keith Woodward (eds.), *Tufala Gavman: Reminiscences From the Anglo-French Condominium of the New Hebrides*, Institute of Pacific Studies, University of the South Pacific, Suva, 2002.

5 Lal and Fortune, p. 621.

6 Margaret Rodman, *Houses Far from Home: British Colonial Space in the New Hebrides*, University of Hawai'i Press, Honolulu, 2001, pp. 1–20.

7 Rodman, p. 53.

8 'Iririki Island Resort Fact File', viewed on 2 March 2008 at <http://www.iririki.com/>.

9 Bresnihan and Woodward (eds.), p. 31.

10 Rodman, p. 53.

11 Ibid, p. 56.

12 Ibid, pp. 61–63.

13 Ibid, p. 36.

14 There is a lobby in Port Vila campaigning to have the building restored. Conversation, Geoffrey Feast of James Ferrie and Partners, architect, Port Vila, 2003.

15 Patrick O'Reilly, *Calédonians: Répertoire bio-bibliographique de la Nouvelle-Calédonie*, Société des Océanistes, Musée de l'homme, Paris 16e, 1953, p. 48.

16 Rodman, p. 36.

17 As with many other early official buildings of the New Hebrides, the authors have been unable to determine the name of the architect.

18 Bresnihan and Woodward, p. 30. The Joint Court House was demolished in 1970, and subsequently, the site was used for the Reserve Bank Building.

19 Rodman, p. 36.

20 Bresnihan and Woodward, p. 43. The building was subsequently destroyed by fire in 2008.

21 This description is based on an early photograph showing the building before alteration. The louvers on the lower part of the building were replaced with flush panelling in the mid-1950s.

22 Bresnihan and Woodward, p. 31.

23 Bresnihan and Woodward, p. 46. The US military installed 2000 Quonset huts at Luganville, the major town on Espiritu Santo.

24 Conversation, Pierre Bourgeois, developer, Port Vila, 2003. Bourgeois died in 2004. The authors would like to acknowledge the introduction to Pierre Bourgeois by Davina Jackson.

25 Bourgeois worked through his company Hebrida Holdings. See also *SPTTN*, May 1970, p. 18.

26 New Hebrides Airways became Melanesian Airways in 1965 and today is Air Vanuatu. David Lyall, 'Airlines: The New Hebrides', The World's Airlines, Past, present & Future, viewed on 19 February 2008 at <http://www.airlinehistory.co.uk/RestofWorld/New%20Hebrides/Airlines.asp>.

27 Unlike the governments of neighbouring countries, the Condominium 'staunchly refused to have anything to do with tourism,' hence it was left in the hands of private enterprise. Ngaire Douglas, *They Came for Savages: 100 Years of Tourism in Melanesia*, Southern Cross University Press, Alstonville, NSW, 1996, p. 218.

28 Bourgeois later became chairman of Air Vanuatu, Bourgeois biography, viewed on 18 February 2010 at <www.oceania.com.vu/presentation.htm>.

29 Bresnihan and Woodward, p. 461.

30 Ibid, p. 53.

31 'The roof was sealed with 1.5-inch-thick plasterboard. On top of that were laid gravel-coated shingles that came in sheets and were not suited to the tropics. It became brittle, ultimately cracked and allowed water to penetrate. We had to re-roof them all – they all went the same way [d'Hauteserre's buildings].' Conversation, Feast, Port Vila, 2003.

32 The church was built by the Presbyterian Women's Missionary Union of Victoria, Australia, in memory of Margaret Whitecross Paton, wife of the missionary John Gibson Paton. They were missionaries on Aniwa 1866–81. There is a commemorative plaque in the church grounds.

33 Advice from the Presbyterian Church Records Office, Melbourne, 2008.

34 'Building safety is getting worse. There are no cyclone codes. No one inspects the plumbing or the steel, and there are no fire regulations.' Conversation, Glen Gibson, Kramer Engineering Group, Port Vila, 2003.

35 'I have never seen anyone knocked back'. Conversation, Gibson, Port Vila, 2003.

36 Feast: 'Then we have the Kramer Group; they call themselves architects.' Taylor: 'Well, the Kramer Group say you call yourself an engineer!' Conversation, Feast, Port Vila, 2003.

37 Vanuatu Statistics Office, census figures, viewed on 18 February 2008 at <http://www.vanuatustatistics.gov.vu/About%20VNSO/Data/Social/Population.htm>.

38 Gregory Rawlings, 'Laws, Liquidity and Eurobonds: The Making of the Vanuatu Tax Haven', *The Journal of Pacific History*, Vol. 39, No. 3, 2004, p. 325.

39 In 2008 the Kramer Engineering Group was still the only engineering firm in Port Vila.

40 The architect Jean Galimard joined d'Hauteserre for a time.

41 The hospital is now the Lands Office. It would appear that Claude Bach had also produced a design for a hospital. O'Reilly states, with reference to Claude Bach, 'He also built the hospital for the Condominium in the New Hebrides'. Patrick O'Reilly and Raoul Teissier, *Tahitiens: Répertoire Biographique de la Polynésie Française*, Publications de la Société des Océanistes, No. 36, Musée de l'homme, Paris, 1975, p. 29.

42 Information on the architects of Vanuatu was provided by Richie Nichols of Fletcher Construction, Geoffrey Feast and Glen Gibson, Port Vila, 2003.

43 Minton was only in practice in Vanuatu for a few years. Conversation, Feast, Port Vila, 2003.

44 The Nasi Tuan phrase means 'we all help each other'. See 'Vanuatu Ministry of Infrastructure and Public Utilities 2011–2013 Corporate Plan and 2011 Business Plan', p. 11, viewed on 23 October 2012 at <www.ausaid.gov.au/countries/pacific/vanuatu/Documents/ministry-of-infrastructure-and-public-utilities-business-and-corporate-plan-part-one.pdf>.

45 Correspondence, Benoit Chassatte, architect, Public Works Department Vanuatu, 20 April 2005.

46 Paul McGillick (ed.), 'Tropical Veranda – Peter Stutchbury's Vanuatu House', *Habitus*, No. 16, July/September 2012, pp. 160–170.

47 Ralph Regenvanu, 'Issues with Land Reform in Vanuatu', *Journal of South Pacific Law*, Vol. 12, No. 1, 2008, pp 63–67, provides an account of current difficulties in administering leased land in Vanuatu and proposed reforms.

48 'This is Disneyland. People fly in with their Gulf Stream aircraft or million-dollar yachts – they are here for a week and then back to the United States. You learn to say 'yes' to everything – it can be done. It's the only way.' Conversation, Nichols, Port Vila, 2005.

49 'See all this land here – it was bought for four Hilux trucks over a beer one night. Bit of extra cash, trucks, beer – and the next generation has lost everything. Now there is resentment coming through.' Conversation, Nichols, Port Vila, 2005.

50 Now named the Grand Hotel and Casino.

51 Conversation, Glen Gibson, Port Vila, 2003. Gibson also reported that they designed it to the New Zealand cyclone code, 'but there is no regulation here that requires that'. The project lay completed but unoccupied for some years.

Chapter 4: Playing Along the Coral Sea

The Tourist: Beginnings 1970-90

p. 99 Toni Stroud quoting James A Michener putting the record straight as to which islands he had drawn his inspiration from in creating Bali Hai. Toni Stroud, 'Where is Bali Hai? In your Mind', *Chicago Tribune*, 7 November 2004, viewed on 3 June 2012 at <http://articles.chicagotribune.com/2004-11-07/travel/0411060325_1_bora-bora-bali-hai-solomon-islands>.

1 Ngaire Douglas, 'Towards a History of Tourism in the Solomon Islands', *Journal of Pacific Studies*, Vol. 26, Nos. 1 and 2, 2004, pp. 29–49.

2 'The holidays were advertised in special company publications with titles such as *Picturesque Travel*, *Picturesque Isles of the South Seas*, and in the Burns Philp magazine which first appeared in 1929 and was issued regularly until World War II threw Pacific tourism into turmoil.' Ann Stephen (ed.), *Pirating the Pacific: Images of Trade, Travel and Tourism*, Powerhouse Publishing, Sydney, 1993, p. 34.

3 'Orly, Wednesday 21 September 1949, 2.45 p.m. The first commercial Air France flight to New Caledonia has just taken off on a journey, lasting 6 days. Tontouta, Tuesday 27 September 1949, 6.40 a.m., the DC4 touches down. With a 65-hour flight time, over a distance of 21 000 km the Paris–Noumea inaugural flight, together with the London–Melbourne and New York–Calcutta services, is the longest air link in the world.' Jacqueline Julien, *Let Me Guide You in Noumea*, Editions Grain de Sable, Noumea, 1999, p. 48.

4 *South Pacific Travel Trade News* (*SPTTN*), May 1968, p. 14.

5 James A Michener, article (unamed), *Philadelphia Sunday Bulletin*, 1970, provided by the James A Michener Library, University of Northern California, Greenly, USA, viewed on 21 February 2009 at <http://www.achievement.org/autodoc/page/micObio-1>.

6 Douglas reports that the hotel was originally built as a printery by Lockhart Bell, but apparently was operating as a hotel when the Reid family purchased it. See Ngaire Douglas, *They Came for Savages: 100 Years of Tourism in Melanesia*, Southern Cross Press, Alstonville, NSW, 1996, p. 62.

7 *SPTTN*, April 1970, p, 30.

8 Conversation, Pierre Bourgeois, developer, Port Vila, 2003.
9 'Times they are changing in Port Vila', Travel section, *The West Australian*, 20 December 2007, viewed on 10 May 2009 at <www.thewest.com.au>.
10 It later became the Hotel Olympic. The first concrete structure was the Silverstone Building. Conversation, Bourgeois, Port Vila, 2003.
11 According to Bourgeois, the workers in the New Hebrides in the early 1960s included Japanese, Hawaiian, Korean and the largest work force of 3000 Vietnamese. These were deported, with the last shipment leaving in 1964 on the 'Eastern Queen'. Bourgeois said only two islanders worked on the Hotel Vate. Conversation, Bourgeois, Port Vila, 2003.
12 Bourgeois biography, viewed 18 February 2010 at < www.oceania.com.vu/presentation.htm>.
13 Douglas, *They Came for Savages: 100 Years of Tourism in Melanesia*, p. 120.
14 Douglas, p. 269. Half of the bedrooms were air conditioned. *SPTTN*, June 1968, pp. 33–36. The hotel went through many extensions, the first being a three-storey block of 102 units, commenced in 1971. *SPTTN*, May 1971, p. 20. Latterly known as the Solomon Kitano Mendana Hotel.
15 *SPTTN*, June 1971, p. 27. When payment was not forthcoming, Brian Derrick, in the name of his company, Naviti Investments, acquired a share in the hotel. Conversation, Ken Grossmith, Honiara, 2005. In 1989 Japanese investment company Kitano Construction Corporation took over the Mendana. It is now known as the Solomon Mendana.
16 In 1974 the hotel accommodation in the Solomon Islands was: Blum's Hometel (fourteen rooms), Honiara Hotel (fifty-three rooms), Hotel Mendana (sixty rooms), Tambea Village (twenty rooms) and Tavanipupu (four fales). *SPTTN*, April 1974, p. 15.
17 It remains common practice today to fly to Vanuatu via Noumea.
18 In 1965 Air Melanesiæ was formed as a joint venture between the British-owned New Hebrides Airways and the French-owned Société Néo-Hébridaise de Transports Aériens (Hebridair). This airline went through various mutations to become Vanair in 1989, and then in 2004 it merged with Air Vanuatu.
19 The InterContinental became the Radisson Royal Palms, then Le Méridien and later the Holiday Inn.
20 Douglas, pp. 239–240.
21 Conversation, Bourgeois, Port Vila, 2003. Bourgeois could not recall the architect's name. The authors have been unable to confirm this in New Caledonia.
22 Conversation, Bourgeois, Port Vila, 2003.
23 Correspondence, Michael Heffernan, architect, March 2010.
24 Trammell Crow was a friend of President Ford and founded one of America's leading property development agencies. See President Ford's diary, 22 August 1976, which records him playing tennis with Trammel Crow, and later that night, Crow and his wife attended dinner with the president. Viewed on 24 February 2010 at <www.ford.utexas.edu/LIBRARY/document/diary/pdd760821.pdf>.
25 Conversation, Bourgeois, Port Vila, 2003. Bourgeois could not recall his name.
26 Conversation, Geoffrey Feast, architect, Port Vila, 2003.
27 The original project was a private venture by Heffernan, his wife and Sydney associates, backed by Japanese funding. In 1990 it was bought by the Japanese Company Narita Golf, and to attract Japanese tourists a further nine holes were added to the golf course. Correspondence, Heffernan, September 2009.
28 Correspondence, Heffernan, November 2002.
29 See White Sands Resort website, viewed on 10 March 2012 at <http://www.wsresort.net/>.
30 Correspondence, Heffernan, November 2002. A chieftain's truss is a three-dimensional truss, unlike the typical two-dimensional truss, and is particularly suitable for small buildings.
31 Douglas, p. 242.
32 UTA (Union de Transport Aériens) was a new company, having commenced operations in 1963. In 1999 it merged with Air France, which had operated since 1933.
33 Conversation, Gabriel Cayrol, architect, Noumea, 2003.
34 *SPTTN*, February 1975, p. 11. A further domestic terminal by Raulet was completed in 2003.
35 *SPTTN*, June 1968, p. 33.
36 *SPTTN*, November 1972, p. 32.
37 It was refurbished by atelier 13 and opened again in February 2011 as the Royal Tera Beach Resort and Spa. See *Varangue*, No. 22, August 2011, p. 22.
38 Correspondence, Cayrol, 6 April 2012.
39 Now known as Le Nouvata.
40 The government bought into the company in 1976 and acquired the remainder in 1984. Substantial investment followed, including a joint venture with Qantas. The company now has regular flights to Brisbane, Nadi, Port Vila, Nauru and Port Moresby.
41 See Table No. 2, p. 34, in Ngaire Douglas, *They Came for Savages: 100 Years of Tourism in Melanesia*, Southern Cross Press, Alstonville, NSW, 1996, where the annual number of tourists coming into the Solomon Islands is shown as about 4000 per year.

The Tourist: Since 1990

p. 106 Attributed to Hugh Possingham, ecologist, in Tom Arup, 'Ocean Parks "Vital to Protect Species"', *The Age*, 8 June 2010.
1 Information on the background of the Windsor International was provided by Fletcher Construction and Geoffrey Feast, architect, Port Vila, 2003.
2 This is now known as Le Parc. A further separate extension of 120 rooms, Le Pacific Complex, was built in 2000.
3 Jean-Marie Charpentier had built many notable buildings, particularly in France and China, including the Shanghai Opera House.
4 Phillipe Thébaud set up his own studio in 1974 in Paris and then in 1986 created the city planning and landscape firm Thébaud Urbanisme & Paysage (TUP) Associated with the Swiss urbanist, landscape designer and botanical expert Marcel Baerfuss. Viewed on 12 May 2011 at <www.thebaud-tup.fr/pdf/plaquette-tup.pdf>.
5 *Varangue*, No. 17, July 2006, pp. 104–107.
6 Sheraton New Caledonia Deva Resort and Spa is opening in 2014. Starwood Hotels, 'Local Area', viewed on 7 June 2012 at <http://www.starwoodhotels.com/sheraton/property/area/index.html?propertyID=3501>.
7 Also seen in the buildings of the Point Cruz Yacht Club, 1980.
8 *Varangue*, No. 19, August 2008, p. 168.
9 Landscaping was carried out by TUP of Paris.
10 In 2006 Philippe Jarcet designed extensions to the reception area, bar and restaurant. *Varangue*, No. 19, August 2008, p. 150.
11 *Varangue*, No. 19, August 2008, p. 79. The original work was designed and constructed by the owner Henri Morini with his construction company NEA.
12 *Varangue*, No. 19, August 2008, p. 60. Coral Palms Island Resort is now known as l'Escapade Island Resort.
13 Conversation, Willy Porcheron, architect, Noumea, 2003.
14 Trevor H B Sofield, *Empowerment for Sustainable Tourism Development*, Emerald Group Publishing, London, 2003, p. 136.
15 'The Marovo Lagoon was nominated for World Heritage classification but the proposed listing was cancelled after the surrounding forests were heavily logged and oil palm plantations established.' World Bank, 'Solomon Islands Rural Development Program' (report), June 2007, paragraph 3.5.5, p. 22, downloaded from <http://documents.worldbank.org/curated/en/2007/06/8484124/solomon-islands-rural-development-project-environmental-assessment-environmental-assessment-environment-social-management-framework>. East Rennell, the southern-most island in the Solomon Islands, has been accepted for World Heritage Listing.
16 The Tavanipupu Resort was mentioned in *SPTTN*, April 1974, p. 15. Conservationist Professor Trevor Sofield developed Vulelua Island Resort.
17 Danny Kennedy, brother of Shane Kennedy, bought Fatboys in 2006, added four beach bungalows to the restaurant and renamed it Fatboys Resort. The role of Australians involved in this stage of the development of the Solomon Islands is of note.
18 Solomon Watersport is one of only six dive operators throughout Asia and the Pacific that is recognized by GO ECO as implementing environmental best practices in their local area. Solomon Watersport website, viewed on 6 March 2010 at <http://www.solomonwatersport.com/>.
19 Conversation, Hans Mergozzi, owner-developer, Sanbis, 2005. Mergozzi trained local people to work in the resort for all duties, including bar and restaurant service. The villagers who live on Mbambanga Island come from the Gilbert Islands.
20 The Gizo Hotel on Ghizo Island and the island of Mbambanga, with Fatboys, Sanbis and the Kennedy house on Naru Island, survived the devastation of the April 2007 tsunami.

Chapter 5: The Special Case of Fiji

Two Colonial Capitals

1 Secretariat of the Pacific Community, 'Mid-2010 Population Estimate', 2010 Pocket Statistical Summary (ISSN 1021-7436), SPC, Noumea, New Caledonia.
2 George Kingsley Roth (ed.), *Fiji: Handbook of the Colony*, Acting Government Printer, Suva, 1937, p. 305.
3 See Part XI, 'India in Microcosm', p. 52, in C W Whonsbon Aston, *Polynesia Patchwork: The Tale of the Pacific Diocese*, Society for the Propagation of the Gospel in Foreign Parts, Westminster, 1948, (transcribed by the Right Reverend Dr Terry Brown, Bishop of Malaita, Church of the Province of Melanesia, 2006), viewed on 23 January 2010 at <http://anglicanhistory.org/oceania/patchwork1948/>.
4 Fiji Islands Bureau of Statistics, '2007 Census of Population and Housing', Secretariat of the Pacific Community, viewed on 4 September 2009 at <http://www.spc.int/prism/country/FJ/Stats/Census2007/census07_index2.htm>. On 12 March 2012 Fiji's military dictator Voreqe Bainimarama formally abolished the Fijian Great Council of Chiefs and decreed that the term Fijian applies to all 837 000 people in the archipelago, including the 37 per cent Indian, while the indigenous people are now to be known as i-Taukei. See Michael Field, 'Fiji's Great Council of Chiefs Abolished', 14 March 2012, Stuff (published by Fairfax Digital), viewed on 20 June 2013 at <http://www.stuff.co.nz/world/south-pacific/6573396/Fijis-Great-Council-of-Chiefs-abolished>.
5 Vanua Levu was formerly known as Sandalwood Island.
6 Ronald Wright (ed.), *On Fiji Islands*, Penguin, New York, 1987, p. 35.
7 Wright, p. 39.
8 Institute of Pacific Studies, University of the South Pacific and Levuka Historical and Cultural Society, *Levuka: Living Heritage*, by the people of Levuka, Suva, 2001, p. 39.
9 'Holy Trinity Church' (pamphlet), 1992, p. 1. As through much of the South Pacific, the first missionaries were from the London Missionary Society. However, in Fiji the name Anglican is more commonly used. Floyd was born in Ireland in 1838 and ordained in Melbourne in 1870.
10 Victor Dove, *Fiji Sketchbook*, Rigby, Brisbane, 1970, p. 11.
11 *The Town of Levuka Heritage Study, 1993–1994*, prepared for the Ministry of Housing, Urban Development and the Environment, Suva, states the firm was established c.1898, and the building is known to have existed in 1900. Percy Morris and Maynard Hedstrom were residents of Levuka.
12 Elsie Stephenson, *Fiji's Past on Picture Postcards*, Caines Jannif Group, Suva, 1997, Figs. 36 and 182.
13 The Masonic Lodge in Suva was built in 1891 in a similar pseudo-Tuscan style. See Stephenson, Fig. 159.
14 For further coverage of Levuka's early buildings see Institute of Pacific Studies, et al., *Levuka: Living Heritage*, and Stephenson, *Fiji's Past on Picture Postcards*.
15 Institute of Pacific Studies, et al., p. 38.

16 The church's early history is mentioned in the pamphlet 'Holy Trinity Cathedral' (mimeographed document), Suva, 1992. See also Stephenson, p. 204.
17 Stephenson, p. 202.
18 *Town of Levuka Heritage Study, 1993–1994*. See also Institute of Pacific Studies, et al., p. 40.
19 *The Town of Levuka Heritage Study, 1993–1994*. p. 41.
20 Leonard Mason and Patricia Hereniko, *In Search of a Home*, Institute of Pacific Studies, University of the South Pacific, Suva, 1987, p. 132.
21 Terence A Donnelly, Max Quanchi, Gavin J A Kerr, *Fiji in the Pacific*, The Jacaranda Press, Brisbane, 1974, p. 125.
22 Albert J Schütz, *Suva: A History and Guide*, Pacific Publications, Sydney, 1978, p. 24.
23 The old village was located in what are now the grounds of Government House.
24 Letter written by Lady Gordon, the governor's wife, 6 December 1875. 'Holy Trinity Church' (pamphlet), 1992, p. 1.
25 Stephenson, pp. 168–170.
26 Ibid, p. 173.
27 Ibid, p. 170.
28 Shütz, p. 23.
29 'The Melbourne Hotel, one of the most select and best appointed residential hotels of Fiji, was established on its present site at the corner of Victoria Parade and McArthur Street, Suva, in 1881, shortly after the removal from there of the seat of government', Archive CD Books Australia, *The Cyclopedia of Fiji, Samoa, Tonga, Tahiti, and the Cook Islands 1907*, Archive CD Books Australia, Modbury, SA, 2006, p. 321.
30 Schütz, p. 24.
31 R Anrep, architect of Suva, is shown in the 1911 *Handbook of Fiji*, but not in the 1907 *Cyclopedia of Fiji*, etc. The fact that he designed the Queen Victoria Memorial Hall in 1904 and the 1909 Carnegie Library might indicate that he went to Fiji only briefly in 1904 to build the memorial hall, was absent for the 1907 Cyclopedia, but returned again for the 1909 library and stayed there until at least 1911.
32 The present porch was not built until after 1920. Stephenson, p. 150.
33 Ibid, pp. 150–151.
34 Ibid, pp. 151–153.
35 The present cable and wireless authority is called the Fiji International Telecommunications Ltd. (FINTEL).
36 Stephenson, p. 155. Stephenson may have taken the term 'concrete sheeting' from an article in the *Fiji Times & Herald*, where it was mentioned.
37 For description of the hotel see Stephenson, pp. 179–181.
38 Schütz, p. 30.
39 The 1893 building replaced the earlier building on the site, which was destroyed by fire in 1891. Original report in *Fiji Times*, 23 May 1891 as reported in 'Celebrating 140 Years: The Great Fire of Suva', *Fiji Times*, 12 June 2009, viewed on 17 March 2012 at <http://www.fijitimes.com/story.aspx?id=123363>.
40 Stephenson, p. 65. The building burnt down in 1998.
41 Joan Beard, *South Pacific Islands*, Little Hills Press, Crows Nest, NSW, 1996, p. 49.
42 Conversation, Arnold Ludolph, Ludolph's grandson, Brisbane, 2005.
43 He married Clare Noell in Melbourne on 29 August 1908 at the age of 25 at St John's Church.
44 Ludolph returned to Suva on a short visit from the United Kingdom on 22 October 1915 on the *SS Omrah* and at that time showed his occupation as Government Architect. Outbound shipping record, National Archives, Kew, UK.
45 Stephenson, p. 181. The building has been occupied by the Ministry of Education.
46 The building has been occupied by the Ministry of Information Communication and Technology.
47 The contractor was Mr Wan of Suva. Stephenson, p. 166.
48 The contractor again was Mr Wan of Suva. Schütz, p. 3.
49 The building bears remarkable similarities to the 1877 National Museum of Colombo. On Ludolph's visit to England in 1915, his ship probably stopped at Colombo, so he could have been familiar with the museum. The Colombo museum was designed by the public works architect J G Smither 'in the Italian architectural style'. Department of National Museums, 'Colombo National Museum', viewed on 24 January 2011 at <http://www.museum.gov.lk/web/index.php?option=com_regionalm&task=regionalmuseum&id=6&Itemid=73&lang=en>.
50 At one time the British Western Pacific Territories consisted of Fiji (until 1952), New Hebrides, Pitcairn (until 1952), Cook Islands and Niue (until 1901), Nauru (until 1921), Union Islands (until 1926), Phoenix Islands (until 1939), Tonga (until 1952), Gilbert and Ellice Islands (until 1971) and the British Solomon Islands (until 1974).
51 National Trust of Fiji Islands, 'Borron House', viewed on 20 May 2012 at <http://www.nationaltrust.org.fj/borron-house.html>.
52 Eleanor Roosevelt was one of the distinguished guests who stayed at Borron House. National Trust of Fiji Islands, 'Borron House'.
53 Members of the public may hire the house for festive occasions. The Fiji Government, 'Borron House in Demand' (cabinet release), 10 August 2010, viewed on 24 January 2011 at <http://www.fiji.gov.fj/index.php?option=com_content&view=article&id=2076:borron-house-in-demand&catid=71:press-releases&Itemid=155>.
54 Conversation, Arnold Ludolph, Brisbane, 2005. He had seen the drawings that his grandfather had submitted for the competition.
55 W F Hedges (FRIBA, MI. Struct. E.). See Building No. 22 at 'Kuala Lumpur', viewed on 27 January 2011 at <http://www.vintagemalaya.com/KL.html>.
56 Kingsford Smith's aeroplane *Southern Cross* on its way from California to Sydney, landed in Albert Park in 1928 after a thirty-four-hour flight from Hawaii on the first flight across the Pacific.
57 The new wing was added in 1967.
58 Note the observations in Rob Ansell, 'Cultural Confidence in Fijian Architecture', *Architecture New Zealand*, September/October 1992, pp. 68–69.
59 Now Westpac Banking Corporation.
60 Louis S Robertson was born in Sydney in 1868 and died there in 1932, whereupon his son Louis Leighton Robertson became principal of the firm. The firm is called Robertson and Marks, and still practises in Sydney.

Shaping Suva

1 Hugh Laracy, 'World War Two', in Kerry R Howe, Robert C Kiste and Brij V Lal (eds.), *Tides of History: The Pacific Islands in the Twentieth Century*, Allen and Unwin, St Leonards, NSW, 1994, p. 158.
2 Previous regular aircraft access to Fiji had been by flying boat from Sydney and New Zealand.
3 As most of the South Pacific countries were under colonial rule, British and French flags and anthems dominated the proceedings!
4 The Indoor Sports Arena is now known as the Vodafone Sports Arena.
5 Conversation, Stuart Huggett, architect, Suva, 2003.
6 Fiji Islands Bureau of Statistics, '2007 Census of Population and Housing', *Statistical News*, No. 45, 15 October 2008, p.34, viewed on 30 January 2010 at <http://www.statsfiji.gov.fj/Census2007/Release%201%20-%20Population%20Size.pdf>. The Suva population figures are from the 1996 census.
7 Conversation, Jitendra Narsey, director, Larsen, Holtom and Maybin, Suva, 2005.
8 Sir Leonard Usher, 'R A Derrick', in Daryl Tarte and Stewart Firth (eds.), *Twentieth Century Fiji: People Who Shaped the Nation*, USP Solutions, University of the South Pacific, Suva, 1944, p. 75. Ronald Derrick's father was an architect, philatelist and secretary to the central Methodist Mission in Victoria. See 'A.J. Derrick, Architect, Philatelist & D.A. Vindin, Stamp Dealer', Australian Postal History and Social Philately, viewed on 24 January 2011 at <www.auspostalhistory.com/articles/1996.shtml>.
9 Ronald A Derrick, A *History of Fiji*, Vol. 1, Print and Stationery Department, Suva, 1946.
10 Conversation, Narsey, Suva, 2005.
11 *Fiji Association of Architects* (Exhibition Catalogue), Fiji Association of Architects, Suva, 1985, p. 25.
12 *SPTTN*, July 1968, pp. 23–28.
13 Ibid, p. 23.
14 These included the 1966 Outrigger Hotel, Suva, the 1966 International Dateline Hotel, Nuku'alofa, Tonga, the 1966 Tanoa Hotel, Nadi, the 1968 Mendana Hotel (Stage 2), Honiara, Solomon Islands, the 1968 Gateway Hotel, Suva, and the 1971 Hotel Kitano Tusitala, Apia, Samoa.
15 Conversation, Tony Sansom, architect, Suva, 2005.
16 Conversation, Sansom, Suva, 2005.
17 Conversation, Narsey, Suva, 2005. Information regarding the firm primarily was provided by Narsey.
18 Larsen retired in 1972 and opened the Suva office of Media 10.
19 Narsey's family were successful Indian merchants in Suva. He attended the Derrick Technical College and in 1972 commenced his architecture degree at the Western Australian Institute of Technology. Narsey was appointed to the firm in 1980.
20 The Courtesy Inn was remodelled by Sharma Architects in 2002 and is operating under the name of the Tanoa Plaza Hotel. Conversation, Narsey, Suva, 2005.
21 Fiji Association of Architects catalogue, Suva, 1985, p. 16. Durrant retired from the firm and moved to Brisbane. Conversation, Narsey, Suva, 2005.
22 The firm was closed following Jaimi's death in 2005.
23 Among these are Huafa Group's Eco Garden housing project in Zhongsan, South China, and the Marriott Hotel at North Ryde, Sydney.
24 Information on Stuart Huggett and Architects Pacific staff was obtained from several interviews with Huggett between 2003 and 2005, and written documentation provided by the firm.
25 The firm has merged with the New Zealand firm MSM Architects but retains the name Architects Pacific. Correspondence, email, Huggett, 30 March 2012.
26 Belt Collins et al., *A Tourism Development Programme for Fiji* (report), United Nations Development Programme, International Bank for Reconstruction and Development, and the Government of Fiji, Hawaii, 1973.

Chapter 6: In Search of Shangri-La

Escaping To Fiji

p. 143 Peter Weir (dir), Andrew Niccol (wr), *The Truman Show* (motion picture), 1998.
1 In 2005 US$ 380 million was injected into the economy through tourism, with an estimated tax value for the government of US$ 73 million. Ministry of Tourism and Transport and Fiji Ministry of Tourism, *Fiji Tourism Development Plan 2007–2016*, Department of Tourism, Ministry of Tourism & Environment, Suva, Fiji, 2007, p. 7. See also Biman Chand Prasad, 'The Fijian Economy: Time to Build Confidence', *East Asia Forum*, 26 November 2010, viewed on 25 January 2011 at <http://www.eastasiaforum.org/2010/11/26/the-fijian-economy-time-to-build-confidence/>.
2 See Native Lands Trust Board, 'Land rights in Fiji', viewed on 29 November 2009 at <http://www.nltb.com.fj/commentary/00_05_02.html>. The situation is currently fluid, however, and a new Land Use Unit has been established within the Ministry of Lands and Mineral Resources in order to enable previously unused land to be brought onto the market and ensure equitable returns to both owners and tenants: viewed on 9 June 2012 at <http://www.lands.gov.fj/land_reform.shtml>.
3 Parts were rebuilt in 1903 by Captain David Robbins, who thickened the walls against hurricanes and rebuilt parts of the hotel. See Elsie Stephenson, *Fiji's Past on Picture Postcards*, Canies Jannif Group, Suva, 1997, pp. 199–200.
4 The Ocean Hotel was renovated in 1974. *SPTTN*, May 1974, p. 9.
5 The hotel is known informally as the GPH. James Louis Salmond (1868–1950) was an English-born architect working

in New Zealand. He subsequently went into practice with Vanes (the authors have been unable to find any information on Vanes).

6 Stephenson, p. 180.

7 The Grand Pacific Hotel was enlarged in 1960 by the addition of two air-conditioned wings, which have since been demolished. In 1998 the hotel was bought by Grand Pacific Hotel Ltd. as a joint venture involving Nauru. When Nauru's financial situation changed in 2002, ownership of the hotel reverted back to the Fiji Government.

8 The partnership was between the Fiji National Provident Fund (FNPF), NASFUND and Lamana Development Limited. Robert F Kay, 'Grand Pacific Hotel (aka GPH) to Finally Get a Facelift', 26 August 2011, Fiji Guide, viewed on 18 March 2012 at <http://fijiguide.com/profiles/blogs/gph>. Architectural design was provided by the BSW (NZ) group in association with Yellow Architects from Fiji.

9 Robert A Kennedy, *Harold Gatty's Legacy: A Photo History of Fiji's National Airline: Fiji Airways 50 years on*, Sigatoka, Fiji, 2002, p. 1. Kennedy's book is a valuable source for further information on air routes of the Pacific.

10 While the service was introduced by NZNAC, it was taken over by TEAL soon after it started. See 'Air Pacific Ltd. History', Funding Universe, viewed on 23 April 2012 at <http://www.fundinguniverse.com/company-histories/Air-Pacific-Ltd-Company-History.html>.

11 'Fiji Isles Get Major Roles in Pacific Defence', *Chicago Daily Tribune*, 22 March 1952.

12 'Nadi International Airport' (history), viewed on 15 January 2010 at <http://en.wikipedia.org/wiki/Nadi_International_Airport>.

13 'Barry Philp had run the old Mocambo airport hotel in Nadi since 1952.' Richard MacMillan, 'Fiji Islands Beautiful, But Need Hotels', Traveller's Guide, *Chicago Daily Tribune*, 8 May 1960, p. D 12.

14 Kennedy, p. 10.

15 Air Pacific changed its name to Fiji Airways in 2013.

16 Visitors walking to and from their flights were to pass between lush tropical gardens planted mostly with hibiscus, Fiji's national flower. The terminal building and runway extensions were funded on a 40/40/20 percentage basis between the United Kingdom, Australia and New Zealand as members of the South Pacific Air Transport Council. 'Australia Helps Fiji to Build an Ultra-Modern Airport', *The Age*, 5 June 1958, p. 2.

17 The Mocambo Hotel is now the Novotel, Nadi.

18 Larry Low, 'Fiji Tourism Update', Suite101, viewed on 2 February 2010 at <http://www.suite101.com/article.cfm/current_events_pacific_islands/110630>.

19 MacMillan, p. D12. The renowned 'Fijian Hotel' was later built on this site.

20 Conversation, Tony Philp, son of Colin Philp, Suva, 2005.

21 In mid-1968 Burns Philp joined Travelodge of Australia and the Trust House Group of London to open Travelodge hotels in Suva, Nadi and Savusavu. See Satya Colpani, *Beyond the Black Waters: A Memoir of Sir Sathi Narain*, Institute of Pacific Studies, University of the South Pacific, Fiji, 1996, p. 121.

22 There was a third brother, David Philp, a naval architect. Colin Philp built the renowned 27-metre ketch *Tau*, which previously had circumnavigated the world and sailed to many islands in the Pacific. Conversation, Philp, Suva, 2005.

23 Vanuatu's 1970 Tassiriki Estate, which was developed with one major hotel together with an extensive residential subdivision of about forty hectares, is the exception, but the scale of the project there is small compared to those in Fiji.

24 'Coral Coast has a New Resort Hotel', *The Age*, 28 April 1975, p. 26. The article mentions that Korolevu celebrated twenty-five years of operation last year, which would mean it came into operation in 1949–50. Place Design Group suggests that it was built in 1948. See Place Design Group, 'Place bring Korolevu back to Life', September 2009, viewed on 25 January 2011 at <http://www.placedesigngroup.com/news.php?n=7>. *The Age* also reported that the Paradise Point Hotel (ninety rooms) had split away from Korolevu (seventy-six rooms) on 1 June 1974.

25 'Sir Hugh Ragg', in Daryl Tarte and Stewart Firth (eds.), *Twentieth Century Fiji: People who Shaped the Nation*, USP Solutions, University of the South Pacific, Suva, 1944, p. 77. According to Colin Taylor, 'Revive the History of the Tropics', *New Zealand Herald*, 5 July 2008, the original proprietor was Bill Clark, who was married to Cathleen, daughter of Hugh Ragg. See 'Clarks Leave Legacy Behind', *Fiji Times Online,* 19 July 2008, viewed on 16 July 2011 at <http://www.fijitimes.com/story.aspx?id=95409>. Ragg's Northern Hotels chain included The Club, The Sigatoka, The Nadi, The Lautoka, The Ba and The Tavua Hotel.

26 Conversation, Lindsay Thorpe, director, Place Design Group, Brisbane, 2009.

27 The *bure* is the name of one of the Fijian vale, or house, types (*vale vakaviti* translates as Fijian-style house). The *bure* form is commonly found in special-use buildings such as visitors' houses or temples, but the name has been adopted by the tourist industry as 'house' and is now in common usage. Paul Gerhard, 'Traditional Fijian Houses', 20 March 2000. Viewed on 3 February 2009 at <http://www.stampsfiji.com.fj/stamps/traditional_fijian_houses/index.html>.

28 Taylor, *New Zealand Herald*, 5 July 2008.

29 Lynn Rogers, 'Fiji is Paradise of South Pacific', *Los Angeles Times*, 9 January 1955, p. A26.

30 Kennedy, pp. 10 and 28.

31 Taylor, 5 July 2008.

32 The new owners are Fiji businessman Hari Punja and Gary Callaghan. Conversation, Thorpe, Brisbane, 2009.

33 Place Design Group employs 140 staff in offices in Australia and overseas. In Fiji the firm is currently preparing town plans for Sigatoka and Nadi and an urban design study for Suva, which includes the winning submission for the Suva Foreshore International Design Competition (in Association with Larson Holtom and Maybin). Conversation, Thorpe, Brisbane, 2009. Thorpe has now resigned as managing director and is currently a director with Place Design Group. See Place Design Group website, viewed on 14 March 2011 at < http://www.placedesigngroup.com/people.php?p=2>.

34 Lynn Rogers, p. A 26. In an advertisement for a hotel clerk, the Beachcomber was described as: 'the glamour tourist resort of the Pacific Islands,' *The Age,* 29 June 1955, p. 28. The advertisement went on to state: 'There are little amenities outside the hotel, but to a self-contained girl fond of tropical beach life and meeting people, it could be an ideal position. She will live with and in the same manner as a guest of the hotel and receive six pounds per week salary, most of which could be saved. Airfare refunded at the end of twelve months' service, together with one month's leave.'

35 *Miami News,* 8 October 1952, p. 8.A, reports Burt Lancaster sending postcards from the Beachcomber, where he was making *His Majesty O'Keefe. The Age,* 5 September 1953, p. 7, reports that to house the film crew of 100, extra rooms had to be built onto the hotel.

36 In 1962 Barry Philp sold the Mocambo Hotel and the lease at Yanuka Island, so it is likely that this was the year he sold the Beachcomber to Ragg.

37 From the Publishers of Pacific Islands Monthly, *South Seas Guide*, Pacific Publications, Sydney, 1979, p. 19.

38 Correspondence, Dean Kawamura, Wimberly, Allison, Tong and Goo, March 2005. The hotel was renamed the Shangri La's Fijian in 1974.

39 Karen Marvell and Glen Craig (eds.), *Fiji Through the Eyes of the Fijian,* Shangri-La's Fijian Resort, Fiji, 1997, p. 25 indicates that the resort was founded by Peter Slimmer and George Wilson along with finance from BOAC, Pan Am, Qantas and a grant from the Fijian government.

40 At the time they were Wimberly, Whisenand, Allison and Tong. Goo joined the firm in 1971. Whisenand left in 1988 and the firm became Wimberly, Allison, Tong and Goo (WATG). The local architects were LHM.

41 *SPTTN*, May 1975, pp. 30–31.

42 The Warwick had a chequered history, as do many Pacific hotels. It opened in the early 1970s as the Coral Gardens Hotel. The construction company, Mainline Constructions, went into receivership when the hotel was 60 per cent completed. At one stage it was also known as the Noah's Ark Hotel. It was taken over by the Hyatt Regency in 1980. *SPTTN*, March 1976, p. 23.

43 Philp had built a house for himself as a part of the Reef Hotel. Some of this complex has been incorporated with the new buildings. Conversation, Philp, Suva, 2005.

44 Conversation, Adrian Sofield, architect, Nadi, 2005.

45 Sofield closed his practice in 2011.

46 Not to be confused with Richard Harold (Dick) Smith who is another perhaps more well-known Australian entrepreneur, businessman, aviator and political activist, born in 1944.

47 Conversation, Philp, Suva, 2005.

48 Bruce Hamby, 'Fiji's Outer Islands Have Their Own Special Charm', *Chicago Daily Tribune*, 6 February 1966, p. H10. Smith went on to develop the resort of Musket Cove in 1976.

49 Advice from Fletcher Construction.

50 It was reported that the island was being totally planned by a six-man team of architects, engineers, an artist, a psychologist and an environmental expert, led by the architect Sam Sloan, who held architecture degrees from the University of Sydney and the University of Nebraska. *SPTTN,* November 1969, p. 19. The artist was Sydney-based Guy Warren. See Norbert Lynton, John McDonald and Deborah Hart, *Searching for Gaia: The Art of Guy Warren*, Palgrave, Macmillan, Australia, 2003, p. 172.

51 'In 1970 100 bures for Stage 1 of a large resort by Neville Price of the architectural partnership Price, Adams, Dodd of Auckland, were completed on Vatulele Island south of Korolevu. The large scheme was planned for 700 rooms'. *SPTTN*, December 1970, p. 11.

52 Henry Crawford first acquired a reputation as director of the TV mini series *A Town Like Alice*, 1981.

53 Herbert Ypma, *Pacific Island,* Stewart, Tabori and Chang, New York, 1996, p. 51.

54 The colour comes from the addition of tandoori food colouring to lime wash. Ypma, p. 66.

55 'Crawford got the idea of the Santa Fe style from a book written by two architects, and he chased them up. I went there to meet them in Santa Fe. They actually did the concept, then Martin did some work on it, and I did some more work on it. The whole style of the interior is Santa Fe.' Conversation, Sofield, Nadi, 2005. A book *Santa Fe Style*, by Christine Mather and Sharon Woods, was published by Rizzoli, 1986.

56 Conversation, Sofield, Nadi, 2005.

57 Jean-Michel is the son of Jacques Cousteau, the noted undersea explorer.

58 Jean-Michel Cousteau – Science – 1993, The Academy of Underwater Arts and Sciences, NOGI, viewed on 31 August 2013 at <http://www.auas-nogi.org/bio-cousteau_jean-michel.html>. In 2005, the resort received the number one ranking in the world on the Condé Nast Traveler's Green List and was the first winner of 'Australasia's Leading Green Hotel' in 2008.

59 Murphy is involved in creating and implementing 'Jean-Cousteau's Ambassadors of the Environment Program'. Richard C Murphy, curriculum vitae, viewed on 23 March 2012 at <http://www.rcmurph.com>.

60 Mosquito control is achieved through planting endemic plants to attract birds and by a series of ponds to lure the mosquitoes away from the resort where their larvae can be eaten by frogs and shrimps. R K Dowling, 'Oceania', in David B Weaver (ed.), *The Encyclopedia of EcoTourism*, CABI Publishing, New York, 2001, pp. 139–154.

61 Vitia Architects Company Profile (mimeographed document), 2005.

62 Information on Namale Fiji Resort and Spa was derived from Conversation, Filipe Tauva, Suva, 2005.

63 Patricia Brown and Erhard Pfieffer, 'Anthony Robbins in Eden', *Architectural Digest*, , Vol. 61, No. 8, August 2004, pp. 144–151.

64 Ahura Resorts of Rosie Group Tourist Company, which is Fiji's largest and most successful tourist operator. The company owns the earlier Malolo Resort, also on Malolo Island. Information on

Likuliku Lagoon Resort from conversation, Tony Whitton, general manager, Nadi, 2005, who provided much useful data.

65 Likuliku offers the first completed example of the Polynesian overwater units in Fiji. The concept seems inappropriate in Fiji, which, like New Caledonia, has large tidal swings. Room service is by traditional canoes!

66 The resort is reputed to have cost US$ 180 million. Fiji Live, 'Developers Mum on Fiji's 7-star Resort, 22 June 2008, viewed 1 December 2009 at <http://www.fijilive.com/realestate/index.php/properties/view_news/46>.

67 Conversation, Stuart Huggett, principal, Architects Pacific and Nicola Vuetilovoni, project architect, Fiji, 2005.

68 'The original subdivision was done by Ralph M Grierson in April 1978, when John MacIntire, one of the world's foremost land planning engineers, bought a 1500-hectare plantation on Taveuni and started what has become Taveuni Estates, a residential community.' Larry Low, *Fiji Times*, 30 August 2004.

69 Conversation, Sofield, Suva, 2005. The Wakaya Club is one of Fiji's more expensive resorts. Gilmour is a noted benefactor, and profits from the resort are used to fund public health and education throughout Fiji.

70 Wakaya Club and Spa website, viewed on 31 January 2010 at <http://www.wakaya.com/>.

71 Stanley Simpson, 'Koro Surprise', *ManuLife*, November 2008, p. 4.

72 Information on Dere Bay Resort and Koro Seaview Estate provided by Elsa Miller, architect, Suva and Koro Island, 2005.

73 *Under One Roof* was a 2002 US reality TV show hosted by Bob Nelson. Conversation, Miller, Koro, 2005.

74 Miller was assisted by associates in Suva including Filipe Tauva, whose office did the working drawings, and Shama, who did the structural drawings. Conversation, Miller, Suva, 2005.

The Mega-Resorts

p. 162 Advertisement, Warwick Hotel, Coral Coast, Fiji, *Explore Fiji*, Aug–Oct 2005, p. 21.

1 Jon Fraenkel, Stewart Firth and Brij V Lal (eds.), *The 2006 Military Takeover in Fiji: A Coup to End All Coups?*, Australian National University E Press, Canberra, 2009, p. 11. 'Fiji's coups regularly set the economy back by years, and this one [i.e. 2006] was no exception, with economic effects worse than those of the coup of 2000. Fiji's economy slumped in the year after the coup that was supposed to revive it. Tourist arrivals contracted by 8.3 per cent and hotel turnover by 6.6 per cent.'

2 The study was commissioned on 23 December 1971 and submitted on 15 March 1973 and covered a ten-year period from 1973 to 1983. It was prepared by Belt Collins et al., *A Tourism Development Programme for Fiji*, United Nations Development Programme, International Bank for Reconstruction and Development and the Government of Fiji, Hawaii, 1973.

3 Belt Collins et al., 'Scope of Study', p. 3.

4 Jerry Hulse, 'On the Go: Three Musketeers Carve South Pacific Paradise', *Los Angeles Times*, 28 January 1973, p. J1. Gilmour later founded the highly successful company Fiji Water.

5 Belt Collins et al., p. 9.

6 'States OKs London Firm's Bid to sell Fiji Land to Californians', *Los Angeles Times*, 16 July 1972, p. K14. Project Planning Associates had designed Canada's Expo 1967.

7 The Beachcomber is now named The Pearl South Pacific Resort & Spa. The Tropic Sands was upgraded in 1979 by Architects Pacific and is now named the Fiji Beach Club and Resort. The Lagoon Resort commenced construction in 1988 as the Atoll Hotel.

8 Construction supervision by LHM. *SPTTN*, November 1972, p. 32 and *SPTTN*, January 1974, p. 9. The hotel initially was licensed to the Americana Group (American Airlines), but soon after it was taken over by Travelodge when American Airlines withdrew from the Pacific area.

9 *Pacific Islands Monthly*, October 1975, pp. 83–84. It also reported that 2428 hectares of its adjacent land had been acquired by Taisei Corporation of Japan and that the Fiji Government has approved, in principle, a plan for development.

10 Such a centre was proposed in Belt Collins et al., p. 119.

11 In association with LHM.

12 Notably, the failure by the Australian project-housing company Pettit and Sevitt, which went into receivership with a US$ 575 000 loss. *Pacific Islands Monthly*, October 1975, pp. 83–84.

13 The new owners were Eddie Phillips and Eric Roberts, Australian property developers in association with American developer Mitch Hagerman. Conversation (phone), Alan Mitchel, architect, 2010.

14 Conversation, Lindsay Thorpe, director, Place Design Group, Brisbane, 2009.

15 The Fiji Regent was renamed the Sheraton Royal Denarau, and after the refurbishing in 2005–06, this was changed to the Westin Denarau Island Resort and Spa.

16 Belt Collins et al., p. 19.

17 The history of the Denarau site can be found on the Tabua website, viewed on 15 November 2010 at <http://www.denarau.com/history>.

18 In association with LHM.

19 Huggett described Pagliuso as 'a genius of an architect.' Conversation, Stuart Huggett, architect, Suva, 2003.

20 The project architect was Peter Rankin.

21 In 1987 Tom Pagliuso left Media Five in Honolulu to establish a branch of the firm in California. The Hawaiian firm became bankrupt and was bought up by the US company Durrant, and became Durrant-Media Five in 2001. The authors are grateful to Michael Ducar for his insights into the history of Media Five. Conversation, Michael Ducar, architect, Gold Coast, 2009. Ducar joined Media Five, Hawaii, in the mid-1970s and moved to Media Five, Australia, in the 1980s. He is a consultant to the firm DBI Design.

22 John R Harper, *SOPAC Training Report 36*, *Proceedings of the CIDA-SOPAC Coastal Investigations and Engineering Workshop*, Fiji, November 1990. One of the case studies reported on in this document is Denarau Island.

23 Harper, p. 4.

24 Harper, p. 2.

25 In 1968 International Telephone and Telegraph purchased the Sheraton Group, after which it is was known as ITT Sheraton.

26 Conversation, Martin Darveniza, Brisbane, 2009. Darveniza was a consultant to Place Design Group.

27 Government of Fiji, *Fiji Today, 2006–07*, p. 39, viewed on 13 September 2009 at <http://www.fiji.gov.fj/>.

28 Ministry of Tourism and Transport and Fiji Ministry of Tourism, *Fiji Tourism Development Plan 2007–2016*, Department of Tourism, Ministry of Tourism & Environment, Fiji, 2007. The study was directed by GRM International and the Ministry of Tourism and was funded principally by the Fiji Government with administrative support from the Ministry of Tourism.

29 Grounds, Lee, Kaba and Partners had previously designed Sonaisali Resort, Sonaisali Island, 1992.

30 *Fiji Times*, 31 May 2005.

31 Now called The Terraces.

32 Now called the Radisson Blu Resort Fiji.

33 'Denarau Beach Resort' (brochure), Tabua Investments Limited, Suva, 2005. At the time of writing, no further new work has been added to this complex.

34 Anne Gibson, 'Paradise Lost for Fiji Investors', *New Zealand Herald*, 29 August 2009, viewed on 12 November 2009 at <http://www.nzherald.co.nz/business/news/print.cfm?c_id=3&objectid=10593870&pnm=0>. As at 2013 the complete project had not been realized.

35 Due to the delay in the opening of the hotel, the first accommodation in overwater *bures* in Fiji was at the Likuliku resort in the Yasawa group of islands, another Architects Pacific project.

36 The Fiji National Provident Fund (FNPF) became a major investor in Fiji's new resorts and was nominated as a principal financier for the Grand Pacific Hotel redevelopment, Momi Bay Resort and the Natadola Bay Estate.

37 'Bridgecorp investors lose NZ$106 million as Fiji takes over Momi Bay.' *New Zealand Herald*, 5 June 2009, viewed on 18 August 2009 at <http://www.nzherald.co.nz/fiji/news/article.cfm?l_id=40&objectid=10576643>.

38 Fiji's superannuation fund would spend US$ 82 million finishing the project. William Mace, 'Fiji Super Fund to Finish Momi Bay Resort', 23 November 2012, Stuff, viewed on 21 July 2013 at <http://www.stuff.co.nz/business/world/7989604/Fiji-super-fund-to-finish-Momi-Bay-Resort>.

39 *SPTTN*, January 1973, p. 3.

40 Belt Collins et al., p. 106.

41 'The next development will be the addition of twenty deluxe rooms to the Mocambo and before three years are out, a minimum of fifty rooms will be added to the Fijian. There is then Natadola Beach ... and we have half the freehold on that.' Captain George Wilson, a Pan Am captain and chairman of Fiji Resorts. *SPTTN*, April 1968, p. 20.

42 *SPTTN*, February 1974, p. 11.

43 *SPTTN*, January 1973, p. 1, reports 'Fiji Resorts has its own master plan for the 638 hectares at Natadola but it has kept it under wraps.'

44 *SPTTN*, February 1974, p. 11. The report also recommended that the Natadola project be undertaken by a development corporation similar to that used in Sentosa Island in Singapore.

45 Laisenia Qarase, former prime minister and Minister for Fijian Affairs, Culture & Heritage. Speech at the inauguration of the Natadola Integrated Resort Project, 25 January 2005, Fiji Government Online Portal, viewed on 15 September 2009 at <http://www.fiji.gov.fj/publish/cat_speeches.shtml>.

46 DBI developed out of Media Five Australia, the Australian branch of Media Five, which was established on the Gold Coast in 1982 by the Australian Desmond Brooks, who had joined Media Five in Hawaii in the early 1970s. In the late 1990s Media Five Australia changed its name to DBI Design Corporation, and in 2002 DBI Design was founded. Conversation, Stuart Shakespeare, managing director, DBI Design, Surfers Paradise, November 2009.

47 Due to internal disputes the project was completed by local architect Adrian Sofield. Conversation, Lindsay Thorpe, director, Place Design Group, Brisbane, 2009.

48 Due to disagreement with the developers, Singh withdrew from the project before it was completed. Conversation, Shakespeare, Surfers Paradise, 2009.

49 Conversation, Thorpe, Brisbane, 2009.

50 'At Natadola, Kuok's Fijian ownership is still sitting there in the wings ready to go. He was clever and left the others to go ahead and get the infrastructure in and the roads.' Conversation, Thorpe, Brisbane, 2009.

PART IV: PLACES OF THE SOUTH PACIFIC: WITHIN THE POLYNESIAN TRIANGLE

THE SCATTERED ISLES OF CENTRAL SEAS

1 Comment by a local villager.

Chapter 7: From Colonies To 'Coconuts'

Colonial Presence: Modern Impact

1 Ministry of Finance and Economic Management, Cook Islands 2011 Census of Population and Dwellings, MFEP, viewed on 20 September 2013 at <http://www.mfem.gov.ck/population-and-social-statistics/census>.

2 Cook Islands Government, Voyage to Statehood, Cook Islands Government Online, viewed on 28 April 2010 at <http://www.cook-islands.gov.ck/history.php>.

3 Archive CD Books Australia, *The Cyclopedia of Fiji, Samoa, Tonga, Tahiti, and the Cook Islands 1907*, Archive CD Books Australia, Modbury, SA, 2006, p. 19. There were seven warships in the harbour when the typhoon struck, three German, three American and one British. Only the British ship escaped.

4 *The Cyclopedia of Samoa, Tonga, Tahiti and the Cook Islands*, pp. 21–22.
5 Ministry of Finance and Economic Management, Cook Islands 2011 Census of Population and Dwellings
6 Brij V Lal and Kate Fortune, *The Pacific Islands: An Encyclopedia,* University of Hawai'i Press, Honolulu, 2000, p. 607.
7 The Second Marine Brigade, consisting of approximately 5600 officers and enlisted men, landed on Tutuila on 20 January 1942. In the same month the approaches to Pago Pago Harbour were mined by the Americans. Gordon L Rottman, *US Marine Corps 1941–45,* Osprey Publishing, New York, 1995, p. 26.
8 Overfishing now threatens the industry, with potentially serious consequences for the tuna population. See 'Overfishing Threatens Two Main Tuna Species', *Islands Business,* April 2008. p. 44.
9 Matori Yamamoto, 'Samoan Diaspora and Ceremonial Exchange', Hosei University, viewed on 6 January 2009, <http://www.t.hosei.ac.jp/~matoriy/paper/migrant.htm>.
10 'Samoa and Tokelau Skip a Day for Dateline Change', BBC World News, viewed on 23 March 2012 at <http://www.bbc.co.uk/news/world-asia-16351377>
11 Fiji has a historic buildings policy, but it is of recent date.
12 *Fita fita* means soldier in Samoan.
13 It later housed the Department of Public Safety.
14 This was later removed and the veranda enclosed.
15 An 8.3 magnitude earthquake struck in the South Pacific between Samoa and American Samoa. 'American Samoa hit by tsunami after earthquake in Pacific', *The Guardian,* 29 September 2009, viewed on 1 April 2012 at <http://www.guardian.co.uk/world/2009/sep/29/american-samoa-tsunami-earthquake>.
16 From the records of the 'Historic Building Register, American Samoa'.
17 John Enright, The Past Surrounds Us (Part 12: Atauloma Girl's School, Origins), American Samoa Historic Preservation Office, viewed on 5 January 2009 at <http://www.ashpo.org/index.php/publications2.html>.
18 Albert Schaaffhausen, Government Architect in Apia, was born in Essen, Germany, in 1876. *The Cyclopaedia of Samoa*, p. 62.
19 *The Cyclopedia of Samoa, Tonga, Tahiti and the Cook Islands*, p. 5.
20 The house had a fireplace that possibly was the only one in the South Pacific. Nelson Eustis, *Samoa Sketchbook*, Hobby Investments Pty Ltd, Adelaide, 1979, p. 32.
21 Harry J Moors, *With Stevenson in Samoa*, Maynard & Co. Publishers, Boston, 1910, pp. 219–223. Moors knew both Stevenson and Kuntz.
22 Miss Robertson, 'A Scotch Woman Climbs the Mountain at Samoa and Describes Her Countryman's Grave', *The New York Times*, 20 July 1901.
23 Moors, p. 223.
24 Advice from Fletcher Construction.
25 During reconstruction each piece of timber was removed, stripped of paint and numbered so that it could be put back in its original position. Advice, Fletcher Construction.
26 Conversation, Dr Letitaia Setu Taule'alo, planner, Apia 2004. Eighty per cent of land in Samoa is customary land, with only 4 per cent freehold, and the rest is common land.
27 Secretariat of the Pacific Community, March 2011 population estimates.
28 Mills' major interest is in anthropology, but his major treatise on Polynesian history, the summation of forty-five years work, was burnt in a fire at his house in the 1990s. Conversation, Ken Mills, architect, Avarua, 2003.
29 Joe Weilenman was preceded by architects in Public Works, but there was a gap of many years before his arrival. Conversation, Joe Weilenman, architect, Pago Pago, 2004. 'At present a young Samoan woman runs the Department of Works.' Conversation, Weilenman, Pago Pago, 2004.
30 The Immaculate Conception of Mary Cathedral was rendered unsafe by the September 2009 earthquake and a new cathedral is under construction on the site.
31 Conversation, George Meredith, engineer, Apia, 2004.
32 Further building gifts from the Chinese Government include the Aquatic Complex for the 2007 Pacific Games, the new 2008 Parliamentary Office Complex next to Parliament, to provide office space for all members, the new 2010 Ministry of Justice and Courts complex in the parliamentary precinct, and the 2012 Convention Centre and government office. Samoa also received the gift of a new Ministry of Education, Sport and Culture office complex, designed by Melbourne architects Whitefield McQueen Irwin Alsop, funded by the Asian Development Bank, AusAID and the NZ Aid Programme. See World Architecture News, viewed on 19 July 2011 at <http://www.worldarchitecturenews.com/index.php?fuseaction=wanappin.projectview&upload_id=16190>.
33 The Chinese Government gave most of the construction machinery to the Public Works Department once the project was completed.
34 Conversation, Meredith, Apia, 2004.

'Staying Over': From Sadie's to Fales

p. 188 'Quatrian for Samoa' (poem No. 11) in 'Poems' in Roger Robinson, *Robert* (introduction and commentaries) *Louis Stevenson: His best Pacific Writings*, University of Queensland Press, St Lucia, 2004, p. 318.
1 Fay Alailima, *Aggie Grey: A Samoan Saga*, Mutual Publishing Company, Honolulu, Hawaii, 1988. p. 115.
2 While not established, it seems likely that such a significant building would have been designed by an architect, and since Albert Schaaffhausen was Government Architect in Apia around that time, the building could have been his.
3 Alailima, pp. 227 and 243. Aggie Grey ran the famous Aggie Grey's Hotel.
4 *Sadie Thompson* tells the story of a 'fallen' woman who comes to Pago Pago on the island of Tutuila to start a new life. The original *Sadie Thompson* starred Gloria Swanson, who delivered what is considered to be one the finest dramatic achievements of the 1920s.
5 The water's edge setting for the 1928 hotel has been replaced by reclaimed land.
6 The American Samoa Historic Preservation Office shows photographs of Sadie Thompson Inn as it looked in 1907, again in 1929, when it was known as the Haleck Hotel, and as it stands today. Viewed on 10 January 2009 at <http://www.ashpo.org/walktour/01.html?>.
7 The following references provide accounts of Aggie Grey's early business: Alailima, pp. 209, 225 and 316; Nelson Eustis, *Samoa Sketchbook*, Hobby Investments, Adelaide, 1979, p. 22; Nelson Eustis, *Aggie Grey of Samoa*, Hobby Investments, Adelaide, 1994. p. 108.
8 The history of TEAL's Coral Route was viewed at Museum of Transport and Technology, The Coral Route, TEAL, viewed on 23 January 2011 at <http://www.teal.co.nz/teal/TEAL%202.htm>.
9 Aggie Grey died in 1988, but her son carries on his long-standing interest in the hotel.
10 By 1969 there were nine InterContinental hotels in the chain in and around the Pacific. The InterContinental Hotel chain was a subsidiary company of Pan Am.
11 The old Rainmaker Hotel continued to operate on a limited basis, catering mainly for government employees. *SPTTN*, April 1968, p. 5.
12 Information on the hotel (Rainmaker Hotel) from correspondence (email), Dean Kawamura, Wimberly, Allison, Tong and Goo, Honolulu, 22 March 2005.
13 The hotel was owned by the American Samoa Development Corporation (ASDC), which was largely backed by small investors and managed under contract by the InterContinental. *SPTTN*, July 1968, p. 31.
14 *SPTTN*, May 1973, p. 15.
15 *SPTTN*, November 1973, p. 26. The hotel was taken over by the Japanese company Kitano Construction Corp. and re-named Kitano (Tusitala) Samoa Hotel. The hotel is now known as the Tanoa Tusitala Hotel.
16 Consolidated Acts of Samoa gives details of the Act of Parliament. Ministry of Finance, Royal Samoan Hotel Act 1984, Pacific Islands Legal Information Institute, viewed on 10 January 2009 at <http://www.paclii.org/ws/legis/consol_act/rsha1984199>.
17 *Islands Business,* May 2004, p. 38, suggests that the resort was themed on James A Michener's writing, due to his friendship with Aggie: 'It is widely believed that the character of 'Bloody Mary' was based on Aggie Grey'. In Alailima, p. 277, she writes that Aggie was not pleased to be associated with the fictional character and wrote to Michener asking him who Bloody Mary really was. Michener replied that she was a figment of his imagination.
18 Secretariat of the Pacific Community, 2010 Pocket Statistical Summary, SPC, viewed on 17 November 2010 at <http://www.spc.int/prism/>. The study indicates that the Cook Islands attracts six tourists per year for every one member of resident population. However, the large number of incoming 'tourists' might well be previous permanent residents of the Cook Islands returning on visits. That this is so is born out by an analysis of the 2001 census results, which showed that of the 18 027 persons enumerated, only 15 017 were permanent residents – thus leaving 3010 persons as tourists or short-term visitors. The study also showed that the Cook Islands population is declining at an average annual growth rate of -3.7 per cent.
19 Correspondence, owner, 5 February 2004.
20 *Islands Business*, April 2008, p. 14. Also, Radio New Zealand International on 12 June 2009 reported that while one of the developers, McEwan, had been bankrupted, the other, Tim Tepaki, indicated that he 'was in the process of finalising a refinancing agreement with a US financier,' and that he hoped to see it opened in 2011. 'Cook Islands Hilton to Welcome First Guests in 2011', Radio New Zealand International, Cook Islands Tourism, Cook Islands Travel Guide, viewed on 16 May 2010 at <http://www.rnzi.com/pages/news.php?op=read&id=47114>.
21 See David Stanley, Discussion on Tourism in the Cook Islands, viewed on 26 March 2012 at <http://cookislands.southpacific.org/cookislands/tourism.html>.
22 'Ghosts of Foreign Investors go Boo', *Samoa Alive News*, 15 July 2008, Samoa Alive, viewed on 12 January 2009 at <http://www.samoalivenews.com/Editor-and-Reader-Opinions/Ghosts-Of-Foreign-Investors-Go-Boo.html>.

Chapter 8: The Kingdom of Tonga

Nuku'alofa: Beyong Vuna Road

1 Statistics Department Tonga, Tonga National Population and Housing Census 2011 (Preliminary Result), SPC, viewed on 26 June 2012 at <http://www.spc.int/prism/tonga/index.php/tonga-documents/cat_view/124-population-census/118-2011>.
2 The highest point above sea level on this island is only about sixty-five metres high, and most of the island is flat and low-lying. This creates substantial difficulties in providing an adequate sewage system. This physical problem curtails major projects. John Connell and John P Lea, *Pacific 2010: Urbanisation in Polynesia,* National Centre for Development Studies, Australian National University, Canberra, 1995, p. 130.
3 Correspondence, John Walls, information officer, Fletcher Construction, 2005.
4 Steven R Fischer, *A History of the Pacific Islands,* Palgrave Macmillan, Basingstoke, 2002, p. 146.
5 Fischer, p. 146.
6 Ibid, p. 148.
7 Palace Archives. As parliament sits so infrequently, the building also serves as a courthouse.
8 Conversation, George Moala, architect, Tonga Public Works Department, Nuku'alofa, 2004. The early building has since been demolished.
9 Queen Sālote used this house when she was a child. Elizabeth Wood-Ellem, *Queen Sālote of Tonga: The Story of an Era, 1900–1965,* University of Hawai'i Press, Honolulu, 1999, p. 173.
10 On the advice of Paul Nessling, the last British High Commissioner, but it has not been possible to confirm this. Conversation, Paul Nessling, Nuku'alofa, 2004.

11 'In the 1930s the house was raised six feet and placed on 150 concrete posts to make it more secure during hurricanes and to reduce the problem of breeding mosquitoes' (Nessling said 'in 1930'. Eustis says 'between 1928 and 1938'). 'This alteration was achieved without mishap by a workforce of sixty Tongans using only simple equipment', Nelson Eustis, *Tonga Sketchbook*, Hobby Investments, Adelaide, 2002, p. 46.
12 Data provided by Fletcher Construction.
13 Conversation, Moala, Nuku'alofa, 2004. This is supported by Wood-Ellem, who says the Post Office and the Treasury were housed in the one building. Wood-Ellem, caption Illustration No. 66.
14 In part funded by Germany and in part by Japan. Eustis, p. 30.
15 Tupou College was later moved out of the town to its present site near the airport.
16 Connell and Lea, p. 33. See also Secretariat of the Pacific Community, 2010 Pocket Statistical Summary, SPC, at <http://www.spc.int/sdp/>.
17 The 1931 population of Nuku'alofa was 4000, and the 1956 population was 9200, so the city's population during the war is estimated to have been between 5000 and 6000 persons. See Connell and Lea, p. 33.
18 For an account of the Americans in Tonga see Ian C Campbell, *Island Kingdom: Tonga Ancient and Modern*, Canterbury University Press, Christchurch, 1992, pp. 156 and 176.
19 Campbell, p. 181.
20 Kurt Düring, *Pathways to the Tongan Present*, Government Printing Department, Nuku'alofa, Tonga, 1990, p. 75.
21 In 2004 Tonga's own airline, Royal Tongan Airlines, went into receivership.
22 The building was demolished in 1999, and the Chinese Embassy built on the site. See Eustis, p. 9.
23 Not only did the coronation mark a new period, but also Tonga became completely independent of Britain in 1970.
24 Extensions and improvements were undertaken in 1977, 1988–89 and 1994–95. Conversation, manager, Dateline Hotel, 2004. Refer to history of the hotel on its own website, viewed on 13 September 2008 at <http://www.datelinehotel.com/>.
25 Now the Paradise International Hotel.
26 More recently, the Puataukanave International Hotel has opened in the heart of Neiafu and overlooks the harbour.
27 'Some Facts for Visitors' brochure, provided by the Tongan Visitors Bureau.
28 Data provided by Fletcher Construction.
29 George Moala died in 2010.
30 The firm's main office was in Suva, Fiji. For information on the Tonga branch the authors are grateful to Solomon Tuita, branch architect, now deceased.
31 *JA Times* (newsletter of Jaimi Associates Architects), April 1997.
32 The dedication plaque on the cathedral credits it to John Rounds, Lee and Partners; however, as Rounds left Tonga before 1982, the later stages of the work would have been undertaken by Lee and Associates.
33 Conversation, Leveni 'Aho, architect, Nuku'alofa, 2004.
34 Eustis, p. 28.
35 A 30 November 2009 Pacific Islands Development Program report indicated that the Chinese Government had extended a loan of some US$ 93.5 million and that construction work had commenced on some major buildings. Pacific Islands Development Program/East-West Center, Pacific Islands Report, viewed on 14 November 2010 at <http://pidp.eastwestcenter.org/pireport/2009/December/12-02-10.htm>.
36 Australian Development Bureau report dated 2 February 2007, viewed on 15 May 2008 at <http://www.tongareview.com/Article.aspx?ID=2466>.
37 Correspondence, Paul Christmas, director, James Cubitt Architects, 31 May 2010.
38 As in so many projects for the Pacific Islands, intentions of low energy usage are foiled by the subsequent insertion of air-conditioning by the clients.
39 Information from Cubitt's website, viewed on 18 May 2008 at <http://www.ukcubitt.demon.co.uk/contact/contact.html>.
40 'Six Found Dead in Tonga Riots', BBC World News, 17 November 2006, viewed on 22 May 2008 at <http://news.bbc.co.uk/2/hi/asia-pacific/6156878.stm>.

Kings and Clerics

1 Steven R Fischer, *A History of the Pacific Islands*, Palgrave Macmillan, Basingstoke, 2002, p. 10.
2 The 2006 census indicated that 11 per cent of the population belong to the Roman Catholic faith, 37.3 per cent to the Free Wesleyan Church of Tonga and 16.8 per cent to the Church of Jesus Christ of Latter-Day Saints. US Department of State, International Religious Freedom Report 2010, viewed on 29 March 2012 at <http://www.state.gov/j/drl/rls/irf/2010/148900.htm>
3 Mike Foley, 'BYU-Hawaii contingent Helps Celebrate Tonga LDS Centennial', Newsroom, Brigham Young University Hawai'i, viewed on 22 May 2008 at <http://newsroom.byuh.edu/?q=node/1260>.
4 The Church of Jesus Christ of Latter-Day Saints, Tonga on the Net, viewed on 11 September 2008 at <http://www.tongatapu.net.to/tonga/convictions/christianity/lds/lds.html>.
5 Noel Rutherford, *Shirley Baker and the King of Tonga,* Pacific Press, Wellington, 1971, p. 169.
6 Rutherford, pp. 224–226
7 Norman Douglas and Ngaire Douglas, *Tonga: A Guide*, Albion Press, Newstead, 1989, pp. 66–67.
8 Rutherford, p. 53, states that 'in 1871 Baker set out to beautify Zion, the oldest and most important church in Tonga, by refurnishing it, shingling the roof and building for it a tower complete with clock and bell' – but the authors are left in some doubt as to whether these works were ever carried out. We have been unable to ascertain what became of the Zion church. Nelson Eustis, *Tonga Sketchbook*, Hobby Investments, Adelaide, 2002, p. 59, maintains that the chapel presently sited at the rear of Sia'atoutai Theological College is the original Zion church, but we have been unable to find evidence to support this.
9 Conversation, George Moala, architect, Public Works Department, Nuku'alofa, 2004.
10 Elizabeth Wood-Ellem, *Queen Sālote of Tonga*, University of Hawai'i Press, Honolulu, 1999. See the caption to illustration No. 98 between pages 208 and 209. Rodger Page was a confidant and close personal advisor to the queen. He had retired and moved to Sydney before being recalled for the moving of the fale church. Wood-Ellem, pp. 118–119. The moving of the church is referred to in Wood-Ellem, see caption to Illustration No. 98.
11 Moala added the surrounding veranda.
12 *Architecture New Zealand*, January/February 1991, pp. 11–12.
13 Conversation, Moala, Tonga, 2004.
14 There is a foundation stone recording the date of an earlier church as 1869.
15 Ian C Campbell, *Island Kingdom: Tonga Ancient and Modern,* Canterbury University Press, Christchurch, 1992, p. 170. For the construction, see Kurt Düring, *Pathways to the Tongan Present,* Government Printing Department, Nuku'alofa, Tonga, 1990, p. 104.
16 The town was divided into three sections and rostered with the responsibility of feeding the workers three meals a day. Eustis, p. 37 (Eustis's information is correct, but the sketch above is of the wrong building as it shows the Centennial Church of the Free Church of Tonga).
17 There had been an earlier church of the same name on this site. David W Mullins, *They Built a Church: Priests of Tonga, R.I.P,* St Bede's College Printery, Christchurch, 2004, p. 18. 'Then the Tu'i Tonga, Laufilitonga was baptised in the Church of St Michael in Lapaha on 7 November 1851 by Bishop Bataillon.'
18 Mullins, p. 32.
19 Conversation, Solomon Tuita of Jaimi and Associates, Nuku'alofa, 2004.
20 Mullins, p. 54. Construction of the church began in 1939 on the first day of World War II.
21 Mullins, p. 54.
22 Conversation, Father Tanicia Foliaki, St Michael's, Lapaha, 2004. The offices of the Catholic dioceses had no further information.
23 'Father Pierre Castagnier', in Mullins, p. 28, where it is stated that he spent the last thirty years of his life, between 1880 and 1910, at Vava'u, where he erected a fine church. It seems likely, therefore, that the 1932 church built by Kermann replaced the earlier one by Castagnier.
24 Ibid, p. 48.
25 Ibid, p. 61.
26 Campbell, p. 170.
27 'His [Callet's] crowning glory is the beautiful Basilica of St. Anthony of Padua in Nuku'alofa.' Mullins. p. 54.
28 *The Basilica of Saint Anthony of Padua, Nuku'alofa, Tonga: A Community Achievement*, Government Printing Office, Nuku'alofa, 1981, p. 3.
29 Detailed information on the building of the basilica is due in part to the church publication *The Basilica of Saint Anthony of Padua, Nuku'alofa, Tonga.*

FRENCH POLYNESIA TO THE EAST

1 Wilmshurst JM, et al., 'High-precision radiocarbon dating shows recent and rapid initial human colonization of East Polynesia', *Proceedings of the National Academy of Sciences of the United States of America*, Vol. 108, No. 5, 2011, pp. 1815–1820.
2 Fischer, pp. 130–135.
3 Colin Newbury, 'Resistance and Collaboration in French Polynesia: The Tahitian War: 1844–7', *Journal of Polynesian Society*, Vol. 82, No. 1, 1973, pp. 5–27.
4 Fischer, pp. 227–229.

Chapter 9: Tahiti: The Polynesian Myth

Eden: After Eden

p. 221 Steven R Fischer, *A History of the Pacific Islands*, Palgrave Macmillan, Basingstoke, 2002, p. 111.
1 Melissa L Hyde and Mark Ledbury (eds.), *Rethinking Boucher*, Getty Research Institute, Los Angeles, 2006. p. 163
2 Janet S Holman, *The Enlightenment and Captain James Cook: The Lono-Cook-Kirk-Regenesis*, AuthorHouse, Bloomington, 2009, p. 52.
3 The French had been major proponents for the Panama Canal, but despite the canal's opening in 1914, Tahiti was still half a world away from Europe, and it made little difference to the accessibility of the French colony.
4 John Borthwick, 'Chasing Gauguin's Ghost', Travel Intelligence, viewed on 2 April 2010 at <http://www.travelintelligence.com/travel-writing/chasing-gauguins-ghost>.
5 The 1935 film *Mutiny on the Bounty* received the Academy Award for Best Picture.
6 Both films, while ostensibly set in Tahiti, were mostly filmed elsewhere. The books on which these films were based were written by Americans Charles Nordhoff and James Norman Hall, who collaborated successfully in writing a number of books, including the *Bounty Trilogy,* when they moved to Tahiti following World War I.
7 Tourist Bureau brochure, Papeete, 2004.
8 First sons had to stay and learn the business; second sons were not so constrained.
9 Robinson returned to America in the war years, during which he built over 200 Liberty Boats for the marines. He returned to Paea in 1945 and was noted for his generous benefactions towards the Tahitian's welfare, including a medical institute. 'William Albert Robinson', in Philippe Mazellier, Bengt Danielsson and Marie-Thérèse Danielsson, *Le Mémorial Polynésien*, Tome VI, Hibiscus Editions, Tahiti, 1977 p. 241.
10 Elizabeth Walker, 'Hazardous Honeymooners Happy now in their South Sea Island Cottage', *Palm Beach Post*, 1 September 1935, p. 16.
11 Christian Gleizal (ed.), *Encyclopédie de la Polynésie: La France en Polynésie 1842–1960*, Vol. 7, Multipress, Tahiti, 1986–88, p. 132. There was also an early Hotel Tahiti located on the site of what

is now the Sheraton Hotel. Previously, the residence of Princess Pomare, daughter of the last king of Tahiti, had stood on this site. Conversation, Michel Prévot, architect, Papeete, 2004.

12 Tiare is a fragrant white blossom and is Tahiti's national flower.

13 Samuel J Rogal, *A William Somerset Maugham Encyclopedia*, Greenwood Publishing, Westport, USA, 1997, p. 274. The name lives on in the Tiare Tahiti, a seven-storey hotel built on the site of the American Embassy, which had been demolished in 1960.

14 Archives, French Polynesia, Slide No. 084-z2, Hôtel de France rue de Rivoli.

15 Philippe Mazellier, *Tahiti Autonome*, Tome I, P Mazellier, Tahiti, 1990, p. 357.

16 Hotel Taire Tahiti, Pacific Island Travel, viewed on 12 February 2009 at < http://www.pacificislandtravel.com/fr_polynesia/hotels/ppt_hoteltiaretahiti.asp>. See also Mazellier, Tome I, p. 357.

17 It is now the Bank Socredo. Mazellier, Tome I, p. 357.

18 Conversation, Prévot, Papeete, 2004.

19 Claude Lestrade, 'Quelques souvenirs de Tahiti entre 1942 et 1945', *Journal de la Société des océanistes*, Vol. 94, No. 1, 1992, pp. 128–129

20 Mazellier, Tome I, p. 357.

21 The site is now that of Le Méridian Hotel.

22 'Her name was Winklestroeter. The two gals built the five overwater here. They had a big business – cruise ships – dances and feasts. But they were going down. Business went by them.' Conversation, 'Muk' McCullum, one of the Bali Hai Boys, Aimeo site (now the Bali Hai Club), Moorea, 2004. Old postcards show the bungalows half on land and half over water. Austin Peterson in *Tahiti with Love: A Love Affair with the 'Island of Love',* Writers Club Press, Lincoln, USA, 2001, p. xi, refers to Mrs Winklestroeter also as the owner of the Air Tahiti Travel Agency.

23 Jean-Louis Saquet, *l'Aviation à Tahiti*, Polymages, Tahiti, 1998, p. 6.

24 James A Michener, Academy of Achievement (article in the Philadelphia Sunday Bulletin in 1970, provided by the James A Michener Library, University of Northern California, Greenly), viewed on 21 February 2009 at <http://www.achievement.org/autodoc/page/mic0bio-1>.

25 See Martin McIntosh (ed.), *Taboo: The Art of Tiki*, Outré Gallery Press, Melbourne, 1999. The Tiki is a Polynesian figurative cult object that became a common element in this Polynesia-derived movement. See also, Sven A Kirsten, *The Book of Tiki: The Cult of Polynesian Pop in Fifties America*, London, 2003. We are grateful to Davina Jackson for alerting us to the Tiki movement.

26 Trader Vic's became well known as the most successful of the Tiki restaurant chains. His Oakland, San Francisco, restaurant started in 1937. The Legacy, Trader Vic's, viewed on 6 June 2010 at <http://www.tradervics.com>.

27 The Polynesian is still in operation. 1970s, Tikiman Pages (the unofficial Polynesian Resort pages), viewed 16 July 2010 at <www.tikimanpages.com/tiki/polynesian-history/seventies>.

28 Information provided by Wimberly, Allison, Tong and Goo, April 2005.

29 Information provided by Wimberly, Allison, Tong and Goo. A 1968 photo at the hotel shows seven over-water bungalows.

30 Conversation, Jean-Hugues Tricard, Papeete, 2004. See also *SPTTN,* November 1968, p. 5.

31 Conversation, Gerald Garnier, Rarotonga, 2004. Prévot agrees, 'Garnier had that idea about glass in the floor'. Conversation, Prévot, Papeete, 2004.

32 The new design will not reflect the original design.' Correspondence (email), Dean Kawamura, associate, Wimberly, Allison, Tong and Goo, 14 July 2011.

33 In 1974 building commenced on the Bali Hyatt, Bora Bora, by Palmer and Turner, but construction did not proceed.

34 The film was not a success despite an all-star cast that included Mia Farrow and Trevor Howard.

35 Jeanine Tehani Sylvain, 'A Life of Joy', viewed on 26 June 2006 at <http://www.vaea.biz/photos/adolphe-sylvain.php>.

36 'Kelley was tired of being a lawyer; McCallum was tired of selling fishing gear; and Carlisle was tired of commuting'. Information regarding the Bali Hai Boys is primarily based on a conversation with 'Muk' McCallum at the Club Bali Hai, Moorea, 2004. Kelley and Carlisle had died.

37 The hotel has since been demolished, and the Moorea Pearl Beach stands on the site.

38 Conversation, McCallum, Moorea, 2004.

39 'Kelly said overwater bungalows. Let's do one and see if it goes down in the storm. We got a couple of big storms, but it was not affected, so we put in a few more. We had to do a brochure, so we said our best view is through a hole in the floor'. Conversation, MacCallum, Moorea, 2004.

40 These large hotels had to install their own electricity-generating plants. InterContinental Hotel Corporation, a subsidiary company of Pan Am, took control of the Tahara'a, and UTH (Union Touristique et Hôtelière), UTA's hotel subsidiary company, managed Maeva Beach.

41 It was financed by American funds from sources including Pan Am and with backing from the French Polynesian government. Mazellier, *Tahiti Autonome*, P. Mazellier, Tahiti, Tome 1, 1989, p. 380. Client: Société de Hôtelière Tahara'a. Joseph Long, who had been highly instrumental in the Hotel Bora Bora, conceived of the idea of the Tahara'a and invested a large part of his personal fortune in it. *SPTTN*, December 1969, p. 27.

42 The hotel has been in a ruinous state for some years.

43 *SPTTN,* March 1969, p. 14.

44 Austin Peterson, Tahiti Report, Writers Club Press, New York, 2000, p. 59.

45 *SPTTN*, November 1970, p. 24.

46 *Travelodger*, May 1974, p. 4.

47 We have not been able to ascertain the architect's forename. The Cook's Bay Resort is now in poor condition.

48 François Merceron, *Atlas de Tahiti et de la Polynésie Français*, Les Éditions du Pacifique, Singapore, 1988. p. 66.

49 Christian Gleizal (ed.), *Encyclopédie de la Polynésie*, Vivre en Polynésie 1, Multipress, Tahiti, 1986–88, p. 126.

Beyond Eden!

p. 232 Julio Cortázar, *Hopscotch*, Pantheon Books, New York, 1966 (Spanish edn: Rayuela, 1953).

1 The same firms had completed an earlier report in 1969 for tourist development in Australia and, in association with Wimberly, Allison, Tong and Goo, undertook a further study with the report *Tourism Development Programme for Fiji* in 1973.

2 School of Travel Industry Management, University of Hawaii at Manoa, *Tourism Development in French Polynesia,* Executive Summary, 1990, p. iv, viewed on 20 June 2012 at <http://www.tim.hawaii.edu/ctps/frenchpolynesia1990_executivesummary.pdf>.

3 French Polynesia's Economy: The Statistics, p. 10, viewed on 8 February 2009 at <http://www.presidence.pf/>. In 1958 there were only 124 hotel beds available in Papeete.

4 The number of tourists visiting Tahiti in 2001 peaked at 255,000, but that number had declined to 162 776 by 2011, reflecting the impact of the global financial crisis. See ISPF, Données détaillées, viewed on 3 April 2012 at <http://www.ispf.pf/bases/Tourisme/EFT/Details.aspx>.

5 See Tony Craig et al., FocusOn Pacific Islands; Well Placed to Lead World Tourism Growth (special report), Hotel Online, December 2002, viewed on 20 June 2012 at <http://www.hotel-online.com/News/PR2002_4th/Dec02_PacificIslands.html>.

6 Conversation, Pierre-Jean Picart, Papeete, 2004.

7 Conversation, Jean-Hugues Tricard, architect, Papeete, 2004

8 Conversation, Tricard, Papeete, 2004.

9 Landscaping by TUP of Paris. The hotel was extended in 2011 with a new sand-bottom pool and twelve overwater bungalows.

10 It was one of the first Tahitian hotels to deliberately cater for the then largely untapped 'convention market' – an increasingly dominant factor in hotel/resort economic survival.

11 This niche market sector of the Tahitian resorts caters specifically for the 'once-in-a-lifetime' and honeymoon couples bracket.

12 The steep volcanic islands have rocky foreshores and mostly black beaches, so rarely are there golden sands. Large expensive resorts, even on the motus, commonly create their own beaches with imported sand.

13 Among the financiers was Harunori Takahashi of the enterprising Japanese company EIE International Corporation (Electronics and Industrial Enterprises), who bought the Tahiti Beachcomber, the Moorea Beachcomber and the Tahara'a Hyatt Regency, spending more than US$70 million to acquire them, and announced a US$ 50 million upgrade programme that was to be managed by Tomas Pagliuso Design Associates. Michael Flagg, 'Pagliuso Wins Pact for French Polynesia', *Los Angeles Times*, 31 October 1989. But the projects did not go ahead as the finances collapsed in 1991 when the Japanese 'bubble' economy crashed.

14 Adequate potable water and power supplies can be limited on the outer islands.

15 Landscaping by TUP of Paris.

16 Conversation, Picart, architect, Papeete, 2004.

17 Later it was to become the Taha'a Relais and Chateaux.

18 Louis Wane is a local tycoon involved in breweries, mass-marketing and the hotel industry, which he manages through his company Société des Hôtels Tahitiens. He is the brother of black pearl magnate Robert Wan. In 2008 Hilton Hotels franchised three hotels from Louis Wane and rebranded them as the Hilton Hotel Tahiti, the Hilton Moorea Lagoon Resort and Spa and the Hilton Bora Bora Nui Resort and Spa. 'Hilton Hotel Enters into Franchise Agreements with Louis Wane for Three Resorts on the Islands of Tahiti, Moorea and Bora Bora, in French Polynesia', Hotel Online, viewed on 18 February 2009 at <http://www.hotel-online.com/News/PR2009_1st/Jan09_HiltonSoPac.html>.

19 Grandou was also the architect for the handsome stepped composition of the University of the French Pacific, 1987, which is now the University of French Polynesia.

20 Peter Haldeman, 'French Polynesia: Bora Bora Nui', *Architectural Digest*, August 2003, pp. 90–95.

21 Conversation, Bruno Hevechon, interior designer, Tropical Architecture, Papeete, 2004.

22 Conversation, Hevechon, Papeete, 2004.

23 'Developer Louis Wane Appoints Starwood's St. Regis Brand to Manage Luxury Bora Bora Resort with 101 Overwater and Beach Villas', Hotel Online, viewed on 27 September 2013 at <http://www.hotel-online.com/archive/archive-15492>.

24 Hoas occur naturally elsewhere in the Polynesian islands. It is described as an inlet that utilizes ocean tides and currents, and provides deep ocean water to the lagoon, replenishing fresh nutrients to sustain the abundant variety of native fish and stingrays.

25 Information on Eden Beach Resort provided by Xavier Lebigre, architect, and Vlad Zidek, on-site manager, Tahiti, 2004.

26 Cleansing the bore water requires three-stage filtering through sand, then 25 micron and 5 micron filters, then ultraviolet light.

27 This, however, consumes considerable energy, and its use is rarely necessary.

28 'The Eighty-Villa InterContinental Resort and Thalasso Spa on Bora Bora Providing New Dimensions to Ecotourism, Escape and Wellness', Hotel Online, viewed on 6 June 2006 at <http://www.hotel-online.com:80/News/PR2006_2nd/May06_IntercontBora.html>.

29 Zbigniew Bromberek, *Eco Resorts: Planning and Design for the Tropics,* Architectural Press (Elsvier), Oxford, 2009, p. 169.

30 Matthew Heller, 'Trouble in Paradise' (*Los Angeles Times,* 23 October 2005), viewed on 21 August 2011 at <www.tetiaroa.com/brando/index.html>.

31 Bernard Judge, *Waltzing with Brando: Planning a Paradise in Tahiti*, Oro Editions, Los Angeles, 2011.

32 Dalya Alberge, 'Marlon Brando Tahitian idyll to become luxury eco-resort', *The Observer*, London, 15 May 2011, viewed on 4 April 2012 at <http://www.guardian.co.uk/film/2011/may/15/marlon-

brando-tahiti-eco-resort>.

33 Barbara Flanagan, Sleeping with the Fishes (a review of the book *Waltzing with Brando*), 8 August 2011, The Designer Observer Group, viewed on 16 December 2012 at <http://changeobserver.designobserver.com/feature/sleeping-with-the-fishes/29218>.

PART V: FAITH ACROSS THE SOUTHERN OCEAN

Chapter 10: Places of Worship

Temples, Shrines, Mosques and Churches

1 The following website gives a comprehensive account of the building of the temple and its background. 'Largest Temple in Fiji Opens', Hinduism Today, September 1994, viewed on 27 September at http://www.hinduismtoday.com/modules/smartsection/item.php?itemid=3328

2 Alfred H Wood, *Overseas Missions of the Australian Methodist Church, Volume III: Fiji-Indian and Rotuma*, Aldersgate Press, Victoria, 1978, p. 15.

3 Hossein Amanat is an Iranian-Canadian Baha'i architect who graduated from the University of Tehran, Iran. See About the Firm, Amanat Architect, viewed on 6 April 2012 at <http://www.amanatarchitect.com/firm.html>.

In the Wake of the Missionaries

1 Daniel Mauer, *Protestant Church at Tahiti,* Dossier 6, Société des Océanistes, Paris, 1970, p. 7.

2 Williams returned to England in 1834, where he supervised the printing of the bible in the Rarotongan language. He returned to Polynesia in 1838 and in 1839, whilst visiting Erromango in what was then the New Hebrides, 'he and [his colleague] James Harris were killed by islanders in apparent retaliation for the previous activities of sandalwood traders.' Brij V Lal and Kate Fortune (eds.), *The Pacific Islands: An Encyclopedia,* University of Hawai'i Press, Honolulu, 2000, p. 196.

3 The Mormons first came formally to the Pacific in 1885. Nelson Eustis, *Samoa Sketchbook,* Hobby Investments, Adelaide, 1979, p. 12.

4 'Once a year they get together and live in tents. So we used that as a design input.' Conversation, George Cowan, Ministry of Infrastructure and Planning, Rarotonga, 2003.

5 The Tahiti temple was designed in collaboration with Pierre-Jean Picart.

6 Conversation, Bill Naylor, Church of Jesus Christ of Latter-Day Saints administration, Apia, 2004. Accreditation of Fetzer as architect for all temples was confirmed by telephone conversation with the Church of Jesus Christ of Latter-Day Saints, Salt Lake City, 27 January 2009. We were also advised that an adaptation of the same design was taken to Santiago, Chile, 1983. The Mormon temple in Sydney, Australia, 1984, is also of similar design.

7 Eustis, p. 6.

8 In February and March 2005, the Cook Islands were hit by five cyclones: Meens, Nancy, Olaf, Percy and Rae, and considerable damage was sustained. Five Weeks of Fury, The Cook Islands, viewed on 20 January 2009 at <http://www.cookislands.org.uk/3cyclones.html>.

9 Wall plaque on the façade.

10 John Williams, *A Narrative of Missionary Enterprises in the South Seas,* John Snow, London, 1837, p. 37.

11 Ebenezer Prout, *Memoirs of the Life of The Rev. John Williams, Missionary to Polynesia,* John Snow, London, 1843, pp. 182–183.

12 Herbert Ypma, *Pacific Island*, Stewart, Tabori and Chang, New York, 1996, p. 89.

13 CICC Churches, Siteseeing Cook Islands, Web Central, The Cook Islands, viewed on 20 January 2009 at <http://www.webcentral.co.ck/asiteseeing.htm>.

14 Cunningham suggested only six timber columns for the interior of the church, but as there were eight chiefs, they objected and requested eight columns, one for each chief. Cunningham's compromise was to obtain two forked posts from the forest nearby, which explains their unique appearance. Two earlier wooden churches existed before this one was built. See *On this Rock* (video) Jeanne Matenga (producer-director), funded by UNESCO in association with Cook Island TV (CITV), 1997.

15 'That church [Titikaveka] originally had three roofs. The two rows of columns – inside you can see where it had three roofs. The early woodcuts show the three roofs. One of the early pastors thought it unsuitable. You got soaked if you sat anywhere near the junctions. Did not know how to have an interior gutter. They then placed one big roof over the whole thing. It has changed from what it was. The original part was built by cannibals – they were converted and once converted they got enthusiastic – got muskets and went along to persuade others to join.' Conversation, Ken Mills, architect, (appointed Government Architect 1962), Rarotonga, 2003.

16 CICC Churches, Siteseeing Cook Islands, Web Central, The Cook Islands, viewed on 20 January 2009 at <http://www.webcentral.co.ck/asiteseeing.htm>.

17 In 1974 the flooring was found to be rotting, and so it was replaced with the present concrete floor. The timber that was found to be sound was reused by lining the interior of the church with vertical boarding up to dado height. *On this Rock* (video).

18 James P Sunderland and Aaron Buzacott (eds.), *Mission Life in the Islands of the Pacific,* John Snow, London, 1866.

19 The church lost its roof in 2005 during Cyclone Nancy.

20 Sunderland and Buzacott, illustration: 'The Avarua Church as built by Aaron Buzacott in 1853', p. 118.

21 Sunderland and Buzacott, p. 106.

22 David Raggs is a talented designer without architectural training, who refers to himself as 'a shade tree architect'. He also created the Black Rock House at Black Rock, Rarotonga, 2000.

23 American Samoa, Must Explore, viewed on 20 January 2009 at <http://www.mustexplore.com/american_samoa/index.html>.

24 The date for the commencement of the church was ascertained by reference to the High Court of American Samoa's report on case No. 88-1948. Gi v. Taetafea, American Samoa Bar Association, viewed on 22 May 2008 at <http://www.asbar.org/Cases/First-Series/2ASR/2ASR401.htm>.

25 John Enright, *A Walking Tour of Historic Fagatogo: Tutuila, American Samoa*, American Samoa Historic Preservation Office, Tutuila, 2001, p. 14. In the 1970s the American Samoa segment of the Congregational Christian Churches of Samoa (CCC of S) broke away, and the Congregational Churches within American Samoa became known as the Congregational Christian Church of American Samoa (CCCAS).

26 '"Mataniu Feagai Ma Le Ata" EFKS church dedication', Newsroom: 01 January – 07 January 2006, Event Polynesia, viewed on 17 January 2009 at <http://www.eventpolynesia.com/news&info/samoa/galleryarchive/SA2_page_gal01jan06.htm>.

Hats and Hymns

1 Cyclones Ofa and Valelia in the early 1990s and Cyclone Heta in 2004, together with the massive earthquake in September 2009, all took a toll on the integrity and soundness of the structure of the building, until a structural engineer's report recommended demolition. It appears from the drawings that the new building is intended to resemble the old building but be larger in size. See Mulivai Catholic Cathedral, viewed on 15 January 2013 at <http://www.mulivaicathedral-donation.org.ws/>.

2 Father Joseph Heslin, Michael B Tyquin (ed.), *A History of the Roman Catholic Church in Samoa: 1845–1995,* Samoa Commercial Printers, Apia, 1995, p. 50.

3 Data obtained from the memorial plaque inside the church foyer.

4 'On April 23, 1929, Father Eduard Bellwald, a Marist Father from Luxemburg and parish priest at Lepua, American Samoa, blessed the cornerstone of the Church of the Immaculate Conception, as construction of the new church began.' Stan Sorenson and Joseph Theroux, *The Samoan Historical Calendar 1606–2007,* 23 April 1929, American Samoa Government, viewed on 26 October 2008 at <http://www.scribd.com/doc/23231966/The-Samoan-Historical-Calendar-1606-2007> (original source: Father Joseph Heslin, [The] Story of [the] Church of Mary Immaculate at Lepua, American Samoa, 1984 [Typescript]).

5 Ibid. The church was built by master builder Fepulea'I Ned Ripley of Leone who agreed to build it for US$ 2600.

6 Patrick O'Reilly, *Tahitian Catholic Church,* Dossier No. 5, Société des Océanistes, Paris, 1969, p. 22.

7 Most Rev. J Quinn Weitzel, MM, Bishop of Samoa-Pago Pago, *Holy Family Cathedral, Diocese of Samoa Pago Pago, American Samoa,* Pago Pago, 10 June 1995, p. 2.

8 Weitzel, pp. 3–5.

9 Vailima Centre, #123 Papeete, The Tahiti Traveller, viewed on 25 May 2010 at <http://www.thetahititraveler.com/islandguide/mooreaintro.asp>.

10 Conversation, George Cowan, Ministry of Infrastructure and Planning, Rarotonga, 2003.

11 The cathedral was renovated in 1989.

12 Correspondence, Jean-Jacques Fernier, architect, 2 May 2011. The firm is now known as Fernier and Associates.

13 The authors are grateful to the late Monsignor Michel-Gaspard Coppenrath, Archbishop of Papeete, for information regarding St Etienne and other churches of his diocese.

14 O'Reilly, p. 7. The church was restored in 1968 and 1985 by Rodolphe Weinmann.

15 Daniel Mauer, *Protestant Church at Tahiti,* Dossier 6, Société des Océanistes, Paris, 1970, p. 7.

16 Ebenezer Prout, *The Memoirs of the Life of The Rev. John Williams, Missionary to Polynesia,* John Snow, London, 1843, p. 70.

17 'They [Tahitians] have never stopped building, pulling down and rebuilding.' Mauer, p. 18. A similar comment was made of the Samoans: 'Here on a whim they will knock the whole church down and build one much bigger'. Conversation, Joe Weilenman, architect, Pago Pago, 2004.

18 Mauer, p. 11.

19 Information on the Bora Bora churches provided by Pastor Teiva Tapu of Vaitape.

Faith and Fantasy: The Later Churches of Wallis and Futuna

1 Mt Puke on Futuna is 524 metres above sea level while Mt Lulu on Wallis is only 151 metres above sea level. 1:25 000 topographic maps of the islands (Series Blue) by the Institut Géographique National, Paris, 1987 are map numbers: Futuna 4902F and Wallis 4901W.

2 Tales have it that in the nineteenth century Alofi was invaded by men from Futuna who ate the entire population. Cannibalism was banned by King Niuliki in the kingdoms of Alo and Futuna in 1830. Wallis & Futuna 1616–1961, World at War, viewed on 21 July 2010 at <www.schudak.de/timelines/wallisandfutuna1616-1961.html>.

3 Frédéric Angleviel et al., 'An Island at the End of the World', in Christian Jost (ed.), *The French-Speaking Pacific: Population, Environment and Development Issues*, Geopacifique, Boombana Publications, Brisbane, 1999, p. 242.

4 Frédéric Angleviel, *Les Missions à Wallis et Futuna au XIXe siècle*, Bordeaux-Talence, France: Centre de recherche des espaces tropicaux de l'Université Michel de Montaigne (Bordeaux III), 1994. p. 27.

5 Angleviel, 1994, pp. 58–76.

6 Angleviel, 1994, p. 43.

7 This was a time of upheaval as Protestant warriors from Tonga fought battles on the island between 1843 and 1851, Angleviel, 1994, pp. 85–98.

8 At its height, the US base on Wallis housed 6000 troops. Angleviel et al. in Jost, pp. 231–244.

9 The current airport terminal building on Wallis was designed by Pierre Lacombe from Tahiti and is more Tahitian in form than Wallisian.

10 'Most Futunians did not know that a war was being fought and only heard of it later.' Conversation with local villagers.
11 Angleviel et al. in Jost, pp. 242–243
12 Frédéric Angleviel (directeur de la publication), *Wallis et Futuna: hommes et espaces: sciences humaines, programmes des colleges*, CTRDP, Noumea, c. 1994, p. 54.
13 Secretariat of the Pacific Community, 2010 Pocket Statistical Summary, SPC, viewed at <http://www.spc.int/sdp/>.
14 Catherine Courvasier, 'The Horn Archipelago Futuna and Alofi', in Christian Jost (ed.) *The French-Speaking Pacific: Population, Environment and Development Issues*, Geopacifique, Boombana Publications, Brisbane, 1999, pp. 245–267.
15 Paul van der Grijp, 'Development Polynesian Style: Contemporary Futunian Social Economy and its Cultural Features', *The Journal of the Polynesian Society*, Vol. 114, No. 4, 2005 p. 312.
16 'The church at Hihifo, though decent, was badly situated, so the parishioners determined to enlarge it and bring it nearer the shore. We have blessed its first stone and foundations. With the well-known ardour and skill of our builders, it will be finished in two years.' The present Church of St Peter and St Paul is built on the site. Reverend Amand Lamaze (Bishop of Olympus, Vicar Apostalic of Central Oceania and Administrator of the Navigation Islands), circular letter, *New Zealand Tablet*, 4 August 1882, p. 21.
17 Lamaze, p. 21.
18 Correspondence (email), Father André Glantenet, Catholic Military Chaplin New Caledonia and Wallis and Futuna, 12 July 2011.
19 No doubt priests contributed much to their designs. Angleviel, 1994, p. 164, quotes Father Dezest as saying in 1878 of the St Joseph's church at Sau Sau, Futuna: 'you understand that [Father] R P Junillon is the architect and mason and that all I have contributed is words of encouragement.' Also, Correspondence (email), Glantenet, 7 July 2011: 'With regard to the more recent churches, mention should be made of Fathers Pelenato Fotofili and Soane Ikauno for their aesthetic and technical contribution and guidance.'
20 In 1882 the churches were described as follows: 'St Joseph's, at Mua, is 60 feet broad and 180 feet long. Its walls are 28 feet high and its steeple 120. People admire its long ogival windows, the bold design of its timber roof, the solidarity of its buttresses, nay, the singular execution of its gargoyles. It is a real monument. Our Lady of Mata'Uta is less graceful but more imposing. Its vast transept, massive tower and brownish colour give it a very becoming appearance of antiquity; it is the mother of all of our churches.' Lamaze, p. 21. Mala'efo'ou was formerly known as Mu'a.
21 Philippe Godard, *Wallis et Futuna: Carnets de route du Pacifique*, Editions Melanesia, Noumea, 1974, p. 198. For assistance in the translation of French texts on Wallis and Futuna, the authors are indebted to Anna Christian.
22 Godard, p. 200.
23 See Godard, p. 198, for a watercolour entitled 'After the Service', by Patrice Nielly that shows two towers on the cathedral.
24 The Maltese Cross is the insignia of the royal house. Godard, p. 200: 'It was said it was inspired by a photo of Vezelay. The completion coincided with the death of Father Hamale and his burial was the first be held in the cathedral.'
25 In 1885 the palace was still a timber building. Godard, p. 97.
26 Godard, p. 20. Angleviel's *Les Missions à Wallis et Futuna au XIXe siècle*, p. 158, states that Mgr. Bataillon, in 1876, arranged to have the palais-royal constructed. This is probably the single-storeyed timber building shown in Godard, p. 97. The palace today bears a resemblance to the two-storeyed seminary building at Lano, see Angleviel, 1994, p. 134.
27 Inscribed on the arch over the nave doorway.
28 Lamaze, p. 21.
29 In 1899 he was beatified and in 1964 was canonised to the status of the Patron Saint of Oceania. St. Peter-Louis-Marie Chanel, The Catholic Encyclopedia, New Advent, viewed on 28 August 2008 at <http://www.newadvent.org/cathen/11769a.htm>.
30 For information and dates of the churches in Futuna the authors wish to acknowledge the assistance of Sister Superior, Sister Mari-Eves from Bretagne, France.
31 Futuna was ravaged by a disastrous cyclone on 17 April 1907, which destroyed the church and the chapel. *Nelson Evening Mail*, Volume XLII, 22 May 1907, p. 2.
32 Lamaze, p. 21.
33 'Oceania', in Nicholas Patrick Wiseman, *The New Glories of the Catholic Church*, Richardson and Son, London, 1859, pp. 244–255.
34 See Angleviel, 1994, p. 164.
35 Information on the Church of St Joseph at Sau Sau provided by a visiting Futunian priest from Fiji.

PART VI: VOICES OF THE SOUTH PACIFIC

D'OÙ VENONS NOUS? QUE SOMMES NOUS? OÙ ALLONS NOUS?

p. 291 As signed on the painting by Paul Gauguin (upper left) on p. 292. 'Where Do We Come From? What Are We? Where Are We Going?' Paul Gauguin, 1897-1898. See Museum of Fine Arts, Boston, viewed on 7 April 2012 at <http://www.mfa.org/collections/object/where-do-we-come-from-what-are-we-where-are-we-going-32558.

Chapter 11: A Matter of Perspective

View From the West: Ambiguous Answers

1 The largest *case* on Lifou, at Hnathalo, was initially built in 1842 and rebuilt after a fire in 1976. Glenn Jowitt and Peter Shaw, *Pacific Island Style*, Lothian, Melbourne, 1999, p. 87.
2 Conversation, Emmanuel Kasarherou, director, Jean-Marie Tjibaou Cultural Centre, Noumea, 2003.
3 Conversation, Kasarherou, Noumea, 2003.
4 It was difficult to find builders to construct the meeting hall at the Jean-Marie Tjibaou Cultural Centre. Conversation, Kasarherou, Noumea, 2003.
5 Correspondence, Jock Stevenson, architect, January 2010. Stevenson could not recall Wassum's first name.
6 'The Americans said we can do the funding for another good one. So they managed to convince the committee to divert the project to the Americans'. Conversation, Osborne Van Gana, architect, Honiara, April 2005. The name Seabees comes from 'construction battalion' (CBs), now operating under the name of NAVFAC.
7 Conversation, Van Gana, April 2005.
8 See illustration, Chapter 3, p. 83
9 The identity of the designer has not been determined.
10 Elven Star or Faerie Star, Technogypsie, viewed on 26 May 2012 at <http://www.technogypsie.com/faeid/elvenstar.html>.
11 Correspondence, Masao Yamagata, project architect for the Japanese construction company that built Parliament House, March 2008.
12 Conversation, Geoffrey Feast, architect, Port Vila, 2003. The forecourt statue is by a Chinese artist and is a further gift from China.
13 Dominique Pechberty, 'les Uvéens en Nouvell-Calédonie', *The Journal of Pacific Studies*, Vol. 27, No. 1, 2004, pp. 63–81. Pechberty's paper speaks of the 20 000 migrants from Wallis and Futuna, or 10 per cent of the population of New Caledonia, living in and around Noumea.
14 The congress was rehabilitated in 1980 by architect Vladimir Perm. Correspondence (email), Isabelle Ohlen, 4th Vice President of Congress, 26 May 2012.
15 For a report of the project, see an interview with Renzo Piano: 'Renzo Piano Workshop', *Architecture and Urbanism*, December 1996, pp. 92–103.
16 Conversation, Kasarherou, Noumea, 2003.
17 *Varangue*, No. 21, August 2010, pp. 78–85. The 1998 Noumea Accord established a senate for Kanak chiefs, and France must consult the Customary Senate on subjects relating to Kanak identity. See Jon Fraenkel, 'Power Sharing in Fiji and New Caledonia', in Stewart Firth (ed.), *Globalisation and Governance in the Pacific Islands*, Australian National University E Press, Canberra, 2006, p. 333.

The Pacific Image of Fiji

1 The Conference Centre now serves as a library.
2 *Leucaena leucocephala* (vaivai tree).
3 A *rara* is a large open green area in which ceremonies can be staged.
4 The Sepik River is in Papua New Guinea, a member country of SPEC..
5 For information on the now Pacific Islands Forum Secretariat complex, the authors are indebted to Stuart Huggett and Elsa Miller, Suva, 2003 and 2005.
6 The building was donated by New Zealand, fitted out by Australia and built on Fiji land.
7 Ryoichi Jinnai is a private Japanese donor.
8 Conversation, Stuart Huggett, Suva, 2005.
9 By an 'over-enthusiastic' welder from New Zealand completing the fire-protection system! Conversation, Elsa Miller, Suva, 2005.
10 Oceania Centre for Arts, Culture and Pacific Studies, University of the South Pacific, viewed on 2 February 2010 at <http://www.usp.ac.fj/index.php?id=2632>.
11 'History', Oceania Centre for Arts, Culture and Pacific Studies, University of the South Pacific, viewed on 2 February 2010 at <http://www.usp.ac.fj/index.php?id=8708>.
12 For an interesting analysis of cultural expressions in contemporary Fijian architecture see Rob Ansell, 'Cultural Confidence in Fijian Architecture', *Architecture New Zealand*, September/October 1992, pp. 68–69.
13 The *bure kalou* in pre-Christian Fijian times was a temple or house of the priests. Usually sited on a hill or mound with a very high roof structure, it was taller than that of the chief's house. See Peter France, 'The Kaunitoni Migration: Notes on the Genesis of a Fijian Tradition', *The Journal of Pacific History*, Vol. 1, 1966, pp. 107–113. Orchid Island is ten kilometres from Suva along Queens Road. An island called Masima has been turned into a lush tropical garden, where hundreds of varieties of indigenous plants flourish. Approximately 150 different types of orchids have also been planted.
14 This decision was contested, with many believing it was more appropriate to leave the chiefs in the soil. Conversation, Huggett, Suva, 2005.
15 When Jaimi died in 2005 the design for the *Bose Levu Vakaturaga* complex was largely completed. The design director, Ulaiasi Baivatu, left the firm to establish his own company, Clearview Architects, and that firm went on to complete the project. See Clearview website, viewed on 25 January 2011 at < http://www.clearview.com.fj/about.php>.
16 The *loru* are usually made of balabala – local tree fern trunks.
17 It has been proposed that the building now be know simply as Meeting House (Vale ni Bose). 'Multi-million dollar Meeting House Opened for Fiji's Great Council of Chiefs', Radio New Zealand International, viewed 10 May 2011 at <http://www.rnzi.com/pages/news.php?op=readandid=49245>.
18 Conversation, Tony Sansom, architect, Fiji, 2005.
19 Conversation, Filipe Tauva, architect, Fiji, 2005.
20 The main contractor was Fletcher-Traditional Décor Ltd. Joint Venture.
21 Information on the design of the Parliament House of Fiji from conversations with architects Tauva and Sansom, Suva, 2005.

Speaking for the Central Isles

1 New Zealand retains responsibility for defence and overseas affairs, in close consultation with the Cook Islands Parliament.
2 There is also a monarchical structure in Wallace and Futuna – three kings with limited powers.
3 Together with the American Peace Corps architect Joseph Snearly and T E Smith McNaught of Auckland. Verbal report, Public Works Department, Apia, 2004.
4 It was being used as the Office of the Ombudsman but was demolished in March 2012.
5 Conversation, Dr Toria Alama, Clerk of the House, Apia, 2004.
6 The building is named after the First Speaker, Luafatasaga Kalapu.
7 In a reply to a comment regarding the low level of security offered by glass walls around the Parliament Chamber, Dr Alama replied, 'I don't see why it had to have any walls at all'.
8 See Pia Sioa, 'Samoa Gets New Courthouse, Compliments China', Pacific Islands Development Program (original source: 4 December

2009, Newsline Samoa Newspaper), viewed on 25 July 2013 at <http://pidp.org/archive/2009/December/12-08-00.htm>.

9 Correspondence, Joe Weilenman, architect, 1985. The Maota Fono was built by Kong Young Korean Builders.

10 To build the project, finance was arranged through the Republic of Nauru Finance Corporation. Shortage of funds caused several delays in the execution of the construction.

11 The architects have been unable to trace their documentation on this complex. Correspondence, Jackson Teece, April 2011. A set of drawings is held at the Cultural Centre, but the authors were unable to gain access to them.

12 See David Arnell and Lisette Wolk, *Visions of the Pacific*, Ministry of Cultural Development, Cook Islands, 1993. The book provides detailed descriptions of the artworks and symbolism in the complex.

Ideology and Identity: French Polynesia

1 Conversation, Michel Prévot, architect, Papeete, 2004.

2 Stephen Henningham, *France and the South Pacific: A Contemporary History*, University of Hawai'i Press, Honolulu, 1992, p. 147. 'The new bi-cultural policy began to emerge in the 1970s but became fully established when it was embodied in the new internal autonomy statute instituted in 1983. Under the new statute, Tahitian joined French as an official language of the territory.' Prior to this time Tahitian had been banned in the schools.

3 'The drawings are completely destroyed. I gave one set of the tracing paper drawings to the authorities, but they have gone, and I had one set and it was dry and crumbling so I threw it out. We did not make any good renderings. We had an agreement with the guy [Sicurani], and once we had the understanding, we got on with it. He saw the way that I worked, and he trusted me. But we did not make money on that. We made 4.5 per cent. That is all. That was *sans fee* architecture.' Conversation, Prévot, Papeete, 2004.

4 Patrick O'Reilly and Raoul Teissier, 'Chabana, Ivan (1902)', in *Tahitiens: Répertoire Biographique de la Polynésie Française*, Publications de la Société des Océanistes No. 36, Musée de l'homme, Paris, 1975, p. 101.

5 O'Reilly and Teissier, 'Chabana, Ivan (1902)', p. 101. Prévot is more dismissive: 'He built in timber and it was all eaten by the termites. He did not do anything after 1942. He returned to nature and lived in a grass hut in the country on the east coast.' Conversation, Michel Prévot, 2004.

6 Conversation, Prévot, and Eric Regaud, architect and son of Christian Regaud, and Alain Prévot, Michel Prévot's nephew. All conversations, Papeete, 2004. Michel Prévot was the design architect for the firm: 'I was the artist and he was the public relations man'.

7 Conversation, Prévot, Papeete, 2004. 'Regaud sailed to Tahiti with an eccentric pianist who put his one-tonne grand piano on the keel and then built the rest of the boat around it.'

8 These projects included the commemorative monument to General de Gaulle and the commemorative monument for the landing of the first Protestant missionaries in Tahiti. O'Reilly and Teissier, 'Weinmann, Rodolphe (1936)', p. 602.

9 Now Tahiti's botanic gardens at Mont Ovini.

10 Philippe Mazellier, 'Difficile Naissance du Musée de Tahiti et des Isles', in *Tahiti Autonome*, Tome 1, Hibiscus Editions, Tahiti, 1989, p. 142.

11 Roger Heim (President, Fondation Singer-Polignac), 'preface', in Patrick O'Reilly, Musée Gauguin, *Catalogue du musée Gauguin, Papeari, Tahiti,* Fondation Singer-Polignac, Papeete, 1964.

12 The museum contains few original works due to the adverse effects of the Polynesian climatic conditions.

13 Philippe Mazellier, *Le Mémorial polynésien,* Tome III, Hibiscus Editions, Tahiti, p. 144.

14 Prévot was familiar with the building as he has a particular interest in Gauguin's art and was writing a book on the subject. He was designer for the exhibition housed at the museum regarding striking parallels between traditional images of Japanese wrestlers and the paintings of Gauguin.

15 The Governor's Palace, 1843, and the Queen's Palace, 1883, were prefabricated in France and assembled in Tahiti by the army (Queen Pomare IV died in 1878 before the palace was constructed). Oak was used for both palaces to resist termite attack. Philippe Mazellier, 'The New Face of Papeete', in *Tahiti: de l'atome à l'autonomie*, Hibiscus Editions, Tahiti, 1979, p. 306.

16 Now the residence of the French High Commissioner.

17 Conversation, Prévot, Papeete, 2004. Prévot had measured and drawn the building.

18 Conversation, Prévot, Papeete, 2004.

19 Known as the René Leboucher Chamber after the first Secretary-General of the assembly.

20 Conversation, Prévot, Papeete, 2004.

21 Information guide to the Assembly of French Polynesia.

22 'Before New Caledonia [Tjibaou] Cultural Centre you didn't have any culturally inspired mileposts. In Tahiti, it could not have happened at all. There was never any directing guy wanting to make architecture. Of course, the building has only a small importance in a small country. The local people were never conscious that it was something worthwhile. They adopted it as their own and lived in it happily for a long time, celebrating and enjoying flower exhibitions, dancing – they never thought of it as modern architecture. That is why it has never been photographed. It is not important.' Conversation, Prévot, Papeete, 2004.

23 Prévot relates that there was little time in which to build the house before de Gaulle arrived. He recounts that as de Gaulle came in the front door the workmen were hastily leaving by the rear, putting on the finishing touches as they left. Conversation, Prévot, Papeete, 2004.

24 Sicurani conceived of the idea for the museum, and the land was purchased in 1966. Sicurani returned to France in 1969 before it was completed.

25 Conversation, Prévot, Papeete, 2004.

26 Traffic in Tahiti has greatly increased since the building of the auditorium, and the building, which is unable to be enclosed and air-conditioned, suffers from acoustic degradation.

27 The title and status of *Pays d'outre-mer,* 'France over the Sea', was granted to French Polynesia in 2004.

28 Flosse was president for the period 1991–2004, in part 2004–05, 2008 and since May 2013. Previously he had been president of the government 1984–87 and president of the assembly 1972–74 and 1976–77. He also represented the territory in the French National Assembly in Paris and was appointed Minister for South Pacific Affairs.

29 Jacques Chirac is godfather to Flosse's youngest son, Jacques. 'Gaston Flosse (Life and Career), Wikipedia, viewed on 6 April 2012 at <http://en.wikipedia.org/wiki/Gaston_Flosse >.

30 French Polynesia is economically dependent on France, which spends US$ 1000 million in French Polynesia per year. This is twice as much as it spends in New Caledonia, which is more self-reliant. Henningham, p. 155.

31 There were forty-one municipal councils established throughout French Polynesia. Henningham, p. 135.

32 Jean-Louis Saquet, *Architecture Tropicale de Tahiti: Te Fare,* Editions Polymages-Scoop, Tahiti, 1991, p. 33. The house was principally of redwood imported from California.

33 Temaru was in political opposition to Flosse and was president of French Polynesia in 2005, 2007 and 2009, and again in 2011–13.

34 Conversation, Jean-Hugues Tricard, architect, Tahiti, 2004.

35 This hall has since been enclosed and air conditioned.

36 Conversation, Jacques Derue, Supervisor, EGT (Etablissement public des grands travaux), Papeete, 2004. 'These buildings did not sit well with Governor Flosse's image of the new French Polynesia, and he has proposed demolishing them to allow for the construction of a more commodious and impressive building for the assembly.'

37 'The old assembly was made in the 1960s, so they wanted to make a place where the whole of the South Pacific would see that French Polynesia is the centre of things.' Conversation, Bruno Hervechon, interior designer, Tropical Architecture, Papeete, 2004.

38 Bengt Danielsson and Marie-Thérèse Danielsson, produced by Christian Gleizal, *Papeete 1818–1990,* C Gleizal/Cobalt – Mairie de Papeete, Papeete, c. 1990, p. 78. 'After the war the municipal council moved into the ancient Convent of the Sisters of St Joseph de Cluny'.

39 Conversation, Prévot, Papeete, 2004.

40 Flosse started his political career in 1965 as the first mayor of Pirae. Before the completion of the building, Flosse was forced to leave this position on 10 March 2000, under the law of the senate limiting the office plurality of mandates. His son-in-law, Edouard Fritch, succeeded him as mayor of Pirae. Jean Louis Saux, 'Polynesia, the Flosse System', *Le Monde*, viewed on 22 May 2004 at <www.politiqueglobale.org//article.php3?id_article=696>.

41 Conversation, Tricard, Papeete, 2004. 'It was a competition so if I wanted to be the winner, I had to do it as the mayor wanted.' Presumably the house to which Flosse referred was the Southern Plantation house 'Tara'.

42 'Commune de Pirae: Observations définitives', viewed on 26 May 2006 at <http://www.ccomptes.fr/crc/votre-region/polynesie-francaise/rods/pfr200420.htm>. With reference to the town hall, the 2004 enquiry into 'the accounts and the management of the commune of Pirea' reported, 'The total amount of expenditure carried out at the end of 2002 thus amounts to 1 245 707 000 Pacific French Francs [US$12.8 million].' It reports in detail on the competition and the work.

43 The columns were of CCV, a combination of black silicone, glass fibre, acrylic polymers and colours. See Hotel de Ville de Pirae (September 2002) at Partner Engineering, viewed on 26 May 2006 at <http://www.partner-engineering.com/Projet/listing/id/9>.

44 French Polynesia, La Presidence, viewed on 22 May 2006 at <http:/www.presidence.pf/index.php?91>.

45 The palace was built to the cost of approximately 3.5 billion Pacific French Francs (in 2006 US$ 37 million): Gaston Flosse announcement, Tahiti Pacifique Magazine, 8 June 2000, viewed 24 May 2006 at <http://www.tahiti-pacifique.com>.

46 Félix Broche was the captain in charge of the Bataillion du Pacifique that fought in Africa against the Germans in 1940.

47 *L'Histoire, 'La Presidence'*, La Presidence de la Polynesie Française, 2000. Unpublished Presidential Palace document.

48 *L'Histoire, 'La Presidence'.*

49 The complex had to be large as the president's office had a staff of 600. Conversation, Tepuanui Snow, department of communication, President's Office, Tahiti, 2004.

50 'The building is something like Directoire style – a melting plot of French old style, and the classical – difficult to explain.' Conversation, Bruno Hervechon, 2004. Directoire style in French interior decoration and costume was popular in the transitional period between Louis XVI and the Empire style at the end of the eighteenth century. The taste for Greco-Roman design heralded the Empire style. Harold Osborne (ed.), *The Oxford Companion to the Decorative Arts*, Oxford at the Clarendon Press, Oxford, 1975, p. 299.

51 Under Flosse's administration the pedestrian crossing of the courtyard was reserved for the use of the president and his guests only. Further, the palace was closed to the public. When Temaru became president in 2004, he determined that the name of the building was to be changed from 'Palace' and the building was to be opened to the public. French Polynesia, La Presidence, viewed 22 May 2006 at <http:/www.presidence.pf/index.php?91>.

52 Conversation, Hervechon, 2004. *L'escalier d'honneur* was only for the use of the president and his guests. Hervechon worked for two years on the design of the staircase.

53 Unpublished presidential palace information.

54 *L'Histoire, 'La Presidence'.*

55 Conversation, Snow, Papeete, 2004.

56 EGT: Etablissement public des grands travaux.

57 The EGT were also charged with managing other large projects, including the new central hospital, to serve the Pacific region. Conversation, Jacques Derue, director, Papeete, 2004.

58 The question posed by the EGT authority was 'what will be the style of architecture for the 21st century here in Papeete – should it be local or should it be international?' Derue, question to the authors, 2004.

OUT OF DIFFERENCE

p. 331 Jean-Marie Tjibaou, interview, *Les Temps modernes*, 1985.

BIBLIOGRAPHY

Alailima, Fay, *Aggie Grey: A Samoan Saga*, Mutual Publishing Company, Honolulu, 1988.

Angleviel, Frédéric, *Les Missions à Wallis et Futuna au XIXe siècle*, Bordeaux-Talence: Centre de recherche des espaces tropicaux de l'Université Michel de Montaigne (Bordeaux III), 1994.

Archive CD Books Australia, *The Cyclopedia of Fiji, Samoa, Tonga, Tahiti and the Cook Islands 1907*. Archive CD Books Australia, Modbury, SA, 2006.

Bellwood, Peter, James J Fox, and Darrell Tryon (eds.), *The Austronesians: Historical and Comparative Perspectives*, Department of Anthropology, Research School of Pacific Studies, Australian National University, 1995.

Belt Collins and Associates et al., *Tourism Development Programme for Fiji*, United Nations Development Programme, International Bank for Reconstruction and Development with the participation of the Fiji Government, Hawai'i, 1973.

Bresnihan, Brian J and Keith Woodwood (eds.), *Tufala Gavman: Reminiscences from the Anglo-French Condominium of the New Hebrides*, Institute of Pacific Studies, University of the South Pacific, Suva, 2002.

Bromberek, Zbigniew, *Eco Resorts: Planning and Design for the Tropics*, Architectural Press (Elsvier), Oxford, 2009.

Campbell, Ian C, *Island Kingdom: Tonga Ancient and Modern*, Canterbury University Press, Christchurch, 1992.

Chevalier, Luc, *Nouméa de l'an 1954 a l'an 2000*, Les Editions Cagou, Noumea, 1998.

Connell, John and John P Lea, *Pacific 2010: Urbanisation in Polynesia*, National Centre for Development Studies, Australian National University, Canberra, 1995.

Daly, Henri, *La Guerre du Pacifique 1941–1945: Nouvelle-Calédonie: porte-avions américain dan les mers du sud*, Société d'Études Historiques de la Nouvelle-Calédonie, Noumea, 2002.

Danielsson, Bengt and Marie-Thérèse Danielsson, produced by Christian Gleizal, *Papeete 1818-1990*, C Gleizal/Cobalt – Mairie de Papeete, Papeete, c. 1990.

de Castillon de Saint-Victor, Arnauld, *Tahiti et l'Avion*, Dossier 18, Société des Océanistes, Paris, 1974.

Derrick, Ronald A, *A History of Fiji*, Print and Stationery Department, Suva, 1946.

Douglas, Ngaire, *They Came for Savages: 100 Years of Tourism in Melanesia*, Southern Cross University Press, Alstonville, NSW, 1996.

Douglas, Norman and Ngaire Douglas, *Tonga: A Guide*, Albion Press, Newstead, 1989.

Dove, Victor, *Fiji Sketchbook*, Rigby, Brisbane, 1970.

Düring, Kurt, *Pathways to the Tongan Present*, Government Printing Department, Nuku'alofa, Tonga, 1990.

Eustis, Nelson, *Samoa Sketchbook*, Hobby Investments, Adelaide, 1979.

Eustis, Nelson, *Aggie Grey of Samoa*, Hobby Investments, Adelaide, 1994.

Eustis, Nelson, *Tonga Sketchbook*, Hyde Park Press, Adelaide, 2002.

Fiji Department of Tourism, *Fiji Tourism Development Plan 2007–2016, Tourism – Fiji's Opportunity*, Sustainable Tourism Development Consortium, Fiji, 2007.

Filippi, Orso and Bernard Fustec, *Le Mémorial de Nouméa, 1859–1999, à travers 140 ans d'histoire du conseil municipal, 1859-1999*, Editions Planéte Mèmo, Noumea, 1999.

Firth, Stewart (ed.), *Globalisation and Governance in the Pacific Islands*, Australian National University E Press, Canberra, 2006.

Fischer, Steven R, *A History of the Pacific Islands*, Palgrave Macmillan, Basingstoke, 2002.

Fraenkel, Jon, Stewart Firth and Brij V Lal (eds.), *The 2006 Military Takeover in Fiji: A Coup to End All Coups?*, Australian National University E Press, Canberra, 2009.

Gleizal, Christian (ed.), *Encyclopédie de la Polynésie*, C Gleizal/Multipress, Tahiti, 1990.

Godard, Phillipe, *Wallis et Futuna: Carnets de route du Pacifique*, Editions Melanesia, Noumea, 1974.

Godard, Philippe and Luc Chevalier, *Le Mémorial Calédonien*, Editions d'Art Calédoniennes, Noumea, 1977.

Harrison, David (ed.), *Pacific Island Tourism*, Cognizant Communication Corporation, New York, 2003.

Hau'ofa, Epeli, *We are the Ocean: Selected Works*, University of Hawai'i Press, Honolulu, 2008.

Henningham, Stephen, *France and the South Pacific: A Contemporary History*, University of Hawai'i Press, Honolulu, 1992.

Heslin, Father Joseph (M B Tyquin ed.), *A History of the Catholic Church in Samoa: 1845–1995*, Apia, 1995.

HJM Consultants and Timothy Hubbard Pty Ltd, *Town of Levuka Heritage Study*, prepared for the Fiji Ministry of Housing, Urban Development and Environment and the Pacific Asia Travel Association, 1994.

Howe, Kerry R, Robert C Kiste, and Brij V Lal (eds.), *Tides of History: The Pacific Islands in the Twentieth Century*, Allen and Unwin, St Leonards, NSW, 1994.

Institute of Pacific Studies, University of the South Pacific and Levuka Historical and Cultural Society, *Levuka: Living Heritage*, by the people of Levuka, Suva, 2001.

Jost, Christian (ed.), *The French-Speaking Pacific: Population, Environment and Development Issues*, Geopacifique Association, Boombana Publications, Mount Nebo, 1998.

Jowitt, Glenn and Peter Shaw, *Pacific Island Style*, Lothian, Melbourne, 1999.

Julien, Jacqueline, *Let Me Guide You in Nouméa*, Editions Grain de sable, Noumea, 1999.

Kennedy, Robert A, *Harold Gatty's Legacy: A Photo History of Fiji's National Airline: Fiji Airways 50 Years on*, Sigatoka, 2002.

Kirsten, Sven A, *The Book of Tiki: The Cult of Polynesian Pop in Fifties America*, Taschen, London, 2003.

Lacourrège, Gérard and Pierre Alibert, *La Présence américaine en Nouvelle-Calédonie*, l'Atelier d'Art Graphique, Noumea, 1981.

Lal, Brij V and Kate Fortune (eds.), *The Pacific Islands: An Encyclopedia*, University of Hawai'i Press, Honolulu, 2000.

McIntosh, Martin (ed.), *Taboo: The Art of Tiki*, Outré Gallery Press, Melbourne, 1999.

Marvell, Karen, and Glen Craig (eds.), *Fiji Through the Eyes of the Fijian*, Shangri-La's Fijian Resort, Fiji, 1997.

Mason, Leonard and Patricia Hereniko, *In Search of a Home*, Institute of Pacific Studies, University of the South Pacific, Suva, 1987.

Mauer, Daniel, *Protestant Church at Tahiti*, Dossier 6, Société des Océanistes, Paris, 1970.

Mazellier, Philippe, *Tahiti: de l'atome à l'autonomie*, Hibiscus Editions, Papeete, 1979.

Mazellier, Philippe, *Tahiti Autonome*, 2 Tomes, M. Mazellier, Tahiti, 1990.

Mazellier, Philippe, Bengt Danielsson and Marie-Thérèse Danielsson, *Le Mémorial Polynésien*, 6 Volumes, Hibiscus Editions, Tahiti, 1977–1980.

Merceron, François, *Atlas de Tahiti et de la Polynésie Français*, Les Éditions du Pacifique, Singapore, 1988.

Moorehead, Alan, *The Fatal Impact: An Account of the Invasion of the South Pacific, 1767–1840*, Tales of the Pacific, Honolulu, 1988.

Mullins, David W, *They Built a Church: Priests of Tonga, R.I.P*, St Bede's College Printery, Christchurch, 2004.

O'Reilly, Patrick, *Tahitian Catholic Church*, Dossier No.5, Société des Océanistes, Paris, 1969.

O'Reilly, Patrick, *Calédoniens: Répertoire bio-bibliographique de la Nouvelle-Calédonie*, Société des Océanistes, Musée de l'homme, Paris, 1980.

O'Reilly, Patrick and Raoul Teissier, *Tahitiens: Répertoire Biographique de la Polynésie Française*, Société des Océanistes, Musée de l'homme, Paris,1975.

Prout, Ebenezer, *Memoirs of The Life of The Rev. John Williams, Missionary to Polynesia*, John Snow, London 1843.

Rodman, Margaret, *Houses Far From Home: British Colonial Space in the New Hebrides*, University of Hawai'i Press, Honolulu, 2001.

Roth, George Kingsley (ed.), *Fiji: Handbook of the Colony*, Acting Government Printer, Suva, 1937,

Rottman, Gordon L, *US Marine Corps 1941–45*, Osprey Publishing, New York, 1995.

Rutherford, Noel, *Shirley Baker and the King of Tonga*, Pacific Press, Wellington, 1971.

Sand, Christophe, *Lapita: The Pottery Collection From the Site at Foué, New Caledonia*, Archaeology Department: Territorial Museums and Heritage Service, Noumea, 1999.

Saquet, Jean-Louis, *Architecture Tropicale de Tahiti: Te Fare*, Editions Polymages-Scoop, Tahiti, 1991.

Saquet, Jean-Louis, *l'Aviation á Tahiti*, Polymages, Tahiti, 1998.

Schütz, Albert J, *Suva: A History and Guide*, Pacific Publications, Sydney, 1978.

Sofield, Trevor H B, *Empowerment for Sustainable Tourism Development*, Emerald Group Publishing, London, 2003.

Stephenson, Elsie, *Fiji's Past on Picture Postcards*, Caines Jannif Group, Suva, 1997.

Sunderland, James P and Aaron Buzacott (eds.), *Mission Life in the Islands of the Pacific*, John Snow, London,1866.

Tarte, Daryl and Stewart Firth (eds.), *Twentieth Century Fiji: People Who Shaped the Nation*, USP Solutions, University of the South Pacific, Fiji, 1944.

Taylor, Jennifer, 'Oceania: Australia, New Zealand, Papua New Guinea and the Smaller Islands of the South Pacific', in Banister Fletcher, *A History of Architecture*, 19th edn., Butterworths, London, 1987 (20th edn., Butterworths, London, 1996).

Taylor, Jennifer and William Lim, Southeast Asia and Oceania, Vol. 10, in Kenneth Frampton, *World Architecture: A Critical Mosaic, 1900–2000*, SpringerWein, New York, 1999.

Thierry, Agostini, *Wallis et Futuna, hommes et espaces: sciences humaines, programmes des collèges*, CTRDP Noumea, c. 1994.

Weaver, David B (ed.), *The Encyclopedia of EcoTourism*, CABI Publishing, New York, 2001.

West, Barbara A, *Encyclopedia of the Peoples of Asia and Oceania*, 2 Vols., Infobase Publishing, New York, 2009.

Whonsbon Aston, C W, *Polynesia Patchwork: The Tale of the Pacific Diocese*, Society for the Propagation of the Gospel in Foreign Parts, Westminster, 1948 (transcribed by the Right Reverend Dr Terry Brown, Bishop of Malaita, Church

of the Province of Melanesia, 2006).
Williams, John, *A Narrative of Missionary Enterprises in the South Seas*, John Snow, London, 1837.
Wiseman, Nicholas Patrick, *The New Glories of the Catholic Church*, Richardson and Son, London, 1859.
Wood, Alfred H, *Overseas Missions of the Australian Methodist Church, Volume 3: Fiji-Indian and Rotuma*, Aldersgate Press, Victoria, 1978.
Wood-Ellem, Elizabeth, *Queen Sālote of Tonga: The Story of an Era, 1900–1965*, University of Hawai'i Press, Honolulu, 1999.
Wright, Ronald (ed.), *On Fiji Islands*, Penguin, New York, 1987.
Ypma, Herbert, *Pacific Island*, Stewart, Tabori and Chang, New York, 1996.

Journals

Architectural Digest
Architecture New Zealand
Journal of Pacific Studies
Journal of South Pacific Law
Journal of the Polynesian Society
Pacific Islands Monthly
Policy Studies
South Pacific Travel Trade News (SPTTN), Vols 1–9, 1967–1974
The Contemporary Pacific
The Journal of Pacific Studies

Catalogues and Pamphlets

Bayol, Dominique, Véronique Defrance and Anny Levanqué, *Coup de Coeur pour le béton: l'architecture moderne à Nouméa, 1930–1970*, Mairie de Nouméa, Noumea, 2009.
Enright, John, *A Walking Tour of Historic Fagatogo: Tutuila, American Samoa*, American Samoa Historic Preservation Office, Tutuila, 2001.
Fiji Association of Architects, *Fiji Association of Architects*, Suva,1985.
Les Bâtisseurs: architecture à Nouméa de 1853 à 1940, Exposition juin 1996/juin 1997, Ville de Nouméa, Musée Archives, Multipress, Noumea, 1996.
O'Reilly, Patrick, Musée Gauguin, *Catalogue du Musée Gauguin, Papeari, Tahiti*, Fondation Singer-Polignac, Papeete, 1965.
Stephen, Ann (ed.), *Pirating the Pacific: Images of Trade, Travel and Tourism*, Powerhouse Publishing, Sydney, 1993.
The Basilica of Saint Anthony of Padua, Nuku'alofa, Tonga: A Community Achievement, Government Printing Office, Nuku'alofa, 1981.

PHOTO CREDITS

All photographs (not otherwise credited in the captions) are taken by the authors, other than the following:

Getty Images: cover (GUIZIOU Franck/hemis.fr) and p.331 (Mako Photo).

OUR THANKS

This book has been fashioned with the generous help, advice and aid provided by numerous people. We can only mention a few here, but our gratitude goes out to all.

For exceptional support, tutoring and guidance beyond any expectation we would like to acknowledge: Isabelle and Kathya Ohlen, Gabriel Cayrol, Don Boykin, Geoffrey Feast, Stuart Huggett, Elsa and David Miller, Adrian Sofield, Ken Mills, Leveni 'Aho, Joe Weilenman, John Enright and Michel Prévot.

Our principal sources of information were found on the ground – the buildings and towns of the South Pacific. Our instructors were the architects, engineers, developers, planners and many others who, in each country, piloted our first footsteps and set us off on trails that expanded into networks of authorities and personal contacts. From these came additional information – the histories and the folk tales – regarding the architectural development of the place, which was pieced together and woven into the material of this book. The virtual absence of any documentation of the background to the early or current buildings of the islands of the South Pacific made their role crucial to the possibility of the study – without their contribution of time, and yet further introductions, this book would not have been possible.

In the search for the limited documentation that did exist, we were highly dependent upon all those who helped us find our way through archives, libraries, newspapers, government administrations and other sources to discover material that would have remained uncovered if it had not been for their courteous and friendly assistance. Thank you also to those from outside the Pacific who, throughout the various stages of the progress of this study, gave freely of their knowledge.

Architecture in the South Pacific is a testimony to all of those who, in one way or another, have shaped the architecture of the new Oceania.

The book has been more than ten years in the making, and sadly some of those who steered us on our way have passed on – we wish they could have seen the fruits of our joint endeavours – RIP Gabriel Cayrol, Pierre Bourgeos, Jaimi Samarawera, George Moala, Solomon Tuita and Monsignor Michel-Gaspard Coppenrath.

Credits for illustrations

All photographs are by the authors except as indicated otherwise. For the graphics of the Pacific maps and town plans we are greatly indebted to Philip Beggs for the very many hours of care and skill spent in preparing and refining the drawings to meet his own and our editor's standards. Also our appreciation goes to the architects, archivists and academics from across the Pacific who kindly provided architectural drawings and archival maps, plans and photographs. All credits are gratefully acknowledged in the relevant captions.

Our particular thanks to the Museum of Fine Arts, Boston, for allowing us to reproduce its painting on p.291. Paul Gauguin, French, 1848–1903. *Where Do We Come From? What Are We? Where Are We Going?*, 1897–98. Oil on canvas. 139.1 x 374.6 cm (54 ¾ x 147 ½ in.). Museum of Fine Arts, Boston. Tompkins Collection – Arthur Gordon Tompkins Fund, 36.270.

INDEX

Note: Numbers in *italic* indicate illustrations